The Case for Legalizing Capitalism

The Case for
Legalizing Capitalism

Kel Kelly

MISES INSTITUTE

Ludwig von Mises Institute
518 West Magnolia Avenue
Auburn, Alabama 36832
mises.org

ISBN: 978-1-933550-62-6

The book is dedicated to the handful of people in the world who truly honor morality, principles, and ethics, consistently, regardless of personal agendas.

Preface

I FIRST BEGAN to learn about economics in college and from reading and studying the topic subsequently on my own. As my studies progressed, I thought I was on the path to learning how the world worked. But one day, while sitting at a café in Paris (where I was doing graduate work), the book I was reading introduced me to the great economist Ludwig von Mises and the so-called Austrian school, which I—like most people—had previously never heard of.[1]

After studying free-market economics, I began to understand how the world *really* worked, and learned that all other explanations of economics could easily be proven incorrect. I soon began to understand how our nation's economic policies in fact actually harm us. I learned that the economic concepts that I, like everyone else, had always thought straightforward and obvious, were completely opposite from what we all simply took on faith. I thought that price controls, wealth redistribution, and government regulation helped and protected people. I had no idea that these things actually harmed those it was intended to help. I further assumed that economic progress was a natural phenomenon: I didn't understand that for over the tens of thousands of centuries that man had existed, improving standards of living had occurred only during a handful of those, and not at all consecutively. Moreover, I didn't know that it was possible for us to cease progressing, at any time, and actually to lose all of the economic gains we have achieved.

As I began to learn true economic cause and effect, I realized that almost everything our government does works against us, and that people unknowingly vote for policies that make

---

[1] The book was *Trader Vic II: Principles of Professional Speculation*, by Victor Sperandeo.

them worse off, not better off, because they, too, falsely assumed that they had a grasp on basic economic concepts. I realized that although the new information I was learning was well documented in academic form in the truly free-market circles, for the most part it was not being disseminated to everyday people. This book has been written in order to try and make the public at large aware that most of what they think is good for their lives, in terms of economic policies, is usually not.

The economic insights that I apply here to our many economic and political problems did not originate with me, but are the culmination of centuries of work performed by great economic and philosophical thinkers. I am simply organizing numerous economic analyses originated by others into a single volume, with the hope of addressing most of the political issues that voters are concerned with. I earnestly try to assign credit to the appropriate sources. Any original thoughts or analysis created by others that I use and fail to acknowledge is purely accidental and I deeply regret the omission.

I would also like to defend my tendency of disproportionately using only a handful of sources for the bulk of the economic concepts I present here. Most of my sources in this book are associated with the Ludwig von Mises Institute because it is the world center of the only true free-market school of economics that exists, namely, Austrian Economics (which includes classical economics to a very large degree). The Mises institute, with its support of Austrian economics is therefore, the premier source of research on, and advocacy of, real capitalism. All other schools of economic thought other than this school of Free-Market economics endorse various forms of government control of the economy and of individuals.

Additionally, I feel no need to pretend to have an "unbiased" presentation and thus to balance capitalistic arguments with anti-capitalistic ones. I do, however, present many anti-capitalistic arguments, and I do so as accurately as possible, but this is for the sole purpose of refuting them, as that is my objective in writing this book. My ultimate goal is not to present all assertions from all competing schools of thought equally, but simply to promote the ones that I have discovered—after years of comparing all arguments—to be correct.

Besides, the public hears the anti-capitalist arguments daily from popular sources, which themselves are very biased, and which also make no attempt to present correct capitalistic arguments to offset the anti-capitalist assertions they are making. What is needed are counter arguments to these commonly espoused views, not a dispassionate, inconclusive, politically correct comparison. In terms of using limited sources, it is a fact that most economists, journalists, publishers, etc. rely on limited sources, indeed mostly on a single source! A dramatically disproportionate amount all of the economic information relayed today comes from one book published in 1936 by John Maynard Keynes; thus the famous saying "We're all Keynesians now." Similarly to how most economists and journalists use this single source as an argument for their economics, I am using 10-15 primary sources from a different school of thought, and one of those sources, Professor George Reisman, is cited more than others (though his views incorporate much of the others).

It should be kept in mind that while most economic schools of thought have political agendas involving the seeking of government power, the Austrian school, as I came to learn, is as close to unbiased as possible. Their only "agenda," like mine, is complete social and economic freedom for all, not political or ideological domination (and I don't regard the goal of freedom as an ideology, but a natural right[2]). Austrians/Capitalists

---

[2] Ideology is defined as 1) *the body of doctrine, myth, belief, etc., that guides an individual, social movement, institution, class, or large group*, 2) *such a body of doctrine, myth, etc., with reference to some political and social plan, as that of fascism, along with the devices for putting it into operation.* The state of utter freedom is a natural, originating state that exists prior to its being altered or eradicated through physical

cheer only those supporting true freedom, and are against all who oppose it; they do not promote political parties per se. It is precisely because they choose these principles and this morality rather than political power and control over other groups that they don't in fact achieve power, influence or recognition, and are thus little known and have little influence. But just because they are unpopular does not mean that they are not economically, and morally, in the right.

I ask all readers to approach the material in this book with an open mind, emotional detachment, and honesty with them-selves. After all, most of us, no matter the political persuasion, have the same ultimate goal: to make the world a better place for everyone, and to help those who are truly in need. What I try to show here is that we can achieve these goals without competing for political power and without harming one group in order to benefit another. And as it turns out, it is in fact precisely the free-dom that I am defending (proposing) that brings prosperity and better lives to everyone.

I would like to thank several groups of people for assisting me in this effort. Christine Perkell greatly supported me not only by discussing and debating the public perception of many topics in the book, and the merits of addressing the topics from differ-ent angles, but by reviewing and editing the entire book. Infelici-ties that remain are due to my own choices.

I would like to thank as well my high school English teacher and close friend Libby Atwell for reviewing and editing several chapters. Additionally, my mother, Pat Kelly, Dennis Campay, and Brian Pinneo kindly read individual chapters and offered valuable feedback, for which I thank them sincerely.

I finally offer thanks to Jeffrey Tucker and Doug French of the Mises Institute for finding my work valuable enough to

---

force by an ideological group. Absent socialism, Marxism, warfare states, and the like, freedom, or, capitalism, would naturally exist.

publish. I thank him for his editing. Thanks also to Paul Wood-ward for creating the graphics and performing proofing and typesetting.

In another category altogether are the thanks I owe my mother and father, my best friends, for supporting me uncon-ditionally and believing in me wholeheartedly, no matter what. Without their love and support throughout my whole life, this book would not have been written.

Contents

PART 1: THE FOUNDATIONS OF OUR ECONOMY

Chapter 1: **Labor: Workers Of The World Unite — and Shoot Yourselves In The Foot** . . . 35

13

PART 2: REGULATION

Chapter 4: Regulation:
The Helping Hand That Harms 161

PART 3: GOVERNMENT CONTROL VERSUS FREE MARKETS

Chapter 9: **Environmentalism—at Any Cost** 377

PART 5: PUTTING IT ALL TOGETHER

Chapter 10: Socialist / Government

Chapter 11: **Political Quotes and News Blurbs**

Introduction

The financial system is collapsing, the stock market is crashing, and retirement funds are evaporating. The auto industry verges on extinction. Home prices have spiraled downwards. Gas prices recently were the highest they have ever been. Jobs are being lost rapidly and unemployment is shooting up. Healthcare costs are reducing some to bankruptcy and even death. Wages are not keeping up with inflation, which until recently has been increasing rapidly. There is fear of a second Great Depression. What in the world is happening?

The answer is simple: Our government is sabotaging the economy. These, and most other economic maladies, are human-made. Specifically, in its attempts to "help" us, the government has managed and regulated the economy and passed laws that *sounded* constructive, but in fact *hurt* the economy and us. Political economic reality is replete with the law of unintended consequences. Our economic problems, in sum, are the natural result of *political* forces, not the natural result of (supposedly evil) *market* forces. We have voted our current problems into existence by having chosen politicians who promised to help us by means of economic intervention and regulation.

For example, we want the government to raise the minimum wage to help the poor, but that only makes the poor too expensive to hire and puts them out of work. We want the government to guarantee competent healthcare and therefore license only a subset of all would-be doctors. Further, we want the government, employers, and insurance companies to pay for most of our healthcare costs.

23

The result is reduced supply and increased demand for healthcare, thus raising prices and making healthcare less affordable year by year. Another example: We want the government to regulate the banking system to prevent depressions like the one in the 1930s. The result, however, is that the government's central bank creates too much money, causes economic booms and busts, financial and real estate market booms and busts, and puts many companies out of business and people out of homes. Similarly, regulations promoted as preventing *monopolies* in fact prevent *competition*, allowing some companies to benefit at the expense of others and the general public. The examples go on and on.

Our leaders are *supposed* to uphold laws that protect our property and insure our freedom; but the regrettable reality is that they do the opposite. The *actual* activity of politicians is to interfere with or outright appropriate the property of one group in order to benefit other groups. This, after all, is how they get elected! Further, even if politicians had the sincere desire to help *everyone*, they could not. First, regardless of whatever expertise they claim, they have little or no accurate understanding of the workings of money and credit, capital investment, production processes, productivity improvements, wages and prices. They are no better informed on these matters than the proverbial man-in-the-street. Second, it is inherently impossible for a finite group of bureaucrats to direct and constructively shape outcomes of entire economies—the actions of millions of people and millions of tools, machines, and factories—as their regulations and controls are intended to do. No supercomputer has yet been invented that can make decisions and calculate optimal outcomes more accurately than can the combined effort of millions of individuals working together, who coordinate their interactions by using market prices that reflect the needs of buyers, the amount sellers should therefore produce, and the price that should be charged. In truth, it's outright arrogant for politicians (or even economists!) to think, and to have us believe, that they can somehow so much as lend a helping or guiding hand to the national economy. The only genuinely helpful thing politicians can do is to undo their previous policies, the ones that have restricted rapid economic growth, distorted market outcomes, and caused thereby a destruction of wealth. As this book will demonstrate, real economic growth and prosperity can come only from free markets.

But perhaps you thought we *had* free markets? We have no such thing! This is true regardless of the fact that politicians of all stripes claim that we do. The government has its hand in every company and every industry in the nation. There are tens *and even hundreds of thousands* of pages of government regulations that dictate what can and cannot be produced, how things should be produced, what prices can or cannot be charged, what workers should be hired and at what prices, and what requirements, approvals, licensing, and reporting must be undertaken or performed for each type of business, product line, or transaction. There are subsidies, tariffs, quotas, tax incentives and disincentives, implied threats, and actual threats that severely alter the actions both companies and individuals would otherwise take. On top of these things, both federal and local governments confiscate portions of the earnings of companies and citizens directly through income taxes, as well as through license taxes, annual tag fees, passport fees, other fees, property taxes, import tariffs, inheritance taxes, capital gains taxes, environmental-affecting taxes, consumption taxes, excise taxes, tolls, retirement taxes, hotel occupancy taxes, payroll taxes, transfer taxes, airport taxes, security taxes, value added taxes, surcharges, commercial rent taxes, etc., as well as by the taxes the government takes by printing money at our expense (the inflation tax). By contrast, a free market is one where anyone is free to live and to do business as they wish—both socially and economically—as long as they do not initiate force upon others or their property. Free markets are not an imaginary utopia—they would exist today if they were not being prevented by law.

Though it may shock you, since you no doubt perceive yourself to largely support democratic capitalism, these types of intervention in the marketplace, which we desire and which are performed presumably *on behalf of society* for the purpose of protecting society and helping to reduce inequality between various social groups, are in fact socialism. *Full* socialism is defined as the *control* by the state of the means of production (companies, and individual producers, and their tools). *Partial* state control of the means of production (as described above) therefore constitutes not free markets but partial socialism! Additionally, any forceful taking of money by one group (taxes) for the purpose of spreading it around to others constitutes the essence of socialism. Thus, since most people believe that the state needs to intervene in the economy to achieve a better outcome, most people in America promote some degree of socialism, and that is what we implicitly demand of our politicians (see footnote[1] below for my definition of socialism).

This constant "helping" of society through attempting to "manage" it has resulted in a constant decline in our ability to produce real wealth and improve our standards of living. As it is now, we are seeing a consistent increase in the wealth of the rich, a moderate improvement in the wealth of the middle class, and stagnation in the living standards of the poor. But there is indeed a better way, a way that has seldom been taken in world history, but, when it has, has succeeded in improving the lives of all involved—rich, poor, black, white, man, or woman. It is called capitalism. Only capitalism, with its true free markets and true freedom for individuals can solve our problems and bring prosperity. (Note: I will henceforth use "capitalism" and "free markets" interchangeably.)

Understand that by "capitalism" I don't mean the right-wing, crony capitalism, corporate welfare economy, or the anti-rich, wealth-redistribution social welfare economy that we have today. In a truly capitalist society businesses *never* receive money or special privileges

---

[1] This book uses the term "socialist" and "socialism" very loosely, yet economically accurately. I call those who do not advocate at least 95 percent capitalism as socialists, because if they do not support this level of capitalism, they are supporting substantial government intervention. The intervention might be in the form of government ownership and operation of companies or industries, or in the form of laws imposing regulations, restrictions, taxes, subsidies, etc., each of which serves to benefit one group at the expense of another. The usual aim of government intervention is to benefit most of society at the expense of the few (usually the rich). Hence, even the United States and Switzerland, since they engage widely in such government intervention, can be called socialist, although most citizens would refuse to accept such a reality and label. Similarly, anyone who proposes government intervention of any kind, which includes Republicans as well as Democrats, and even many Libertarians, is thus labeled socialist in this book. It should be kept in mind, however, that *when I apply the term socialist, I am usually referring to those with a more intense desire for government control and wealth redistribution.*

Ideally, we should all seek 100 percent capitalism, but such a proposal, which includes such notions as private ownership and control of things like roads and schools, is hard for most to swallow. Thus, I am happy proposing and settling for "95 percent capitalism," which, in my definition, would consist of government providing such basic services as law enforcement, road-building, etc., but having absolutely no influence whatever on the way in which individuals and companies operate, *providing that they cause no physical harm to others or their property or person.*

from government: they succeed if they please consumers in offering them what they want, and they fail if they do not. Analogously, in a truly capitalist society, individuals never receive special privileges or transfer payments. Instead, they have an abundance of jobs and of wages commensurate with the value of people's work (more than a "living" wage). Under free market capitalism, it is virtually impossible for things like inflation, shortages, booms and busts, recessions, unemployment, starvation, and unaffordable healthcare to exist. Why? Because competition and the threat of competition serve as iron-clad shackles on companies, preventing them from underpaying, overcharging, or under-supplying and guaranteeing the safest, lowest-priced, highest-quality products that can possibly be produced at any particular state of technology and development.

Decade after decade our politicians, both Republicans and Democrats, have continuously implemented more of the same policies that have increasingly *slowed* our economic progress. Both ancient Greece in the fourth century B.C., as well as the Roman Empire of the second century A.D., through relatively free markets, reached a state of development that brought them close to an industrial revolution similar to that which ultimately occurred in Britain in the late 1600s. But ever-encroaching socialism (i.e., military warfare, class warfare, crushing taxation, inflation, and regulations) ate away at and economically reversed these advanced societies; Rome dwindled into nothingness, into absolute poverty, where most people produced and consumed, if lucky, the minimal necessities of a day-to-day subsistence. It was more than a thousand years before civilization again reached a state of improving standards of living. Similarly, the Western world today is on the verge not only of no longer progressing but even of retrogressing. The policies we have voted for have had the unintended consequence of increasingly restricting our ability to accumulate, and keep capital—savings that become factories, machines, tools, computers, etc.—the sole means by which we can produce and create wealth. Without essential changes—and soon—we will begin (or continue, as the case might be) sinking slowly into an economic abyss. The decline will not be noticeable, as it will be gradual, since things that change subtly and slowly are not noticed day by day or even decade by decade.

Consider this remarkable irony: we citizens put our faith in *government*—the entity that steals from us, causes wars, imprisons and starves innocent citizens, and is an absolute monopoly—to provide for us and keep us safe. At the same time, we see *businesses*—which have eradicated diseases and starvation,[2] engaged in peaceful exchanges instead of war, are fully restrained by hungry competitors (in free markets), produce virtually everything we currently own and enjoy, and pay us our wages and provide capital for us to improve our productivity—as our enemies from whom we need protection. These commonly held but irrational prejudices form the very foundation of the political arguments espoused by professional anti-capitalist "thinkers."

Most economists, especially those associated in any capacity with government, subscribe to one or the other variations of non-free-market economics[3]—despite the economic ills, including the Great Depression, caused by these policies over the last hundred years. Their economics, primarily Marxist and Keynesian and, to a lesser degree, supply-side economics, and even Milton Friedman's monetarist school, are in many cases, despite their differences, fundamentally flawed in their shared belief that markets can be profitably managed by the government. They fail to grasp that the success of markets is a function of their freedom. Therefore they promote theories to "fix" things, assuming that the current economic problems were caused by insufficient, instead of too much, outside intervention. Since these mainstream economists devise government intervention, or benefit from it in other ways, I will hereafter call them "mainstream" or "government" economists.

---

[2] Contrary to popular notions, most diseases were not eradicated by government. For evidence of this, see: Timothy Terrell, "A Pox on Government Vaccines!," *The Free Market* (April 2001). Additionally, even where disease eradication was performed by government-funded scientists, the funding unambiguously originated with for-profit, wealth-producing entities. Had these entities not first created the wealth that the government then confiscated, it would not have had funding with which to perform research and pay researchers.

[3] This includes economists at think tanks, banks and investment firms, the World Bank, the IMF, the Treasury Department, the Federal Reserve Bank, and virtually every economist in Washington, D.C., because they are all tightly linked with, or constitute, the government.

It may seem outrageous for me to propose that numerous Ph.D.-certified, Nobel Prize-winning university professors do not understand correctly how economies progress and produce in a synchronized manner, but this is in fact the case. I don't intend to be pompous, for these economists are very intelligent people. It's just that they have learned incorrect explanations of economic cause and effect, even if their schools of thought are the most common and popular world-wide. Likewise, the scores of journalists and authors who claim that we currently have capitalism and that it has failed us are outright ignorant of what capitalism actually is.

The most prominent of the early incorrect theories came from Karl Marx,[4] who most proposed that workers were exploited and forced by capitalists to a subsistence level of existence,[5] the remedy being state ownership of the means of production. Then, during the Great Depression, John Maynard Keynes incorrectly identified the crises as stemming from "animal spirits" and from a failure of markets to work properly, when in fact it was brought on by previous government intervention. He thus channeled his personal socialist feelings into thinking up, on the spot, his theories of how markets fail and of how government can fix them.[6] Since his theories *seemed* to make sense, and since they gave government the green light to intervene in the economy, the theories caught on like wildfire. Today we have multiple variations of these two dominant theories, along with plenty of new ones. But none of these economic schools, unlike the free market school, explain how an unhampered economy can progress effectively. They only explain (incorrectly) how things can go wrong and how markets can be manipulated for the better so as to protect

---

[4] Based on flaws in Adam Smith, *The Wealth of Nations*, Edwin Cannan, ed. (London: Methuen, 1776).

[5] Though he later, for all practical purposes, indirectly admitted his wrong thinking in the third edition of his work. Karl Marx, *Das Kapital* (Hamburg: Verlag von Otto Meissner, 1867).

[6] John Maynard Keynes, *The General Theory of Employment, Interest and Money* (London: Macmillan, 1936). His previously concocted theories from several years earlier were promptly refuted by Austrian economist Friedrich Hayek. The second time around Hayek decided it was not worth the trouble because he knew that once he spent the time and energy refuting Keynes again, Keynes would—as Keynes admitted he had a tendency to do—simply change his mind and come up with a new theory.

citizens. But it is precisely markets free of interference that actually *do* protect citizens.

When our current government-managed economy experiences problems, there is huge pressure on government to "do *something*." It is a difficult-to-accept truth, however, that the best action is no action—i.e., to allow the market to self-correct. But politicians pursue the easy and popular course of intervention, instead of the correct course of being hands off—as there used to be in the 1800s (and even in 1921) when recessions were thus fleeting. In the face of any current crisis, they feel compelled to implement new "policies," which necessarily become the seeds of the next crisis about which they will soon have to once again "do something." It is understandably difficult to accept the notion that nothing should be done when millions are suffering during economic downturns. But the quickest road to recovery is not to interfere with the corrective processes markets undertake. Better yet, we should abolish the policies that *cause* financial crises and recessions.

The economic achievements of today's society came from capitalism, while the recessions, inflations, unemployment, and lack of increasing real wages came from anti-capitalistic interventions in the market. This book aims to prove these assertions by explaining the relationship among human action, labor and the production of goods, and money in accessible terms that require no previous study of economics. An economic whistleblower for the many, I will disabuse readers of false notions about the causes of economic prosperity, and provide them instead with an understanding of markets sufficient to enable them to vote themselves into increasing standards of living.

In this undertaking, I am indebted primarily to the works of David Ricardo, John Stuart Mill, and Jean-Baptiste Say (generally associated with the British Classical School of economics), and even more so to the works of Eugen von Böhm-Bawerk, Carl Menger, Ludwig von Mises, Friedrich Hayek, and Murray Rothbard, among others, who represent the Austrian School of economics. Economist George Reisman, who represents both schools, has had the most influence on my economic understanding. It is these economists' fundamental insights into the nature of the economic common good that underlie the material and arguments of this book.

By giving readers an easily understood presentation of these various brilliant economists' combined insights, this book seeks to change the general public's view of the pervasive incorrect assumptions about the sources and causes of economic well-being and to do so by addressing the social and economic issues most relevant to the average voter in our world today.[7] I do this by explaining cause and effect through logic and deductive reasoning; for the most part I leave aside statistics, since they can complicate the story and confuse readers, and because they can be easily manipulated to tell whatever story one wants them to. My hope is that if people understand the logic of how free markets bring prosperity and benefits to *all* of us, they will vote for politicians who will allow markets to be free, or else demand it of them.

---

[7] I make little attempt to speak to the die-hard socialist because their views will not be altered no matter what logic, reason, and facts are presented to them; their views are driven by emotions, not economic reality.

PART ONE

The Foundations of Our Economy

Chapter 1

Labor: Workers of the World Unite — And Shoot Yourselves in the Foot

Blaming greedy companies for exploiting workers…it's all the rage these days, and actually has been for several hundred years. Popular as well are politicians promising to resolve workers' woes. Presidential candidates on the campaign trail in 2008 were trying to win votes by telling us how they planned to create jobs for us, and help us receive higher wages by boosting the economy. They promised to raise minimum wages and strengthen our unions. Democratic primary contenders, Barack Obama and Hillary Clinton both supported higher taxes on the wealthy with which to "pay" for lower taxes on the middle class, as Republican candidate John McCain had also once proposed. Most of our politicians support government taxpayer spending on programs that they believe will create jobs. But can the government really create jobs? Can it really help workers bring in higher wages? How does it all work?

You might think that a discussion of how workers earn wages must necessarily be dry and boring. This chapter will delve into some technical detail in the first half, but only enough to provide a framework for the following, decidedly less technical material in most of the other chapters in this book (and the book becomes more dynamic as it progresses). But understanding clearly how jobs and wages come about is crucial for comprehending how workers, economies, and standards of living improve. That process forms the very foundation of this book and of economics as a whole. Comprehending the economics of labor is important because most Marxist and Communist countries, and most left-wing ideologies in general, exist largely because of the very belief that workers are exploited by evil and greedy capitalistic companies.

This ambitious goal of the chapter—to prove that nothing could be further from the truth—will show that companies tend not only to pay workers the maximum amount they can bear, but that they are the creators of most jobs, provide the capital to improve productivity and raise real salaries, increase the quantity and quality of consumer goods, and bestow upon us a permanently higher standard of living, all while *paying* us in the process. At the same time, companies' gains, though very large initially, are not as permanent as the workers' gains. Further, this chapter will demonstrate why such a phenomenon as unemployment would never exist in a completely free market, and is in fact caused by the policies of the politicians who purport to help us workers.

What is an Economy and How Does it Work?

To understand how workers get paid, you need a basic knowledge of how an economy works. We hear a lot about the economy: that it's strong, or it's slowing, or that we need to improve it. We see it as a *thing* that we must somehow manage and grow as though it's a wild animal. But the economy is not a thing: it is simply us and our lives. The economy embodies each of us working, producing things we all need for our lives, and exchanging these things with others who are doing the same. Whether as individuals producing, or as thousands of people grouped into a company and producing together, we all make "stuff" that businesses and individuals need, and we get compensated for the stuff we produce (and "producing" includes any of the activities that individuals and employees engage in that contribute towards creating a final product). We then exchange our stuff or our salaries for different stuff made by others. That's an economy—it's as simple as that.

Imagine that you are stuck on a desert island. To survive, you catch fish by hand in the ocean. Since they are fast and slippery, it's a difficult job, taking you 12 hours to catch two fish; 6 hours per fish. You can therefore catch only two fish per day. But then you get smart: you decide to make a net. Yet making a fishing net by hand takes time, too, as it involves many steps: searching the island for raw materials like grasses and vines; finding something to serve as the handle; twining and bending strong but pliable vines or twigs into a rim to support the netting; and finally braiding and weaving vines into netting and tying it to the frame to form a sieve-like scoop. With no tools available, this process will take you five days by hand. To take five days off of fishing without going hungry, you must save some of your caught fish for a couple of days by eating only one fish per day instead of two. The saved fish will sustain you for the five days it takes to build the net, and once the net is complete, you can catch 50 fish per day.

This example introduces some basic components of an economy. You have *savings* (the fish you set aside to eat over the course of several days) that sustained you while you produced a *capital good* (the net). The capital good, which, in this case, was also a new *technology*, allowed you to improve your *productivity* (the number of fish you "produced" per day). Now that you have plenty of food to keep you from starving, you have more free time and labor available. You can use this to improve your standard of living by building a hut, a bed, clothes, and maybe even a boat. In addition to time and labor, though, you will need tools (more capital goods) with which to build these things. That means that it will take a lot of time, savings, and production of capital goods to improve your standard of living.

Now, suppose that several other people also landed on the desert island. With a division of labor, each person can focus on making the things they are best at (given what *needs* to be made), which increases the total amount that all islanders can produce, and each person can trade most of what they produce for the goods made by the others. Obviously, the more capital goods (e.g., knives, hammers, nails, shovels, nets, axes) that get produced, the more consumer goods (e.g., bowls, fish, beds, huts, hammocks, clothes) that can be produced in a given amount of time. With this division of labor among the castaways resulting in increased productivity, and with the existence of a *capital*

*structure, which consists of an organized collection of tools and technolo-
gies used to make things,* there will be more goods produced overall in
the island economy, which means higher standards of living. Obviously,
part of the success of this process involves each person producing *what
others want or need*; making something just for the sake of making it
will not necessarily satisfy the needs of others in the community. This
concept will be discussed in more detail throughout the book.

In this division of labor society, what each person produces
becomes that individual's *purchasing power.* The things people make
that they don't directly consume they can trade for other goods they
need or want. In this hypothetical deserted island economy, the castaways' amount of consumption is based on their amount of production: the value of what they *produce* becomes the value of the amount
they can *consume*; and to the degree that their production adds to the
supply of goods in the economy, prices (barter exchange ratios) fall in
proportion, increasing their purchasing power. This notion that supply (things produced) creates its own demand (the *means* with which
to consume) is known as *Say's Law.*[8]

Notice specifically that what people on the island gain from producing and exchanging becomes their *profit*, not their *wages.* In this
example, *individual producers* do not pay themselves or each other
wages when they produce for themselves or when they trade for
other goods. If the island's cloth maker sells a shirt, or if the berry
picker sells some berries, they are traded (they are "paid") other goods
in exchange for the *full amount of their production.*[9]

Now, back to the real world. Today's complex, modern economy
still contains the same basic functionality. In our modern, advanced
economy, most of us produce a single thing—hair cutting, electri-
cian services, sales or marketing services, etc.—and we then exchange
our salary for everything else we want. We still have many individual

---

[8] Jean-Baptiste Say, , *Traité d'économie politique, ou simple exposition de la manière dont se
forment, se distribuent, et se composent les richesses* (1803); English translation *A Treatise on
Political Economy*, C.R. Prinsep, trans. and Clement C. Biddle, ed. (Philadelphia: Lippin-
cott, Grambo, 1855).

[9] George Reisman, *Capitalism: A Treatise on Economics* (Ottawa, Ill.: Jameson Books,
1996). The fact that a single producer/sole proprietor earns a profit, and not a wage, is a
truism, but is not a commonly accepted notion.

producers such as hot dog vendors, farmers, painters, lawyers, and, of course, economists. But most production takes place in companies. The primary difference here is that in addition to profits, *wages* are also present. In contrast to individual production where all income consists of profit, wages appear once there is *combined production* (groups of people working together in companies) and individual producers within the group are *paid in advance* for producing an input, or an *intermediate product,* by *businesspeople/employers/managers*—that is, someone in charge of orchestrating the production of individual intermediate products to combine them into a *final product.* The final product is partly composed of each individual worker's contribution; their contribution is only an intermediate step towards completion of the product (except for the product of those few workers who are involved in the very last stages of production). In combined production entities, workers have *freely chosen* to work for someone else in exchange for wages, instead of producing on their own for profit. They would only choose to do this if they felt they could make more income by accepting wages than in producing by themselves and earning profits.[10]

How We Progress as an Economy

Most of our rising standards of living can be attributed not to us single workers, but to entrepreneurs, capitalists (e.g., stock holders, bond holders, venture capitalists, individual wealthy investors) and businesspeople who create, finance, and run these companies.[11] Innovative entrepreneurs seeking profits think up ingenious ideas for ways to make our lives more enjoyable or to produce things we currently produce more efficiently: mattresses, ovens, picture frames, computers, cell phones, and video games (consumer goods), or conveyer belts, nail guns, adhesive materials, and building cranes (capital goods). Individuals or other companies will buy these innovative products for the

---

[10] Based purely on money incomes, which is without question the biggest factor in choosing between various employment opportunities. There are, of course, other factors such as commute distance, type of work, perks, career benefits, camaraderie with coworkers, etc.

[11] These three entities may or may not be the same person, or any two of them could be the same person. Were they the same person, the one who is running the business also had the idea and vision to create the company's product, and also wholly or partly financed the business and its production.

right price if they believe they will benefit from having or using them. A good idea can easily be made into a product because if the idea is potentially profitable—that is, if consumers will pay more for something than it costs to produce it—people with money to lend (capitalists) will do so in order to earn more money. Innovators / entrepreneurs will use this money to start businesses producing these products, or use part of the loaned funds to hire others who know how to do it for them.

To design, produce, market, and distribute the products, the businesspeople (once entrepreneurs begin producing they become businesspeople) hire laborers. They direct and manage the laborers, likely with the help of other managers reporting to them, who each oversee particular areas of production. When the final products are complete, the businesspeople will (hopefully) sell the products for more than the costs of production (including labor) and earn a profit.

A *large* profit,[12] one significantly higher than the "average" profit (in percentage terms), is possible when a product is new and different, and has no competitors (think of the first personal computer, hula hoop, automobile, etc.). If a profit is very large, it is because sales revenues *far exceed* the total costs of producing the product. Costs consist of workers' wages plus the cost of all the capital goods and materials (e.g., tools, machinery, building, raw materials, supplies). This large profit generally makes the entrepreneurs and capitalists who provided the funding for the ventures very wealthy. If a businessman was hired to run the company by the entrepreneur, that person most likely received a salary, but could also have shared in some of the profits. These high profits should be celebrated and seen as a good thing— after all, they signify the creation of something that customers desired so much that they preferred to have the product than their money— but in fact profits are generally frowned upon in our socialist-oriented society as evidence of greed and selfishness. But fret not, socialist friends, there is good news: these often-called "obscene" profits will not last long.

Large profits are fleeting because of the economy's *tendency to shift toward a uniform rate of profit* throughout the economic system.

---

[12] Profit is always discussed in percentage terms—in terms of the dollar amount of profit as a percentage of the dollar amount of sales revenues.

The steps involved are simple and logical: (1) capitalists flock toward those products or industries where they see or anticipate the greatest percentage profits; (2) more capitalists in one product or industry means more money invested there; (3) increased investment creates a corresponding increase in demand for labor and the capital goods required for production; (4a) increased demand for labor and capital goods drives up the costs of labor and capital goods and simultaneously (4b) increased production and supply drives down the selling price of the products; thus (5) higher costs and lower selling prices mean lower profits. The same process works in reverse: if profits are low, fewer capitalists invest, causing monetary capital (e.g., monetary savings cum financial investment) to flow elsewhere; the resulting lower production means reduced supplies, which drives up selling prices, leading to increased profits. With money constantly shifting away from areas of low profits toward areas of high profits, rates of profit tend to equalize throughout the economy. There are many things that cause profits on companies' *income statements* to vary widely in different industries, but the *effective rate of return on monetary capital invested* tends toward equality across industries.

With the understanding of the *uniformity of profit principle,* we can visualize what will happen to an entrepreneur's successful company: others will notice the high profits from the entrepreneur's new product, and will rush to produce the same product or, even more likely, either a cheaper or an improved version of the product. We see new examples of this daily. For example, once Apple came out with its Newton hand-held device, Palm soon followed up with its Pilot, and then Nokia with the first "smart phone," the 9000 Communicator. Soon after, there were hundreds of models of smart phones from many companies, each competing by offering additional attributes. This kind of competition leads to each new round of products delivering versions that usually improve on the previous ones, and at lower costs.

As an example of profits being competed away, take the simple ballpoint pen. It first came to market in October 1945 at a selling price of $12.50 (over $50 in today's money), with production costs per pen of 80¢—a 94 percent profit![13] The following October, after several competitors entered the market, ballpoint pens sold for $3.85, and the production costs averaged 30¢ per pen. By December 1946—just a few months later—there were over 100 pen manufacturers competing, causing pen prices to fall to 99¢ by February 1947. In 1948, pens sold for 39¢, and cost 10¢ to produce. Average profits had fallen to 74 percent. Within several years, average ballpoint pen profits were reduced such that they were in line with profits in other industries, which was probably about 10 percent to 12 percent (before taxes). The fact that pens have been sold an average of 57 times per minute since 1950[14] reveals the dramatic increase in supply. Today, *Bic*®, perhaps the best known pen manufacturer, has average profits of just over 10 percent.[15]

Clearly, once competitors arrive, big profits disappear quickly. But even older, established companies still have *some* rate of profit; they still have revenues that exceed their total costs. This profit is the "standard" uniform economy-wide profit, and it is *this* remaining profit that is generally seen as the problem associated with "exploitation," as famously argued by Karl Marx.[16] The charge of exploitation will be addressed below.

There are only two ways for companies earning the normal rate of profit to possibly—and temporarily—achieve large or excess profits. They must either develop a new, innovative, and original product, or they must find ways to produce current products more efficiently and cheaply. The former will raise sales revenues above costs, and the latter will lower costs below sales revenues.

---

[13] Joseph T. Salerno, "Pricing of the Factors of Production and the Labor Market" (a lecture from Introduction to Austrian Economic Analysis with Joseph Salerno, 2006); http://video.google.com/videoplay?docid=5503610910224878764#.

[14] Tim Hepher, "Bic makes a point with 100th billion-ballpoint milestone," *The San Diego Union-Tribune* (September 9, 2005).

[15] Societe Bic (Bic) *2008 Income Statement*, http://www.bicworld.com/inter_en/investor/index.asp#.

[16] Marx, *Das Kapital* (1867). Marx's argument is rooted in the idea that something is worth the amount of labor hours used to produce it, whereas in reality a thing is worth what one is willing to pay for it based on their subjective view of how much it would benefit them to have it. Thus, by calculating the number of hours needed to produce something, depending on how one calculates the cost per hour of labor (which is a separate issue up for debate), it could be calculated that workers are not paid for the total number of hours worked, and the money owed them is instead kept by capitalists as profit.

To be able to constantly create new products for us consumers, and to be able to continually produce them more efficiently, new and additional physical capital (i.e., capital goods), paid for by monetary capital, must be employed.[17] It is this capital—which, as we saw in our deserted island economy, comes from savings (i.e., production which is not yet consumed)—that sustains companies while they develop new and better ways to produce, and often, while they simultaneously use their current resources to continue producing in the current fashion. For example, for General Motors to have the ability to build a newer, more advanced factory while still producing vehicles in the current factory, it must obtain additional funding, since its current money is tied up in producing this year's cars (it can't use its profits as they are either paid out to owners or reinvested in production). The capital goods that are purchased with monetary capital, combined with new science and technologies, ultimately lead to increased productivity. These new capital goods and new technology allow each worker to produce more things during a given period.

Think about, for example, our large factories of today with automated equipment producing items en masse versus the small shops of years past where workers produced goods by hand. Or consider how much more efficiently 4,000-horsepower diesel-powered trains a half-mile long transport supplies versus the historical method of horse-drawn wagons. Think also about the fact that today's car companies can produce an entire automobile in 18 hours mostly with automated means: machines. These machines, these capital goods, help humans produce many more things much more quickly. The capital goods do most of the work. People may run the machines, but the machines perform most of the actual production. Even office workers produce most of their work on machines: computers. To produce the same quantity of work by hand would take us hundreds or thousands of hours longer.

The following conclusion is one of the most important that could be understood in all of economics: *The continually increasing rates*

---

[17] In a world where government did not create money to add to the economy, additional savings per se would not be needed to fund economic progress, only the sufficient devotion of saving to capital goods production versus consumption. The need for actual savings results largely from the effects of inflation, since inflation destroys capital. See Chapter 3 for more insight.

of productivity enabled by tools and machines bought through savings and investment are what allow us to continually increase the amount of goods and services available. This increase in goods and services serves to reduce prices relative to our incomes, and thus increase our real wealth and standard of living. What counts is whether we are able to produce more wealth each year than we consume or that deteriorates.

Real Wealth

Money as we know it is not real wealth; money is only a medium of exchange that shows us the relative prices of different things. We have money so that we can exchange it for *real* stuff. The more real stuff we have—houses, refrigerators, medicine, food, diapers, soap, televisions, etc.—the richer we are and the fewer hours we have to work to maintain a particular standard of living. The more stuff we produce, the cheaper everything becomes relative to our incomes— that is, *in real terms*. That, in sum, is how an economy works.

Probably not one member of Congress (besides Ron Paul) fully understands this concept or else the government would be doing everything in its power to help companies grow their capital to build more tools and machines. Or perhaps they merely fear that doing so would not get them votes since they assume the public doesn't understand the concept. They in fact do the opposite, as is chronicled throughout this book. If the government truly wanted to create economic progress, the best way would be to create capital. This is done by lowering tax rates, abstaining from printing money and inflating prices, undoing burdensome regulation, taking off price controls, etc. All of these forms of capital destruction will be discussed in detail.

The idea that goods get cheaper needs some explanation since we see prices around us rising, not falling. Though inflation raises the *money* price of goods, the *real* price—the price as a proportion of our income—falls as production and supply increase. The average automobile, for example, used to cost more than five times the average person's income; now the average price of a new car sold in the United States is $28,400[18] or a little less than three quarters of the average person's

---

[18] Federal Trade Commission, *FTC Facts For Consumers: Buying a New Car* (April 2006).

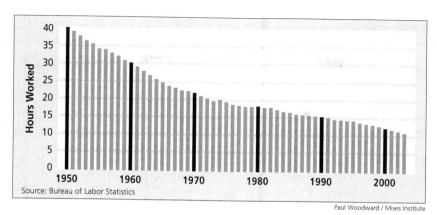

Figure 1.1: A comparison between the work hours required today versus those in 1950 to produce the same results.

income of $39,430.[19] Looked at another way, the number of hours of labor it takes to purchase a certain item or the number of hours of labor it takes to achieve a particular standard of living constantly declines through time as our productivity rises. **Figure 1.1** shows that the average worker today needs to spend only 11 hours per week to produce what took an average worker in 1950 a full 40 hours per week; European data is comparable.[20]

This reduction in labor hours can be even better understood by looking at individual products as in **Figure 1.2**.

The prices of goods, *and wages*, rise because the government prints more money and adds it to the quantity already existing in the economy—that's what inflation is, and nothing else. When the amount of money in an economy increases at a faster rate than the amount of goods and services, prices rise. But in real terms, *if productivity is increasing*, prices fall relative to wages, even if both are rising in "outside," or nominal, prices (the increase in the quantity of money does not lower wages along with prices because the supply of workers does not increase along with goods and services).

---

[19] "The Economist Intelligence Unit," *Pocket World in Figures 2007* (pamphlet from The Economist).

[20] This data, like most government data, is likely fudged or inaccurate due to methodology flaws, but it is directionally correct.

Cost in Time
Hours worked at the average wage to purchase typical household goods

	1950	2009
Sofa	57.7	22.0
Sofa Bed	69.2	19.4
Arm Chair	28.4	8.9
Mattress	34.6	33.3
Four-Drawer Chest	43.5	3.3
Desk	150.0	33.3
Vacuum Cleaner	34.6	5.6
Dryer	127.0	20.0
Freezer	244.2	23.3
Refrigerator	153.7	21.7
Toaster	10.0	1.9
Gas Range	65.3	23.2
AM-FM Radio	26.9	0.6
Recliner Chair	38.4	6.7
32-piece Silverware Set	22.7	0.8
Television	161.5	30.5
Total Hours of Work	1,267.0	254.5
Weeks of Work	31.7	6.4
Months of Work	7.9	1.6

Source: mjperry.blogspot.com[21]

Figure 1.2: A comparison between the work hours required today versus those in 1950 to produce the same results

If there were a constant supply of money, if government did not *increase* the number of bills floating around, prices would necessarily fall because the same quantity of money in the economy would have to be spread across more and more goods. Think of it this way: if we have 100 dollars in an economy to purchase 100 items, each item would cost on average $1 ($100/100 items = $1). If we increase production such that we have 200 items in the economy, the same $100 must now buy, or "cover," twice the items. This means that each item would cost on average 50 cents ($100/200 items = 50¢). The

[21] Mark J. Perry, "The Miracle of the Market," http://mjperry.blogspot.com/2009/03/miracle-of-market.html.

important point to remember is that in *real* terms (or, in a world of an unchanging supply of money), as we increase our production of goods, prices fall while our wages stay the same. This is how increased standards of living come about.

Since an economy is simply each of us producing things in the ways in which we decide is best for us, politicians can do nothing to improve our decision making—any intervention will necessarily reduce the optimization of the process and slow it down. Any "policy" the government promotes, unless it is one removing restrictions previously placed on capital accumulation and production, will cause *fewer* jobs to be created and *fewer* goods to be produced, and thus lower our standards of living. Neither the Democrats nor the Republicans, or any political party, including one composed of free marketers, have the ability to create wealth for us. Nor can any economist, including myself, orchestrate a better outcome for millions of people than individuals can create for themselves using their labor, incomes, capital, and the price system.

Profits Don't Really Exist

I mentioned above that it is this standard rate of profit that Marxists and socialists (and most of society today) view as the means of worker exploitation. They argue that some or all of the profits should instead be paid to all the workers in a company instead of being kept by the capitalists. They suggest that workers are not being paid for the full value of what they produce. This is a grave misconception.

To see why we must understand what this standard rate of profit is and why it exists. The answer will tell us why workers don't receive this profit in the form of additional wages. In reality, this standard rate of profit is not a profit at all—it is a mix of two different things. The first, inflation is in a class of its own. When the government creates new money and inserts it into the economy, the new money increases sales revenues of companies before it increases their costs; when sales revenues rise faster than costs, profit margins increase.

New money, which is created electronically by the government and loaned out through banks, is spent by borrowing companies.[22] The expenditures show up as new and additional sales revenues for businesses. But much of the corresponding costs associated with the new revenues lag behind in time because of technical accounting procedures such as the act of spreading asset costs across the useful life of the asset (*depreciation*) and not recognizing inventory costs until the product is sold (*cost of goods sold*). These practices delay the recognition of costs on the profit and loss statements, or income statement.

Since costs are recognized on company's income statements months or years after they are actually incurred, their monetary value is diminished by inflation by the time they are recognized. For example, if a company recognizes $1 million in costs for equipment purchased in 1999, that $1 million would be worth less today than in 1999, but on the income statement the corresponding revenues recognized today are in today's purchasing power. There is an equivalently greater amount of revenues spent today for the same items than there were ten years ago (since it takes more money to buy the same good, due to the devaluation of the currency). Another way of looking at it is that with more money being created through time, the amount of revenues will always be greater than the amount of costs, since most costs were incurred when there was less money existing. Thus, because of inflation, the total monetary value of business costs in a given time frame is smaller than the total monetary value of the corresponding business revenues. Were there no inflation, costs would more closely equal revenues, even if their recognition were delayed. In summary, a majority of profits "earned" by businesses are actually inflation effects; thus, government gives companies much of their paper profits.

Since business sales revenues increase before business costs, with every round of new money printed, business profit margins stay widened; they also increase in line with an increased rate of inflation. This is one reason why countries with high rates of inflation have such

---

[22] Most funds are borrowed from banks for the purpose of business investment; only a small amount is borrowed for the purpose of consumption. Even borrowing for long-term consumer consumption, such as for housing or automobiles, is a minority of total borrowing from banks.

high rates of profit.[23] During bad economic times, when the government has quit printing money at a high rate, profits shrink, and during times of deflation sales revenues fall faster than do costs.

Bear in mind that these apparent profits are not real but a monetary illusion. Due to higher costs from inflation companies must at some point replace their plants, equipment, and inventories at much higher prices, which wipes out most of their paper profits, even though this cannot be seen on an income statement (companies often consume capital without even knowing it). Since businesses have their increased profits from inflation taxed, but have to replace inventory, plant, and equipment at higher costs than last time, the profits needed to replace the equipment at higher costs are diminished because a portion of them has been taxed away; companies thus have about the same, or likely, less real purchasing power with which to replace assets. In short, the increased profits that inflation provides companies do not constitute real increased wealth for these companies; at best, companies come out even.

Since the inflation effect is one derived solely by the government's increasing the amount of dollars circulating in the economy, let's look at what would constitute profit in the absence of the inflation effect. This second source of profits is the deduction of costs from sales revenues to compensate capitalists, whose money the companies are using to operate. In this way, the difference between revenues and total costs is not really profit, but a return on investment "paid" *to those who really own the company*: capitalists. More specifically, profit compensates the capitalists for waiting for a return on their investment, since the investment is made long before the final production it generates. Stated another way, the companies themselves do not make profits on what they sell; the profits are payments—like any other of the company's payments to suppliers—to the suppliers of capital as a return on their investments. Without their investments, the company would not exist.

Income statements are set up in such a way that *capitalists* can see their returns—a view of the business as seen by the capitalists. The business's view as seen by the *company* would theoretically include the

---

[23] The other main reason for this, if the country is poor, is the fact that there is a lack of capital: the more capital, the lower the rate of profit will be, and vice versa (though it can never go to zero).

capitalists' required return as normal business cost alongside invento-ries, machines, or labor. Though this is never done, if it were, profits would not generally be left over after subtracting all business costs.[24]

In most cases, massive outlays of money are invested before any product exists. It can easily be years or even decades between the start of a business's operations and when the business gets paid for the prod-uct it makes. For example, consider the aircraft industry: the amount of time required to plan and design a large plane, properly build and tool the factory, and to actually produce the plane can add up to many years or decades. Similarly, a nuclear plant takes 5 to 7 years just to build—and that does not include the time spent putting in place the company's business and operations. Though less time is needed for the development and production of many items (e.g., shoes, furniture, candy), the same concept of production taking time still applies.

It is the capitalist who pays for labor (and machines) *in advance* in anticipation of future production. Can you imagine how long employ-ees at the airplane factory would have to wait if they could not be paid until the product was sold? They would have to work for decades before receiving any income, and they would not be fully compen-sated until the very last plane was sold, many years after the first one. How would they purchase food, clothing, and housing? The capitalists take on the role of doing the waiting for the workers, by paying them in advance for their future production. This is why true cooperatives—those financed solely by the workers—rarely exist. Since the capitalists have their money tied up for several years, they are not able to use it, and have to forego their own immediate consumption. In short, they are compensated for the time spent without that money at their dis-posal. For this, they receive interest, just as a bank receives interest for lending out money. They also receive a bad rap as greedy, money-hun-gry pigs because they do not give away their money for free.

In the end, real profits do not exist on an ongoing basis. The cost of wages, supplies, machinery, land, *and the money used for operations* (*capital*), are all subtracted from revenues. After the subtraction of

---

[24] Interest payments on borrowed funds, which are listed as items on an income state-ment, are different than interest to stock holders. In general, I am referring to profits prior to interest, taxes, etc. Interest payments can only be made if there are profits.

		Revenues	$1,000,000	100%
Cost of Labor		Wages	$365,000	37%
	Other Capital	Product Input Costs	$160,000	16%
		Supplies & Administrative	$80,000	8%
Cost of Capital	Capital Goods	Plant / equipment / machinery / tools	$295,000	30%
		Profit	$100,000	10%

Figure 1.3: Simple income statement showing sales revenues, costs, and profits for a sample company

these items, *nothing* is left, except in those instances discussed earlier where exceptional profits can be made temporarily from introducing a new product or a new efficient production method.

Capitalist Exploitation of Workers: The Myth

To return to the original question, how can we be so sure that the total wages a company pays are as high as they can be? How do we really know that workers (and machines) aren't destined to be ripped off by their employers? Consider all the aspects of profitability and costs of a company's income statement as shown in **Figure 1.3.** This sample company has sales revenues of $1,000,000, total costs of $900,000 and a profit of $100,000, or 10 percent. After allowing for the 10 percent profit, and after payment for other physical capital, $365,000 is the amount available to pay for labor (in reality, capital and labor purchases are chosen simultaneously). How do we know that all company employees combined will receive a total of $365,000 in salaries?

We know workers will be paid the full $365,000, the most they can be paid without the company losing its profit, because of the competitive nature of a capitalist economy. Labor is the scarcest resource we have. Thus, it will all be put to use (the existence of unemployment will be discussed below) by businesses competing for its limited supply. Individual workers tend to be paid according to the amount of sales revenue they can bring in based on their productivity. There is a going market wage for each type of worker and each level of productivity. Workers use capital goods to create their products, and both they and the capital goods get compensated according to the value of what they produce.

If a worker with a particular skill set, knowledge base, and education can produce work that brings in $40,000 in revenues, tight competition in the labor market will cause that laborer's wage to be bid up to $40,000 as well, minus the amount needed to achieve the going rate of profit. If one firm tried to underpay the worker with a salary of $35,000, (ignoring, for the moment, the discount needed to achieve the required rate of profit) that person would be an undervalued asset because their associated revenues will be higher than their compensation/cost. Another firm would be inclined to offer the worker $38,000, another $39,000, and so on until the workers' wage is ultimately bid up to $40,000. But the price will not be bid higher because if a firm paid more than the $40,000 the worker is capable of producing, it would lose money. Similarly, all workers together (along with supplies, machines, etc.) are paid the most that can be paid for them without losing a moderate profit margin. Total costs for a company, on average, will be equal to the amount of money the company takes in, except for the amount discounted from costs that is equal to the average, economy-wide rate of profit.[25] Were there no waiting and no capital involved, a company's costs would equal the amount of money it brought in.

What does all this led up to? Simply this: far from exploiting workers, companies do exactly the opposite. They (1) create jobs, (2) pay workers more than they would make on their own by being self-employed, and (3) provide the tools, technology, and machines to improve productivity and increase profits, thereby raising wages. All of this is thanks to entrepreneurs, business owners, and capitalists (who in some cases may be one and the same). While their big profits are short-lived, in the long run their actions result in permanent gains

---

[25] Again, except for those firms temporarily making high profits from introducing new products or cheaper production methods, and, except by firms making below average profits because of the fact that they are uncompetitive.

for the wage earners. That should make businesspeople the workers' best friends, not their worst enemies.

Given these truths, it is ironic if not indeed tragic that the exploitation of labor is at the heart of many arguments for why we need government protection from companies that would supposedly otherwise abuse workers and pay them unfair salaries. We can see now that, on average, this could not be the case. Businesses would certainly like to pay lower wages and to take advantage of the workers, and in fact most care nothing about the workers personally beyond making sure that they are happy enough to be productive and help bring in revenues for the company. But businesses are not *able* to underpay workers because of the market forces explained above. If companies pay too little, workers can instead choose to work for other employers who will pay higher wages. The same principle applies to workers who want to earn more money—though they would like to earn more, they cannot ask for more than they are worth in the marketplace because their price will be uncompetitive: other workers with similar skills and abilities will sell their labor services for less money (i.e., the market wage). As with the prices of anything else in the economy, the price of labor is ultimately determined by supply and demand, not by individual greedy employers.

Capital Structure as the Driving Force of Rising Wages

It should be clear at this point that what helps workers, besides the ideas of entrepreneurs and the expertise of the business owners, is *capital*. The availability of capital derived from savings makes possible the transformation of an idea into real, physical goods and services, and the ability to produce these goods at faster rates, and with increasing salaries. Countries that experience a continually rising standard of living do so only because of a growing capital structure.

Since we now know that a capital *structure* is the collection of physical buildings, factories, machinery, and tools in place that make not only the consumer goods we buy, but also additional capital goods that allow us to make even more consumer goods, it should be clear that the bigger the capital structure, the more we can make of everything we need, and the more real wealth we have.

The key to using this capital structure is the existence of a division of labor in producing things (remember our castaways, with one fishing and another making fishing nets). Think of all the plants and factories we have and how there is a division of labor of industrial producers, just as there is a division of labor of workers. Any product you buy is assembled from individual parts, possibly thousands of parts, which are often made by different companies in different places. For an automobile, for example, sheet metal might be made by one company, leather by another, screws, radios, wiring, glass, rubber, and plastic each by other individual companies.

These companies are all part of a division of labor involved in the production of capital goods. The greater the division of labor of these capital goods, the more capital goods that can be made; this will ultimately result in more consumer goods. Each of the individual automobile components listed above was in turn produced by multiple companies: for example, raw materials dug out of the ground by one company get sent to another company to be cleaned and processed, then to another company to be mixed with other raw materials from yet another company and transformed into a new semi-finished material, and so on. For instance, it takes a combination of iron, carbon, silicon, graphite, chromium, nickel, and molybdenum to produce stainless steel. Semi-finished materials may go through several more stages before becoming something like sheet metal or screws. Now, think of all the tools, materials, and machines needed to process these raw materials—which themselves were made from thousands of different components from multiple sources—just to make them available for the original mining company to use in extracting the original raw materials which were later fed into these other goods. This complex web of production facilities, this subdivided capital structure, is what makes possible the standard of living we have today. It is also what is at risk of being diminished by the proposed policies of socialist-leaning politicians (which includes most Democrats *and* Republicans) and environmentalists—policies which tax, regulate, and restrict production to the point of suppressing it even more than has occurred already.

Economist Murray Rothbard[26] often used a fascinating example of what was involved just to get a ham sandwich on his kitchen counter, and the number of years it took. The steps included such things as building a farm to raise cows that produce milk with which to make cheese, and growing rubber trees in order to produce rubber that would become tires for trucks that would deliver supplies such as wheat to the baking company that would bake the bread. This type of production structure consists entirely of capital goods (tens of thousands of them)—goods used to make things that will make other things that will eventually make consumer goods. Every factory producing the capital goods that go into producing other factories and machines all exist ultimately for the production of consumer goods—the "stuff" we have in our lives. The larger the production structure, the more "stuff" that can be made. In short, the bigger the capital structure, the wealthier, healthier, safer, and more comfortable we can be. Think of the process of production described above in contrast to production in some poor countries in Africa or Asia where people are producing only simple things, and all largely by hand, with crude, simple tools. They lack our modern factories, machines, tools, and technologies. It is for the lack of capital goods, not because of exploitive companies, that these peoples do not have our standard of living.

How Wealth Redistribution Harms the Poor

From the explanation on how the capital structure provides wealth, it should be clear that things our government does to support a growing capital structure will help us, and things that inhibit or especially reverse the growth of a capital structure will harm us. Since savings (monies we citizens have in banks, investment accounts, savings accounts, CDs, pensions, 401Ks, etc.,) and monies that come from companies reinvesting their profits instead of paying them out to the owners of the companies are used to build this capital structure, it should be obvious that the more savings we have, the bigger the capital structure we will have.

---

[26] Murray N. Rothbard, *Man, Economy, and State: A Treatise on Economic Principles* (1962; Auburn, Ala.: Ludwig von Mises Institute, 2009) and *For A New Liberty: The Libertarian Manifesto* (1973; Auburn, Ala.: Ludwig von Mises Institute, 2006).

Taxing the rich, who have the most savings and monetary capital, is among the most damaging things that could be done for the overall economic health of the economy. When we take money from the rich, that money goes to our government and is spent. Whether it is given by the government to other people to spend or is spent by the government itself on behalf of all of us, it is consumed. This is somewhat true even when government spends on roads, bridges, and other infrastructure. Since government does not operate with profit and loss statements, it is a virtual certainty that it usually consumes more resources in producing something than society gets out of it.[27, 28] This will be explained in detail later. Regardless, most government spending does not go toward infrastructure, but to thinly disguised wealth-redistribution schemes that are, most unhelpfully, a net consumption of wealth.

As a rule, we can consider that when the wealth of the rich, or of any of us, goes to pay taxes to the government, it is consumed. When wealth stays with its rightful owners, that portion not consumed is mostly used by businesses as monetary capital, which is transformed into capital goods. This is especially true for the rich, who save an overwhelming majority of their wealth.

Money in banks, savings institutions, and investment firms is loaned out or invested in places where it is ultimately used for the production of consumer goods (including services).[29] Again, the more consumer goods we create, the more our real wages rise relative to the costs of things we buy—things become cheaper in real terms.

---

[27] Nonetheless, government spending on infrastructure is far more productive than outright consuming all of the money at once.

[28] If this comes as a surprise, consider that virtually every instance of a government service that is privatized (and not subsidized) results in reduced operating costs. This means that the operations under previous government management were much more inefficient and therefore less profitable, and almost certainly unprofitable. Similarly, socialist economist John Maynard Keynes promoted government funding of social projects because of the very fact that private companies would not engage in them due to their unprofitability.

[29] The majority of firms who take on investment capital operate in the capital goods industries where large-scale investment in factories and equipment with lives of 20 or more years are required. Consumer goods industries, for the most part, do not require such heavy investment. The use of monetary capital by the capital goods industries far outweighs monetary capital used by both the consumer goods industries and by individual consumers (for purposes of financing homes, automobiles, etc.).

We can generally think, somewhat abstractly, of things in the following fashion: Every $1 *not* paid in taxes becomes $1.20 if left in the hands of its owners. If that same $1 goes to the government through taxes and is consumed, it becomes $0. The additional 20 cents created by capitalists can be thought of as a new tool with which to produce, and therefore a new consumer good or service, while the $0 can be thought of as a tool or good never having been created to begin with. Wealth kept by its owners, when saved, creates new jobs and products for us. Wealth taken and given to someone else is spent and disappears forever. It cannot be emphasized enough that the spending for capital goods and labor is paid for by savings, not by consumer spending! For when we go to purchase a car, home, or television set, these things have already been made before we arrive at the store. The necessary spending for production takes place long before we consumers show up, and is funded by savings/monetary capital. Without capital, there would be no money or tools with which to make things—we would all have to produce individually by hand. This would include even our cars and homes, as it is savings that pays for both the home and cars to be built in the first place and to finance them once they are built (since most of us could not afford to pay cash up front).

Think of the effect this has on individual workers. Consider that most politicians propose taking money from the rich to give to those who don't earn as much. When this occurs, the redistributed money serves as a subsidy (or entire income) for those with lower salaries. But once they spend the money, it's gone forever. How will this money be reproduced? Can the rich just somehow "make" more? No, they can't, not for each portion of wealth taken from them. Even if the rich earn more afterward, the total amount of wealth existing in society is already diminished by the amount that was consumed. In fact, the rich need the monetary capital—i.e., the money that the government gives away in benefits to the poor—to make more money for themselves and thereby create new jobs and wealth for the rest of us.

The less savings and monetary capital businesses receive with which to operate, the less wealth the businesses can create for us. This means fewer jobs, and fewer goods being produced. If the lower income groups did not receive free money from (mostly) the rich, they would instead receive ongoing (and rising) salaries and a constant increase in goods available to them at constantly lower prices. *Only capital creates jobs and pays wages.* This is why wealth redistribution does not work. Taking from the rich will indeed harm the rich, but it will harm the poor considerably more.

How Government Creates Unemployment with Minimum Wage Laws

Politicians like to tell us that if we elect them, they will create jobs for us. This is impossible, unless they intend to expand government and have taxpayers pay more government workers to produce unprofitable services, or, to directly finance the creation of specific jobs in a specific marketplace with taxpayers' money. In either case, a destruction of wealth is involved, and the jobs—unlike private sector jobs—do not pay for themselves and thus require yet new taxpayer funding each year, which further reduces capital in the economy. Except for the few wealth-destroying activities such as building space stations[30] and military bases, government creates and builds nothing. It thus has no power to create real jobs in the marketplace; it can only "manage" and regulate. It is only individuals and individual companies that produce and create; their ideas and capital are what *profitably* create jobs. *The only way politicians can create beneficial jobs for us in the marketplace is by undoing the existing policies that create unemployment.*

That's right, the government (and only the government) creates unemployment, except for unemployment that arises from temporary factors such as switching between jobs. The notion that there could not be enough jobs for everyone is absurd. Think back to the desert island example: can we imagine that regardless of whether there is one person or many people on the island that they could ever run out of things to do to improve their standards of living? The same is true in our economy today. There are many more things needing to be done than we have people to do them. Most companies operating

---

[30] The space stations might *eventually* help us produce wealth, but do not currently. Even if they did, consumers would likely prefer to have other things for their lives instead of space stations. If space stations were to be a consumer preference (i.e., cost effective), they would likely be so decades or centuries down the road, not now. Plus, many things NASA is associated with having created were actually created by others. On this, see Tim Swanson, "What won't NASA Build Next," http://mises.org/daily/2434.

today, given available monetary capital, would expand production of what they are currently producing, or create new lines of businesses if only they had additional workers available to do this new work. And the more people we would have producing, the more things we could produce.

So then why is there unemployment? Primarily because some workers are prevented from working by having the cost of their labor fixed artificially high, above the market price, by law.[31] This is done in two primary ways. The first way is by the existence of a minimum wage. As we learned earlier, workers are compensated based on the expected value of what they can produce. If the government prevents companies from hiring workers for less than a given wage, and if workers are not capable of contributing enough to company revenues to be able to cover the cost of their wages, they will not be hired. If a worker's contribution to production brings in $5 of company revenues per hour, then paying the worker $7 per hour will mean a loss of $2 per hour to the company. Such workers will thus be left out of the workforce because they are unprofitable.

One might counter-argue that companies should pay a minimum hourly wage of $7 simply in order for the worker to survive given the cost of living. This argument will be addressed later in the section on poverty. It could also be argued that companies could pay more to workers by paying the difference out of profit, or by raising their prices. Neither of these is possible. As was explained earlier, businesses pay the maximum amount they can afford to pay for both labor and physical capital. Paying more will cut into the capitalists' returns, or eliminate their profit altogether, which will drive them away toward other ventures; the entire company could thus go under (not to mention that companies must reinvest much of their profit in order to produce next year's goods). Similarly, businesses cannot raise their prices to pay for higher labor costs. If they were able to raise prices at all, they would have already done so simply to make a higher profit. Businesses charge as much as the market will bear given a particular amount

---

[31] And to a lesser degree by other labor laws such as those dictating maximum hours one can work as well as laws restricting the hiring and firing of workers, both of which are more intensely implemented and destructive in Western Europe and South America, where unemployment rates often reach over 20 percent.

of money in the economy; if they charge more, they will make less money because demand will drop. Businesses across the entire economy will only raise prices if there is an increase in the quantity of money in the economy—i.e., the government prints more money. The current discussion is based on a fixed quantity of money in the economy at a given time.

If companies charge more, people will purchase a lower dollar amount (higher price times a lower overall quantity purchased). If companies charge less, their customers will purchase a higher dollar amount (lower price times a higher overall quantity purchased). Which way is optimal? Companies charge an amount that maximizes the total revenue they receive based on a price/quantity mix that results in the highest amount of revenue. If they charge more than the optimal amount, the total dollar amount of goods purchased by customers at that particular price/quantity level will be lower than the total dollar amount purchased at the optimal point possessing a lower price and higher quantity.

As an example, consider a theoretical burger joint where the owner is wondering whether raising prices would make it possible to pay more to the workers. **Figure 1.4** reveals the different amounts of revenues that would result from various prices of hamburger plates. Lowering the prices of each burger plate results in more burger plates sold. Raising the prices of each burger plate results in fewer burger plates sold. We can see that this owner's optimal price to charge for a burger plate is $5.10. Charging more than this will result in lower *revenues* because the increase in price causes customers to buy fewer burger plates. Charging less than $5.10 will also result in lower *revenues* because even though the lower price leads to greater volume, it also means that fewer total dollars make it into the till. This example shows us that if the restaurant owner tried to charge more in order to pay workers more, the entire restaurant would lose business. The likely result would be the laying off of at least one worker in order to maintain profitability.

The minimum wage can help no one except those remaining workers who receive increased pay at the expense of the ones let go. Ultimately, having a minimum wage harms those it purports to help. But it's more than ineffectual; it's damaging. Those who are hurt the

	Price of Burger Plate		Number of Burger Plates Purchased at the Given Price		Total Amount Spent / Total Revenues
	$5.70	x	482	=	$2,749
	$5.55	x	511	=	$2,837
	$5.40	x	537	=	$2,899
Optimal Amount to Charge	$5.25	x	558	=	$2,931
	$5.10	x	575	=	$2,933
	$4.95	x	587	=	$2,903
	$4.80	x	592	=	$2,843
	$4.65	x	594	=	$2,760

Figure 1.4: Optimal Amount to Charge: Companies, in selling their products, will choose the price and quantity combination which maximizes total revenues.

most are those with the lowest productivity—younger, less educated, inexperienced workers. Every time the minimum wage is increased, unemployment rates rise for this group, particularly for black, male teenagers. Further, as unskilled labor becomes too expensive to hire, businesses find it cheaper to replace labor with technology (automation, etc.). This is a primary reason why, for the most part, we no longer have many gas station attendants, maids or doormen.

Most economists, free market-oriented or not, do not support minimum wage: it's one of the few topics nearly all agree on. Those who do support the minimum wage usually do so for ideological or political reasons. The ideological reasons are based on emotions, not economic facts. The political reasons are obvious: to most politicians it seems not to matter whether they truly help or harm citizens. What is important to politicians is to be *perceived* as helping people. When Congress approves minimum wage legislation after hearing testimony from economists, most, if not all, of them voting in favor of it must surely be aware that the law will not help workers. The only explanation seems to be that they pass the law simply to look good to constituents who don't understand the harm done.

In his 1993 textbook,[32] Joseph Stiglitz wrote detailed explanations of how minimum wages, which are a type of price floor, cause unemployment. Yet after being appointed chairman of President Clinton's Council of Economic Advisors (CEA), he suddenly changed his opinion and supported minimum wage legislation. Perhaps he did this to be seen a "team player." President Clinton in turn said that *he* supported the legislation because his CEA supported it. Stiglitz, as leader of the CEA, pointed to the fact that a handful of economists had signed a petition in support of the legislation as the main reason that he had chosen to support it. In the end, this minority of economists all supported it simply because they all supported it.[33]

The economists who come up with obscure and often methodologically and theoretically questionable statistical studies that contradict most other studies on the minimum wage and conclude that increasing the cost of labor can somehow improve the lot of workers, are either ignorant of economics or are attempting to circumvent economic laws. Logic alone tells us that if the price of labor is raised above the value of its usefulness, there will be less of a demand for it.

After all, if raising wages will help workers, then why not apply the minimum wage to everyone, and make the minimum wage $100 per hour? Or $1,000,000 per hour?[34] Our politicians do not do this because they know that most of us would then be unemployed. We will see in Chapter 6 that artificially high wage rates were the primary reason the Great Depression lasted so long, and why it even evolved from a simple recession into a depression.

How Government Creates Unemployment by Sponsoring Union Coercion

The second way government causes workers to be unemployed is by allowing unions to, in effect, extort companies and by preventing

---

[32] Joseph E. Stiglitz, *Economics* (New York: W.W. Norton, 1993).

[33] Vedran Vuk, "Professor Stiglitz and the Minimum Wage" (2006), http://mises.org/daily/2266.

[34] Naturally, pro-minimum wage economists managed to come up with "studies" where numbers were manipulated to show that a low minimum wage is helpful, but a high minimum wage is not.

companies from dismissing workers who extort them. This is another form of unemployment caused by forcing companies to pay artificially high wages. Since companies have a fixed and limited amount of money they can expend on labor, they end up paying the same dollar amount of labor costs, but to fewer workers. Again, some workers benefit at the expense of others. And it's not only the workers who get laid off from unionized companies who suffer: when union workers get laid off, they often have to find jobs in the non-unionized part of the economy, adding to the number of workers competing for jobs elsewhere and thus lowering wages of jobs outside of "union shops." In the end, union workers gain at the expense of all other workers in the economy.

How do unions make companies pay workers more money against their will and best interest? The government forces companies to do so. The Norris-LaGuardia Act of 1932 deprived employers of the ability to obtain federal court injunctions against labor-union coercion. The National Recovery Act and the Wagner Act of 1935 made it mandatory for companies to recognize labor unions and to bargain with them (to pay higher wages than they want to pay or can afford to pay) or else be found guilty of "unfair labor practices." Imagine that you run a business and employ people who have agreed to work for a certain wage. Then, they all come to you and tell you that they demand 10 percent higher wages than they agreed to, or they will stop working and effectively shut down your business. You know that you can't afford to pay more, so your only choice is to replace them with other workers. But then you find out that you can't because they have unionized and the government therefore forces you to negotiate with the original workers—to pay them somewhere between their current price and the 10 percent higher wages they want. In the end, you will be forced to pay more than you can afford. It's your company and your property, but the government tells you that you must give in to threats or be taken to prison. Since you only have so much money you can spend on labor, in order to pay workers a higher wage, you must fire workers, so that the remaining workers can have the salaries of the ones who are fired.

Unions would be incapable on their own of imposing uncompetitive costs on employers. Only by preventing employers from replacing them with workers willing to accept the wages offered can union workers hold wages artificially high. This is why they threaten and torment non-union workers who consider taking their jobs for the market wage, and why they use the government to prevent employers and non-union employees from negotiating market wages (i.e., from freely exchanging money for labor services in a free market).

Many people who understand the damage that unions do today still maintain that unions somehow helped in the "old days." They often argue that it was only because of unions in the early part of the twentieth century in America or during the industrial revolution in the U.K. that workers managed to get ahead. This is a fallacy. Unions have *never* helped any group as a whole. Mines and factories in the old days had competition too, from traditional self-sufficient farming as well as from other employers. They thus had to pay competitive wages in order to attract workers. Workers *chose* to leave farming and to instead work in mines or factories because they felt they benefited by doing so; they were free to leave at any moment. Mines and factories paid much lower wages then relative to today because they did not have the productivity-improving capital goods we have today.

Since it is *employers* that raise the productivity of labor and thus wages and not the unions, unions can only *prevent* the increased productivity of labor. They are against technology because they falsely believe it will obviate the need for workers. They prevent progress by preventing the implementation of labor-saving machinery—but what this actually prevents is an increase in productivity. Since it is increased productivity that raises wages, not coercion, unions prevent higher standards of living for *all* of us.

But unions do more damage than just cause unemployment. They also run companies out of business. Since they prevent companies from adopting more efficient methods of production, they cause them to lose their competitiveness. Part of this entails the production of lower quality goods brought about by the prevention of technological advancement. They can also force companies to raise selling prices to the point where the companies' revenues decline because their prices are higher than those of competitors. These things have crippled America's steel, shipping, and textile industries, to name just a few, and are currently threatening the automobile industry. Unions are a primary reason Ford and GM make lower quality cars at higher prices than their foreign competitors.

Union demands and government-forced compliance with these demands drag companies down in other ways, too. In 2006, after GM's assembly plant in Oklahoma City shut down, the company was actually obliged by its UAW contract to pay 2,300 employees full salaries and benefits for doing no work at all. They reported to work each day to read, watch TV, or chat.[35] Without the UAW, GM would have had an average cost per automobile similar to that of non-unionized Toyota, which makes an average profit per car of $2,000, while GM makes no profit per car. In 2005, the *Cincinnati Enquirer* reported that the UAW contract costs GM $2,500 per car. [36] According to CNBC television, the costs of future union healthcare burdens alone total $1,500 per car.[37] These costs equal the difference in competitiveness between GM and Toyota. The Center for Automotive Research estimates that the Detroit automakers spend an average of $63.65 per hour on production (excluding buyout and jobs bank costs) while non-unionized Toyota spends an average of $47.50.[38]

Because of government-imposed union power, companies are often prevented from making decisions that are best for the company because many decisions must be approved by union bosses. Employers must obtain union approval for new investments and strategies, on top of jumping through other union hoops (for example, purchasing goods only from unionized companies and thus paying higher prices). Unions are parasitic organizations that thrive only by weakening and ultimately destroying companies. The ultimate goal of unions is to forcefully transfer wealth to unions from these companies by making the companies pay higher-than-market salaries and benefits for doing as little work as possible. Unionization is literally legalized theft.

---

[35] George Reisman, "Where Would General Motors Be Without the United Automobile Workers Union?" (April 19, 2006), http://mises.org/daily/2124.

[36] Ibid.

[37] Phil LeBeau, "GM and UAW Seal Deal: Was Strike Worth It?" *CNBC* (September 26, 2007).

[38] Katie Merx, "UAW contract: Nuts and Bolts," *Free Press* (September 29, 2007).

When unions face resistance from companies in getting what they want, they resort to violence. Union violence is well detailed in a 540-page 1983 book from the Industrial Research Unit of the Wharton School at the University of Pennsylvania entitled *Union Violence: The Record and the Response by Courts, Legislatures, and the NLRB.*[39] The book cites over 2,598 incidents, including murder, attempted murder, destruction of property, arson, sabotage, stoning, shooting, stabbing, chaos, beating, dynamiting, intimidation, and threats.[40] Police forces are well known for looking the other way and not getting involved in these incidents. The police, who are usually unionized themselves, are often sympathetic to unions since they consider them "brothers" who are fighting for their "rights."

Union *members* are either gamblers or oblivious to the results of their own actions. This must be so because by forcing companies to raises wages for some of their members, they force other members to be unemployed. If union members are aware of this consequence of forcing their wages higher, they are playing Russian roulette with their jobs given that they don't know which ones of them will be let go and which will be kept on. If they are not aware of the consequences, then they simply don't understand the dangers that unions pose to them.

The only union members who have mostly secure jobs are the union bosses and economists. The bosses negotiate how many workers they will lose for a given pay and benefits increase. The role of the so-called labor economists is to perform the calculations that estimate the costs and benefits of the proposed trade-off. Union bosses are known to be concerned primarily with their "senior" members. The newer or less experienced members are easily disposable to union bosses (except, of course, that the loss of their membership fees will be mourned).

What about the politicians who support unions? Are they aware of the damage that unions cause to companies, employees, and

---

[39] Armand J. Thieblot, Jr., Thomas R. Haggard, and Herbert R. Northrup, *Union Violence: The Record and the Response of the Courts, Legislators and NLRB* (1999).

[40] Ibid. (The list of offenses, and the book itself, was recently raised by Thomas J. DiLorenzo, "The Myth of Voluntary Unions," Mises Daily (September 14, 2004) http://mises.org/daily/1604).

consumers? Those who are aware are guilty of knowingly supporting something that harms the very workers they proclaim to protect.
Those who are not aware are *still* guilty of intervening in the free
market by preventing the voluntary labor arrangements entered into
between employers and workers, and tampering with something they
know nothing about. But why would politicians support something
that either they know harms workers or something they are uncertain will produce a better outcome than would a free market? Because
they care more about votes than they do about the gains or losses of
others. Unions represent a major constituent with large-scale voting
power. This is why Democrats fall all over themselves to convince
unions they will support them. Even Republicans pay homage: in the
2008 Republican debates, Mitt Romney rather moderately stated that
there are good and bad unions, and Rudolph Giuliani proudly stated
that he recognized the good that unions have done, and cited his
grandmother as having progressed out of poverty in her career as a
garment worker because of unions. In this ongoing struggle for political power, it is the workers who suffer.

If one argues that it is not true that unemployment arises only
because government has forced wage rates to be higher than the value
of what workers could produce (and above the price at which they
would voluntarily work), one has to explain why employers would
not hire more people at lower wage rates, while still paying the same
amount of total labor costs they incur currently. So for example, if
there are 10 people in an economy available for work and employers who have $100 available to pay out in wages have hired only nine
of these people for an average wage of $11.11 ($11.11 × 9 people =
$100), why would they not instead hire all ten people for $10 each ($10
× 10 people = $100).[41] With one additional person working, the com-
pany could produce more goods. Why would an evil capitalist willingly pay this current higher wage rate instead of a lower one? Only
because the government does not permit the workers to accept a
lower wage.

---

[41] Skill level does not apply: there is always work available for unskilled people, and their
salary will be in accordance to their skills.

To argue that at any given point in time there is only so much work to do is illogical. If there will be more work to do next year, why couldn't we do some of that work this year? We produce twice the amount of goods today that we did in 1970. Why couldn't we have used some of the unemployed labor in 1971, 1972, etc. to produce some of the additional amount of goods that were later produced in 1975 or 1980 or today in excess of what we produced in 1970? Why couldn't we use some of the unemployed people who exist today to produce more lumber, automobiles, nails, hula hoops, doorman services, garbage pickup services, construction services, McDonalds hamburgers, janitorial services, etc. (labor requiring mostly unskilled, unknowledgeable laborers)? Construction companies, for example, would like to have more workers who could hammer more nails. They could certainly use these unemployed people if it didn't cost them anything. Wouldn't they also pay $1 per day or $1 per hour? Or even $3 per hour? Of course they would. Saying that there is no more work to be done is simultaneously saying that there are no more goods and services we individuals want to consume (i.e., that as consumers we would have no more need or want of the additional things we would make as workers).

How Other Government Regulations Create Lower Wages and Unemployment

The consequences of any regulation that government imposes in the workplace are ultimately borne by workers and/or consumers. The more costs imposed on employers—for example, requiring better workplace health and safety regulations—the lower salary workers receive. As we've seen above, the costs cannot come out of profits, or else the companies will go under.

It is a mistake to think that workers need "protective" regulation at all; it is a fallacy to believe that workplaces will not improve without forced regulation. OSHA and EPA regulations came about only in the 1960s and 1970s as workplaces had already reached a state similar to what they are today. In other words, workplaces have been improving for hundreds of years without government force. Employers have a natural incentive to make workplaces safer, healthier, and more comfortable in order to attract laborers. For example, if company A has air conditioning and a safer environment than workplace B, which is uncomfortably hot and less safe, workers will choose workplace A as long as they are paid the same. Companies with less desirable workplaces will have to pay more for labor, but since they can't easily afford to pay higher salaries, they compete with more satisfactory workplaces. This is why many workplaces today offer gyms, free food and drinks, entertainment, and other amenities voluntarily, without government force. In India, the outsourcing boom has resulted in a lack of qualified workers, and companies are not only bidding up wages to the point that they are increasing at over 30 percent per year, but they are also competing by offering myriad other benefits such as defined career paths, quicker promotions, more workplace amenities and services (such as transportation to work), more holidays, and flexible work schedules.

But when government tries to force such improvements before they are economically viable, workers will foot the bill with lower salaries. Think of the American textile factories in the early part of last century. They were hot in the summer and cold in the winter. They had poor lighting and bathrooms (if they had any bathrooms at all). Now suppose the government had forced employers to install central air, which since it was invented only in 1902, was still enormously costly even in, say, 1910. Suppose further that the employers were forced to install nicer, bigger bathrooms with a minimum number of stalls. In addition, imagine they were compelled to put in carpet, more windows, cutting edge technology lighting, and a break room stocked with food. Clearly, the less developed workplaces of those days could not have afforded such luxuries. They would have had to lay off many workers to pay for the additions, or else paid workers much less money. To have paid for improvements out of profits would have resulted in business losses, and thus the entire business would have gone under.

Why Sweatshops, Child Labor, and Dollar-a-Day Wages Should Be Embraced

In the same way that companies 100 years ago could prosper only by developing workplaces that were in line with the level of development of the economy as a whole, people and companies in third-world countries today can only prosper by having such things as so-called sweat shops and child labor—living and working conditions that are the norm in those countries. To force improvements in working conditions or to prevent children from working means, at best, a reduced standard of living for these workers, children included.

The name "sweat shop" implies that those workplaces are of less-than-average quality. They are not. They are in line with (actually, usually nicer than) other workplaces in those countries. These workplaces are not more developed because the country in which they operate is not more developed. Companies there can simply not afford to have nicer shops, factories, or offices. While much criticism has been leveled at companies like Nike that outsource work to supposed sweat shops in undeveloped countries, the truth is that Nike employees' working conditions are usually an improvement over competing local companies, and the wages they pay are significantly higher than local market wages. In fact, the supposedly greedy and exploitative multinational companies we hear that conduct sweatshop operations in undeveloped countries usually pay about double the local wage.[42]

Were companies such as Nike to insist that their suppliers have first-world quality workplaces and pay developed-world-level wages, the result would be that any cost savings that caused them to select the undeveloped country in question would disappear. Thus, the local supplier producing and then selling shoes to Nike could not provide the shoes at the price they do currently under "sweatshop and child labor conditions." As a result, you, the consumer, would not buy as many of Nike's products, since the price would not be as low as it is, and you would therefore put the workers in these developed countries out of work. To the extent we keep paying for goods from so-called sweatshops, we not only help provide jobs for these poor workers, we help raise their standard of living by causing more investment and capital to flow to these locations (for the purpose of increased and more efficient production). We can also understand from the discussion on wages above, that paying "fair wages" to coffee growers in Latin

---

[42] Thomas Sowell, "Third World Sweatshops: Why Cambodian Workers Bribe for 'Sweatshop' Jobs," (January 27, 2004), http://www.capmag.com/article.asp?ID=3487.

America means that some farmers receive above-average selling prices at the expense of other local farmers who get nothing.

Child laborers are necessary in developing countries, as they were in developed countries when they were poorer, because many poor families in undeveloped countries rely on multiple incomes simply to survive. And just as it was more important for my grandfather to drop out of school in the 7th grade in 1907 to support his family so they would not go hungry, so it is more important for many children in undeveloped countries to work than to have the luxury of learning about science or history in school. If the working children of these countries did not have the employment they currently do, their likely alternative would be prostitution, begging, stealing, or starvation. Readers who have traveled to third-world countries will be more easily convinced of this. I, for example, witnessed scores of children in India whose parents cut off their fingers or hands so they would appear more pathetic and thus more likely to be given money by rich tourists; it's why these children appear mostly at stop lights soliciting people in taxis. Make no mistake: children should never be forced to work against their will; it should always be done voluntarily and with the permission of the parents.

Abraham Lincoln had less than one year of formal education because he was needed by his parents to work as a farm hand.[43] American society historically accepted child labor as necessity; it only became a "terrible" thing *after* child labor largely disappeared during the great depression. This was brought about by women's unions, which wanted to reduce the competition they faced from child laborers. It was actually parents and clergy, not companies, who fought the movement to ban child labor.[44] As prosperity increased in America, families were better off and did not need to have their children work as much. By 1930, only 6.4 percent of children of ages 10 to 15 were employed compared with about 30 percent in 1900. Though unions had tried for many years to prevent competition from children, they

---

[43] Thomas J. DiLorenzo, "How "Sweatshops" Help the Poor," *Mises Daily* (November 9, 2006), http://mises.org/daily/2384.

[44] Jeffrey Tucker, (The Problem with Child Labor Laws), http://insidecatholic.com/Joomla/index.php?option=com_content&task=view&id=2339&Itemid=48&limit=1&limitstart=1.

succeeded only *after* most children no longer worked anyway. The law that brought about the end of child labor served as a helpful political tool for politicians. As Jeffrey Tucker states:

> It was the same law that gave us a minimum wage and defined what constitutes full-time and part-time work. It was a handy way to raise wages and lower the unemployment rate: simply define whole sectors of the potential workforce as unemployable.[45]

Most laws that the government passes—laws that are usually cloaked in rhetoric claiming to help citizens—in fact constitute the use of government by one group to reap benefits at the expense of another group.

The media like to tell us that workers in third-world countries are living on "only a dollar a day." While it may be true, it is very misleading. A dollar a day in sub-Saharan Africa or Central America is not *worth* what it is in the United States. It is worth significantly more in real terms, and will buy workers there many things to enhance their lives. Houses in Ecuador, for example, average $820 per square meter;[46] while houses in the U.S. average $14,898 per square meter.[47] Wages adjusted for costs of living in Ecuador are indeed still disproportionately low relative to those in U.S., but this reflects the relative lack of capital accumulation there.

Though workers in poor countries earn lower wages than those in developed countries, they are nevertheless, on average, paid in accordance with the value of what they produce (where markets are permitted). Since the capital structure and thus labor productivity is lower in these countries, individual workers are unable to produce as much as workers in developed countries. But their wages are still market wages. Given the lack of work available overall in these poorer countries due to government actions, most workers are glad to receive the wages they do, which is why they often go

---

[45] Ibid.

[46] Global Property Guide, Square Meter Prices in Ecuador, http://www.globalproperty-guide.com/North-America/Ecuador/square-meter-prices/b.

[47] Global Property Guide, Square Meter Prices in The United States, http://www.global-propertyguide.com/North-America/United-States/square-meter-prices.

so far as to bribe factory managers to hire them.[48] It has also been shown that workers in these countries tend to choose a job in a factory at lower wages to a job working outside in the heat (or cold)—in nature—paying higher wages. It is not the workers who claim to be exploited and complain about slave wages, it is those of us in developed countries ignoring economic reality that try to "protect them" by preventing their getting the factory jobs they so desperately need and want.

The outrage over working conditions and wages of workers of poor countries should be targeted not at the employers who provide the opportunity for work and wages to these citizens but at the governments responsible for the general state of poverty in undeveloped countries. These governments usually (1) fail to either permit ownership of private property or to protect those ownership rights; (2) prevent foreign investment and capital from flowing into the country or confiscate it for themselves; (3) steal citizens' wealth every way they can (including direct, physical confiscation); (4) intervene heavily in their economies in the form of absurd rules, restrictions, tariffs, price controls, and printing of money to the point of causing hyperinflation; and (5) prohibit or heavily restrict not only international trade but even domestic trade. In these and other ways they run their economies into the ground and leave their citizens with few tools with which to improve their lives and standard of living.

Zimbabwe is a prime example. Today Zimbabwe's annual inflation is over 4 million percent, or 10,000 percent per day (it has a paper currency with a face value of $10,000,000), excluding compounding. Property has been literally stolen from certain groups and given to others, and grocery store shelves are empty and mass starvation is prevalent. Even in countries such as Guatemala where conditions are calm but people are generally poor, the blame should be directed at the government leaders who prevent their citizens from freely producing, trading, and borrowing foreign capital, and who prevent foreign firms from investing in their country, creating jobs, and sharing production knowledge with local businesspeople.

---

[48] Thomas Sowell, (Third World Sweatshops: Why Cambodian Workers Bribe for 'Sweatshop' Jobs), http://www.capmag.com/article.asp?ID=3487.

If people in any nation are poor, if they have not already increased their production of goods to the point that they have a decent standard of living, the only reason is that they have been prevented by governments or by some other coercive entity (e.g., mafia, warlords). There is plenty of proof—logical, circumstantial, and empirical—that any country, regardless of its starting level or level of education, will grow and flourish if given the freedom to do so. There is even more proof that governments cannot grow a country or its economy, only individuals can. Blame the local government leaders for sweatshop conditions and low wages; don't blame the only party that is not only capable of helping poor workers but actually doing so—the business leaders—for only they are providing capital investment in these countries and raising workers' productivity and wages (and most poor countries around the world are experiencing increasing standards of living).

The Notion of Inequality: Our Achilles's Heel

The ultimate goal of socialism and communism is to make us all equal or, at the very least, to redistribute wealth Robin Hood[49] style by taking from those who have more and giving it to those who have less. In seeking equality, socialists are not concerned with having everyone looking or acting the same (indeed, in these respects they often tout diversity, even by force); they care only about equality in financial terms (though many of them pretend to abhor money and disdain those who openly desire it). By understanding how wages rise and why we each receive the salaries we do, we can see not only that government-imposed transfers of wealth will not bring equality, but that such transfers will make things worse for the intended beneficiaries.

There is a tendency for us all to be paid in accordance with the value of what we are able to produce, and in accordance with the supply of available competition among each type of producer (secretary, veterinarian, store clerk, etc.). Teachers are paid less than athletes because there are many people capable of teaching, but relatively few capable of providing the entertainment athletes do. Since athletes bring in millions of dollars in revenues to their organizations, they

---

[49] Who was probably justified, incidentally, in stealing, because those he stole from had stolen it from society.

are paid the value of their production. The fact that there is as much demand for basketball—and thus high basketball salaries, as there are—simply reflects the preferences of consumers. Were there little demand for basketball, players would be paid very little.

In the same way, individual workers are paid based on what they can produce. A worker who can produce twice that of another will, on average, end up being paid twice as much, depending on the number of people with similar capabilities. Naturally, entrepreneurs and business leaders are paid much more than workers because they provide the guiding and directing intelligence[50] in the economy. Generally speaking, workers do not develop money-making ideas for consumers—businesses and entrepreneurs do. Workers do not provide the capital to companies and bear the risks of failure—capitalists do. Workers do not manage and design the specific and changing-as-needed divisions of labor within companies that lead to optimal production. Workers do not create the strategies and visions that allow companies to out-perform competitors. To the extent that workers are capable of contributing to any of these processes, they are recognized and rewarded accordingly, and will themselves then become business leaders and entrepreneurs. Examples of this abound; it seems that half of the business success stories are based on such instances.

It is not just blue-collar workers who are laborers: every person in an organization up to the CEO is a laborer. Naturally, those who contribute less to the creation of wealth are paid less; those who contribute most are paid the most. A laborer who uses a computer is likely to produce more than a laborer repairing machinery or answering telephones. Even laborers who use computers but perform only narrow tasks or manage only small groups—me included—are likely to produce less wealth for an organization than will those directing larger overall portions of a company or directing entire companies. Still, politicians continue to remark that it is the hard-working lower and middle classes that bring prosperity, as though business leaders and entrepreneurs do not work (or do not work very hard). President Obama went so far as to highlight the distinction between "the working class, as

---

[50] George Reisman, "Classical Economics vs. The Exploitation Theory," *Mises Daily*, (January 24, 2005).

opposed to the wealthy."[51] Yet these supposed slackers in reality spend an extra 30–40 hours on top of the standard 40-hour workweek, while the rest of us spend that time eating out and watching Celebrity Fit Club and Project Runway.

To take money from those who make more and give it to those who make less results in less wealth for everyone—*particularly* for the so-called poor—for three reasons: (1) as the possibility for business leaders and entrepreneurs to maintain ownership of their accumulated wealth is diminished, the incentive to take both monetary risks and career risks to create wealth are similarly diminished; (2) when there are fewer innovations and fewer new products and companies created by entrepreneurs looking to make a profit, there are also fewer new goods, new jobs, and new ways of raising labor productivity; and (3) as wealth is taken from the rich and given to the "poor," it is consumed instead of being transformed into physical capital and used to continually reproduce wealth. Wealth redistribution means that the poor receive one-time payments that disappear rather than ongoing payments in the form of wages. It also means that they miss out on receiving the additional and continual production of many more goods they would have at their disposal, goods that would reduce their real costs of living.

Capitalism may leave people far from equal in wealth, yet it leaves everyone better off than they would otherwise be. The poor today live better than most people in history ever have. Yet it seems that leftists of all variations cannot stand the idea that the poor (and often themselves) are not living as well as do some others.[52] They are willing to make everyone, including themselves, worse off just to attempt to bring about equality. Equality is an impossible goal because individual human beings are unequal in multiple dimensions: we each have different goals, intelligence, capabilities, interests, and ways of thinking.

---

[51] As stated in the question and answer session of his speech to the nation on April 29, 2009, upon his first 100 days in office.

[52] I am reminded of lyrics from one of my favorite musicians (the musical group James) which states, *"if I hadn't seen such riches I could live with being poor."*

It has been proven time and again that pure socialism or communism, while they do in fact result in a kind of equality of most citizens, does so only by way of making all citizens equally poor and equally suffering in their miserable level of existence from a lack of food, health, security, and personal freedoms. And again, ironically, even in socialist countries the term equality applies not to *all* citizens, but only to most. For the wealthy still exist in the form of the citizens' supposedly benevolent leaders who live lavishly while the citizens suffer with their truly slave wages. These great leaders, who impose equality and meager lives upon their subjects, live like kings off the production of the starving citizens.

Jealousy and the mistaken notion that financial equality is both desirable and achievable prevent all of us from having better lives. If we would all accept that most of us will never live like Bill Gates or Warren Buffet, or even the guy in the neighborhood down the street with the big house and the new tricked-out BMW, we will all be better off than we are now. No matter what rung of the ladder we are currently on, as long as we have the will and the freedom to do so, we can move up and increase not only our absolute wealth, but our wealth relative to that of others. As we will see in the following chapters, there is nothing holding us back. But if we're not careful, the simple emotion of jealousy resulting from a misguided desire for economic equality will destroy the economy we currently have. It might sound noble or benevolent to try to help one group by taking from another, but such an approach simply cannot work and will only result in harming most people—particularly the lower-wage group we intend to help. If we will permit and accept inequality, we can all realize consistently increasing standards of living for *everyone*.

Chapter 2

Trade:
What it is and How it Works

The more trade we have, the better off we are. The public generally supports the notion of free trade in theory, but if the average person is asked whether there should be no government restrictions on trade whatsoever (another way of asking if they support free trade) they default to the position that we still need government to regulate and control trade. In the same way, politicians, for the most part claim to support free trade, yet they spend considerable time and energy preventing it by implementing tariffs, quotas, subsidies, embargos, sanctions, and other types of trade restrictions, not to mention verbally criticizing America's trading partners for allegedly not trading "fairly" (there is no such thing as being able to trade unfairly, as we'll see below).

Trade is misunderstood by the lay person and politicians alike. While politicians don't care how trade really works, since their only goal is to impose whatever trade restrictions are perceived to help their constituents in order to gain votes, it is still important for the average voter to understand it, so that they can demand of their politicians to have the government cease using the tools it implements to reduce trade. This chapter will first cover the basics of how trade works, and then apply these principles to popular political issues related to trade.

The Basics of Trade

Specialization in production is the key to creating wealth for every single country. It was explained in the desert island example in Chapter 1 that individuals produce what they are best at making and they exchange what they produce for what others produce. The same concept applies to world trade. Each country specializes in the things it can produce most efficiently and it trades with other countries for what they produce.

The table in **Figure 2.1** shows two different hypothetical scenarios of both trade and lack of trade between two countries, China and Greece. In the first scenario, i.e., the top part of the table, there is no trade. Each country produces its own supply of both shirts and olive oil. Greece is a somewhat more advanced country with higher labor productivity than China; therefore it can produce more of both products than can China: $600 worth of shirts versus China's $500 worth, and $700 worth of olive oil versus China's $200 worth. If each country produces both products, Greece can produce $650 worth of goods and China $350. Both countries together can produce a total of $1,000 ($650 + $350) worth of goods.

In the second scenario, in the bottom part of the table, each country produces only the product at which it is best at producing: it specializes. Since China can produce a greater amount of shirts relative to olive oil, it produces shirts. Since Greece can produce more olive oil than shirts, it produces olive oil. With each country specializing in what it is best at, the two countries can produce more goods in total: $1,200 worth. Note that the total amount of production between the two countries is higher with only China producing shirts even though Greece is *better* at producing *both* shirts and olive oil. With Greece concentrating on the product in which it has a *comparative* versus *absolute* advantage, and letting China do the same, both countries benefit. The same concept applies to all countries and all things they produce.

Figure 2.1: Countries that specialize in making products in which they have a comparative advantage are able to increase their total production.

Domestic/Local Trade (Domestic/Local Specialization)

Trade is commonly thought of as taking place only at the international level between different countries, as shown above. But of course, it takes place at every level of society, even at our work places.

Just as countries specialize in producing what they're best at, so do individuals in an advanced society. Specialization of individual labor applies not only to self employment such as being a barber or free-lance photographer—where haircuts and photographs are exchanged in return for money with which goods and services are bought—but also to work within a company. A machine operator, packing specialist, marketing assistant, and CEO, all work together for a particular firm to produce a specific final product. The money which the company receives for the product is distributed amongst these laborers, and they in turn exchange their incomes for other goods from other companies. But even within this structure, each worker focuses on producing what he or she is relatively best at (as decided largely by supply, demand, and market prices for the jobs in question). If the marketing assistant were to also try and run the assembly line machines, while the CEO tried also to package the product for shipping, neither of them would accomplish as much as they could if each focused on the work in which they have a *comparative advantage*—it would not be nearly as efficient.

Trade also takes place at our doorsteps. Instead of spending your working hours only at work performing in your job, and then trading your salary for things you need, what if you tried to be self-sufficient? What if you tried to produce your own home, clothes, food, bed, television set, cell phone, medicines, automobile, and hot water heater? Your standard of living would be drastically lower than it is now. This is why specialization, or a *division of labor*, is so important. The more of a division of labor we have, both domestically and internationally, the more things we can have in our lives. Trade is simply the result of having a division of labor.

This logic would dictate that the worst thing we could do is try to be self sufficient and not exchange with those either near us or far away. If we aimed at self-sufficiency, we would not have specific knowledge of how to produce particular products. Instead, by having specialized knowledge, we can excel at being able to improve the things we produce and the ways we produce them. For example, one who makes picture frames constantly advances the technologies, machines, glues, types of wood and metal used in producing, etc., and can figure out how to make frames more cheaply and efficiently through the years, and with higher quality. Further, the more people there are involved in trade, the more specialists there are, the more brains that are involved, and the more unique ideas that come about. This alone is a reason why centralized command economies cannot work: government officials, or even regional officials and "industry" managers have no way to acquire the specialized knowledge needed for progress. Only profit-seeking, specialized, individuals build better mousetraps, not government bureaucrats or self-sufficient farmers.

Understanding how trade really works has very important implications for both social conditioning and government policy. The rest of this chapter will address common misperceptions about trade by both the man on the street and by political economists.

Don't Buy American—Buy What's Best

One of the consequences deducible from the principles stated above is that having the goal of "buying locally" does not help anyone. To take the logic to its end destination, buying everything locally would mean having our local economy entirely self sufficient. This absence of trade would severely diminish our standards of living.

This lesson includes understanding that it does not help to "buy American." To be clear, it helps to "buy American" for those products which America has a comparative advantage in making, and to "buy foreign" those products which it does not. The question naturally arises as to which is which, and how we should make purchasing decisions. The answer is that we can't know, so we should just buy in a way that we feel that we benefit on a case by case basis instead of purchasing for illogical political or emotional reasons. We don't know in advance which products should be produced by whom, but the market will tell us, but *only if* the marketplace is not distorted by government interference or consumers' deliberate attempt to change their buying patterns in the name of ineffective political "buy local" mentalities.

By listening to leftists or ultra-patriotic people who think they're helping the laborers in their country, consumers who deliberately buy American when foreign products are less expensive, and/or higher quality, keep the world production structure as it is. What's wrong with that, one might ask? The problem with an artificial production structure that it is not arranged in such a way that countries are producing what they are best at is less overall production and thus higher consumer prices and lower real wages; it means a reduction in our standard of living.

Intentionally buying only American goods when one would otherwise choose foreign products keeps American workers employed—temporarily—in jobs where they are producing goods which should be produced by other countries, while their labor would be more beneficial in another line of work. Because of this, there are fewer total goods produced and lower real salaries for both the laborers and the consumers.

For the same misguided reasons of trying to protect American jobs, governments apply import tariffs to foreign products to make them more expensive, causing consumers to buy [then] cheaper American products instead, when they otherwise would not. But this only hurts consumers, because without the tariffs, the foreign products would be cheaper. Consumers could instead buy the foreign products, and the domestic producers could instead make something else—something that they could make more cheaply than foreign producers. We would have a drastically higher standard of living today if it were not for the fact that world governments apply trade restrictions that prevent the optimal world production structure from taking shape, all in an attempt to protect their (inefficient) producers from competition or to increase government revenue. Just because the word "optimal" is used, or just because there was "only" a 20 percent difference in total production in our theoretical example in **Figure 2.1**, does not mean that the difference between our world production structure today and what it could ideally be has only a small effect on our lives. The difference between restricted trade and free trade is immense.

In either of these scenarios above, if domestic workers are in jobs that are truly not competitive, the day of reckoning is only being delayed by these policies, and money is wasted in the meantime in trying to keep an the economy artificially manipulated. In sum, trying to protect workers or trying to help the American economy by intentionally buying local goods when one would not otherwise, does not help the workers or the economy.

We Don't Need Energy Independence

By understanding the workings of trade, it is plain to see that there is no need for energy independence. America can always obtain oil by trading what we produce in exchange for oil produced by others. An often raised objection, that we could be held hostage by being deprived of oil by those who produce it is unfounded and will be discussed in detail in Chapter 4. America is obsessed with the idea that we should be energy independent, yet no one worries that we are not "shoe independent" or "television independent" (since most shoes and all televisions are made outside America). Living by being independent means a life of poverty. Living by engaging in trade means a life of prosperity.

The Economic Threat from China

As China is becoming more capitalistic and prospering, and as America is becoming more socialistic and falling behind, there is a popular concern that China will overtake us. To the extent that this theory hints ultimately at China's ability to have greater military power over the U.S. and the world, the concerns are valid. In that case, the roles will reverse: America would now fear China's military might just as China has feared America's potential military aggression for many years (as did the Soviets, who saw America as aggressors).

As far as the possibility of China harming us *economically* as it becomes economically stronger, all fears are unjustified. Whether or not the U.S. progresses economically, having China or any other country in the world become dramatically stronger economically is a *benefit* to America and every other country, because it will add to the world-wide production of goods and services, creating more useful things for citizens in every country, and lowering world prices. Additionally, another country with billions of brains and new ideas creating new inventions and new technologies, can only improve our lives. Consider how much worse off the rest of the world would be if they didn't have American (or western) technologies and goods. We can observe from documentaries and movies showing poor backward countries that their lives are improved by having western medicines, automobiles, telecommunications equipment, airplanes and the like.

New creations from China would further our own prosperity. Having not one, but tens of new countries rising into economic adulthood is a thing we should wish for.

In order for China to interact with us economically, they must *trade* with us. Free trade *never* involves one group gaining at the expense of another. Trade is beneficial to both sides; each side is willingly giving up what it has for what the other side has, because it feels that it will be better off. If one side does not think it will benefit from trade, it will not willingly engage in it.

Additionally, though the average person thinks we are being taken over by China and forced to take its cheap goods, it must be understood that less than 16 percent of US imports come from China, and only about 20 percent of China's exports go to the U.S.; about 80 percent go to other countries.

As a side note, China's rapid economic growth in the last three decades should serve to show that having a large or increasing population does not cause impoverishment. China was a nation of starving people under the communist policies of the 1970s, at which time the population was a little under a billion. After capitalism began to be allowed in modest increments starting in 1976, China became more prosperous, improving the lives of most citizens, including subsistence farmers. Today, its population is over 1.3 billion, and there is an abundance of food, consumer goods, and capital. The more people a nation has, the more hands and brains there are to engage in producing the things a country needs—assuming technology increases, which is almost certainly the case in a capitalist society. An increased population should increase economic growth and prosperity. Some socialists today comment that China is now growing by way of exploiting its workers. Besides the fact that such a notion is untrue, if it really were exploitation that brings increased wealth to a society, shouldn't all of us workers want to be exploited?

Trade Deficits Don't Persist in Free Markets

A common economic concern in the media is the size of America's trade deficit. What's seldom revealed is that the deficit is a result of government paper money. In a free market, under which gold would serve as money or would fully back money, trade deficits could not exist on an ongoing basis because of the free-market self-correction process that would take place under a gold standard. Historically, when countries were on gold standards, their trade balance tended towards zero. Gold would exist as money in a free market because it is the money that societies have chosen over and over through history, based on its possessing the ideal characteristics of a medium of exchange. Were it not for our government's preventing gold from being used in exchange (by making paper money legal tender, and by not legally enforcing contracts made in gold), our money today would be based on gold.

The self correcting mechanism, termed the Price Specie Flow Mechanism by classical economist David Hume, works as follows. If country A imports more than it exports, gold would flow out of the country, so as to pay for the goods being imported from country B, causing prices to fall in importing country A (and to rise in exporting country B). With prices becoming lower in country A than in country B, country A could not afford to import as many higher-priced goods, and would instead begin to *export* goods to country B, since country B would then want to purchase (import) more of the lower-priced goods from country A with its increased amount of gold. With goods then flowing from country A to country B, gold would flow back from country B to country A. Over time, prices would equalize between the two countries, and each country would have a zero balance of trade.

In our government controlled world, things don't work according to natural market forces. Instead, since America's central bank constantly adds to the quantity of paper money in the economy, our balance of trade is skewed, and we persistently import more than we export. Much of the money our central bank prints goes to pay for goods we import from foreign countries. Exporting countries are often willing to accept only our paper bills as payment, choosing not to in turn exchange them for our goods. In this case, they usually invest their dollars in American assets such as stocks, bonds, and factories. Many observers consider the amount our imports exceed our exports the amount by which foreigners "finance" us, since we Americans, in this case, are seen as buying beyond our means. But the trade imbalance can also be seen as the amount of excess consumption Americans can undertake *because* foreigners are willingly handing over goods to us without requiring that we produce and exchange something of value, since printing up paper bills creates purchasing power without having to produce in order to achieve that purchasing power. These are all problems arising from government intervention in the free market.

Who is "We" and Who is "Us"?

Let's take a moment and look more deeply at the structure of our trade deficit. We will soon see that the mere fact that a trade deficit exists is not necessarily meaningful in and of itself.

When defending the massive debts the U.S. government incurs, right wing economists and politicians (and now left wingers too, since *they* are now once again spending us into oblivion) usually state that "deficits don't matter" because "we owe it to ourselves." But the "we" who are spending the money (the government), and the "we" benefitting from the receipt of it (the poor), are different people than the "ourselves" who finance most of the debts (the rich). In the same way, our trade actions are comprised of different entities, the primary ones being the government, private businesses and private individuals. Some of these entities export more than they import, and some import more than they export. The total trade figures are really an amalgamation of multiple unrelated trades. The sum, or the net, is simply just that, and is for the most part meaningless.

The fact that trade totals do not tell the whole story can be more clearly understood by realizing the facts. Economist Sudha Shenoy[53] has shown by careful analysis of the official trade figures that the private sector trade deficit is actually balanced.[54] It is the government's particular trade position that is out of whack. Shenoy shows that government capital inflows—U.S. government borrowings which are an accounting counterpart to a trade deficit—started rising in the early 1980s, the same period in which America's trade deficit began

---

[53] University of Newcastle (Australia).

[54] Sudha Shenoy, "The Case Against Neo-Protectionism" (lecture), http://mises.org/multimedia/mp3/ss06/Shenoy.mp3.

to appear. Since that time, government capital inflows have risen 2.5 times faster than private capital inflows (and thus government trade deficits have increased in proportion).[55] Between 1980 and 1985, 17.3 percent of total capital inflows consisted of US government borrowings, on average. Between 2002 and 2004 34.4 percent of total capital inflows consisted of government borrowings, on average. Thus, the share of total capital imports belonging to the government almost doubled over that 24 year period. This increase reflects the government's borrowing in order to spend money it does not have. Understanding that the "state" is different from the individual should also help us see that the notion of a "national interest" is not necessarily a healthy one. What's important is not the interest of the state per se— the government and its officials—but of individuals citizens and their ability to improve their lives. The two are usually not in synch.

Additionally, it is usually stated that our trade deficits, which result in America's importing much more than it exports, reflect the lavish consumption of American consumers in excess of what they can really afford.[56] But this is not the case. The truth is that the bulk of *private* U.S. imports has always consisted of capital goods (factories, tools, machines, etc.), not consumer goods. In fact, as the trade deficit has grown, the proportion of consumer goods imported has *fallen.*[57] Therefore, it is completely wrong to say that American consumers are binging on imported consumer goods.

The Misconceived Notion that Trade Surpluses are Ideal

While much is made of America's trade deficits, and while they are viewed by most as a bad thing, in truth, our deficits are not necessarily harmful, because they are largely offset by *capital* surpluses. The flip side of importing more goods than we export is that we receive

---

[55] Sudha Shenoy, "'Is America Living Beyond its Means?'—Is That the Right Question?" http://hnn.us/blogs/entries/30606.html.

[56] It is true that Americans, due to government spending and tax policies, save very little of their incomes these days. But that shortfall has been made up for by savings from overseas, mainly Europe.

[57] Sudha Shenoy, "'Is America Living Beyond its Means?'—Is That the Right Question?" http://hnn.us/blogs/entries/30606.html.

Type of investment in the U.S. conducted by foreigners

	Percentage of All Capital Flows
Private portfolio investment (i.e., purchase of stocks & shares by foreigners)	31.4 percent
Private FDI (Foreign Direct Investment), i.e., purchase/construction of factories, purchase of machinery, etc., for such factories	18.0 percent
Other private investment (loans to companies, private purchase of shares, etc.)	10.2 percent
Private bank deposits & holdings	14.6 percent
Foreign official holdings of Federal US government debt	13.8 percent
Private holdings of Federal US government debt	8.7 percent

Figure 2.2: Allocation of Investments by Foreigners in the U.S., 1983–2004.

more investment capital than we send to other countries. A country which has a trade deficit (of goods) tends to have a capital surplus (of money—investments in stocks, bonds, real estate, businesses, etc.), and vice versa. These inflows serve as capital that America desperately needs. They are real savings, i.e., unconsumed production, which serve to promote a further expansion of real wealth in the U.S.

It is often argued that much of the capital inflows to the U.S. are not very helpful because they flow mainly into government coffers, not into the private, productive, sector. But the official figures tell a different story. Shenoy showed (**Figure 2.2**) that for the 22 years between 1983 and 2004 more than 75 percent of all capital flows into the U.S. have been private investments in the private sector.[58]

Additionally, even though capital going to the private sector where wealth is created is always more beneficial than that going to fund government consumption, having foreign capital flow into treasury bonds does help the country, *given our government's penchant for spending*. When government spends, it takes capital away from the private sector. The government's being funded to a large degree by

---

[58] Sudha Shenoy, "Foreigners and Those Vast US Dollar Holdings," http://blog.mises.org/archives/006487.asp.

foreign savings means the government needs to take less capital from domestic private enterprise. Foreign money flowing into the U.S. treasury has prevented increased destructive effects on capital accumulation that would have otherwise resulted from the government's policy of deficit financing. Then again, it could be argued that the foreign savings consumed by our government could instead go to the private sector in foreigners' own countries, so that *they* can create more wealth; in this case, both foreigners and Americans would be better off.[59]

Most people, economists included, believe that a country gains jobs by exporting more than it imports. This leads most governments to tax and regulate the economy in a way that artificially increases exporting sector. But both deficits and surpluses can be beneficial. By exporting heavily, economies can gain (monetary) purchasing power in order to acquire the things they need: a country buys imports by offering its exports in exchange. On the other hand, incurring trade deficits by importing more than it exports means an economy can receive large quantities of (physical) capital goods it needs. And, since trade deficits result in capital surpluses, investment capital also enters the economy in the form of monetary investment.

Different countries benefit from different types of trade balances. Britain has had a trade deficit since the end of the seventeenth century. It was also the largest single exporter of capital in the nineteenth century. Australia has been a net capital importer since the 1860s, with a trade deficit of 6.2 percent of GDP in 2007 versus America's 5.7 percent. Canada, New Zealand, and South Africa also import capital. Countries can continue developing with both surpluses and deficits. What's important for any particular country is not whether it imports or exports more goods, but whether it is importing or exporting in a way that helps it attain capital goods as much or more than consumer goods—that helps it produce rather than consume.

The conventional mercantilist notion that a nation's exports should exceed its imports merits a deeper analysis. We should undertake this

---

[59] It could also be argued that this is not true since the foreigners have actually already kept their savings, which were given to them in the form of local currency printed by the local central bank.

by first remembering that real wealth is not money, but what money exchanges for—goods. The goal of both production and exchange is to accumulate goods. Therefore, let's consider what would happen if a country exported *everything* it produces, and imported *nothing*. It would ship all of its goods abroad, and would take none in. It would get rid of all amounts of the very thing it is trying to end up with—goods. We can see from this that government policies which cause a country to export much more than it imports are not necessarily a good thing.

Remember, a country's trade balance reflects the net trade of multiple parties, each having different goals. It is really not useful to be concerned with an overall balance of trade, since it does not reflect the state of *individuals* and does not relay whether or not they are accumulating capital. After all, in our own lives, we are not so concerned with trade balances. I have massive trade deficits with Walmart, Pet City, and my local pizza place, importing lots of goods and services from them and exporting nothing to them in return. All of my employers have had large trade deficits with me. Yet all of us with trade deficits are saving, producing, and obtaining wealth.

Does Trade Harm Poor Countries?

Leftists often complain that free trade harms poor countries and disproportionately helps rich ones. This is not true in any way. Poor countries can only benefit from trade—their workers and entrepreneurs are paid for what they produce and sell to others, and all of their citizens gain access to additional goods they otherwise would not have access to, an occurrence which also lowers consumer prices in their country. There is no country that has ever become poorer by engaging in world trade. Quite the opposite is true: Many of the now first-world Asian countries experienced strong economic development only after they opened their markets. Japan has few natural resources, but became wealthy by exchanging labor services, and acquiring know-how and capital investment in the process.[60] Hong Kong, a country with an area of only 427 square miles built on hills that slide into the ocean, was a very poor country in the middle of last century. Within 40 years it became one of the wealthiest countries

---

[60] Though it did steal resources for a while from neighboring countries such as China.

in the world because it engaged in almost completely free trade. It is the only country that to this day has no direct trade restrictions at all, and it exports more than most developed countries. Hong Kong is a prime example of the fact that trade agreements are unnecessary. Any country can and will benefit even from unilateral free trade, letting their trade "partners" impose restrictions without taking any similar action themselves. The country with trade restrictions will get fewer goods at higher costs than they need to, while the country with no trade restrictions will be able to buy more goods at world prices.

In light of this fact, it should be understood that trade agreements are all about politics and protecting industries from competition and protecting workers from having to move to more appropriate employment—they are not about free trade in the least. Like most things political, the terms and descriptions used are contrary to the truth. Free trade means *free trade*: it is not necessary to write 1000-page-long trade agreements in order to freely trade without restriction. Truly free trade would require zero words and zero agreements.

Poor countries remain poor because they are un-free. Their lack of external free trade reflects (in part) their lack of economic freedom. For many decades, western "development" economists have taught poor countries that subsidies, tariffs, planning, and regulation will bring them prosperity. But those countries that have ceased adhering to the central planning suggestions of these economists and have instead opened their borders to competition and trade—such as many of the Asian nations—have realized dramatic economic growth.

Many left-wing economists point to the fact that America became prosperous while having government-restricted trade as a reason for not needing free trade. But two things should be considered. First, America had free internal trade between its various states which were not yet a consolidated single nation. Second, just because America intervened to prevent its economy from being free does not mean intervention brought prosperity. America progressed *in spite of* the government's obstruction. The case is no different today. We do not have free trade; we do not have free industries or free businesses. The government has its long arm in everything that takes place in such a way that we produce less than we otherwise would and have salaries lower than we otherwise would. So far, we have managed to progress even with this wind—or blizzard—in our faces. A dog with a missing leg can still run, just not as well and as fast as if it had four legs. Thus, three legs is *not* better than four. (Similarly, arguments that Sweden prospers while being socialist in a different way than America is socialist does not mean socialism brings wealth. It means that Sweden has enough capitalism to move forward despite socialist policies that hinder it.[61])

Another false accusation is that prices in poor countries are low because western buyers are paying less for foreign goods than they should be. But the fact is that prices there are set by the market. The prices of many goods exported by poor countries are due to low labor costs, which in turn are due to low productivity levels, which in turn are due to a lack of capital and lack of freedom to produce capital. But it also is very often the case that export prices are lower than they would otherwise be because governments in these countries subsidize production of the exported products. This is often the case with farmers. With monetary encouragement by governments in these countries to enter the industry, too many people become farmers, causing production to be artificially high and prices and profits artificially low. Because of this, Indian farmers, for example, have been committing suicide at astonishing rates. Yet socialists, in wanting, through misguided desires, to help these farmers, constantly promote more of the same government actions as before that will actually make them worse off, not better. Some would argue that the farmers need to farm because there are no other jobs. This argument is absurd. There are not enough *other* jobs because local governments have not allowed the economic freedom needed that would create capital and jobs economy-wide. They have instead chosen such wealth prohibiting policies as trade restrictions, including farm subsidies—policies that socialists promote as wealth creating. These will be addressed next.

---

[61] Not to mention that Sweden, importantly, permits *low* corporate tax rates, which prevents the consumption of capital.

Restrictions on Trade

Interference with trade harms poor and rich countries alike. Any policy that prevents as many goods from being exchanged as otherwise would be the case reduces supply and raises prices. It also prevents people from having the things they would desire but are prevented from doing so. These policies usually exist to "protect" workers and industries in the home countries, but in the long run, they do the opposite. This can be seen quite easily by observing the demise of our steel industry, which has been "protected" for years by labor laws and trade restrictions. Still, earlier this decade president Bush imposed new steel tariffs, raising the cost of steel to U.S. (and world) producers and consumers, and reducing the supply. Then, in retaliation, Europe imposed restrictions on imports, thus hurting European citizens. Who was better off? No one but workers, temporarily, and politicians who could claim to have saved jobs; at least for a year or two.

In spring 2009, Mexico slapped tariffs on 90 agricultural products coming from the U.S., thus depriving its citizens of more food at lower costs. Why? Because the U.S. failed to comply with North American Free Trade Agreement (NAFTA) requirements that Mexican trucks be allowed on American highways.[62] The U.S. reneged on its previous agreements because the trucking unions were upset about having to face competition. Therefore the government allowed the teamsters to benefit at the expense of the rest of the American people. The Obama administration said that it would work to create a new cross-border, long-distance trucking program between the two countries. The white house stated that:

> The president has tasked the Department of Transportation to work with the U.S. trade representative and the Department of State, along with leaders in Congress and Mexican officials to propose legislation creating a new trucking project that will meet the legitimate concerns of Congress and our NAFTA commitments.

What "legitimate concerns" does congress have, you might ask? Getting re-elected. It needs to have the unions' support to do this.

---

[62] Post-Chronicle staff writer, "Facing Mexican Tariffs, U.S. Seeks New Trucking Pact," *The Post-Chronicle* (March 16, 2009).

Therefore, congress is saying to hell with the American people and to "free trade" agreements that it had *already agreed to*. It wants to re-write the rules in its favor at the expense of both the American and Mexican economies.

Often, countries impose restrictions for no apparent reason. The U.S. protects rice and mohair in the name of "national defense." Many poor countries have very stiff tariffs on goods *they don't even make*, when they have no workers needing to be "protected." For example, many poor countries have tariffs of 20 percent, 50 percent, 100 percent and higher on automobiles. The same used Ford Taurus for which you might pay $15,000 for could cost as much as $30,000 or more in some countries. I had a friend in graduate school from Haiti who would take a different used car with him every time he returned home, so that he could smuggle it in to sell for a profit. The selling price would be higher than the purchase price in the U.S., but less than the market price in Haiti. Without the tariffs, more people could afford automobiles, and more money would be available for investment.

The United States, like many poor countries, pays farmers to farm, when otherwise many would not, since limited profits would exclude many farmers. The main argument for subsidies is that we need to protect our poor farmers from "low" prices and incomes. But most subsidies go to commercial farms with incomes of $200,000 and net worth of nearly $2 million.[63] Plus, the average farm household earns $81,420 (29 percent above the national average), and has a net worth of $838,875 (over 8 times the national average). The resulting overproduction of food in the U.S. means that many farmers from poor countries can't compete. In a free market, poor countries would provide much more of the world food supply. American (and European) farmers, instead of being paid to produce food that other countries could produce for less, would instead be employed producing things developed countries are relatively better at. In this case, all world citizens would be better off.

We should all be so lucky as to have our jobs protected just because we prefer to do a particular job instead of another. For

---

[63] Brian M. Riedl, "How Farm Subsidies Harm Taxpayers, Consumers, and Farmers, Too," http://www.heritage.org/research/agriculture/bg2043.cfm.

instance, if I would rather be a rock star than an office worker, why shouldn't the government pay/subsidize me to do that? If someone else wants to write poetry instead of working at the bakery, why shouldn't we all pay taxes to support her? If a doctor would rather be paid to race cars rather than perform surgeries, why shouldn't we contribute to his cause for "labor freedom" and "worker's rights"? The answer: besides the fact that most of us don't want to give part of our incomes to others just so that they can do what they want, if we all did the work we would *like* instead of doing the work that market prices tell us needs to be done, we would all be producing little that people wanted to buy. Therefore, we would receive little or no income from customers, and thus would have little or no money to pay in taxes, taxes that the government would use to pay everyone for doing "nothing." The whole system would collapse.

Preventing goods from being moved between borders, by means of quotas, tariffs, or subsidies, results in diminished capacity to acquire goods, and thus a reduction in standards of living. Importing fewer capital goods and materials to be used as inputs results in less of an ability to produce still more goods. Subsidies and tariffs also prevent day-to-day adjustments that are needed to meet the changing conditions of production abilities in various other parts of the world. Since these incremental adjustments are not allowed, market forces usually bring about sudden, drastic changes that cause a shock to countries with regulated economies. In these cases, ironically, the free market— and speculators—not government intervention, is seen as the cause of the problem. Further, the prevention of trade between countries often tends to create conflict between nations and thus promotes war.

Globalization

In light of the facts stated here about world trade, it should be seen that globalization is simply that—world trade. It is an increased interconnectedness of various countries (just as our individual states are interconnected). Though ignorant leftists see Globalization as harmful to the world, this is not the case. World trade benefits entire countries just as it benefits individual people, towns, and states. For few people in Florida are upset that they import forest products from Wisconsin. Most Oklahomans are not concerned that they are dependent on telecommunications products from other states. Illinois does not fear the import of cheaper cotton from Mississippi (although it used to, and used government control to prevent competition). Ohio does not impose trade restrictions against other states when jobs move to those states. Economic changes that result from globalization are part of the normal process of trade, both domestically and internationally. In the early 1990s, "experts" predicted that Columbus, Georgia would become a ghost town after its textile jobs were lost to Mexico upon trade restrictions being taken down due to the NAFTA. Indeed, textile work moved to a more efficient location, but Columbus reinvented itself as a financial services city (its comparative advantage).

Trade is beneficial between any two regions. Just because there is a geographical border—an imaginary line dividing two areas— does not mean that the concept of trade changes in the slightest. If this were the case, New York City should impose trade restrictions against other states, and even against the rest of its own state, because it imports most of the goods it consumes across a body of water.

Nonetheless, some of the concerns of anti-globalists are in fact valid. For example, trade restrictions such as subsidies in so-called "Northern" (rich) countries harm so-called "Southern" (poor) countries. And debt accumulation in poor countries does indeed put them at a great disadvantage. But these issues are derived from government intervention and influence, and are unrelated to free markets. For instance, increasing massive accumulations of third-world debt would not and could not exist in free markets where government had nothing to do with production and exchange. Still, Bono insists that we in the west should give away yet more of our money to third-world dictators so that they can make their people worse off. He cozies up with government officials on both sides in this effort, yet apparently spends little time learning how the poor of the world can truly escape poverty. If he did, he would be encouraging leaders on both sides to open their borders to *private* capital and goods. He would demand the protection of private property rights of third world citizens and demand the legalization of capital accumulation in the third world, instead of trying to force both sides to exchange *other people's* money.

The anti-globalists also blame the World Trade Organization (WTO), the International Monetary Fund (IMF), the World Bank, the Organisation for Economic Co-operation and Development (OECD), as well as free trade agreements for harming world citizens. It is valid to hold strong opposition to these organizations, but not for the reasons leftists contend. They see these groups as agents of classical liberals (true free marketers), promoting (somehow) harmful free trade. In fact, these are all government organizations which exist to *prevent* free trade. They exist to impose trade restrictions, to allow "Northern" governments to hold sway over "Southern" governments and to manipulate their economies, and to try and achieve a centralized world government.[64] Even to the extent that these organizations are really and truly attempting to help developing countries, they do more harm than good, because they alter, via government force, what individuals in all of the participating countries would otherwise choose for themselves if left to their free will.

If world citizens would stop voting for world governments to manipulate world economies and if they would ignore illogical leftist ideologies, they might see that globalization has the potential to raise the productivity of labor, and thus living standards, across the entire planet.

Not only can globalization bring poor countries to the level of development that currently exists in the developed world, but it can much more drastically develop the developed world. If we will allow ourselves to progress, we could achieve a fantastic level of inequality. Within a generation or two, the poor could be in a position to drive new Mercedes and live in one of their several four-bedroom homes, and the rich could all own private planes or flying cars, and take excursions to Mars for the weekend to get away from their boring private islands, personal skyscrapers or underwater homes. In this more prosperous future world, everyone, of course, would have medical care that is a quantum leap ahead of today's antiquated technology, and they would pay a fraction of today's costs. The inequality description is used tongue-in-cheek (since inequality would still exist), but the scenario is

---

[64] A quintessential example is the IMF's attempt to create a new world money, the SDR, or Special Drawing Rights, in 1968, which would establish the IMF as the central bank of all world central banks, just as any nations' central bank is the bank where all individual banks bank.

a very realistic one. But if we prevent globalization, we can expect our economic progression to be slowed, if not arrested.

World integration at the private level—as opposed to the government level—promotes capital accumulation that allows for increased production capabilities. Globalization is the process of including the entire world into the division of labor. Today, only a small portion of the world's citizens—the hand-full of developed countries—produce an overwhelming majority of its goods. With everyone—including all of Asia, Africa, the Middle East, and Latin America—involved in production, and especially if complete economic freedom were universal, the poor and the rich alike could live an order of magnitude above the highest standard of living today.

It is often thought that low-wage developing countries will begin producing everything, leaving no production and thus no jobs in the developed world. This is a fallacy. The developing nations have comparative advantages, but only in some areas. Not only does every nation have work they can perform comparatively more efficiently than another nation (per our example in **Figure 2.1**, this is a mathematical truism), developed countries are capable of producing many things that other nations are not advanced enough to handle (and poor countries have comparative advantages *because* they are poor—in labor-intensive work, etc.). Also, developing nations often don't have the same particular natural resources many developed nations have. These types of considerations mean that North America and Europe will be leaders in many fields. The United States produces and exports electrical machinery, appliances, vehicles, office machines, transport equipment, scientific instruments, telecommunications equipment, chemicals, and other technology, among many other items, that most nations could not begin to compete with. Even those poorer nations which do compete in many of these areas are years away from being able to produce the same quality of product. Quality and productivity both affect wage rates; wage rates are in fact in proportion to them. For example, a $50,000 per year bulldozer driver in Ohio can compete with $500 per year workers with shovels in Mozambique, because he can move 100 more times dirt per hour than the workers with shovels. The key, again, is capital accumulation and technology.

Economic Arguments Against Globalization[65]

One of the most prominent academic economic arguments against globalization is the concern that there will be a downward pull on sales revenues and GDP if poor countries become richer. This is in fact true in terms of having a static quantity of money, but not in real terms. Recall, that if the quantity of money in a society is constant, prices will fall. In a world with a static global quantity of money, as other nations begin to produce more goods, since the same quantity of money must cover the increased amount of goods, prices in developed countries will fall not only in normal nominal terms, *but also in relative proportion to other countries' production volume.* In other words, in economic terms, a greater proportion of global income will accrue to developing countries, and a smaller proportion of global income will accrue to developed countries, *in terms of money.* This is simply a mathematical necessity. But economists who argue this point as something detrimental are way off base. For these money incomes *are not related to the income of physical goods or standards of living.* The reality is that the quantity of goods produced and existing in developed countries, along with developing countries, will *increase.* The increase in the quantity of goods will serve to *decrease* our costs in real terms, and *increase our buying power.*

If the developed world did not increase its production of goods at all, the increase in the quantity of goods produced in the developing world would *cause reduced prices that exactly offset* the reduced incomes of the developed world.[66] But, in reality, the developed world will also be increasing its production of goods—this increase will cause prices to fall well in excess of incomes, just as increases in domestic production makes prices fall as explained in Chapter 1 (and further explained in Chapter 3). In sum, additional production from the rest of the world lowers both our real incomes and our costs equally, but the additional production created in our own country lowers our prices relative to our incomes. Real wealth is still increased.

---

[65] Most of the insights in this section are based on George Reisman, "Globalization: The Long-Run Big Picture," http://mises.org/daily/2361.

[66] For a detailed understanding of this, see George Reisman, "Globalization: the Long-Run Big Picture," http://mises.org/daily/2361.

But in fact the quantity of money will *not* stay that same in the future: its supply will be expanded by the government. Thus, the decreasing proportion of domestic nominal incomes relative to developing countries will not be noticed because nominal incomes will rise. In other words, we will continue to progress in real terms, but the *real* changes in purchasing power or relative purchasing power will not be noticed because they will be masked by the increase in prices and incomes, just as they have been for 100 years.

A second prominent concern over globalization by economists is that it results in the loss of capital of advanced countries. It has always been acknowledged by most economists that *the products that are made* might be switched from being produced in one country to another; but the concern now, in light of modern technology, is that the actual movement of *the tools that make the products*, the capital goods, will move from one country to another, leaving workers in the former country without anything to produce or any tools to produce with.

The concerns make sense on the surface. If a company can save millions by having products made or services provided by lower wage labor overseas, then indeed, companies will move factories and office buildings to the location of the cheap labor (as they are currently doing). But, first, the money companies save by operating overseas becomes additional capital available at home. The additional funding serves to bring about more production and thus more goods and lower prices for us at home.

Second, we are not in actuality losing capital on net. America has been exporting capital since the late 1800s and that has not yet made us poor because we import more capital than we export. This truth is revealed in the very fact that we have a trade deficit; and it was shown above that we import more capital than we export, and that 75 percent of what we import is in fact capital goods. With these capital goods we create and then export the materials, equipment, and machinery to supply the workers in developing countries who are now producing for us: any capital we send overseas is in the form of exports. Therefore, if we were currently losing capital, we would be exporting much more than we are importing. These facts show that we are not depleting our capital base by moving it overseas—we are doing the opposite.

The world does not stand still. Changes in technology, production, tastes, and trends, along with economic development in various regions, mean that jobs, factories, or even entire companies might move to a new location, change what they produce, or go out of business all together. These changes cause changes in the comparative advantages between countries. Thus, we should not expect that jobs, companies, and products, will remain the same.

Outsource Everything Possible[67]

Outsourcing, in the general sense, is the act of retaining an outside party to perform a service. A localized example is having a plumber to fix a leaky faucet because he or she can do it better or more cheaply or efficiently (in the latter case, we're talking about cost in terms of time out of our day—an opportunity cost—which translates into a monetary cost). Companies outsource many of their services, including telephone-support services (sales, reservations, information, etc.) and the reading of MRIs by radiologists. Also prominent for many companies is the outsourcing of back-office processing such as accounting tasks, IT support, analysis work, procurement, and human resources activities. This work is outsourced because, given both the lower labor costs overseas, as well as the current state of technology which enables the movement of the work, it can be done much more cheaply in this manner.

The immediate concern most people have about outsourcing is the loss of jobs by those whose work is moved overseas (along with the already-discussed concern that there will be no jobs left for us in the U.S.). This topic will be addressed in the next section. The larger problem that will be addressed currently is the fear that because higher-wage jobs here are being moved to lower-wage areas, average salaries in the U.S., and the developed world in general, will decline. These fears are unmerited: while salaries might in fact decline, *prices*, as just noted, will decline more than salaries. As costs of production decline, selling prices—due to competition—will decline in line with costs. (If companies did not reduce selling prices as their production

---

[67] Most of the insights in this section are based on George Reisman, "Globalization: The Long-Run Big Picture," http://mises.org/daily/2361.

costs declined, opportunities would arise for a host of competitors to exploit the large profit margins now available in the industry, and thus reduce the market share of the original firms experiencing lower costs; the new, additional firms would simultaneously expand production and supply, forcing all firms to reduce costs).

If economy-wide salaries were to fall due to outsourcing, we would currently be observing workers' wages falling as more outsourcing is taking place, but we are not. In today's outsourcing world, overall salaries are not falling as much as costs because higher paid workers are not dropping the level of salary they are willing to work for to the low level of those overseas—their new competitors—who are now taking their jobs. Our outsourcing-induced displaced workers are settling for replacement jobs paying 90 percent, 70 percent, or even 60 percent of their previous salary, not 10 percent or 20 percent as would be the case if they were having to meet the wage levels of the overseas workers. This is because there are *other* jobs available to them that do not have comparable competition overseas (jobs in industries that other countries are not capable of competing in). Most people are already in these other industries that do not have overseas competition and are thus not losing their jobs to overseas workers, and most people are therefore having their salaries remain at their historical level. Thus, overall wage rates in the American economy fall very slightly, while prices fall by a much greater degree. It should be obvious that having our economy-wide costs decline by a much greater degree than our wages is sign of increasing, not decreasing, prosperity.

Additionally, the increased incomes offshore workers in India and China acquire from outsourcing results in more money they will have with which to import goods from the U.S. Thus, our exporting industries benefit. And, as poor countries develop economically their wages will rise toward our level. So socialists who want to stop outsourcing should support capitalism in poor countries, so that workers there will not remain competitors salary-wise.

The economic effects of outsourcing are really no different than the effects of having technology and machines replacing workers, something that has been happening for over three hundred years. These workers have always had to move to other jobs for which they were then best suited. From time to time the public fears that all of our jobs will be taken by computers and machines. Clearly this never happens; the computers and machines free up labor that is then available to be used in producing the next best thing that should be produced, or for producing more of the current things being produced. Besides, what if all our jobs were eventually taken by computers and machines? This would be fantastic! We do not hold jobs for the purpose of simply performing labor for the fun of it; we hold jobs in order to acquire money to exchange for things we need. We need *things*, not money. If we had computers and machines automatically producing everything for us, we would not need to work, since we would have all the goods and services that we would ever need created for us for free without having to make them ourselves. What a great world that would be.

Outsourcing began happening in Britain, Australia, and Europe 20 and 25 years ago. The U.S. has been adjusting to this phenomenon only for a few years, for the most part (however, some types of outsourcing took place in America starting in the 1970s when American [along with Japanese] electronics firms began moving their production facilities to low cost locations such as Taiwan and Singapore). Though these other early outsourcing nations experienced uproars from their citizens who complained that low-cost nations would undercut everything they did, that it would be impossible to sell to these nations, and that industries in the developed world would be destroyed, none of these concerns ever became reality.

What About the Lost Jobs?

It has been stated already that many of our jobs need to be ended or changed in order for us to engage in outsourcing and in world trade in general. This is of course seen as a terrible thing by most people. In reality, it is a bad thing only for those who lose their jobs, since the rest of society benefits from this process. Losing one's job is not an easy thing, and should not be taken lightly (and has happened to this author *because* of outsourcing). However, it should be seen as a necessity for economic progress and improved standards of living for everyone.

People tend to regard jobs as though the jobs themselves are what one needs to survive. Instead, what is important about jobs are the things the jobs bring us—the ability to produce goods and services we need. Therefore, jobs need to be structured in a way that are profitable and most productive (yes, it is, and *should* be all about profits, as I will explain in later chapters). Attempting to make sure jobs are not allowed to change or disappear, which can only be done by using government force to control the private property of privately-owned companies, results not only in making everyone worse off immediately, but simply delaying the changes and challenges that market forces will eventually bring protected workers.

Almost all jobs in this country used to consist of agriculture. What if we had prevented farmers and field workers from having to leave their jobs (to a greater degree than we previously have)? We would have an overabundance of food and little else in our lives. We would have very little to buy because people would not be producing things like beds, stereos, satellite TV, and medicines, since they would instead be producing food. What if we had tried to save horse-and-buggy jobs when the automobile came along by subsidizing those jobs or by making it illegal for the automobile companies to exist since they would steal jobs? Even if we had simply subsidized the horse-and-buggy makers, it would have been a loss to all in society. More money would need to have been taken from incomes and productive sectors of the economy in the form of taxes in order to support workers producing things people no longer want to pay a profitable price for. If the workers were instead allowed to experience change, most could have been re-employed in the profitable automobile industry.

These types of changes have been taking place for hundreds of years now. There are always new jobs and new careers available for those unemployed; there has certainly been an abundance of jobs in countries and during eras where labor regulation did not prevent jobs from being available. Indeed, switching jobs and learning new skills might not be easy, and it might take some time. But life is not easy; we have to do what we need to do in order to progress. The first settlers of this country had no choice of employment; they simply had to do what was needed in order to survive. There is no way incomes can be guaranteed to us; we must create incomes by creating products that people want, or relying on others to create these jobs for us. At least today we have more choices than times past, thanks to entrepreneurs and rich savers. We would have many more choices if the government would allow it, or, more specifically, if you would vote for free markets.

The fact is, jobs are lost and created daily, and people voluntarily and involuntarily leave their current employment constantly. According to the Bureau of Labor Statistics, each month roughly 11.8 million people take a job, leave a job, or switch jobs, all while the official unemployment usually stays virtually unchanged.[68] A study by economists Clair Brown, John Haltiwanger and Julia Lane regarding employment trends over a 20-year period shows that (1) over the period in question, the proportion of low-income jobs fell in proportion relative to high-income jobs, (2) though job seekers faced tough times at first, the long-run job change usually led to improved circumstances for workers, 3) in low-end jobs, workers generally moved up into better jobs, and 4) "Firm entry and exit tended to reduce dramatically the percentage of low-income workers."[69] The freer economy we have, the more jobs and more choices there would be, and at higher income levels.

Change is inevitable. Individuals around the world are taking actions to try to further their lives on a daily basis. Their individual attempts at progressing result in changing what is being produced and therefore in the types of work needing to be done. The more we allow change to take place, the faster our lives improve. This is why unprofitable companies such as the faltering car and airline companies should be allowed to fail. These companies have been protected from competition for years by the government, and their workers have been protected from both other workers and from marketplace wages their employers needed to pay them in order to prosper. These policies have obviously failed by causing the firms to be inefficient: their costs are so high that their operations are not profitable. Looked

---

[68] Terry Fitzgerald, "Book Review: Economic Turbulence: Is a Volatile Economy Good for America?" http://www.minneapolisfed.org/publications_papers/pub_display.cfm?id=1144.

[69] Clair Brown, John Haltiwanger and Julia Lane, *Economic Turbulence: Is a Volatile Economy Good for America?* (2006).

at another way, people are not willing to pay enough for the products these companies have to offer. These products should therefore not be made by the current companies since doing so means an economic loss for all of society.

Instead of handing out more taxpayer money to workers simply in order for them to keep their unprofitable jobs, the labor and capital used by these failing companies should be allowed to move to places where they can instead be employed to make profitable things. The job losses would not be as bad as it seems. The likely scenario is that (1) the assets of the car companies would be purchased in bankruptcy by German, Japanese, or South Korean automobile companies, and (2) most of the laid-off workers would be hired by these companies,[70] but at market labor rates, not artificially high labor rates paid for by the rest of society. Think this is a terrible idea because the U.S. should produce automobiles? Well, the U.S. would probably still be producing automobiles profitably had these companies and their workers not been regulated and protected through the decades (and had they designed cars that were more attractive). In short, this is what you have voted for. Alternatively, if these firms would somehow need to go out of business even without having had government help, then that fact would reveal to us that the U.S. does not have a comparative advantage in producing autos and should not attempt to do so.

The airline companies that we would let fail (not all would) would similarly have their assets acquired by more efficient domestic competitors such as Southwest Airlines and Allegiant Air. If the United States would allow foreign competitors to compete in the country, many European, Asian, and Gulf Region airlines might take the place of the previous inefficient competitors.[71] However, some of the most profitable airlines in the world that might end up dominating the U.S. airspace are profitable because *they* receive subsidies from *their* governments. One might ask why these subsidized airlines should operate in place of domestically subsidized airlines. The answer is that by having foreign subsidized airlines operating instead

---

[70] Or maybe even by American investors who would buy the failed businesses, or parts of them.

[71] The same concept applies to letting banks fail, instead of bailing out their incompetent owners at the expense of the rest of society.

of our own, we will waste fewer people and resources domestically, resulting in increased standards of living here at home. If the French taxpayers, for example, want to throw away their money for the purpose of transporting American passengers around the United States on Air France,[72] by all means we should let them.

By letting unprofitable companies go bust and moving labor and machines into more useful hands, domestic productivity will improve, ultimately raising wage rates relative to prices. This is positive progress, this is *real* change. We must understand that change is inevitable, and we must not fight it. Even if we are able to protect a small group of people, they will gain at the expense of the rest of society, and only temporarily. By allowing companies and individuals to adjust as needed to market forces, *everyone* benefits in the long-run.

It should now be a logical conclusion that using taxpayer money to keep people in their jobs, or preventing economic progress for the sake of keeping things the same, reduces our quality of life. Workers around the world who constantly protest their employer's actions or seek government assistance to this end prevent economic progress.

Free Trade is Good

There should really be no debating that free trade is good for everyone. Most economists actually agree on this, even though many of them often advise *foreign* countries to restrict trade. Even most left-wing economists are decent on the trade question, including Paul Krugman, of all people. These economists still try to get governments to manipulate trade because they erroneously believe they can arrange more beneficial scenarios, but they generally agree with other economists and true free marketers on the concept of competitive advantage and the general notion that free trade is best. So the next time you hear your politicians claiming a country is not trading fairly or that we need to "protect" workers from foreign competition, send them a message that you know they are trying to fool you and that you want free trade.

---

[72] Though it used to be wholly owned by the French government, after its merger with KLM, Air France became only partially owned by the government.

PART TWO

Regulation

Chapter 3

Inflation:
The Printing of Money is
the Root of Most Evil

Consumers blame greedy oil companies for high gas prices, mercenary Wall Street moguls for the decline of the markets, biofuel crops for higher food prices, mortgage lenders for falling home prices, and profit-hungry businesses for other rising prices. All this blame is misdirected: the real culprits are governments and the printing of money.

This chapter will show that the only explanation for annual economy-wide price increases is that the government, through its central bank, continually adds more money to the economic system. It will show that this increase in money is the sole cause of consumer price inflation—especially healthcare costs—and rising oil and food prices, as well as increasing stock and bond markets, real estate, corporate revenues, and even the gross domestic product (GDP). It also will show that the central bank is solely responsible for the regular occurrence of recessions, rapidly rising unemployment, and devaluation of the currency, and is the cause of crises around the world—to mention only a few of its ill effects.

Inflation, created and continually exacerbated by the government's printing presses, has immense and pervasive negative effects on all sectors of the national and global economy. But because the general public doesn't easily recognize the consequences of printing money as actual inflation, the practice continues unabated and unopposed. Hence, inflation spreads like an insidious, invisible disease that infects our daily lives.

In the movie *My Big Fat Greek Wedding*, the father of the Greek bride-to-be proudly claims that for any particular word mentioned, he could show how that word was derived from the Greek language. Similarly, but without the claims being exaggerated, for so many of the ills our economy and society suffer today, I could show you how the printing of money by the government is the originating cause. This chapter discusses some of these ailments, and shows the damage we do to ourselves by supporting politicians who try to manipulate the economy by printing money.

The History of Banking

A brief foray into the history of banking will be both interesting in itself and key to understanding our current economic crises. Though various forms of banks have existed for well over 2,000 years,[73] it is helpful for our purposes to learn how goldsmiths became bankers. In the Middle Ages, people took their gold and silver wealth for safekeeping to goldsmiths who had storage vaults. The goldsmiths would issue receipts, or promises to pay, as claims for the stored wealth (deposits), and these receipts became history's first bank notes. After some time, goldsmiths noticed that few people came on a daily basis to claim their gold and silver and that most of the time it simply sat unused in storage. The goldsmiths realized that they could make money by loaning out idle gold and silver, charging interest for the loan—in other words, they engaged in what should legitimately be termed fraud and counterfeiting by issuing claims to money that already was spoken for. They would loan out as much as 90 percent of the stored wealth, given that no more than 10 percent at a time was withdrawn. This lending of some portion of customers' wealth while keeping available some other proportion for redemption purposes is

---

[73] For a detailed account of the history of banking, see Jesus Huerta De Soto, *Money, Bank Credit, and Economic Cycles* (2006).

called fractional reserve banking. Banks engage in substantially the same type of operations today. The process of creating new loans from deposits is called "credit expansion," "money creation," "loan creation," "expanding the money supply," and "printing money," among other things.

One of the important things to understand is that when banks allow a third party to use the funds another person has placed in the bank for safekeeping—as opposed to placing them there for the express purpose of having the bank assign the use of the funds to someone else[74]—two different parties believe they have purchasing power with the very same funds. When more people gain additional purchasing power which is not brought about by previous production, and without new goods having been created to meet the additional demand of the new purchasing power, problems, as we shall see, arise.

Many banks throughout history began as deposit banks, offering true safekeeping storage units to warehouse wealth for clients, who *paid* for the service. Banks also were paid for transporting the wealth from one city to another to settle exchanges of money for goods. But most banks, once they obtained government permission, eventually began to lend out the wealth they had promised to hold in safekeeping[75]—and most of them eventually collapsed. There is a natural tendency towards insolvency of *fractional reserve* banks, since they give claims to multiple people for the very same money. When too many people come to the bank to claim their money at one time, there is not enough to go around, and banks go bust.

This was the problem with our banking system in the United States in the 1800s when banks issued their own bank notes—their own currency. Having multiple currencies would have worked fine, given that the these currencies were backed by gold, except that the banks, with government permission and encouragement, also engaged in fractional reserve banking—promising their clients that their money was safe in the bank, while in reality lending it out to others. Banks regularly expanded their loans by pyramiding them on top

---

[74] In which case the depositor knowingly and intentionally gives up and forgoes the use of the funds for a specified time period.

[75] It was usually governments who began doing so before banks themselves.

of a given quantity of real money on deposit with the bank, taking a risk on both the rate of default on loans and on the rate at which clients would reclaim their money. It should be understood that for a bank to loan out clients' funds that are there for safekeeping (deposits) is different from the situation in which clients *knowingly* agree to give up the use of their funds for some period of time (bonds, CDs, savings accounts, etc.).

These banks expanded the supply of money (i.e., in the form of loans, the receipts/claims to the money stored in the "warehouse") by issuing receipts for gold to ever more people. The new receivers of credit (borrowers) then used the claims to purchase goods. The sellers of the goods would then deposit the claims in their banks, which would present the claims to the original issuing banks to be paid in real gold. The more claims presented to the issuing banks, the more gold they were required to pay out. Naturally, those banks that printed the most money (wrote up claims to gold and loaned them out) lost the most gold. Ultimately, they were unable to return their clients' money and thus went bankrupt, often dragging their clients down with them.

Most banks in this period were careful not to exceed the pace of other banks in creating new loans from depositors' funds so that their depositors would not come to distrust them and thus withdraw their funds. Therefore, each bank was frustrated that it could not create money as fast as it wished. So the banks did what most businesses do that dislike being restrained by the marketplace from making excess profits: they collaborated in turning to the government to seek special privileges.

The banks worked out a deal with the government to be regulated whereby they would form a cartel with government sponsorship in the form of a *central bank*. This government-sponsored monopoly to create money as a single official body allowed all the banks to synchronize money creation so as to grow their loans at a higher but uniform pace, reducing the chances of any particular bank's going bust from printing money more quickly than others. But if a bank did get in trouble, the monopoly central bank could create more money with which the ailing bank could be nursed back to health (socialism for banks). Most importantly, the average rate at which banks could create money would be greatly increased (thereby causing inflation), even though a primary public argument promoting this monopoly was that the central bank could better control inflation.

Central Banks: Creators of Money "Out of Thin Air"

Central banks appeared on the scene in the 1600s in Europe, primarily as a means for kings to steal additional money from citizens above and beyond what they could manage to collect in taxes. Rulers have stolen from citizens for centuries. Historically the theft was in the form of such tactics as coin clipping (shaving down the size of gold or silver coins so as to make additional coins from the clippings while keeping the face value of the coin the same) and diluting the content of coins by replacing some of the gold or silver with cheaper metals. The more modern way for rulers to steal from their citizens in the monetary fashion is to form a central bank. Central banks typically came about in the following way: a king would want, as usual, to extract more money from his subjects than they would allow through taxation without rebelling. So the king set up a national bank that was given the authority to provide the only money that legally could be used—the "legal tender"—in the country. The king would instruct the bank to print new money for him to "borrow," and for this he would issue an IOU to the bank. In this way, the king could create his own money to spend.

Today, central banks work largely the same way, but the money-creating process is more formalized so as to appear more legitimate. In order for our government to obtain new money from our central bank, the Federal Reserve (Fed), the central bank buys government bonds (IOUs) from the US Treasury. The U.S. Treasury issues bonds that are both bought and sold in the marketplace, and many of these eventually are purchased by the Fed. In order for the banks to create new money, all the Fed needs to do is to buy *something* from someone. For many reasons, it chooses to buy primarily government bonds from banks and from the Treasury. Since the Fed is the bankers' bank and acts as a clearinghouse for all bank transactions, when the Fed buys government bonds (or anything else, from paper clips to a big new marble building), it pays for them simply by issuing a credit to the seller's account at the seller's bank, which becomes a sum of money that appears in their bank account. The credit is not real money: it consists merely of keystrokes on a computer keyboard. This process is still commonly referred to as "printing money" (as well as being called the various other terms mentioned above) even though the technique of money creation has become more technologically sophisticated.

The bank that sold the bond to the Fed now has more "money" in the form of credit (since it was paid for the bond it sold to the Fed). The bank legally is obligated to keep 10 percent of the new money on deposit with the Fed as reserves (for those few people who come to claim their funds in cash) but can loan out the other 90 percent. This 90 percent, once it's loaned out, represents new money in the actual economy that never existed previously—it is an addition to the stock of money. It represents immediate new purchasing power in the marketplace that someone has with a new bank account, with money which still belongs to its original owner who also has purchasing power with the very same money. When the 90 percent is loaned out, it is usually deposited in a bank different from the originating one. This second bank also keeps 10 percent on deposit and loans out 90 percent (81 percent of the original amount). This second 90 percent arrives in yet a third bank, which loans out 90 percent (72.9 percent of the original amount). This process, of "credit expansion," continues to a point where the amount of new money created in the banking system amounts to *10 times* the original amount created by the Fed. In other words, a new $100 dollars created by the Fed results in the creation of a new $1,000 in the economy. This money- and inflation-creating system of holding fractional reserves is not only fraudulent but also the cause of many of our economic ills.

Banks should keep not 10 percent, and not 50 percent, but 100 percent of the money they hold for us; it should be backed by something of real wealth (like gold), and we should have the right to convert our banknotes and bank accounts into this real wealth. Yet the government forces us to accept only Federal Reserve paper money and electronic credit for paper money (bank accounts), and fully supports and encourages the fractional reserve system. In absence of this government endorsement, people would lose money constantly and it would not be long until they would refrain from putting their money in banks until they were sure that their money was actually being stored in the bank. Alternatively, there would be true banking insurance, and insurance companies would force banks to act morally. England attempted to force banks to have 100 percent gold backing for money in the 19th century. The Peel Act, as it was known, was unsuccessful in preventing artificial creation of money because lawmakers applied the 100 percent backing only to *banknotes* and not to bank *accounts*, which have the same purchasing power (think checks, debit cards, etc.) as paper bills. Today, most of the money supply is in the form not of cash, but in bank deposit accounts, which are simply IOUs issued by our respective banks for particular dollar amounts. Most of your money, even if it consists of millions of dollars, is simply electronic credits for money, not real money. A wide-scale financial catastrophe could wipe out every bit of your net worth. You may technically be owed that amount if your failed bank is taken over by another or by the government, but good luck actually getting your hands on the money.

And FDIC insurance could not help. The government's FDIC exists simply to make your money *appear* safe so that you will have faith in the pyramid scheme. In reality the FDIC has only enough money to save a handful of small or medium-sized banks (FYI: during the Great Depression 9,000 banks collapsed). In fact, the entire U.S. government does not have enough money to save more than a fraction of all banks should there be mass failure—without printing it, as they have been doing recently. In 2007, the *entire government budget* was $2.8 trillion,[76] while the total value of commercial bank deposits (which does not include investment accounts and other types of deposits) was $6.6 trillion.[77] The government could print trillions of dollars to give to us all, but that would result in hyperinflation, effectively voiding the effect of recouping your funds.[78]

In general, there is nothing to keep the government's central bank from printing as much money as it wants except the fear that

---

[76] The U.S. Congressional Budget office, Fiscal Year 2007, http://www.gpoaccess.gov/usbudget/fy07/browse.html#budget.

[77] Thorston Polleit, "Inflation Is a Policy That Cannot Last," http://mises.org/daily/2901.

[78] For various reasons, printing trillions and giving them to the banks does NOT necessarily cause high price inflation. It can also cause rapid asset inflation while causing little increased consumer price inflation.

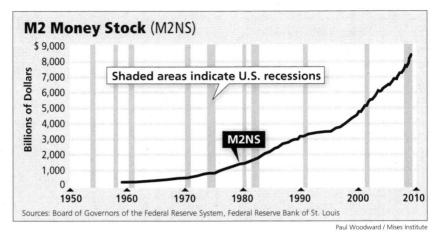

Figure 3.1: The total (and increasing) amount of money in the U.S. economy, as measured by the Federal Reserve Board's M2 calculation.

the public will not tolerate prices rising too quickly. The Fed and the banks are entrusted to do the right thing. But how many people or businesses would limit the amount of money they would print if the government gave *them* a monopoly to print paper dollar bills?

This process of credit creation brings many problems to the real economy; some we see, and some we don't. The rest of the chapter will look at the major problems associated with credit creation, the "printing" of money.

How New Money Causes Inflation

Historically, inflation was accurately defined not as rising prices, but as an increase in the quantity of money in circulation. This definition has changed over time in such way as to conceal the real source of the rising prices—credit creation and expansion.

We learned in Chapter 1 that expanding the quantity of money in circulation makes prices rise because more money is then chasing the same quantity of goods. There are only two ways in which the average selling price of all the goods across the economy can each sell for a higher price: (1) there are fewer goods to be sold, or (2) more money is spent to buy the goods. It is a statistical fact that we produce many more goods each year than the year before. We also can

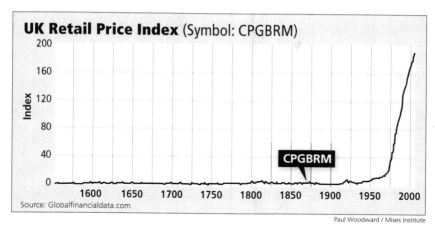

Figure 3.2: Historical price levels in the United Kingdom.

look around us and see that we don't have fewer goods each and every year; we obviously have more. The quantity of goods expands, on average, about 3–5 percent per year. Therefore, the explanation for rising prices must be the existence of more money each year; money must be added to our economy at a rate in excess of 3–5 percent per year. In fact it is: **Figure 3.1** reveals a chart of one measure of the supply of money in our economy, called M2.[79] Money supply growth in the U.S., while varying from year to year, now averages about 7.5 percent per year (reaching 12.5 percent in some years).

Figure 3.2 reveals the historical rate of inflation in the United Kingdom since the 1500s in the form of the retail price index. A comparable price index for the United States since 1800s is in **Figure 3.3**. From these charts, it is clear that once our governments' central banks began regulating banks and the amount of credit they could create, the money supply grew rapidly, resulting in unprecedented inflation rates never before seen in the history of the world. From 1750 to 1914

---

[79] M1 to M3 are money supply measures used by the Fed. M1 is restricted to the most liquid forms of money: currency in the hands of the public, travelers checks, demand deposits, and other deposits against which checks can be written. M2 is a wider definition of M1, which also includes savings accounts, CDs under $100,000, and balances in retail money market mutual funds. M3 includes M2 and cash deposits, deposits of euros, and repurchase agreements. As such, M2 represents the aggregate money supply.

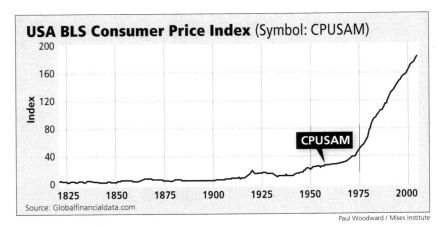

USA BLS Consumer Price Index (Symbol: CPUSAM)

Source: Globalfinancialdata.com

Paul Woodward / Mises Institute

Figure 3.3: Historical price levels in the United States.

(the year after the Federal Reserve was created in the United States[80]), inflation rates in the United Kingdom averaged 0.63 percent. Since 1914, they have averaged 4.91 percent, and since 1950 they have averaged 5.61 percent.

To get an idea of the compounding effect of inflation growing at 5 percent per year, consider that something that costs $100 in any particular year would cost $1,146 after 50 years of 5 percent inflation. Conversely, consider that $100 worth of wealth in any given year would be worth only $8.72 after 50 years of 5 percent inflation. At 10 percent inflation, the respective numbers would be $11,739 and 85 cents. The present U.S. dollar is worth no more than 10 cents of the 1970 dollar and 50 cents of the 1980 dollar! This is the case even though politicians always claim that "a strong dollar is in our nation's interest."

Our economy does not need more money to grow, although Keynesians, monetarists, supply siders, and other mainstream economists apparently fail to grasp this point. If printing money brought prosperity, we would have alleviated world poverty by now. Any static quantity of money can fulfill the needs of exchange in society, year

---

[80] Though the technical explanation is beyond the scope of this book, it should be understood that inflation from the U.S. central bank causes inflation to be increased in foreign countries as well. This is truer today than ever before.

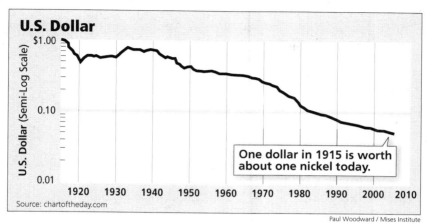

Source: chartoftheday.com

Paul Woodward / Mises Institute

Figure 3.4: The purchasing power today of a 1915 dollar.

after year, as prices adjust to the quantity of goods existing. In fact, if the quantity of money remained stable through time, we would be wealthier: imagine that the quantity of goods continued to increase, as it does every year, but that the quantity of money did *not* increase. Prices would then *decline* every year! This is precisely what happened in the United States during most of the 1800s, except for periods of large discoveries of gold and when the government printed money to pay for the Civil War. Since goods were added to the economy faster than money was (the production of goods outpaced the production of money), prices declined.

The quantity of new goods outpaced the quantity of new money created during most of the 1800s because our money was backed by something real and tangible—gold and silver. Though individual banks were creating money, they were more constrained than are today's banks because they faced the threat of ultimately having to pay depositors in real gold and silver. They could expand the money supply only until the risks of losses or customer demands for redemption of gold threatened their financial viability, at which point the money supply would collapse (causing only regional recessions). It was impossible for individual banks to constantly increase the supply of money over long periods of time.

Ultimately, however, our government chose to abolish the restraint on credit creation by dropping the gold backing precisely

Figure 3.5: An example of historical dollars, which used to actually represent claims on real gold and silver.— Source: collectselltrade.com

because it limited the creation of money—more money was what the government needed. The government even went so far as to make possession of gold illegal from 1933 to 1976 except in small amounts and in the form of jewelry, fillings, etc. Thus the government prohibited Americans from owning real money and instead forced them to hold only paper dollar bills, which it continuously devalued and does so to this day (as shown in **Figure. 3.4**). The government thus reneged on its obligation to pay holders of dollar bills the gold to which the dollar bills entitled them.

Today, there is *nothing* backing our currency except the belief on the part of the people that the paper bills will retain their purchasing power. Our dollar bills *used to* bear the inscription *"This certifies that there is on deposit In the Treasury of the United States Of America one dollar in silver payable to the bearer on demand."* Look closely at the text of the dollar bill from 1957 (**Figure 3.5**). Now, without gold or silver backing our currency, our dollars say no such thing, and the Fed can print as much money as it wants, as fast as it wants to, without any legal restraints whatsoever—as long as people en masse accept paper and electronic bank accounts as real money.

How Printing Money Constitutes Theft and Forced Wealth Redistribution

When new money is created, it enters the economy—technically—in the form of loans to businesses and individuals. The government gets money by selling bonds, which the Fed later buys, and which gives reserves to new banks, reserves that will back new loans to businesses and individuals. But since those bonds are bought by the Fed for the very purpose of funding the government, government spending is effectively new money entering the economy as well. The receivers of the new money spend it by buying things from others. Then, those who sold goods to the new borrowers take their increased sales revenues and spend the money, in their turn. As the money is spent and re-spent, prices begin to rise from the increase in demand. Once the new round of money has fully flowed through the economy, prices will be higher than before the new money was created. But here is the tricky fact: those who receive the new money first spend *before* prices rise. Those who receive the money last spend *after* prices rise. The late spenders and those who did not borrow and spend part of the new money are left with less purchasing power and a devaluation of their assets. Thus wealth is transferred from the last receivers of money to the first. The ones who are hurt most are the poor and the retired and elderly citizens, who live on fixed incomes.

Naturally, as a first receiver of money, government gets to spend new money before prices rise, financing a large portion of its deficit by printing money. Without the central bank, deficits would be impossible because the government would have to rely solely on the amount of taxes it could force citizens to pay. By using the Fed, the government can have all of us subsidize it further by having it gain more income at our expense—the higher costs we pay for goods each year constitutes the amount that we are losing and the government is gaining. This is what is known as the "inflation tax."

Most government spending consists of social programs[81] that transfer wealth from one group to another—most taxes are not spent on schools and infrastructure and fighting unnecessary wars. Therefore, the higher costs you and I pay for goods and services each year mostly reflect what we are paying to give money to someone else. The *receiver* of wealth distribution is taking money from citizens through the government's monopoly printing press. As we learned in

---

[81] The term in this case is not limited to programs such as Social Security, Medicaid, Medicare, etc. It includes any spending that effectively serves as income for any party that is paid for by another party.

Chapter 1, this ultimately causes them to be poorer, not richer. Either way, forcing money away from one group by devaluing their money, and giving it to another group, constitutes theft: a forced tax that no one voted for.

Another group that suffers from the wealth redistribution effects of the government's inflation is the holders of the government bonds (almost 50 percent of whom are foreigners), bonds which enable the entire process. The money the government owes to holders of its bonds is devalued during the inflation process, allowing the government to benefit from borrowing at the expense of the lenders, who are repaid in money worth less than it was at the time the bonds were purchased.[82]

The Inflation Rate:
Lies, Damn Lies, and Statistics

Most people think of inflation as a natural and inevitable phenomenon. But it is not. In an economy without government intervention, most prices would constantly go *down*; it is only *with* government regulation and control that inflation occurs. Ironically, people who give any thought at all to the central bank believe that it is there to, among other things, *prevent* inflation. But the inflation it is to prevent is the very inflation the bank itself creates! The Museum of the Federal Reserve Bank of Atlanta celebrates the efforts of the Fed (where, hypocritically, the guide explains how the banks in the 1800s created too much money!) in taking the decisive action of stepping in to stop our high inflation in the early 1980s. Yet it says nothing about how the inflation came about to begin with. There is no mention of how the Fed had printed so much money in the 1970s that by the early 1980s inflation was out of control. The Fed got rid of the Federal Reserve Chairman who created the inflation (along with his predecessor), G. William Miller, and brought in a new one, Paul A. Volker, who did the only thing that could stop inflation—he simply

---

[82] The interest rate does not compensate the borrower as would be the case in a free market, because interest rates are kept artificially low by the government, as will be explained below. It should also be noted that with inflation, borrowers typically always benefit at the expense of lenders.

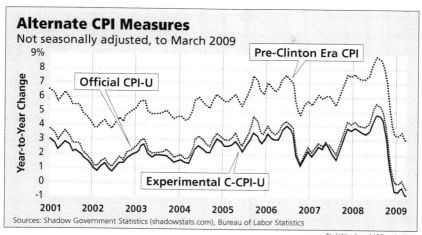

Figure 3.6: Inflation rates manipulated by government to show less inflation.

quit printing money, at least for a while. Inflation is neither natural nor inevitable.

Government-published statistics about inflation are deceptive. Since most people have no idea why consumer prices rise, they accept inflation—as long as it remains below 2–3 percent—as a necessary evil, trusting that their seemingly benevolent government tells the truth with its statistics on the rate of inflation. But the government *rarely* tells the truth.

Take the so-called Consumer Price Index (CPI). The CPI claims to be a barometer of the true rate of consumer price increases. But it is not, for many reasons. First, the government does not count all prices. Omitted from the CPI, for example, are the prices of houses—the single-largest expense most people have. Instead it uses something called "equivalent rent," which is supposed to represent the cost of renting one's own home. This, however, is a misleading figure, because as housing prices rise from more people buying houses, rental prices fall since fewer are renting. Other sly calculations such as what is known as "hedonics," or quality adjustments, make prices appear lower than they are. With this calculation method, the government can *claim* that prices of goods have fallen even though their retail prices have *risen!* For example, a Honda Accord may cost 8 percent more this year than last, but the government, in its opinion, might consider that after taking quality improvements into consideration (airbags, satellite radio, etc.), the price actually fell by 10 percent. It is this reduction of 10 percent that goes into calculating the CPI. Though we see with our own eyes prices on the store shelves rise by 6 percent in a given year, the government will tell us through the CPI number that prices have risen only 1.5 percent. Similarly, and to the same effect, when the government reports inflation, it always focuses on the "core" CPI, which excludes "volatile food and energy prices." In this case, *volatile* of course means *rising*, because we all see that food and energy prices do not *fall* over time.

These few examples, along with many more that could be mentioned, allow the government's CPI numbers always to understate inflation, and they tend to understate it increasingly through time. CPI calculations have changed dramatically just in the last ten years. Consumer inflation, when measured with the same techniques used until several years ago, shows prices rising currently at close to 3 percent, even though the government is telling us that they are hovering around 0 percent as of the time of this writing. **Figure 3.6** shows the difference in CPI calculations just since 2001. It shows the old CPI calculation, the current one, and the calculation currently being considered.

With tactics like these, the government can always misrepresent the real rate of inflation. Further, it can even make money from artificially low CPI rates by reducing the amount it owes. The government promises many groups to whom it pays money, such as welfare and social security recipients[83] and buyers of inflation-indexed bonds, to adjust the payments each year by the amount of inflation. But since it does not compensate them for the *true* rate of inflation, those receiving the government payments still lose out. Another example is income taxes. As inflation raises wages, it pushes individual salaries into higher tax brackets ("bracket creep"). But even where government adjusts tax brackets to increase with the rate of inflation, salaries will not increase along with the *true* rate of inflation; the artificially

---

[83] Social security thus results in a rate of return of about 1.23 percent for the average middle class family, and is often *negative* for minorities. See William W. Beach and Gareth E. Davis, "Social Security's Rate of Return," http://www.heritage.org/research/social security/cda98-01.cfm.

low CPI will not adjust brackets enough each year to keep up with this real rate—brackets still creep!

Consumer price inflation, however, does not always exist in the form of rising prices. When producer input costs rise and companies cannot afford to pass on costs to consumers, they reduce the amount or quality of their products: a cereal producer may put less cereal in the boxes, or soda makers may replace real sugar with artificial sugar (as Coca-Cola did in the 1970s because of rising commodities prices). I have observed that my favorite brand of frozen chicken patties now comes four to a box instead of five, but the price remains the same. The box became more expensive even though the price tag did not budge. This year, my nutrition bar shrank by about 10 percent, leaving spare space in the package and the price the same. During times of high oil prices, and when they can't raise prices due to competitive pressures, airlines often move seats closer together to squeeze more people on a plane. Many restaurants that used to give cloth napkins now give paper ones. The examples of hidden inflation go on and on.

Bet You Didn't Know That *This* Was Inflation!

All prices, not just consumer prices, are affected by the central bank. The average person does not associate rising stock and bond prices, rising house prices, rising corporate revenues, gasoline / oil prices, or even GDP itself with inflation—and certainly not with the government printing money. But as we saw in the chart above, it is impossible for prices of any sort to rise continually without more money being inserted into the economy. For example, what is there to cause an inflow of money into the stock market year after year to push it higher? One might argue that, as more people continue to earn wages, they save more and invest more. But while some are investing funds in the market, others, such as older people no longer working, are withdrawing funds. What is there to cause a *net* inflow of money into the market? Theoretically, larger proportions of future savings could go into the market, but then spending on other items would necessarily be reduced, and the prices of those other items would necessarily decline. In other words, prices of other goods would have to fall to enable a rise in the stock market.

Similarly, how can housing prices continually rise through time without additional money existing? Many argued during our recent housing bubble that prices could not fall because there was an increasing demand for houses. It is true that "demand" is what was raising the prices, but what exactly is "demand"? Does an increase in population necessarily mean an increase in demand? No, it doesn't. An increase in demand requires more money in people's hands. When that money is no longer there, neither will be the demand.

As a concept, "demand" is subject to misunderstanding because we use the term in several different ways. I might have a demand (desire) for a house in the south of France in order to have a place to park the yacht I also demand (desire). In this case demand is without consequence because I do not have the means with which to actually *pay* for these items. Real demand can affect prices only if there is real purchasing power, in the form of money, to support the demand. Consumers cannot demand and, thus, pay for increased consumption of food, houses, gasoline, and stocks without more money, which can only arrive in their pockets after being printed by their central bank. They can have an increased real demand by way of producing more goods with which to pay for more things, but this would serve to reduce prices, not raise them.

To be clear, it is not the companies that people work for that are producing money because companies don't produce money that they pay out as wages—they produce only goods. For all companies to have more money (i.e., sell their goods at higher prices than the previous year) and pay out more money in wages to workers, more money has to be created by the government in the form of credit expansion.

In the bigger picture, for salaries to rise and consumer goods to increase in price while simultaneously stocks, bonds, real estate, commodities, company revenues, and oil all increase in price as well, more money has to be coming into existence to enable companies and consumers to continually bid up prices. If we all, in the aggregate, earned the same amount each year (the sum of all our wages stayed the same), how could we all bid prices higher year after year? We couldn't.

To make sure this very important point regarding the cause of inflation is understood, let's take a brief look at a more detailed mathematical example. **Figure 3.7** and **Figure 3.8** below show two different scenarios of a progressing economy—an economy in which the amount of both consumer and producer goods is increasing. Both figures show a sample economy or, at least, sample goods in an economy. (You can imagine that these are all the goods existing in an economy.)

In **Figure 3.7**, the amount of money in the economy stays static while, in **Figure 3.8**, the quantity of money increases. In both examples, the production of goods increases by 10 percent. In **Figure 3.7**, the price of each good falls because the same $1,000,000 of spending must buy more goods. In this scenario, the rate of inflation—the average percentage price change of all goods—falls by 9 percent. In the second scenario, **Figure 3.8**, the government increases the money supply by 20 percent to $1,200,000 in year 2. In this scenario, even though production increased by 10 percent, the pace of money creation was higher at 20 percent, and prices thus rose by 9 percent (prices rose by 20 percent due to the increase in money supply and fell by 9 percent due to the increase in goods produced). It is this second scenario that is more similar to our economy today. The first scenario largely represents what an economy would be like in a true free market where the government did not expand the quantity of money in the economy, and even in the case that we returned to the gold standard.[84]

It should now be clear that for the price of *anything* to increase, in absence of a decrease in the price of other goods, there must be more money entering the economy to push up prices. This "quantity of money" explanation for rising prices is the true one, no matter what other explanations are offered by those who supposedly understand economics. Even most economists naively argue that rising oil prices can raise the price of all other goods because oil goes into making these other goods. But this is demonstrably wrong. If the quantity of money in the economy were static and our demand for purchasing goods was not expanding due to newly printed money, then as the price of oil rose, the price of other goods (or the quantity purchased)

---

[84] Though with the gold standard, since the quantity would increase to some degree, prices would fall more slowly. The production of gold, however, would not keep pace with the rate of increase of other goods.

Scenario 1:
The quantity of money remains unchanged
Assumptions:
Quantity of money = $1,000,000 in Year 1, and remains $1,000,000 in Year 2
Production of all goods increases by 10 percent per year
Demand for each product relative to other products stays the same every year*

Year 1

Goods In the Economy	Units Produced	Share of Total Spending	Total Amount Spent for the Good	Unit Price
Shirts	400	1 percent	$10,000	$25
Microwave Ovens	100	2 percent	20,000	200
Electric Generators	4	5 percent	50,000	12,500
Steel Sheet	70	15 percent	150,000	2,143
Sandwiches	4,000	2 percent	20,000	5
Shares of stocks	2,000	10 percent	100,000	50
Tons of Grains	50	30 percent	300,000	6,000
Barrels of Oil	450	5 percent	50,000	111
Houses	3	30 percent	300,000	100,000
Total	7,077	100 percent	1,000,000	

Year 2

Shirts	440	1 percent	10,000	23
Microwave Ovens	110	2 percent	20,000	182
Electric Generators	4.4	5 percent	50,000	11,364
Steel Sheet	77	15 percent	150,000	1,948
Sandwiches	4,400	2 percent	20,000	4.5
Shares of stocks	2,200	10 percent	100,000	45
Tons of Grains	55	30 percent	300,000	5,455
Barrels of Oil	495	5 percent	50,000	101
Houses	3.3	30 percent	300,000	90,909
Total	7,784.7	100 percent	1,000,000	

- **Increase in quantity produced: 10 percent**
- **Rate of inflation: −9 percent**

* Even if production of goods did not increase equally and/or if the share of total spending of each good did not stay the same from one year to the next, the overall amount of spending would not be influenced.

Figure 3.7: Consumer price changes in an economy with a static amount of money.

Scenario 2:
The quantity of money expands by 20 percent

Assumptions:

Quantity of money = $1,000,000 in Year 1, but increases to $1,200,000 in Year 2

Production of all goods increases by 10 percent per year

Demand for each product relative to other products stays the same every year*

Year 1

Goods In the Economy	Units Produced	Share of Total Spending	Total Amount Spent for the Good	Unit Price
Shirts	400	1 percent	$10,000	$25
Microwave Ovens	100	2 percent	20,000	200
Electric Generators	4	5 percent	50,000	12,500
Steel Sheet	70	15 percent	150,000	2,143
Sandwiches	4,000	2 percent	20,000	5
Shares of stocks	2,000	10 percent	100,000	50
Tons of Grains	50	30 percent	300,000	6,000
Barrels of Oil	450	5 percent	50,000	111
Houses	3	30 percent	300,000	100,000
Total	7,077	100 percent	1,000,000	

Year 2

Shirts	440	1 percent	12,000	27
Microwave Ovens	110	2 percent	24,000	218
Electric Generators	4.4	5 percent	60,000	13,636
Steel Sheet	77	15 percent	180,000	2,338
Sandwiches	4,400	2 percent	24,000	5.5
Shares of stocks	2,200	10 percent	120,000	55
Tons of Grains	55	30 percent	360,000	6,545
Barrels of Oil	495	5 percent	60,000	121
Houses	3.3	30 percent	360,000	109,091
Total	7,784.7	100 percent	1,200,000	

- **Increase in quantity produced: 10 percent**
- **Rate of inflation: 9 percent**

* Even if production of goods did not increase equally and/or if the share of total spending of each good did not stay the same from one year to the next, the overall amount of spending would not be influenced.

Figure 3.8: Consumer price changes in an economy with an increasing amount of money.

would necessarily *fall*. As the higher cost of gasoline and the higher cost of oil-dependent products took a greater portion of our paychecks each month, we could not buy the same amount of other goods we previously bought and would, thus, cut back on other things—eating out, movies, travel, and so on. With less demand for these other goods, the prices would fall (or fewer quantities would be purchased).

Perhaps you might argue that you and people you know *did* cut back on other goods because of high gas prices, and yet all prices kept rising. This does not mean that the quantity explanation of money is wrong. It means that there are still other people bidding up the prices. Somebody somewhere has newly printed money they are spending.

It was newly printed money flowing into the stock market in the 1990s that caused the NASDAQ bubble to expand and then burst. This money then flowing into housing prices, along with the existence of artificially low interest rates resulting from printing lots of still more new money, is what caused the recent housing bubble. The cost of home financing fell dramatically as the interest rate fell while the newly printed money financed the actual purchase of the houses. Because much of the new money created in the last few years also flowed into the commodities markets, oil and food prices rose dramatically. It is true that there were legitimate supply-and-demand issues with respect to commodities and agriculture, but in a world with a fixed quantity of money, any fundamental decrease in the supply of oil and other commodities would cause their prices to rise while other prices would necessarily fall—the *overall CPI* could not rise.

To better understand the effects of more money pushing up prices, consider the charts below. In each set of charts, the first one is plotted using dollars as the measure of value while the second plots values in gold grams. Gold is used as an alternative pricing mechanism because it represents the amount of the decline in value of the dollar relative to gold. The dollar's decline relative to gold, in turn, largely represents the increase in the supply of dollars relative to the increase in the supply of gold. Gold, unlike paper money, cannot be created so easily. It must be dug out of the ground at great cost, time, and energy. Therefore, the supply of gold increases by only about 3 percent or 4 percent per year.

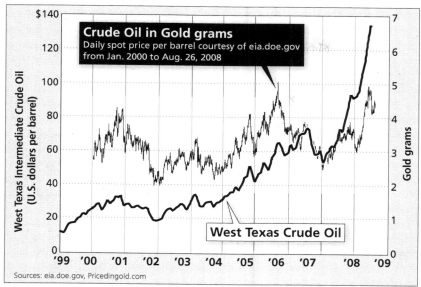

Figure 3.9: Oil priced in dollars; Oil priced in gold.

Figure 3.9 shows the price of oil in dollars and the price of oil in gold. It should be understood that all commodity prices, not just oil, rose throughout most of the past decade as the Fed printed new money and devalued our currency. With more money existing, the purchasing power of each existing dollar diminishes, particularly against other currencies that are not being printed as quickly as ours. Because commodities are priced in dollars, as our currency declines against other currencies, commodity prices become cheaper to foreigners, who, thus, increase their purchases. This is precisely what has been happening in recent years. But since the dollar also declined in value against gold, the gold price reveals how little the price of oil has increased in "real" terms.[85]

The oil charts in **Figure 3.9** reveal the real misguided politics behind commodity prices. *While consumers blame greedy oil companies for high gas prices and biofuel crops for a food shortage in many coun-*

---

[85] True real terms would consist of adjusting prices for true (not CPI) purchasing power. The comparison to gold gives an idea of what true purchasing power *could* be. In reality, gold has not adjusted to dollar/gold supply differences in many years for various reasons. Had the price of gold adjusted to reveal the true extent of supply increases of dollars over gold, the charts would be even more dramatic.

tries, the real culprit is the governments and the printing of money. As explained in Chapter 1, due to competition and absent new money being printed, it is impossible for companies to constantly raise prices. American oil companies, in particular, would not have that pricing power as they are a very small minority of global oil producers and gasoline providers. Even OPEC could not substantially raise prices to the rest of the world without causing demand (and thus their revenues) to fall off. The government(s) gave the oil companies their profits by printing money. Yet congress keeps putting oil CEOs on in the hot seat in televised hearings, scolding them for their large profits!

Figure 3.10 shows the price of the stock market, as represented by the Dow Jones Industrial Average, in dollars and in gold. The price of the stock market in gold is a good representation of what the real stock market performance has been this decade. While investors thought they had big gains during the bull market of 2003–2008, in real terms—that is, in terms of how much the value of their currency has declined and how much inflation has eaten into their gains—they made very little, even before the current sell-off. Clearly, not only would gold have been a better investment vehicle in the 2000s, but so would stocks in other countries whose currencies have risen in value against the dollar. So would have been European or Asian money markets. For example, between 2002 and 2008, on average, one would have gained more money by simply putting their money in a European bank account and having it sit there in cash, rather than having it invested in the U.S. market. The Dow Jones saw an increase of 52 percent over this time period, while the Euro saw an increase of 71 percent.

The phenomenon of people saving and investing part of their income for the future would mostly not exist were it not for inflation.[86] We are all forced to try and save because we know that the value of our wealth today will be worth less in the future when everything costs more. Imagine that we had a free market in money and prices actually did fall each year. How much money would you need to save

---

[86] This does not mean that people would not save, as they would still have incentives to for many reasons. It means that they would not *have* to save specifically to afford increased future prices. Additionally, less saving would be needed to fund companies because less capital would have been previously destroyed through inflation. See below for further effect of inflation on capital accumulation.

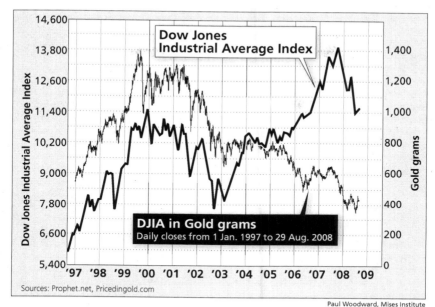

Sources: Prophet.net, Pricedingold.com

Paul Woodward, Mises Institute

Figure 3.10: Dow Jones Industrials priced in dollars; Dow Jones Industrials priced in gold.

if the lifestyle you have today (mortgage, food, vacations, medicine, entertainment, etc.) costs you, say, $50,000 per year, but that same lifestyle in 30 years would cost you $15,000, because everything became cheaper? This would be a very realistic scenario since, without government printing money, the production of goods would increase about 4 percent per year, and prices would therefore fall by almost 4 percent per year. We save and invest for the future mostly just to keep our purchasing power in the future equal to today's buying power.

But of course, any gains we make from investing, even in our own houses, are unnecessarily taxed by the government (capital gains tax), pushing us further behind. Still, what harms us the most is not the loss of our own savings, but the loss of the savings of the rich.

Alternative Excuses Offered for Rising Prices

Given the by now clearly unarguable truth that the government's printing of money causes inflation, we must ask why there are alternative explanations offered as to how and why prices rise and what the motives are of those who offer them. In the first instance, there are those who were mis-taught and misled by government textbooks and socialist professors calling themselves economists who firmly believe inflation is good.

There are still others who fully comprehend the quantity theory of money but choose to accept the effects of government money creation for political reasons or for reasons that allow them to advance in their careers by "consulting" governments on the issue or even to actually run the government printing presses. For example, Alan Greenspan, the previous Federal Reserve chairman, is not only extremely knowledgeable about the quantity theory of money and its devastating effects on prices and on the economy, but actually used to write scathing critiques of the central bank and of creating money. Consider for example the following quotation from him in 1967:

> The law of supply and demand is not to be conned. As the supply of money (of claims) increases relative to the supply of tangible assets in the economy, prices must eventually rise. Thus the earnings saved by the productive members of the society lose value in terms of goods. When the economy's books are finally balanced, one finds that this loss in value represents the goods purchased by the government for welfare or other purposes with the money proceeds of the government bonds financed by bank credit expansion.[87]

Clearly, Greenspan, given the chance to run a prestigious and economically powerful governmental agency, pursued policies inconsistent with the above-cited insight. He is thus responsible for creating trillions of dollars in fake money, thereby helping the government steal from citizens and creating multiple financial-asset bubbles and economic collapses (including the housing market bust and the current recession).

Shockingly, the most common alternative explanations offered by professional economists and academic textbooks for the cause of rising prices are based on the notion that inflation will appear simply because people expect it—that is, the "inflation expectations" argument. I kid

---

[87] Alan Greenspan, "Gold and Economic Freedom," in Ayn Rand, *Capitalism: The Unknown Ideal* (1966).

you not—this is a real proposed argument, actually discussed regularly in the academic world. For example, in a 2007 speech, Fed Chairman Ben Bernanke relayed that it's possible for "people [to] set prices and wages with reference to the rate of inflation they expect in the long run."[88] Supposedly, according to this argument, workers expect inflation and, therefore, start demanding higher wages, or consumers begin paying higher prices for goods, even in the absence of these two groups having received additional monetary purchasing power with which to bid up wages and prices. Thus, this ridiculous argument does not take into consideration that there would be no additional money in the economy with which to pay higher wages or higher consumer prices. These economists live in an imaginary world of mathematics and statistics that are not bound by reality.

Several years ago I was invited to a debate/discussion with economists at the Federal Reserve Bank of Atlanta. The visit confirmed my suspicion that these economists know some of the basic causes and effects of their intrusions into the economy and that they undertake these moves with cynical clarity. One of the economists at the meeting said, "We could stop inflation tomorrow if we wanted." (In reality, they could *begin* the process tomorrow, but it would take a year or more to actually *stop* it.)

Most revealing was their answer to my question of why they enact inflationary policies, namely that "market participants have contracts where inflation is expected." Presumably this meant that *unions* were expecting inflation. Workers cannot demand *and get paid* higher wages without causing unemployment for themselves. But with the help of the Fed bringing about an increase in general prices, unions can ask for and receive seemingly higher wages because economy-wide prices would be rising along with union wage increases. Unbeknownst to union workers, therefore, an important goal of the Fed is to have union members believe they are actually earning more money as a result of demanding higher wages when in fact they usually are just keeping up with inflation (while non-union workers usually experience wage increases below the rate of inflation).

---

[88] Federal Reserve Chairman Ben Bernanke, "Inflation Expectations and Inflation Forecasting" (speech), http://www.federalreserve.gov/newsevents/speech/bernanke20070710a.htm.

These economists at the Federal Reserve also told me that they were not the only ones creating inflation, but that private businesses were as well. Unfortunately, they did not have the opportunity to explain to me how this can happen, but had they, they might have cited one of the many other supposed explanations typically offered for rising prices. The most common of these are the following:

1. The "cost-push" doctrine: rising business costs bring rising prices

2. The "wage-push" doctrine: unions (primarily) force business to pay higher wages

3. The "profit-push" doctrine: greedy businesses raise prices in seeking higher profits

4. The "crisis-push" doctrine: temporary economic "shocks" raise prices permanently

5. The "demand-pull" doctrine: an "overheated economy" raises prices

6. The "velocity" doctrine: consumers start spending the very same money more quickly (for no reason), increasing demand

7. Credit cards: spending rises because of increased spending ability with plastic

8. Installment credit: consumer home, auto, and other personal loans increase spending

9. Derivatives: options, futures, swaps, and so on (financial market products that provide leverage) create increased spending

10. Government budget deficits: excess spending by government

All of these arguments are fallacious. For each of these, and any others that could be offered for higher prices, it can be easily proven that the hypothesis is faulty and that inflation could not be created by the means proposed. In fact, if the items listed above were investigated thoroughly, it would be found that most *further prove* the quantity of money theory. For instance, it can be easily shown that quantity of money is the factor that affects velocity the most and that the ability to use credit cards or alternative payment systems and derivatives requires that more money be created and credit extended. In a world with an invariable quantity of money, and in the absence of a reduction of spending that would bring about increased saving, it would be impossible for more credit to become available. I will not digress further in order to disprove each of these alternative explanations, but rest assured that disproving them is easily done.[89]

How the Government's Central Bank Creates Recessions and Financial Crises

The most damaging effects of the central bank are the economic crises it creates through its creation of credit—that is, by printing money. Recessions and depressions, along with the associated job losses and financial hardships that accompany them, are not normal occurrences in any economy. They are government made. The following sections explain the deleterious effects of the government's inflationary policies on various sectors of the economy: the first focuses on the real economy (production of goods, payment of wages, etc.) and the second on the financial system (banks, financial markets, etc.). In the former case, problems are manifest as declining output, job cuts, and business failures. In the latter case, problems are manifest as banks going bust; stock, bond, and real estate markets falling in value; currency exchange rates collapsing; and credit generally disappearing.

The Creation of Recessions

Nationwide recurrent recessions and expansions—that is, the business cycle, as it is known—did not exist before central banking and centralized banking systems became institutionalized in the 17th century. Even now, business cycles don't occur in either communist countries or in developing countries that lack centralized fractional-reserve banking systems.

The expansion of credit by the central bank, and in particular the banking system's government-endorsed fractional-reserve system, cause large-scale economic imbalances in the real economy—imbalances that must eventually be corrected—because the money that

---

[89] For a complete and devastating critique of all of these explanations, see George Reisman, *Capitalism: A Treatise on Economics* (1995), pp. 895–921.

banks create and push out into the economy in the form of loans does not affect all prices and all sectors of the economy equally.

New money entering the economy, in the form of credit, lowers interest rates artificially (i.e., lower than those rates would be without the additional money), thereby increasing capital investment disproportionately in the capital goods industries relative to the consumer goods industries. Why? Because capital goods industries require large-scale investment in factories, equipment, technology, and so forth and can always benefit from more and new investment, and thus additional funds available at low interest rates. The lower the cost of borrowing monetary capital, the more these industries borrow, especially because of what is called "net present value" calculations in the world of corporate finance: the method of discounting the future value of investments via prevailing interest rates. With artificially low interest rates, the profitability of investments is artificially increased. Businesspeople, unaware that artificial money is causing their projects to look more profitable than they are, assume that the interest rate reflects the true amount of savings and money (i.e., real physical materials, tools, supplies, etc.) available to fund their investments when, in fact, it does not.

New money entering the economy competes with real savings for a limited amount of real resources. Businesses, therefore, compete with their new funds for these limited resources whose prices do not reflect their real cost. This situation is similar to the game of musical chairs, which ends with too many people trying to obtain too few chairs, except that, in this case, the number of chairs would remain the same while more people joined the game. With interest rates misrepresenting the real price and availability of resources, some of the borrowed new money is used in investments that appear to be profitable, but in reality are not. Were the interest rate higher (i.e., at the *real* rate determined by the market instead of by the government), the real threshold of profitability would be revealed, and if fake money were not competing with real money for limited profitable investments, only the truly profitable investments would be undertaken (with, of course, some natural margin of error).

Additionally, many of the investments being made are not in accordance with consumers' desires. More true money would be available to invest in capital goods only if consumers had decided to consume less in the present and more in the future. They would have *saved* more of their income and made it available as *real* monetary capital to be used in producing more capital goods. Because it is capital goods that make consumer goods, an increase in capital goods would eventually provide consumers more consumer goods in the future. But, in fact, consumers have *not* abstained from spending at the time the Fed pushes credit out to capital goods firms, and they have not saved more money that can be used in increased capital goods production.

The economy is, therefore, being pulled in two directions: businesses are trying to use the limited savings available to invest for the future while consumers are not curtailing spending so as to make the savings available, as businesspeople are led to believe. But as long as businesses have access to more and additional credit (fake savings masked as real savings), they can get by without losses. This additional availability of credit from the Fed also encourages them to rely on its constant availability; thus, they minimize the cash they keep on hand (worsening the ensuing "credit crunch").

However, after some period of time, all the new money that has entered the economy through business loans begins to make prices rise. Costs of producer goods rise because companies are buying them. Costs of consumer goods rise because more workers working and receiving higher salaries (as more companies compete to hire them with their newly borrowed funds) are spending more money on goods. Consumer goods also rise because, since the investment of new resources has been primarily in the capital goods industry, the consumer goods industry has not yet expanded its capacity to produce current goods and is, thus, not creating many more goods each year than the last. With more consumer money chasing a steady or even declining volume of consumer goods, prices rise. Moreover, prices of financial assets also rise when too much of the new money makes its way into the financial markets, and asset bubbles sometimes appear. It is for fear of either increasing price inflation or of asset bubbles that the Fed stops printing money because regulators know that it is the money being printed that is causing these occurrences.

Once the Fed's credit creation comes to a halt, or even slows down, like a public water fountain that falls after the force of water shooting up below it is diminished, there is not enough money to keep funding the ever-more-costly investments; similarly, as the quantity of money falls or accelerates too slowly, there is not enough money to support asset prices, and they fall. It follows, then, that once the pace of credit expansion slows, that business projects cannot be completed or become unprofitable, and asset prices, which also often serve as collateral for business for loans supporting these investments, must fall. Losses naturally ensue.

Business losses become widespread after the money stops flowing and the pace of spending declines. Projects already undertaken are often abandoned, unfinished, due to lack of funds and higher costs. Many businesses that were profitable during the boom become unprofitable once less credit is created because the flow of new money itself was a source of demand for products and services. Without that demand, business revenues fall while costs remain the same or decline more slowly.

A Monetary Perspective of Recessions

It is also important to understand booms and busts from a purely monetary perspective. Since Reisman has explained this so brilliantly, it is well worth summarizing here.

Recessions come about only by a preceding expansion of money which leads to an artificial elevation of spending brought about by the increased money in the economy (A credit-induced boom leads to an inevitable bust).

When credit expansion begins, it raises the velocity of circulation: as new money enters the economy, it appears that credit is cheap and easy to come by, causing people to hold fewer dollars, because they feel they can easily access funds when they need them. But the availability of funds leaves businesses less liquid. Why? Since businesses can easily obtain money, they don't need to hold as much of it, and they therefore spend the money they were keeping in checking accounts. With businesses (and people) holding less money and spending it more rapidly, the velocity of circulation increases. As velocity increases, demand increases.

But an increase in the money supply has another important effect: it increases debt in the economic system. This is because as the quantity of money is expanded, interest rates, and thus borrowing costs fall. But the rate of profit for businesses remains the same as before. As interest rates fall relative to business profits, which remain the same, it becomes more profitable to borrow. Thus both businesses and (individuals) take on more debt and extend their leverage.

But when the credit expansion ends or slows, debt becomes harder to repay. The belief that people can operate with lower cash holdings is predicated on the continuation of credit expansion. When credit expansion ceases, velocity falls, and this alone can cause serious problems, as those who relied on cheap and easy credit, instead of holding adequate cash, scurry to build up their cash holdings. With reduced velocity and spending, increased cash holdings, and less credit available at higher prices (interest rates rise with a cessation or reduction in credit expansion), payment of all outstanding debt can't be maintained. With outstanding debt levels too great to be repaid; bankruptcies inevitably ensue.

But things really get bad when unpaid debts cause business firms to default on their debts to banks, which lowers the value of bank assets. Due to fractional reserves, bank deposits—the bank's liabilities—are backed, via currency on hand, by only 10% of the value of the deposit. The rest of their assets are in the form of loans and securities. If loans go bad, leaving fewer total assets backing bank liabilities, banks can't pay depositors all their money—they go bankrupt.

When banks go bankrupt, their checking account money— promises to pay on demand—no longer have value; they are worthless. Those checking deposits are no longer part of the quantity of money. When the money supply is reduced in this way, there is less money spent. The ability to repay debts is thus reduced further, setting up more bank failures and more money supply declines. Due to reduced demand and business losses, unemployment ensues. This is the vicious cycle that took place during the bank failures of the Great Depression.

A Recession's Aftermath

Capital goods companies, and other companies that produce intermediate goods, experience steeper losses of revenues and profits during recessions than consumer goods companies—retailers, service-oriented companies, and so on—that hold up relatively well during tough economic times. Companies in areas such as manufacturing, infrastructure, materials, and construction are hardest hit. Likewise, it is primarily workers from these industries, not those from the consumer goods industries, who are laid off. Many of these businesses go bust, resulting in layoffs, the closing of factories, and unused idle capacity of plants and equipment (for example, steel mills, dot-coms and the housing industry).

Companies that become less profitable or go bust cannot repay loans to banks. Banks must write off loans and close accounts. Deposit accounts then evaporate into thin air just as they were created out of thin air. Banks are then forced to call in other loans in order to meet reserve and capital requirements. At some point, at least one or two banks go under. The bankruptcy of one bank causes many others to fail because they are all interconnected through the pyramided financial payments system. Just as money was created with a multiplier effect, it is destroyed with a reverse multiplier effect. The lack of credit available to businesses leaves them in still worse shape, and this downward spiral continues until the bad investments are cleared out and banks' balance sheets are restored (when permitted; when bailouts do not occur).

The inflationary booms and busts bring about lasting damage to our capital structure. The misallocated capital resulting from the business cycle described above entails a destruction of real wealth and thus of the ability to create new and additional tools, technology, and machinery. The result is lower real productivity, lower salaries, fewer goods, higher real prices, and a reduced standard of living. Had this wealth never been destroyed, we would all have a much higher standard of living than we do currently. Instead of average household incomes of about $44,000, as we have today, we could have average incomes of $60,000, $80,000, or $100,000, with the *same* cost of living we have today.[90]

In sum, recessions are not a natural phenomenon. There is a reason that thousands of companies, most of which do a great job of forecasting and planning most of the time, suddenly all experience bad investments and losses simultaneously. The mainstream pro-government economists, such as Keynesians, have no clear and logical explanations for business cycles: their best theory for business cycles is that wild "animal spirits" cause businesspeople and investors to spend crazily but then suddenly stop without reason.[91] It is simply spending and re-spending, they hold, not saving and investing, that causes economies to grow. It should be apparent from Chapter 1 that it is real savings, not paper bills being passed from one person to the next, that grow our economy. Instead of some unpredictable wild animal spirits, it is fake government money that causes the boom and then the bust.

These pro-government economists also argue that during the boom there is economic overinvestment and overproduction. This cannot be true, of course, because we could never produce more goods than we could use (not to mention, that if we did overproduce, the "excess" goods would be free, since no one would want them). Even if we somehow could overproduce, prices would fall to adjust to our purchasing power—along the way, not all of a sudden. The reality is that we overproduce in some industries and under-produce in others. The government distorts the price system that coordinates resources and causes a misallocation of capital. Recessions are actually the corrective healing process wherein workers and materials are reallocated to where they should be, based on consumers' ultimate wishes as revealed by their spending patterns. Even so, much capital and real savings are destroyed in the process.

---

[90] To be technically correct, the increased wealth would actually be in the form of lower costs of living. I stated the gains in terms of higher salaries in order to describe it in a way most people can relate to. Either scenario is accurate in terms of the point being made because increased real wealth would bring higher salaries relative to the things we buy.

[91] The reduction in spending actually arises from a decrease in the volume of spending, available credit and a decrease in the quantity of money, both of which result from a reduction in the rate of credit creation.

The Creation of Financial Crises

Soon after the first central bank arrived in the Netherlands in 1609, so did the first known financial bubble. The famous "tulip mania" occurred in the 1630s and consisted of dramatically rising prices of Tulip bulbs.[92] New money created by the Dutch central bank (much of it pyramided on new gold and silver flowing in from America) was funneled into, among other things, tulip prices, just as new money is funneled into particular stock and bond prices today. The Dutch sold homes, farms, and many acres of land just to buy as little as a single tulip bulb, with hopes of becoming rich, until the tulip bubble collapsed and prices came crashing down.

Perhaps the most famous bubbles are those of the South Sea and Mississippi Companies from 1717–1720, which were associated with the origination of the first state-chartered bank of France. Here, un-backed currency was created in the form of loans, many of which were used to buy shares in two companies that were run by the central banker himself. Again, after extraordinary gains, share prices plummeted in what was probably history's first market crash.

More recent asset bubbles include the 1989 property boom and bust accompanied by the S&L bailout; the Japanese economic boom and, as of now, 19-year bust; the 1990s economic boom and collapse of the "Asian Miracle" countries; the late 1990s dot.com stock market bubble and subsequent collapse; and the recent world real-estate boom and current bust. All of these financial/economic booms and busts are the result of the worldwide printing of money, which originates predominantly in the United States with the Federal Reserve Bank. Our inflationary trade imbalance, as will be explained below, causes money to leave the U.S. and flow into other countries, *causing* other countries to print money. Additionally, money created by the Fed (as well as the E.U. central bank) and loaned out to institutional investors, flows into other countries as investment capital, and swells asset prices and bank balance sheets in those countries.

---

[92] For a full explanation, see Doug French, "The Truth about Tulipmania," http://mises.org/daily/2564.

Financial bubbles result from new money being channeled into financial markets and remaining there (i.e., not leaking out into the real economy). As more and more money flows into financial assets, their prices rise, often at an increasing rate. Because rapidly rising asset prices are such a profitable endeavor, not only do individual investors invest more of their savings, but institutional players (hedge funds, insurance companies, mutual funds, etc.) borrow increased amounts of the new money in order to participate, often using a large degree of leverage to multiply their returns. Particularly in the later stages of the "game," the prices of the assets involved in the bubble become completely divorced from the underlying fundamentals and true amount of risk involved in the purchase of the assets. The driving force is simply the flow of money. Then, as is the case with inflation in the real economy, once the Fed's money stops flowing, the asset fountains fall back to the ground. No matter what the talking heads on television say about "the new economy" or about housing prices being solely a function of population and demographics, the inescapable truth is that when the money that has been pushing up asset prices begins to flow less strongly prices will fall.

Prior to the recent real estate bubble, physical and monetary over-investment took place in dot-com companies. When the Fed's fake money stopped flowing, hundreds of these companies—many of which should never have received funding to begin with, and would not have without the Fed's monetary manipulation—ceased to exist and real capital was lost. In fact, the housing market, which was already hot at that time, became a bubble precisely because the Fed was trying to save the economy in the early 2000s from being negatively affected by the collapsing dot-com bubble. The Fed's money-pumping actions, beginning in 2001, prevented the economy from healing from the massive imbalances that existed, making them drastically worse over the next six years as it created a new bubble, this time in real estate.

During the recent real-estate bubble, the Fed began slowing its rate of credit expansion in 2004. Though interest rates rose for almost two more years, by pumping enough money to keep them at still artificially low levels, Alan Greenspan and company were continuing to expand credit at high (but decelerating) rates. By mid-2006, interest rates had risen to a rate of over 5 percent, up from their two-years-prior low of

1 percent. Within a year's time, the slowing availability of money for financing real estate and rising interest costs caused homebuyers to slow their pace of buying. With less affordability and less money from the Fed with which to bid up prices, housing prices began to fall. When homeowners' variable-rate mortgages purchased when interest rates were lower were reset to higher market interest rates, many of those who had bought houses they could not really afford were unable to make mortgage payments at the higher rates. This caused losses on the balance sheets of banks and investment firms that held the leveraged mortgages or mortgage-backed securities (groups of mortgages packaged together to be traded on financial markets; also now known as "toxic assets").

As real estate prices fell, banks' balance sheets began to deteriorate because the houses themselves, which were falling in value, served as collateral for loans, and, because many customers were not repaying their mortgage loans. Additionally, many investment banks owned mortgage-backed securities, which were declining in value for the same reasons. Their deteriorating state of finances caused widespread bank insolvencies.

In 2008, we witnessed U.S. and U.K banks going bust left and right. One-hundred-fifty-year-old financial institutions went out of business overnight. Most major Wall Street banks either failed and were taken over by others or transformed themselves into deposit banks (where they can always create their own money). Quasi-governmental mortgage agencies Fannie Mae and Freddie Mac, already government sponsored, imploded and were (unconstitutionally) nationalized by the government. The same happened to AIG, one of the largest insurance companies in the world.

For fear of these events resulting in widespread credit contraction and a failure of the entire American financial system, the Federal Reserve has been trying to paper over current credit losses with more new money and new debt. But it is not yet clear as to whether its successes so far will be permanent. If the injections of newly printed money and bailouts work, we can expect higher inflation and less real economic growth—even though the stock markets and GDP will register a considerable increase (see more on the meaninglessness of GDP in Chapter 10). If the bailouts fail, we can expect rapidly falling prices (not in a good way) and less real economic growth. Either way, we have incurred a reduction in standards of living (whether we notice it or not!) due to the latest effects of the government's money machine.

But there is one essential thing that should be understood: there is no way that the housing bubble and burst, mortgage implosion, financial crisis, and recession could ever have occurred without an expansion of the money supply by the government, no matter what derivatives were used or what bad choices were made. In fact, the derivatives went bad because the underlying assets went bad. And as we have seen, it was the manipulation of money and credit which caused the underlying assets to go bad (and for seemingly uncorrelated assets to suddenly become correlated). It was government intervention—in the form of regulation—that caused the crisis.

Consequences of a Financial Implosion

It could be the case currently that the imbalances in the whole of the economy have been large enough to cause such a destruction of real savings and capital that new credit is not enough to cover up the problems. In this case, it is possible that an implosion of the money supply, resulting deflation (falling prices arising from money disappearing), could cause a nasty economic downward spiral. Many have pooh-poohed the notion that this deflation could happen today and dismiss those who claim that it could as doom-and-gloom crackpots. But it is precisely for fear of this implosion that our "leaders" are desperately trying to prop up the system.

Bernanke has said previously that a 1930s-style money supply collapse could not happen today because the Fed would print enough money to prevent it. This is questionable, however, because the same strategy failed in the 1930s. Contrary to popular opinion, the Federal Reserve did try to expand the money supply back then by pumping bank reserves into the system. As evidence of this attempt, the Fed's holdings of bonds purchased from member banks for the purposes of expanding reserves increased by 400 percent between 1929 and 1931.[93] However, this maneuver did not stop the falling market and the

---

[93] For detailed statistics, see Murray Newton Rothbard, *America's Great Depression* (2000).

collapsing economy, mainly because citizens withdrew their deposits from banks, which reduces the money supply. But as long as people believe the government will and can compensate them for their deposits in a bankrupt bank, they will not withdraw their funds. As long as this continues, the government, by creating credit, can always replenish the amount of money that evaporates in the system as a result of bankruptcies and lack of debt repayment.

The other reason the money supply could not be re-inflated in the 1930s was because much of the newly-created money was not loaned out and did not enter into the money supply. In order for the new money to make it into the money supply, banks have to feel financially healthy enough to lend their excess reserves[94] to the public, and the public has to feel financially healthy enough to borrow the new money.

The banks did not initially lend out their bailout funds in 2008 and 2009 precisely because they were not healthy enough to do so; they first needed to recapitalize themselves with the funds merely in order to survive. In the same way, the public will be reluctant to borrow more money if they already feel that they're under water from their current debt. If neither the banks nor the public make use of the new funds, the money will not make it into the money supply to push prices up. When the demand to hold money is strong and when large amounts of credit have been destroyed while at the same time banks refuse to lend more credit due to ongoing losses from the previous credit, what exists is commonly known as a "credit crunch." When business and bank losses are not liquidated, credit can remain frozen, bringing the wheels of the economy to a standstill. This is why it's imperative for losses to be realized and for institutions that would otherwise collapse not be propped up with taxpayer money—it's all for naught, as it throws good money after bad, and results in a net loss of wealth.

If the Fed manages to save the banking system, it will be all of us who pay the price. "Being saved" means having money printed,

---

[94] This is where the proposal for a government bailout comes in. The idea is for the government to buy the bad loans so as to remove them from the books of the banks, so that the banks can become healthier and resume loaning out money.

borrowed, or taken in additional taxes in order to recapitalize the banks and to pay for losses the Fed and the Treasury will take on from buying the banks' deteriorating assets. All of this will result not only in higher consumer price inflation, but in less capital available for us to use to improve our standards of living, and more crises in the future. Nobel Prize-winning economist Friedrich A. Hayek had this to say in 1928:

> To combat the Depression by a forced credit expansion is to attempt to cure the evil by the very means which brought it about; because we are suffering from a misdirection of production, we want to create further misdirection—a procedure that can only lead to a much more severe crisis as soon as the credit expansion comes to an end.[95]

This is the cost we will pay to compensate financial institutions for the mistakes they made in using the money they stole from the rest of us (remember, they are intertwined with the Federal Reserve). The Fed's existence encourages these firms to take on risky gambles over and over, because they know that the Fed will bail them out with our savings. It is very possible—though not a certainty[96]—that the large price tag will be in the form of the highest inflation rates in many years.

Bankers have spent over a hundred years arguing that fractional-reserve banking is a natural product of the free market and is harmful to the economy only when it isn't properly regulated by the government. We have nothing resembling a free market in banking and finance, however, and clearly fractional-reserve banking is tantamount to fraud, since it is selling claims to someone else's money. Inevitably, our current problems will result in politicians arguing we need *more* regulation to prevent crises, while they will make sure to leave fractional reserve banking in place to fund wealth redistribution.

---

[95] Friedrich Hayek, *Monetary Theory and the Trade Cycle* (1929).

[96] Because new money might flow disproportionately into asset prices instead of consumer prices.

International Financial Crises

Since the last remnants of the gold standard were snuffed out by the U.S. government in the early 1970s, worldwide creation of money—and with it the frequency of financial bubbles[97]—has grown at the fastest pace in history. While few large-scale financial and economic calamities simultaneously affecting multiple countries occurred prior to the 1970s, crises have been popping up around the world ever since, and are becoming more common. The Latin American runaway inflation of the 1970s and 1980s and subsequent debt crisis in the early 1980s, the 1989 S&L crisis, the 1995 Mexican "tequila" crisis, the 1997 Asian currency crisis, the 1998 Russian debt crisis, the 2002 Argentine debt crisis and subsequent economic implosion, the competitive currency devaluations between countries, currency collapses, and the many more worldwide events of financial destruction were all caused by the massive amounts of debt the world's central banks created.

It should be pointed out that much of the debt created by various central banks in the world is a direct result of America's trade imbalances. Foreign exporters who receive our dollars as payments for goods they shipped to us exchange those dollars for local currency at banks in their countries. But most of the local currency paid to the exporters by their banks is newly created money: for each dollar they collect from us, foreign central banks create an equivalent amount of money in their currency in order to pay their exporters. The dollars, instead of being converted into local currency, are reinvested by foreign central banks in the United States, mainly in financial assets, so as to keep their currency low so that their exports will be more competitive. These dollars held by foreign central banks are known as *foreign exchange reserves* or *reserve assets*. The international central banking system revolves in this away around the dollar because of the government-installed Bretton Woods regulated monetary system that preceded the current state of affairs.

Not only does the money that flows back to the United States become a driving force pushing up U.S. asset prices, but money foreign central banks print in their own countries creates asset bubbles and

---

[97] More realistically, the *origination* of modern financial bubbles.

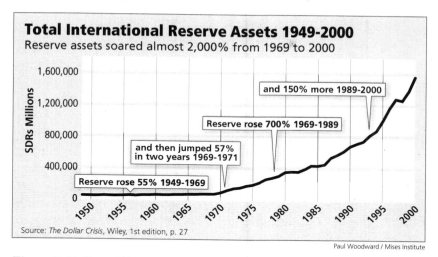

Figure 3.11: The rapid increase in world reserve assets since going off the gold standard in 1971.

distorts economic growth in the same way that it does in this country. This, along with international investment capital flows created in both the United States and Europe, is the "fuel" that causes the types of booms and busts described above. As evidence, consider the chart in **Figure 3.11** showing the increase in total world reserve assets since going off the gold standard in 1971. The increase in reserve assets reflects the increase in world money supply. No wonder international crises have been so predominant since the early 1970s. Though the total reserve assets in this chart, which goes through 2000, are just shy of $1.6 trillion, the total as of 2010 is over $9 trillion (up $1 trillion over mid-2008).[98]

The massive world inflation created by central banks shapes the events in our daily economic lives, even though the only measure of inflation you probably are aware of—the CPI—states that inflation is tame. The above-mentioned crises are all caused by inflation that you do not see, affecting your well-being, and reducing your wealth and your standard of living in the multiple ways described above.

---

[98] Wikipedia, List of Countries by Foreign Exchange Rates, http://en.wikipedia.org/wiki/List_of_countries_by_foreign_exchange_reserves.

The Crazed Desire for Price Stability

In "managing" our economy, most central banks supposedly aim for stable prices. More specifically, they aim for a stable, positive, but low rate of inflation. Most economists fear falling prices because they associate them with deflation. They believe there should be *some* inflation for fear that if the inflation rate gets too close to zero, it will slip into deflation. This fear is misguided, however, as deflation comes about only with a collapse of the money supply. Deflation—prices collapsing from a collapse in the money supply—is in no way related to falling prices that arise from the production of goods and services. Further, even stable prices (an inflation rate of zero) constitute inflation because without the printing of more money, as we have learned, prices would fall. Therefore, the amount of money that is printed in order to keep prices unchanged still has the same negative effects on the business cycles and financial markets described above.

Still, central bankers believe that having price stability—instead of merely letting prices fall—is a panacea for all inflationary ills, even though inflation would still be prevalent in the form of an expanding quantity of money and rising asset prices, *in addition* to the 2 percent to 3 percent inflation they plan for. Even with their intended goal of a positive rate of inflation, they often get more than they bargained for. An example is Iceland's recent inflation rate of 14 percent, even

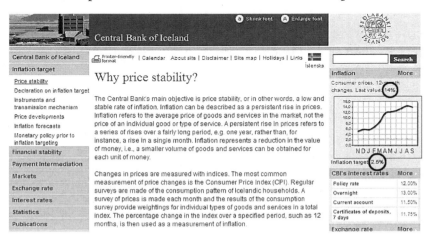

Figure 3.12: Iceland's inflation level of 14 percent versus its stated goal of 2.5 percent. Source: Central Bank of Iceland: http://www.cb.is/.

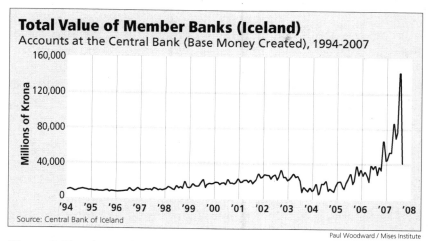

Total Value of Member Banks (Iceland)
Accounts at the Central Bank (Base Money Created), 1994-2007

Paul Woodward / Mises Institute

Figure 3.13: Iceland's inflation level of 14 percent versus its stated goal of 2.5 percent.
Source: Central Bank of Iceland: http://www.cb.is/

though its central bank's stated inflation target is 2.5 percent, as shown in **Figure 3.12**.

The primary reason that Iceland's inflation rate achieved 14 percent was its increase in the money supply. **Figure 3.13** shows that the amount of money in Iceland's economy increased dramatically between 2004 and 2007.

The reality is that for many reasons central banks can't maintain a particular target rate of inflation. The inflation rate will vary widely around the targeted number. Additionally, there is every political incentive to print money at a faster rate than planned, as the government never has enough money, and it always needs to try and pump up the economy so that politicians can get re-elected. We would all be better off if the government simply quit printing money and let prices fall.

Stop the Insanity!

It should be seen how ridiculous the whole system of creating money is. There is no need for it. It does not help true economic growth—i.e., the increasing production of goods and services and rising real wages. Only real savings can grow the economy. Diluting the amount of limited real savings with paper money results only in some portion of the real savings and real wealth being destroyed. If money were never printed, or if we were legally allowed to use the money that the marketplace has chosen for hundreds of years—gold—money would never be at risk of disappearing because it would not be based on debt, it would be real. Deflation, credit collapses, multiple bank failures, and recessions come about only as a result of the central bank.[99]

It is probably safe to say that voters are not aware that by supporting the current policies of today's politicians, they are voting for inflation and a destruction of wealth. If voters let their politicians know that they are as upset about inflation, recessions, and economic crises as they are about reproductive, immigration, and civil rights (not that these issues are not important!), politicians would respond accordingly in order to get elected. The sad reality is that voters rely on the politicians to somehow fix the economy. Voters have no idea that the economy is already in a mess precisely because of what the politicians have been up to. It is the printing of money that helps pay for wealth redistribution, finances wars, temporarily causes higher employment, and makes the so-called GDP rise—the things voters think benefit them. Only with an understanding of what really helps us become wealthier as citizens can we encourage our politicians to do the *real* right thing.

---

[99] Even after all this detailed explanation, government economists would simply say that much of it is hogwash, that these assertions are not proven in "the data" (as I was told by central bankers at the Atlanta Fed).

Chapter 4:

Regulation:
The Helping Hand That Harms

ost people believe that the United States is a free country with free markets. Whenever economic problems arise, they blame unfettered capitalism. The truth is that the entire U.S. economy is controlled to a very large degree by government intervention. The intervention, or regulation, consists of anything from anti-trust laws and price controls, to actions forcing companies to or prohibiting them from engaging in particular activities.[100] The Federal Register, the book which lists government regulations, now has more than 73,000 pages, which is an increase of 10,000 pages or 16 percent over the last thirty years. Still, socialists claim that our economy has been deregulated.

Every instance of intervention constitutes the government's prohibiting individuals or companies from acting in a way they choose, by way of threatening the use of physical force. People believe that if individuals and companies were left to their own devices, they would harm others. In some small percentage of cases they would (but

---

[100] I call regulation any form of government intervention. Though this might not be customary, I feel that it is 100 percent appropriate: anything the government does to alter market processes is in fact some form of governing—regulating—the economy.

much less than under our current system of regulation). In these cases there should indeed be laws that promise and carry out punishment of those who physically harm others or their property (including the government) in the form of making them (or their insurance company, as it would be) pay compensation.

Most people mistakenly believe that harm can be done from the normal procedures of carrying out production and exchange, in other words, by individuals doing business with each other. They believe that all of our laws and regulations exist simply to protect innocent people from being harmed. Nothing could be further from the truth. As we have seen to some degree already and will continue to learn, businesses, unless they break simple capitalistic laws aimed at preventing the forceful taking of private property (including by way of fraud), cannot harm us by hiring us, producing for us, or selling to us.[101] We need only these basic laws protecting property rights—which includes one's person—and a court system in order to deter or punish acts of harm to one's property; we do not need 73,000 pages to do it. If an individual's property has been taken or harmed by a company or employer, they would have a legal claim to compensation.[102] Don't

---

[101] This statement excludes such murky issues such as the fact that McDonald's can "hurt" us by selling us food that will make us fat or cause high blood pressure. One does not need to take the argument to that level—they can simply choose not to purchase the food. Similarly, one might think companies harm us by polluting. But most of us implicitly approve of this because we choose to continue buying the resulting products. Plus, we know that if we don't pollute at all we will die for lack of food and medicines. These kinds of arguments lead us down the road of believing that any of our neighbors or competitors are doing something that is "harming" us, and thus we need government to intervene for what we believe.

[102] A primary problem with regulation is that it allows "harm" to constitute virtually anything. For example, if a Jewish-owned company wanted to hire only Jews, they should be able to. But labor regulation makes it illegal for a privately owned firm to hire whom it wants; regulation makes such an act something that "harms" others who were intentionally not chosen because they are not Jewish, even though there really was no harm involved. (Though it is beyond the scope of this book to prove, it should be understood that in a free market, racial, gender, or ethnic discrimination would hardly exist: competition and the desire to achieve high profits would force employers to hire the most capable and suitable people for the job, not those they simply like best. As proof of this, consider that for all that we hear about women not making as much as men, in fact they do. Women with the same level of education, skills, number of years in the workforce, etc., make more on average than their male counterpart.)

confuse political law (regulation) with civil and merchant laws (protection of person and property).

Most of the myriad regulations on our books, however, do not protect private property, rather, they allow one group to benefit at the expense of another group and to thus *take* their property. The regulations prevent companies from operating in a fashion that would offer too much competition to other politically favored groups. There is no net benefit to society at all from these regulations, but only harm and injustice.

Consider the list of government departments below, of which defense departments are not listed:

Administration for Children and Families (ACF)
Administration for Native Americans
Administration on Aging (AoA)
Administration on Developmental Disabilities
Agency for Healthcare Research and Quality (AHRQ)
Agency for Toxic Substances and Disease Registry
Agricultural Marketing Service
Agricultural Research Service
Alcohol and Tobacco Tax and Trade Bureau
Alcohol, Tobacco, Firearms, and Explosives
Animal and Plant Health Inspection Service
Arms Control and International Security
Bureau of Economic Analysis (BEA)
Bureau of Engraving and Printing
Bureau of Indian Affairs (BIA)
Bureau of Industry and Security (formerly Export Patent & Trademark Office)
Bureau of International Labor Affairs
Bureau of Labor Statistics (BLS)
Bureau of Land Management (BLM)
Bureau of Public Debt
Bureau of Reclamation
Bureau of the Census
Bureau of Transportation Statistics
Center for Nutrition Policy and Promotion
Centers for Disease Control and Prevention (CDC)
Centers for Medicare & Medicaid Services (formerly the Research, Education and Economics)
Community Oriented Policing Services (COPS)
Community Planning and Development

Computer Emergency Readiness Team (US CERT)
Cooperative State Research, Education and Extension
Domestic Nuclear Detection Office
Drug Enforcement Administration (DEA)
Economic Development Administration
Economic Research Service
Economic, Business, and Agricultural Affairs(SAMHSA)
Economics & Statistics Administration
Elementary and Secondary Education
Employee Benefits Security Administration (formerly U.S. Citizenship and Immigration Services)
Employment and Training Administration (ETA)
Employment Standards Administration
Executive Office for Immigration Review
Executive Office for U.S. Attorneys
Farm Service Agency
Federal Aviation Administration (FAA)
Federal Bureau of Investigation (FBI)
Federal Bureau of Prisons
Federal Emergency Management Agency (FEMA)
Federal Highway Administration
Federal Law Enforcement Training Center
Federal Motor Carrier Safety Administration
Federal Railroad Administration
Federal Student Aid
Federal Transit Administration
Financial Management Service (FMS)
Fish & Wildlife Service
Food and Drug Administration (FDA)
Food and Nutrition Service
Food Safety and Inspection Service

Food, Nutrition and Consumer Services
Foreign Agricultural Service
Foreign Claims Settlement Commission
Forest Service
Geological Survey (USGS)
Global Affairs
Government National Mortgage Association (Ginnie Mae)
Grain Inspection, Packers and Stockyards Administration
Health Care Financing Administration
Health Resources and Services Administration (HRSA)
Indian Health Service (IHS)
Institute of Education Sciences
Internal Revenue Service (IRS)
International Trade Administration (ITA)
Management Under Secretary
Maritime Administration
Marketing and Regulatory Programs
Mine Safety and Health Administration
Mineral Management Service
Minority Business Development Agency
Multifamily Housing
National Agricultural Statistics Service
National Cemetery Administration Service
National Drug Intelligence Center
National Highway Traffic Safety Administration
National Institute of Standards & Technology (NIST)
National Institutes of Health (NIH)
National Interagency Fire Center
National Marine Fisheries
National Oceanic & Atmospheric Administration (NOAA)
National Park Service

National Technical Information Service
National Telecommunications & Information Administration
National Weather Service
Natural Resources Conservation Service
Occupational Safety & Health Administration (OSHA)
Office for Civil Rights
Office of Disability Employment Policy
Office of Enforcement
Office of English Language Acquisition
Office of Fair Housing and Equal Opportunity
Office of Federal Housing Enterprise Oversight
Office of Healthy Homes and Lead Hazard Control
Office of Housing
Office of Innovation and Improvement
Office of Intergovernmental and Interagency Affairs
Office of Justice Programs (Juvenile Justice, Victims of Crime, Violence Against Women and more)
Office of Management
Office of Public and Indian Housing

Office of Refugee Resettlement
Office of Safe and Drug-Free Schools
Office of Surface Mining, Reclamation & Enforcement
Office of the Chief Financial Officer
Office of the Chief Information Officer
Office of the Comptroller of the Currency
Office of the Pardon Attorney
Office of Thrift Supervision (OTS)
Operations Coordination Office
Pension and Welfare Benefits Administration
Pipeline and Hazardous Materials Safety Administration
Policy Development and Research
Policy Office
Political Affairs
Postsecondary Education
Preparedness Directorate
Program Support Center
Public Diplomacy and Public Affairs
Research and Innovative Technology Administration
Risk Management Agency
Rural Business-Cooperative Service
Rural Development
Rural Housing Service
Rural Utilities Service

Saint Lawrence Seaway Development Corporation
Science and Technology Directorate
Special Education and Rehabilitative Services
Substance Abuse and Mental Health Services Administration
Surface Transportation Board
Transportation Security Administration
U.S. Coast Guard
U.S. Customs and Border Protection
U.S. Immigration and Customs Enforcement
U.S. Marshals Service
U.S. Mint
U.S. Mission to the United Nations
U.S. National Central Bureau of Interpol
U.S. Parole Commission
U.S. Secret Service
U.S. Trustee Program
Veterans Benefits Administration
Veterans Health Administration
Veterans' Employment and Training Service (VETS)
Vocational and Adult Education
Women's Bureau

Almost every one of these departments exists to tamper with the marketplace in such a way that government can have the outcome it wants. Most of these interventions do not protect citizens or increase their standards of living one iota.

The notion that regulations give voters what they truly want is an incorrect one. First, voters are able to get what they *want* as consumers, as will be explained in Chapter 5. The price system, if allowed to operate freely, puts individuals in charge of the marketplace. Regulation, on the other hand, allows a *minority* group of voters to benefit at the expense of other voters who have not shown as consumers that they want what the minority voters want. For example, if consumers truly wanted "greener" vehicles or other alternative forms of energy, they would have shown, through their buying habits, that they were willing to pay higher prices for these less economical means of production. But they haven't. Environmentalists, intent on pushing their unreasonable environmental restrictions upon all members of society, persuade the average voter to believe that going green is good for everyone. Thinking that it sounds reasonable and could do no harm, the average voter goes along with environmental regulation. But it does do harm by imposing the higher costs on them—costs that they chose not to vote for as consumers—harm for which they later blame the free market (more on environmentalism in Chapter 8).

One might argue that voters did in fact go along with the proposals, revealing that they in fact wanted the regulations. But that is the nature of the problem: the average uninformed voter goes along with all "reasonable sounding" proposals, without understanding the real damage to themselves. An example of this, as discussed in Chapter 1, is that it sounds reasonable to voters that the poor and the unions need a minimum wage and that imposing one would seem to do no harm; in fact it does. Similarly, forcing companies to incur higher costs for regulation x, y, or z *would seem* to not affect the voters' own employment, wage level or standard of living, but it does. The voter just can't see the negative consequences occurring.

Average voters, by going along with "reasonable sounding" proposals, almost always worsen their own lives. The cost of any particular regulation is one that they will pay for in the end, sooner rather than later. Making the means of production more costly and less efficient hurts everyone in numerous ways. The average voter would agree that environmental regulation is good. But if you asked them whether they were willing to have their family pay $5,000, $10,000, or $20,000 per year, or whatever the actual cost is, for this regulation, most would undoubtedly say no. Yet this is what they do to themselves by going along with regulations (via foregone higher wages or purchasing power).

But it gets worse: regulation breeds more regulation. Because government's first intervention in the marketplace has unexpected negative consequences, politicians and average voters think yet more regulation is needed to fix the problem. Instead, more regulation makes things still worse. For example, as part of the commodities boom caused by the central bank (regulation), milk prices rose dramatically and then fell. Farmers increased supply when prices were rising, but they were left with an excess supply of milk when prices collapsed, causing losses. Milk farmers now believe that their oversupply of milk (selling at losses) was caused by an inability of the market to match supply with demand. They don't realize that 1) "demand" was simply increased prices, not a real need to consume significantly more milk, and 2) that "demand" could never change so quickly and drastically in absence of the printing of money. Now the farmers, not knowing that their problems were caused by previous regulation, want new regulation in the form of government help in managing the industry, matching supply and demand for them, and providing yet more subsidies for their losses with taxpayer money. The additional subsidies will then help cause an oversupply of milk, and government control will have resulted in even more distorted prices and production—and losses. Soon the industry will need bailouts, price controls, and still more subsidies! At that point, many will call for outright communism (as they do today for healthcare) so that the government can have full control. The results from that measure will be the same as they were with food production in communist China, Russia, North Korea, and Cuba: death and starvation, economic retrogression, and a totalitarian state that kills its own people. Government intervention is like a disease—it starts tearing up what it touches and causes it to deteriorate.

In Cuba, regulation intended to protect and help citizens includes making air conditioners, toasters, and microwaves illegal. In Belize, citizens are protected by regulation giving one company a monopoly on cell phone service, making its owner very wealthy. Naturally, it is very costly to make calls.

Regulation is socialism. Karl Marx rightly stated that socialism is that state of transition between capitalism and communism. "Socialism;" "the third way;" "a regulated free market;" whatever the terms used, cannot be a lasting phenomenon, because the policies enacted inevitably cause more problems that then necessarily must be controlled with yet more regulation and more policies. Socialism must continually slide down the spectrum to communism.

With that being said, let's take a look at our current state of socialist regulation and see what results can be identified from it. The few examples in this chapter summarize the imposition of prior regulation and the resulting problems. Both the lists below and their cause-and-effect scenarios are far from exhaustive. To fully expose the effects of all regulations would take years and years of writing by many people.

How Anti-Trust Regulation Brings About Monopolies

Most Americans, and most economists as well, believe that anti-trust regulation prevents monopolies and fosters competition. They believe consumers are protected by the government from big corporations that reduce their production in order to raise prices, or run smaller weaker companies out of business, so that they can enjoy high profits at the expense of the rest of society. This argument is fallacious.

The truth is that anti-trust laws exist in order to allow the creation of monopolies that could not otherwise exist: the government protects less efficient but politically favored companies from more efficient competition. The companies themselves are usually the ones to originate and promote the regulation. Companies use government power to prevent the mergers, acquisitions, expansions, or particular investments or production of rival firms so as to make them less competitive. In some cases, two firms that would have as small as a combined 3 percent market share in their industry have been prevented by the government from merging.[103] The government also prevents newer, smaller competitors from competing with larger corporations because the immense amount of time, money and hurdles required under regulation is often unaffordable to smaller companies that have not yet acquired as much capital as their larger competitors. The resulting failure of these small firms is, of course, the intention of the regulation.

Trust-Busting

But surely, you must be thinking, what about all the historical cases you've heard about concerning the large trusts (early forms of corporations) of the late 1800s that were broken up because of their monopoly control and presumed damage to citizens, right? The stories are myths...complete myths. Indeed, the government broke up these companies and destroyed or diminished their productive capabilities, but the trusts were not harmful economic entities; they contributed greatly to increased prosperity for all. It is true that some

---

[103] An example is the 1962 case of Kinney Shoes being prevented from acquiring the Brown Shoe Company.

of those who owned or ran the trusts eventually asked the government for protection from competitors (regulation), and this is shameful. It is also true that many other companies became powerful and wealthy through government-trust-assigned privileges. But without question, the trusts did not become large and successful by somehow "unfairly" competing in an otherwise free market.

Thomas J. DiLorenzo showed in the June 1985 issue of the International Review of Law and Economics[104] that the industries accused of being monopolies at the initiation of the Sherman Antitrust Act were expanding production four times more rapidly (some as much as ten times faster) than the economy as a whole for the entire decade leading up to the Sherman Act. These firms were also dropping their prices faster than the general price level (remember that prices fell during most of the 1800s). One of the senators in favor of antitrust laws at the time, Representative William Mason, admitted that the trusts "have made products cheaper, have reduced prices."[105] Nonetheless, he argued that in accomplishing this, the trusts put honest competitors out of business, which implies that the trusts were dishonest and that they had engaged in wrongful acts by simply competing in business. He stated this because he, along with most congressmen at the time, wanted to protect less efficient companies in their districts from the more efficient competition of the trusts.[106] Economic policy actions are almost always taken for political reasons.

Similarly, Dominick Armentano found that of the fifty-five most famous antitrust cases in U.S. history, in every single one, the firms accused of monopolistic behavior were lowering prices, expanding production, innovating, and typically benefiting consumers.[107] He found that it was their less efficient competitors, not consumers, who were harmed.

As further evidence of the lack of any harm trusts caused individuals, economic historians Robert Gray and James Peterson pointed

---

[104] Thomas J.DiLorenzo, "The origins of antitrust: An interest-group perspective," *International Review of Law and Economics* (June 1985), pp. 73–90

[105] Thomas J. DiLorenzo, "Anti-trust, Anti-truth," Mises Daily (June 1, 2000).

[106] Ibid.

[107] Dominick T. Armentano, *Antitrust and Monopoly: Anatomy of a Policy Failure* (1990).

out that between 1840 and 1900, the proportion of national income received by workers remained unchanged: Labor received 70 percent and owners of capital, property, and materials received 30 percent. This means that companies did not gain at the expense of the public.

The most famous trust is probably that of John D. Rockefeller's Standard Oil. The company refined oil that was mostly used in kerosene products (gasoline and automobiles were just being developed). The oil business was very small as compared to today. Standard Oil began as a smaller company, and grew in size through normal business competition—providing a better product at lower prices. As a result of its innovation and the competition it fostered, the price of refined petroleum fell from over 30 cents per gallon in 1869 to 5.9 cents in 1897.[108] Competition did in fact force many companies into bankruptcy, which is what happens to any company that fails to compete effectively. Still, such occurrences formed the basis of accusations of wrongdoing against Standard Oil in court. However, unlike most cases, companies that could not compete with Rockefeller were usually able to sell their assets to him. One man so benefitted from Rockefeller's buying him out that every time he went out of business, he started a new oil company that Standard Oil could once again outcompete and buy out. He became very wealthy by having Rockefeller buy him out eleven times.[109] Even though Rockefeller outcompeted most companies, there were other companies that in fact gained ground on Standard Oil and prevented it from having a monopoly—in the free market, without government help.

What is a Monopoly?

A key way in which the government finds firms guilty of being monopolies is in defining monopoly in both vague and unrealistic terms. According to the government's and government economists' view, there should always exist a world they describe as having "pure and perfect competition," in which there are numerous firms in an industry, selling identical products, each having a small market share,

---

[108] Thomas J. DiLorenzo, *How Capitalism Saved America* (2004).

[109] Robert LeFevre, "The Age of the Robber Barons" (lecture), http://mises.org/mp3/lefevre/131.mp3.

operating in fluid, continuous markets, where there is a constantly fluctuating market price, where no single firm has any pricing power, and where there are no barriers to entry of the market (of any kind, even those which are natural ones).

In government economists' view, if this description of a marketplace does not actually exist, there instead exists a monopoly, duopoly, or oligopoly, with unnatural pricing and competitive powers. As we all know, industries with this profile rarely exist; which is why the government always has an excuse to find firms guilty of being monopolistic. Additionally, it is very difficult in many cases to determine exactly what the industry is. Does Coca Cola compete only with other soft drinks, or does it also compete with iced tea, fruit drinks, coffee, water, and beer? Depending on how the definitions are used, any firm could be a monopoly. For example, Wendy's could be a monopoly even though so many other burger places exist, since only Wendy's has a menu offering large square beef patties with baked potatoes offered as a side dish. In fact, companies normally compete in part by means of intentionally differentiating themselves. And in the bigger picture, all products compete with all products. For example, if you win the lottery, you might choose between a boat, an RV, and a diamond ring.

The reality of the case is that there can be very tight competition in different industries with five, two, or even *one* competitor. Additionally, there might exist only *one* business in an entire industry! But having only a single "monopoly" firm in an industry does not mean that it has the power to restrict output or raise prices. *An industry, even with only one company, is competitive as long as competition is a threat.* This is the case, for example, with the NFL, which does not act monopolistic in the least: it constantly creates new product attributes such as instant replay for questionable referee calls, and it expands supply by adding new teams. Additionally, it always has indirect competitors (the CFL, sitcoms, other forms of entertainment, etc.), and sometimes has direct competitors, such as the XFL football league which attempted to compete in 2001. But it always has the threat of competition.

In the same fashion, Alcoa was the only producer of aluminum ingot for many years, but did not constitute a monopoly in the traditional sense, because it did not prevent competitors from entering the marketplace, and its rate of profit, at 10 percent, was not an extremely large one.[110] It earned its position in the marketplace by honestly and fairly out-competing other previously-existing firms. Nonetheless, the U.S. Court of Appeals found the company guilty of employing "superior skill and foresight"[111] that the court felt "forestalled" competition by less efficient businesses. Alcoa was accused of being "exclusionary," since not all firms in its industry had equal skill and foresight.[112] In other words, Alcoa was guilty of outcompeting in the marketplace by offering a superior product at lower prices.

Conversely, *harmful* monopolies can exist while numerous companies operate in a market. In New York and many other cities, larger, more efficient taxi cab operators are prevented from competing against smaller, costlier ones through the government's limiting of the number of licenses it *sells* (at over $100,000 each). Were supply not limited, profits would fall, and cost savings would be initiated; only the most efficient competitors would remain, and they would do so by being larger (like car rental companies). In the end, fewer firms would provide more, higher quality, and cheaper services. A *harmful* monopoly exists whenever government prevents even one competitor from entering a market.

Why Harmful Monopolies Can't Exist in Free Markets

The reason that even a single firm cannot act monopolistic is rather simple. The higher the prices a company charges, the more profit it makes. The higher the profit, the more competition is invited into the market, *as long as other firms are permitted to freely enter the market*. The more firms that enter the given market, the more likely the existing firms will lose market share. Therefore, not only do existing firms (or a would-be monopolistic firm) try to prevent possible competitors by keeping the selling prices of their products not too far above costs, but they continually try to find ways to reduce their costs. For if existing firms remained inefficient, they would lose market share to new entrants who would come to take advantage of the

---

[110] Randal C. Picker, "Monopolization under Sec. 2" (powerpoint lecture), picker.uchicago.edu/antitrust/AT13Post.ppt.

[111] Thomas J. DiLorenzo, "Anti-trust, Anti-truth," Mises Daily (June 1, 2000).

[112] Ibid.

fact that they could make larger profits by producing with lower costs than the current firms, while maintaining the same selling price, or even *lowering* the selling price. As long as even a sole competitor has the *threat* of a new competitor, it will sell for as low a price as possible, which it could achieve more easily with economies of scale that come from *increased* production.

It is for this reason that we have products that are very important to us, but that still sell for relatively low costs. For example, one would think that automobile batteries or the on/off switch to an air conditioning unit would cost thousands, since the overall machines could not function without these small parts. But instead of being expensive, these parts are easily affordable because they are priced based on their costs of production plus a reasonable profit;[113] their costs of production, in turn, are based mostly on the market prices for each individual subcomponent, which themselves are based on cost of production resulting from supply and demand of the individual "factors of production," along with the product's "marginal utility." If firms tried to sell these parts for more than potential competitors could sell them for, they would be facing stiff competition.

On that note, it should be pointed out that product prices on the retail side, which are largely based on the value that consumers attribute to their enjoyment of the product (marginal utility), can sometimes enjoy higher profit margins in cases where direct, comparable competition is impossible. For example, a restaurant whose particular ambiance, recipes, flavors, and taste of food, cannot be easily replicated by competitors could earn very high rates of profit. According to the government, the restaurant would constitute a monopoly even by providing such a great product that consumers go out of their way to pay the asking prices (which could still not be too high without causing a decline in the restaurant's revenues and profits).

Since the key to the prevention of monopolistic practices is the freedom to compete, another argument government economists often put forth should be considered. This is that if the barriers to

---

[113] Contrary to what the entire world of academic economics supposes, (manufactured goods) businesses in the real world do not assess marginal revenues and set prices equal to marginal cost. They set them on a cost-plus basis.

entry are too high, the market is not competitive. This thinking is wrongheaded. Just because one is free to enter a market does not mean that one has the means to do so. High capital requirements, typically seen as a barrier to entry, in reality just mean that in order to be profitable, the producers must operate with low costs. Many industries require this large scale and efficiency, which requires an immense amount of investment. The need for large investments and large scale is the reason that so many industries end up with only two or three firms. Would-be smaller competitors are not able to achieve such a high quantity of production and low selling prices.

Predatory Pricing

One of the most influential theories with regard to monopolies is that of so-called predatory pricing. Under this theory, a company, particularly a large, wealthy one, could temporarily slash its prices in order to undercut the smaller firms and drive them out of business, at which time the large firm woud be able to reduce its production and raise its prices. The idea is that the large firm, more than the small, can afford to sell at a loss for a while, and then make up the loss later with its higher prices. After the large firm becomes the sole supplier in the industry, it is held, other firms will not attempt to compete for fear of incurring losses in the same way again. The list below comprises the primary reasons why this predatory pricing doctrine is completely unrealistic.[114] Though the list is somewhat technical and infused with economic jargon, it is important at least to present these arguments to the reader, because the predatory pricing doctrine has such a profound influence on the world of political economics; it is a primary cause of harm to millions of consumers:

1. Though the large firm has more money, any loss incurred would be in the same proportion as that of the small firm; the large firm is thus hurt just as much (even if the marketplace in question is that of a particular operating location, and the large firm has many other locations to support the one location in question,

---

[114] Condensed, summarized, and paraphrased from Reisman's writings on predatory pricing: George Reisman, *Capitalism: A Treatise on Economics* (1995), pp. 399–402.

it cannot afford to maintain an unprofitable operating location which reduces its overall profits).

2.   If the relative proportion of capital of the small firm is larger than that of the large firm, it can afford to sustain losses for a longer period.

3.   In order to recoup previous losses, the large firm has to raise prices to such a degree that their very large profits would attract new competitors that could even possibly compete at lower costs, due to the lack of losses to make up. But in fact it is restrained from raising prices due to this fact. Also, once the large firm succeeds, its new profits are limited because if it raises prices too high, demand will fall (since customers can choose to buy less or buy alternative products).

4.   Depending on the remaining productive capacity of the large firm as well as the so-called elasticity of demand (the extent to which buyers will continue to buy more, less, or the same quantities at higher and lower prices), a lower price could cause increased demand which would drive the price higher because there would not be enough capacity to meet the new demand. If the large firm increases capacity in order to meet the new demand, it has to keep funding that new capacity after all market manipulation is complete. The resulting costs could outweigh the gains from possible higher prices later.

5.   The large firm must sell below the variable operating costs, not the largely fixed total costs. As long as the small firm can produce above operating costs, it pays to continue operations. If much of the costs of the small firm are fixed, it might be able to profitably operate for quite a while.

6.   Suppliers to the competing firms, who would be harmed by decreased demand resulting from the large firm's future higher prices, would have an incentive to subsidize the small firm so as to prevent the large firm from raising prices.

7.   Were the large firm really to try and continually lower prices to harm smaller firms, the small firm could profit by shorting the stock of the large firm every time it re-entered the market where

the large firm was operating, making the money needed to support its other losses.

8. Were the now sole large firm to continually lower prices, every time small firms tried to compete, the small firms could encourage buyers to wait until they entered the industry and the large firm reduced prices. At this point the withheld demand would be so high that the small firm could sell at higher prices and profit.

9. Were buyers to see that only a single firm would be left, they would require contractual agreements in order to deal with such a price-manipulating company; otherwise, they would stand to be harmed financially.

10. If the small firm goes out of business, its assets are worth less. They can be bought at bargain prices in bankruptcy, thus offering a low cost basis with which the new small firm owner can be competitive.

The occurrence of any particular one of the above events would likely make attempted predatory pricing unprofitable. The reality is that the large firm would suffer extreme losses and would, in fact, be more profitable by sharing the industry with competitors.

Predatory pricing does not really occur, even though some economists like to pretend it does. Examples abound of supposed companies that engage in predatory pricing, but are instead simply better competitors. One example is the former A&P grocery store chain, which used to be a very prominent national chain that was accused of predatory pricing. But in the end, they were outcompeted, likely *because* they were prevented by government from offering their own private labels like grocery stores do today; the government saw that act as monopolistic at the time.

It should occur to readers at this point that companies can easily be held guilty by the government of *raising prices* too much on the one hand, and of *lowering* them too much on the other. They often are accused of at least one of these.

The Only Real Monopolies — Government Monopolies

The only way firms can be the sole company in an industry and not face the threat of possible competition is by having the government prohibit (i.e., threaten to use physical force) others from entering a particular market. Indeed, the government engages in such action; it is therefore instructive for us to look at the results of such efforts. The most common occurrences of true monopolies are in the areas of railways, telecommunications, water services, electricity services, mail delivery, and public schools. These are industries where frequent train wrecks (Amtrak), power blackouts, and water shortages (public utilities) occur, along with constantly increasing prices (post office and schools & universities), long lines, and poor services (post office), as well as underachieving students and dramatically increasing taxes and tuitions (schools and universities).

It is argued by government economists that most of these are "natural monopolies" where the existence of a single provider is more efficient than multiple providers. This argument, just like the predatory pricing argument, is not only fallacious, but is based purely on preconceived false notions, not on observation from reality. In fact, the theory was made up *after* the fact (i.e., it is a rationale for actions previously undertaken).

Before the government decided that government-imposed monopolies should exist, there was in fact competition in these markets; in most of them, there was more robust competition: Six electric light companies operated in New York City prior to 1890; 45 had a legal right to operate in Chicago in 1907; prior to 1905, Duluth Minnessota had 5 electric light companies, and Scranton Pennsylvania had 4. After monopoly regulation was implemented in these cities, prices (and profits) usually stayed the same or went up (this was during a period where prices were falling).[115] University of Illinois economist Walter Primeaux found that those cities which allowed two or more

---

[115] Based on research performed by economist George Stigler. http://mises.org/journals/rae/pdf/rae9_2_3.pdf.

competing utilities firms (some for over 80 years) had prices that were on average 33 percent lower than those that didn't.[116]

Until the early 1900s, many large cities had at least two telephone companies. Once AT&T's patents on telephone service expired in 1893, more than 80 competitors cropped up within a year, and by 1900, over 3,000 telephone companies existed.[117] Prices fell dramatically and call volume increased exponentially. But upon the initiation of World War I, the government nationalized the phone company in the name of "national security." Until it was again denationalized 80 years later, Americans faced punishingly expensive telephone service that made calling long distance a rare event. Once deregulation arrived again in the 1980s, prices fell dramatically; now, cheap long distance calls are made by all of us daily without our giving it a second thought. Many state telephone companies in foreign countries were forced into privatization in the 1990s as cell phones became competition: the rigid, overpriced hard lines could not compete with the cheaper, higher quality service of mobile phones.

The government's antitrust department is a massive bureaucracy constantly searching for companies to harm. A prime example is its prohibiting RCA Corporation from charging royalties to American licensees in the 1950s, a practice deemed to be monopolistic. RCA instead licensed to many Japanese companies, which gave rise to the Japanese electronics industry, which ended up outcompeting the American industry.[118] RCA was eventually bought by a Japanese company in 1990.

Pan American World Airways was destroyed by antitrust regulation because it was forbidden to acquire domestic routes, action that was deemed to be unfair competition to other airlines. Since it had no "feeder traffic" for its international flights, Pan Am also went bankrupt in 1990.

---

[116] Howard Baetjer Jr., (Deregulate the Utilities), http://www.thefreemanonline.org/columns/deregulate-the-utilities/.

[117] http://www.cato.org/pubs/journal/cjv14n2-6.html.

[118] Thomas J. DiLorenzo, "The Origins of Antitrust: An Interest-Group Perspective." *International Review of Law and Economics* 5 (June 1985).

Examples such as these belong to the long list of harm done to companies, employees, investors, and mostly consumers by the federal government. Normal competition is often deemed anti-competitive by government bureaucrats; companies that are more successful than others are deemed to have an unfair advantage. Government officials and contributing Harvard and Yale socialist economists always believe that they know better than the marketplace what actions should be taken to please the most number of people in society, and they believe they know the exact prices that should be charged for thousands of products. Some economists have even gone so far as to argue that a company that creates an innovative new product from which consumers can benefit is a monopoly until competitors come along. Thus, the government, they say, should regulate companies' research and development spending in such a way that all companies can produce new products in synch.[119] In other words, it is argued that competition should be abolished, and companies should instead spend time and money lobbying the government for the right to produce the particular things that they want to produce with their own private property.

Typically, politicians call new monopoly regulation—as well as most other types of regulation—"deregulation" (most laws government passes are titled in ways that describe the opposite of what they are). Deregulation often involves the government's setting prices at below-market prices, with the outcome that new companies will not enter the market to compete since they can't make profits by charging market prices. When this happens, politicians and socialists say that deregulation has failed and that government control is needed. Regulation is *regulation*, not *de*regulation.

A typical way that government economists determine that a company is monopolistic is by assessing whether it is making "high" profits. Armies of economists are trained to be able to perform such "scientific analysis." These economists take a snapshot of company data at one point in time, make assumptions to fill in the gaps, and determine whether profits are too high. But research has shown that when the same company data is studied over time, those with higher rates of profit tend to have profits fall to the average rate, while

---

[119] For example see Profile: Dennis C. Mueller, http://ideas.repec.org/e/pmu110.html.

companies with lower rates of profit tend to see profits rise towards the average rate, just as was discussed with the uniformity of profit principle in Chapter 1.[120]

Government should be kept out of the marketplace and companies should be allowed to compete without regulation. Unfair competition and exploitation of consumers is not possible. Successful companies can only run other competitors out of business, which, contrary to the government's beliefs, is not an act which causes harm to society.

Regulation of the Financial Industry

In the midst of the most recent financial crisis, dishonest socialists cry that financial deregulation caused the mess. The public, due to either ignorance or dishonesty or both, echo the same cries. But it should be clear from Chapter 3 that our financial markets have not been free. When government controls both the quantity and price of money—the very basis of the financial markets—there is almost complete government control. Indeed, the Financial Services Modernization Act of 1999 repealed much of the Glass-Stegall Act[121] in 1999, but it did not constitute deregulation, considering our non-gold-backed currency.[122] Instead, it amounted to corporate welfare for financial institutions, giving them incentives to take on risks for which bank account holders and tax payers would be liable. Other (valid) financial deregulation in recent years resulted in things such as drastically reducing transaction fees (stock trades that used to cost $300 per 100 shares can now be executed for $1.00), among others. In our "deregulated" environment, although the government allows market participants to deal with one another, the guidelines for every action that

---

[120] For example: Yale Brozen, "The Antitrust Task Force Deconcentration Recommendation," *Journal of Law and Economics 13* (October 1970): pp. 279–92; Yale Brozen, "The Persistence of 'High Rates of Return' in High-Stable Concentration Industries," *Journal of Law and Economics 14* (October 1971): pp. 501–12.

[121] Which was originally enacted to enable Rockefeller-dominated Roosevelt administration to cripple the Morgan financial empire: Alexander Tabarok, "The Separation of Commercial and Investment Banking: The Morgans vs. The Rockefellers," http://mises.org/journals/qjae/pdf/qjae1_1_1.pdf.

[122] As explained by Robert B. Eukland and Mark Thornton, "More Awful Truths About Republicans," http://mises.org/daily/3098.

banks, brokerages, and other financial firms may or may not engage in are dictated by the government (i.e., regulation).

How could the financial markets be called free when they are controlled on a daily basis by the Federal Reserve, the Treasury department, the SEC, the Comptroller of the Currency, the FDIC, the Bank of International Settlements, the Office of Thrift Supervision, the Office of Federal Housing Enterprise Oversight, the Federal Home Loan Board, the Federal Financing Housing Board, the Department of Housing and Urban Development, the states Superintendent of Banking, the National Credit Union Administration, the Federal Financing Bank, the Federal Financial Institutions Examination Council, the Thrift Depositor Protection Oversight Board, and the Community Development Financial Institutions Fund, among others? For more on this, see the housing discussions in Chapter 11.

All of these regulatory institutions are supposedly there to protect investors, bank account holders, and consumers. Instead, they protect the banks and financial institutions and harm everyone else in society. Consider also what D.W. MacKenzie says about regulation protecting the public:

> Those who claim that more regulation will stabilize financial markets ignore the obvious fact that corporations lobby those who write regulations. They ignore the less obvious truth that special interests, corporate or otherwise, hold inherent advantages in politics. It is much easier for narrow special interests to organize lobbying efforts. Proponents of increased regulation dream of a world where the state promotes the public interest, but this runs counter to the nature of large activist governments.[123]

The obvious solution, then, is to get government out of the business of intervening in business.

As for cases like Bernie Madoff's ponzi scheme, it should be realized that the SEC had been notified by individual investors from 1999 on about his suspicious actions and financial statements. But Madoff used his close family ties with the SEC to keep investigations at bay. The SEC has failed to catch numerous other financial crimes.

---

[123] http://mises.org/daily/3162.

It has also failed to be in compliance with regulation it must adhere to, and received failing marks from the government's own auditing arm. But due to its failures, it will now receive larger budgets and more power.

There is one very important thing to understand and remember: without fractional reserve banking, any derivatives and mortgages losses could NOT have affected the entire financial system and put all individual bank account deposits at risk. Any losses incurred by lenders and investors would affect *only* those parties, not you and me and the entire national and world economy.

Regulation of the Shrimp Industry

It was stated previously that it is usually individual companies that bring about regulation for their own benefit. The following is a prime example of this. But in this case, it should be added that it is not just companies per se, but often entire industries that benefit most from regulation.[124]

Several decades ago, shrimp were considered a delicacy and were very expensive, but today, can easily be obtained at moderate prices in stores and restaurants. Americans currently consume more than four times the amount of shrimp they did in 1970.

American shrimp trawlers, who operate mainly in the Gulf of Mexico, have suffered economic losses in the process. This is because of industry innovations consisting of shrimp farming, which produces much more shrimp at lower costs and effort, as well as increased shrimp supplies from many other countries. The shrimp industry of eight southern states, as represented by their lobbying organization, the Southern Shrimp Alliance, filed an anti-dumping petition with the U.S. Department of Commerce (DOC) against shrimp farms in six other countries providing shrimp imports to the U.S. It was a typical case of companies turning to the government to help them at the

---

[124] This section is condensed from two articles, Don Matthews, "The Fallacies of Shrimp Protectionism," http://mises.org/daily/1551 and Aleksandra Dunaeva and Don Matthews, (How the Shrimp Tariff Backfired), http://mises.org/daily/2644.

expense of both other companies and consumers, since anti-dumping laws are pure protectionism.

The supposed act of dumping involves foreign firms' setting of prices in their export market either below their cost of production, or below the prices they charge in their own markets; it would be another instance of so-called predatory pricing. Similar to what was described above, the theory is that foreign firms would dump their products on the U.S. market at below-market prices, and therefore gain increased market share and drive their competitors out of business. These predatory firms would then raise their prices to recoup the losses they incurred and would gouge American consumers by forcing them to pay whatever price they asked.

But the idea of dumping is absurd, because it implies that hundreds of firms from multiple different countries were somehow communicating and organizing to coordinate precisely when and how much to cut their prices, and in order to target a particular single price—without any single colluder cheating by selling at a higher price! Further, even if it was actually possible to communicate and coordinate and not cheat, all of these firms would incur massive losses that would grow larger as their market shares grew. The companies would realistically not be able to raise their prices later to such a degree that they would recoup their losses, much less bring additional profits. With any substantial increase in shrimp prices, U.S. consumers would quickly turn to sellers in one of the other 44 shrimp exporting countries. Additionally, they would choose not to buy shrimp, or to buy other types of seafood or meat instead.

But the government does not consider any such logic. Instead, the DOC and government economists engage in their own brand of economic assessments of whether foreign exporters were harming domestic businesses. It compared the price of exporters' shrimp sold in the U.S. to other locations, including its home country. But, businesses often sell the same product for different prices in different countries, often because of the costs of various regulations, requirements, transportation costs, taxes, and tariffs in different countries. In two of the countries in question, exporters didn't even sell frozen shrimp in their own countries. When there are no prices to compare to, the DOC *estimates* what the price would be if the exporter *did* sell the same shrimp at home! It is, of course, impossible to know what the price would be if it existed, since it does not in fact exist. Any estimated price is purely arbitrary, and likely one made up to arrive at the most needed for the politics at hand (since the DOC has almost always ruled in favor of the antidumping petitioner).

The possibility of price dumping is also often assessed on the basis of profit margins. Supposedly, if a firm is selling for a loss, it is likely price dumping. But under this logic, the very firms supposedly needing protection, the American shrimp trawlers, since they are barely breaking even or incurring losses, are themselves price dumping!

No matter: the shrimp trawlers got their government protection in 2005 when the DOC imposed tariffs of up to 112 percent on the six countries in question, because the DOC determined that the American shrimpers had been caused "material injury" by the foreign exporters. It was naturally expected that the tariff would protect US shrimpers from competition by reducing shrimp imports; this would, like most regulation, increase the prices we consumers have to pay.

But in this particular case, the tariffs were placed against six particular shrimp exporting countries, not all countries. Thus, American shrimp importers turned to the other 44 foreign exporters. Additionally, the six exporters named in the suit began exporting other types of shrimp, such as breaded shrimp (instead of plain frozen shrimp), that were not named in the anti-dumping law. The result was that shrimp imports into the U.S. have *increased* by 14 percent since the tariff was imposed, and shrimp prices have *declined* by 9 percent (It is fortunate that tariffs were not placed on *all* shrimp imports).[125]

The monies collected from the tariffs were distributed among the American shrimpers. But then, newly enacted laws stopped this activity. Thus, the Southern Shrimp Alliance (SSA) used high-priced lawyers to file a special appeal with the DOC that threatened foreign shrimp producers with more extensive tariffs. More than 100 foreign shrimp suppliers thus paid the SSA millions of dollars in return for

---

[125] At least as of the time of the research this story is based on, which was in 2004 and 2006.

its promise to drop the petition. The SSA used the money to pay its lawyers, to pay lobbyists to rally government support for the industry, and to pay office expenses. The domestic shrimpers, its clients, now receive nothing. The beneficiaries of the shrimp tariff are lawyers and lobbyists, not shrimpers.

Government Price Controls

In Praise of Price Gouging

There is not really such a thing as price gouging, as long as there are competitive markets. In competitive markets, any rise in price, even if labeled price gouging by consumers and politicians, is in fact the market price. During hurricanes and other natural disasters, shortages of goods often appear due to a lack of supplies (which itself is often due to government's preventing the free movement of goods in the name of safety of those otherwise willing to transport goods). In such times, government imposes price-gouging laws. But in these cases, more than in most, what's needed is for the price accurately to reflect the supply of goods relative to their demand; what's needed is for prices to rise (so-called price gouging).

Consider a gas station convenience store along a relatively isolated highway after a hurricane. If the price of gas rose extremely high—to the market price—people would only take as much of the expensive gas as they felt they needed, leaving spare gas for others. But if the price is set artificially low, those that arrive first will fill their tanks "just to be safe." The same applies for the goods inside the store. Those first on the scene would take, say, five boxes of cereal apiece at a price of, say, $5. But if, due to scarcity, the price of the cereal box instead rose to, say, $95, each customer would likely take only one box. And just because the price increases does not mean that only the rich could afford the cereal. Poorer people could afford the first $95 box they really needed more easily than the rich could afford a second, third, or fifth box they don't really need. Government-imposed price ceilings cause goods to become unavailable, whereas supplies would otherwise be available at *some* price.

The Worldwide Food Shortage

The same concept applies to the recent food shortages many countries experienced. Government imposed price caps on food and gasoline (food is made and transported with the use of gasoline) resulted in a lack of supply of food in these countries. The cost of making the food had risen considerably—by way of high commodity prices—but food producers were not allowed to sell their product for a profit, since government limited their selling price. They therefore quit bringing food to market. People thus starved, fought each other for food, and engaged in riots.

Paul Krugman blamed the price of food on, among other things, new food demand from China, and diversion of farmland from growing food to growing biofuel crops. Krugman did not, however, mention that the underlying cause of food shortages must necessarily be the lack of a free market, since shortages could not exist in a free market. Under free markets, while prices of goods would likely rise at the onset of reduced supplies, the goods in question would always be available at some price—and the higher the price, the more the supply would increase to meet demand, which would then of course reduce the price. If we had free world markets, food would be exported from some countries, such as the U.S. and Europe, where food is plentiful, to countries where it is needed. This is because it would be profitable to ship goods to needy areas where selling prices were higher. Yes, the poor countries could afford higher prices because 1) they would be buying less at the higher prices, 2) they would curtail other consumption and 3) just because they are poor does not mean they have no purchasing power at all.

The fact that this was not happening can be a result only of government price controls (that prevented prices from rising in needy countries), trade restrictions, or some other government barrier which prevents people from getting what they need. The World Bank, at the time, had cited a list of 21 countries which had price controls on basic staples. We all remember the stories of people in Ethiopia starving in the 1980s, when 3 million people went hungry. What was unreported was that there were 60 million people in Ethiopia *at the same time* who were unaffected by famine. The moving of food from one part of the country, where it was plentiful, to the other part, affected by drought, was prevented by fighting between the government and rebel groups near the area of the drought. Economic incentives were prohibited by 1) the government's forced withholding of food shipments (so that rebel soldiers would not have access to supplies), 2) price controls, 3) the prohibition of grain wholesaling in much of the country, and 4) by the prohibition of the private selling of farm produce or machinery (based on communist economic planning). A similar situation occurred in Zimbabwe in the early 2000s. Indian economist Amartya Sen won a Nobel Prize for demonstrating that most famines are caused not by lack of food but by governments' ill-advised intrusions into the functioning of markets. The rising food prices, as we discussed in Chapter 3, could only come from government printing presses. Otherwise, prices could not rise dramatically unless the real supply of food was quickly disappearing.

To be clear: for various fundamental reasons related to production, supply, and demand, there was a lack of supply of some commodities available relative to the growing real demand for them. Still, this lack of supply was not the root cause either of the occurrence of shortages or of the extreme increase in world food prices (by over 80 percent in three years). Additionally, though many commodities such as wheat had been stagnant or in reduced production over the prior several years, other commodities had seen continued increases in production. And other food groups such as cereals, fruits, livestock, and fish/seafood products had seen mostly increased supply. Data from The Food and Agriculture Organization of the United Nations showed that both world agriculture production and food production per capita had risen since 1990, and stayed steady since 2000.[126] In comparison, commodities' *prices* constantly rose between 2000 and 2008.

Any *real* "new demand" for food from China (the increased "demand" was actually only an increase in the printing of money by the Chinese central bank, putting more money in its citizens hands) would necessarily have resulted not only in the Chinese themselves producing more food to meet this demand, but in the rest of the world doing so as well. In fact, China had increased agricultural production

---

[126] The Food and Agriculture Organization of the United Nations, Food Production Indices (2006) http://faostat.fao.org/site/612/default.aspx#ancor.

per capita by 22 percent between 2000 and 2007. Can we really imagine that world food producers would not have spotted this demand and tried to make profits by satisfying it? They had, and had therefore been producing more food. The Chinese population is increasing by just over one-half of one percent per year. How, then, could the Chinese suddenly have a desire and need for 30 percent or so more food per year in recent years? Further: how could they pay for it, even if they had the want of more food? The answer: they didn't have that much of an increased real demand, they simply *paid* 30 percent more for it with the additional paper currency their government printed. If there were as much of a new demand for food in China as Krugman claimed, given a *constant amount of money in the economy*, there would necessarily be a corresponding *reduction* in the demand and prices of other goods. Therefore, the Chinese may well be consuming more food, but this increased consumption would not be responsible for (absolute) higher prices or shortages. The higher prices were the manifestation of inflation created by the world government's printing of money, and shortages arose from price controls imposed because of the inflation.

As for Krugman's last argument—that farmland usable for food was being diverted to the growing of biofuel feedstock instead—this is a question mark. In a free market, if there were a shortage of food and if the (necessarily) associated high prices of food gave that market signal, land used for any other item—biofuel feedstock, car lots, movie theatres, houses, or whatever—would be converted to use for farming. If we experienced sustained food shortages in the United States, for example, this is what would happen. Indeed, agriculture used to represent 50 percent of GDP at the beginning of last century, but is now less than 1 percent. Land use has changed to meet changing demands. But if we needed food, we could and would build agriculture back up towards that 50 percent level. On a world-wide scale, as food prices rose, land would be turned to the more profitable growing of food instead of the less profitable growing of biofuel feedstock.

Only if government subsidies were high enough to obscure these market signals, or if government required energy companies to purchase feedstock (which this author is told is the case in the U.S.), could the agriculture production structure be deformed so that this market response would not take place. Similarly, if agricultural lands became difficult to develop due to government regulations to, e.g., protect current farmers, increased production could become difficult.

In sum, the real cause for the previously rising food prices was the printing of money by world governments: since they slowed the printing presses in the last couple of years, and since commodities prices fell as a result, food prices have stabilized and fallen. The real cause of actual food shortages was the prevention of profitable global trade in food by the ill-advised policies of governments of the very people who are starving. To the extent that any other causes proposed contributed to a reduced supply more than temporarily, this must be because governments prevented the market from working. To ignore these primary drivers of recent world food shortages is either willfully to dismiss economic logic, or to be unaware of it.

The Gasoline Crisis of the 1970s[127]

A gasoline shortage occurred in the U.S. in the early 1970s due to price controls. When an Arab-led OPEC embargo raised the price of oil in the west, the U.S. government imposed price controls in the North Eastern United States. Whereas OPEC could not have otherwise harmed us, our politicians allowed them to do so. Had our government allowed prices to rise, oil would have flowed from other parts of the U.S. (and the world), to the North East. But since it was unprofitable to do so, this did not happen. The result was cars lined up for hours waiting to obtain some of the little gasoline that very few gas stations had.

We should not be bothered about a possible refusal by Arab or all OPEC countries to sell to the United States harming us—a concern often voiced by those who cry that we should not be oil-dependent. As prices rose in the United States, non-OPEC oil-producing countries, along with other countries that also purchase oil from OPEC and non-OPEC countries, would export oil to the U.S. because they could profit by doing so. Besides, even if there were no indirect means of obtaining OPEC oil, OPEC would not refuse to sell to us for long.

---

[127] As explained by George Reisman, *Capitalism: A Treatise on Economics* (1990), Chapters 12 and 19.

For doing so would cut off much of their revenues and profits. They would be engaging in economic suicide.

In fact, an OPEC boycott would help us, and it would have done so in the 1970s had we not had price controls, and had the American oil industry been otherwise unregulated (i.e., free).[128] As world oil prices shot up, American oil companies would have made tremendous profits, and would have therefore been in a position to locate, develop and produce much more oil, as well as other forms of energy, such as shale. Additionally, oil-dependent Western Europe would have needed to turn to the U.S. for their oil. The U.S. would have established itself as a much larger oil producing country and exporter. The OPEC countries, on the other hand, would have been deprived of oil revenues, and the smarter countries of the group would have broken from the OPEC alliance so as to resume bringing income into their country. All of these actions would have served to bring oil prices back down, and probably to a point lower than where they previously were.

A Personal Example of Being Harmed by Price Controls

Permit me to offer a personal example of what it means to be harmed by price controls. Upon the death of a family member several years ago, we as beneficiaries hired an accountant to help settle the estate. Upon interviewing this particular accountant recommended by my deceased family member, we inquired as to his estimated charges. He gave a reasonable figure and we accepted. Had the estimate been higher, we would have instead employed another accountant whom we knew personally, and who had given a similar cost estimate. Ultimately, the bill we received from the accountant was about four or five times larger than he had estimated. Further, he could not account for the details of the charges; he could not explain what was done hour-by-hour, so as to account for the number of hours he charged. I proceeded to make a formal complaint and appeared before a judge to make my case. No matter that the accountant clearly seemed to have lied and cheated us (an accusation he never contested), I lost the case,

---

[128] The following argument was derived from George Reisman, *Capitalism: A Treatise on Economics* (1990).

because of the fact that *the charges were within the official range, as a percentage of the total estate, accorded by state law.*

What's notable is that the state effectively gives the accountants and lawyers themselves the power to write the law, as it is only they, supposedly, who know the "appropriate" charges. The law is presented as a means of protecting the consumer from price gouging, but in fact sets a price floor for the transaction. Though the lawyers, in the laws they write, cite a maximum percentage to be charged, they also cite a minimum percentage—at a price which represents very nice profits for themselves. In a free market any price could be charged, but competition would dictate that it is kept low. Of course there could be cases where an accountant figures a client to be a sucker, and charges him or her way too much. But, such a case would be rare, and most other clients, unlike today, would be charged appropriately based on true costs. Secondly, even if overcharged, clients would have first had to agree willingly to the charges (or could legally contest them), which means the charges were to a large degree acceptable to them. Otherwise, they could have hired one of the many other accountants and lawyers who could perform the same service for less. But because of today's regulations, my family members lost money to others who could legally swindle us (and the estate was not a large one).

Rent Controls

The government sometimes imposes a maximum rental price so that renters will not be overcharged. The result is a lack of housing and deteriorating quality of current housing. If rental prices are capped, owners cannot adjust revenues to their higher costs as inflation rises. Thus, new housing will not be built. Existing owners invest little in maintaining their units, because they are not rewarded for doing so since 1) they can't raise rents, and 2) they do not have to compete with other housing units in order to attract renters—given that the scarcity of new apartments leads to more renters competing for the same quantity of housing as the population increases. Whenever something seems screwy, look for the existence of government intervention and regulation.

The results of such regulation can be easily seen in New York City, one of the few cities in the U.S. still under heavy rent control laws. New York is famous for a shortage of housing, with renters competing for old, out-of-date, run-down apartments. It is common for the superintendents of these buildings, who are in charge of letting the apartments, to take bribes of tens of thousands of dollars from renters competing for the housing that's available (at low monthly rates). Naturally, the poor can't compete.

Were rent control abolished, thousands of old buildings would be torn down and replaced with well-maintained high-rise apartments, due to the very high prices that would suddenly take effect. After the supply of apartments increased, however, there is no question that overall rental prices would fall.

Pay Day Loans

I have a socialist aunt who insisted several years ago that the poor should never be charged a higher interest rate than other people. She was referring to the pay day lending business. She didn't understand that pay day lenders were helping the poor, not hurting them.

Pay day lenders lend to those to whom others deem an unacceptable risk. Borrowers typically have very bad credit, which means they have not always repaid the money they owe on time, if at all. Predictably, many who borrow through pay day lenders do not repay their loans. Thus, the lenders must charge high rates in order to cover the losses they incur from those who don't repay. The rates they charge are certainly high, typically well over 100-200 percent on an annualized basis (they usually lend money for a matter of weeks, until the borrowers receive their next paycheck, which is then used to repay the loan).

If the borrowers could have obtained loans at a bank, they would have. But since they were high risk, and since they likely had no collateral, banks do not typically lend (unless forced to and/or subsidized by government programs, as they are to a large extent). Thus, pay day lenders make money available to borrowers who otherwise would have no immediate means to obtain needed cash.

To a large degree credit card lenders work the same way; high rates cover the losses they incur from those who do not pay. Were such lenders forced to loan at official interest rates through some type of "fair lending" laws (new laws in addition to the current ones that have already put lenders out of business or ones that force the taxpayer to subsidize loans), they would either go out of business, lend only to borrowers with exceptional credit, or require some type of collateral in order to extend credit. For those who don't believe these logical explanations and feel that these lenders are still gouging consumers, let them open a business lending to consumers at lower rates and see if they could take market share away from the current "greedy" lenders. Obviously, if this were possible, people would already be doing such things. In fact they have, and they brought interest rates down to the current market rates, the rates which are deemed excessive.

A friend recently equated credit card companies to the IRS. In correcting his understanding, I explained that for it to be the same thing, he would have to be forced by the government to borrow from a single government-run monopoly lender at the high rates they dictate (in order for there to be lower rates, the lender would have to be subsidized the equivalent amount by extra income taxes). In reality, if my friend does not like his current lender he can shift to others, or, choose not to borrow at all. With the IRS, we can't choose not to deal with them.

Regulation of the Healthcare Industry

The AMA Monopoly

While most people believe that our healthcare industry is one comprised of free markets, it is anything but. The industry is completely distorted by government manipulation.[129]

To start with, the American Medical Association (AMA) has had a government-granted monopoly on the healthcare system for over 100 years. It has intentionally restricted the number of doctors

---

[129] The introductory paragraphs that follow, and most historical facts and figures are taken from the following authors and papers: Dale Steinreich, Ph.D., "100 Years of Medical Robbery," http://mises.org/daily/1547#_8_, and "Real Medical Freedom," http://mises.org/daily/1588; Henry E. Jones, MD, "How Medical Boards Nationalized Health Care," http://mises.org/daily/1749.

allowed to practice medicine so as to raise physician incomes artificially. The primary way it does this is by using the coercive power of the state to restrict the number of approved medical schools in operation. After the AMA created its Council on Medical Education in 1904, state medical boards complied with the AMA's recommendation to close down medical schools. Within three years, 25 schools had been shut down, and the number of students at remaining schools was reduced by 50 percent. After three more years, 10 more schools were closed. Since that time, the U.S. population has increased by 284 percent, while the number of medical schools has declined by 26 percent to 123.[130] In 1996, the peak year for applications, only 16,500 candidates were accepted out of 47,000. While high rejection rates can be common in many schools, applicants to medical schools are usually among the brightest and highest quality students who have put themselves through a very costly admissions process. High rejection rates are why so many aspiring doctors attend medical schools in the Caribbean, where they are prepared to be American doctors. The medical monopoly also marginalizes or outlaws alternative or slightly alternative (i.e., competing) medical practices, along with nurses and midwives, who could perform many of the tasks doctors do today.

The AMA also has monopoly power over the state boards which issue licenses. A physician can practice only by having a state license (licenses in general exist primarily to prevent competition). Each state has licensing boards consisting of AMA members who decide which applicants, according to them, are competent and morally fit. The boards also have police and enforcement powers to monitor their own kind, and keep as many nasty incidents as possible out of the public eye. The state medical boards masquerade as consumer protection agencies. Instead of revealing competition to the public as something that lowers doctor's incomes, the AMA and medical boards present it as something that must be stopped in the name of keeping patients safe.

---

[130] This actually understates continual declines. Paul Starr, *The Social Transformation of American Medicine* (1982), p. 421, reports that in 1965 only 88 schools existed, meaning that the Council almost reached its goal of a more than 50 percent closure of schools.

As a further understanding of the intertwining of government and our healthcare system, consider the following summary by Henry E. Jones, MD:

> Most members of the state medical boards are appointed by the governor. State and county medical associations, medical specialty societies, large medical group practices, HMO's, health insurance companies, chain and wholesale pharmacies, and large hospital chains contribute heavily to the campaigns of candidates for governor and attorney general. Thus, the governor appoints to the state medical board those desired by the medical monopoly. Doctors selected by the medical monopoly for appointment to the state medical board can be counted on to cooperate. And it works the same way with the State Board of Pharmacy.
>
> The medical monopoly contributes heavily to congressmen and maintains one of the best-financed and most effective lobbying programs in Washington, D.C. It is important that the AMA, the state medical board, and the state attorney general in each state work hand-in-glove to further the interest of the medical monopoly. [131]

Do We Need To Be Protected?

One might retort that restricting the supply of doctors is good, because only the smartest, most knowledgeable, and safest people should be responsible for our very lives. But under this argument, we could ask "why stop at the doctor-limiting threshold at which we currently operate?" Why not restrict the supply further so that we have only the top thousand or even the top ten doctors in the nation to take care of us? In that case of having only the most qualified doctors, even more people would die each year for lack of affordability as well as lack of opportunity to actually get in to see the doctor.

Look at it another way, what if we limited the number of automobiles in the same way? What if we were only allowed to produce cars with the quality and safety of the top Mercedes, BMWs, and Rolls Royce's, as well as prohibiting cars older than three years old (since they are less safe)?

---

[131] http://mises.org/story/1749.

In terms of assigning grades to the quality and capability of the doctors: what if we *should* restrict the number of doctors to those who are grade B and above, but we have already placed restrictions at a higher level such that we only accept A+ doctors?

Just as a Saturn Astra or a used Ford Escort deliver a valuable service to many, so would a B- or even a C grade doctor, particularly for non-life-threatening issues. There are many of us who would pay, say, $30 to visit a C grade doctor for a cold, versus $100 to visit an A grade doctor.

In a free market, *any* doctor could practice medicine. But would we then have any and everyone hanging out shingles calling themselves doctors only to kill someone due to misdiagnosis or by removing the heart instead of the spleen? No, we wouldn't, as I explain shortly. But even if that did happen on rare occasion, the number of deaths resulting from such an event would likely be much less than the number who die currently from current doctor's mistakes (see below), or from the number of those who die from a lack of affordable healthcare (I know of one person who because he couldn't afford treatment for his Parkinson's disease committed suicide last year). Besides, in those terrible rare cases, individuals would have at least had the opportunity to choose what they thought was best for them.

In reality, the doctors who would practice would be those who are educated to do so. Besides, any unqualified doctor who did bad work would lose clients and go out of business, as word got around. Above all, there would be private ratings agencies comparable to other consumer reports services telling us how various doctors rank, and which doctors have high accident or casualty rates.

At the least, why not allow *competing* medical associations? We could have 4 or 5 other associations with the same criteria of competency as the AMA. We could allow an absolute rather than a rank-ordered threshold to be met in order to practice medicine. Or, why not permit many more less qualified people to practice medicine, and then let individuals choose between higher-priced AMA-certified and lower-priced non-AMA certified doctors?

Healthcare "Insurance"

The other major problem with our healthcare system is our third-party payer system, where we rely on someone else to pay most of our bills; i.e., we use "insurance" that is funded mostly by corporations and the government. Though this system originated with the Blue Cross and Blue Shield entities early last century (which obtained government-supported advantages over competing private systems), the third-party payer system really took hold with the advent of government regulation during WWII. Since economy-wide prices were rising due to the government's printing of money that paid for the war, politicians imposed universal price and wage controls. Since, then, businesses could not compete for labor by bidding up wages, they began to compete by offering special benefits, including paying employees' healthcare costs (which socialists now see as something incumbent on large companies).

When something is free or mostly free, people demand more of it. With someone else paying their bills, people make more trips to the doctor, they don't negotiate against increasing prices they face, and they don't balk at more and more superfluous tests and more specialist visits being required of them. This constitutes more demand for healthcare services and equipment, the owners of which raise prices in response, not only to take advantage of their increased pricing power, but to try to reduce their workload, since more people start to demand healthcare than providers have the time and resources to address. Prices are used to equate supply with demand. With the supply of doctors restricted by the AMA, and increasing demand for relatively free healthcare on the part of consumers, prices began to rise rapidly, and waiting times to see doctors became longer.

Since healthcare then became unaffordable to many (whereas previously it was not), politicians, in the name of helping people in order to get votes, set up government agencies to offer Medicare and Medicaid to pay for the healthcare costs of those who could not afford it. With the government spending additional billions of dollars to compete for the limited amount of healthcare services, prices began to increase all the more. With every new instance of government's paying for citizens' healthcare, such as the Medicare Part D program enacted in 2003 to pay for prescription drugs, healthcare costs rise still

Insurance and Managed Care Industry Profits, 2007

United Health Group	5.8 percent
Wellpoint	5.4 percent
Aetna	6.7 percent
Humana	2.3 percent
Cigna	7.0 percent
Health Net	2.5 percent
Coventry Health Care	7.2 percent
WellCare Health Plans	3.7 percent
Amerigroup	3.8 percent
Centene	−1.9 percent
Medical Mutual of Ohio	4.9 percent
Molina Healthcare	2.3 percent
Sierra Health Services	8.1 percent
Median Profits	**4.9 percent**
Fortune 500 Median Profits	**7.6 percent**

Source: *Fortune Magazine*, 2007: http://money.cnn.com/magazines/fortune/fortune500/2006/industries/Health_Care_Insurance_Managed_Care/1.html

Figure 4.1: Profits in the insurance industry.

further. Had the companies facing price controls in the 1940s chosen to pay for employees' food instead of their healthcare, we would likely have grocery prices rising at phenomenal rates today, causing a "food-care" crisis supposedly brought about by free market failures.

It is very important to understand that, since the government funds one of every two healthcare dollars spent, and since much of the government's spending comes from the printing press, a substantial portion of the demand for healthcare consists of money being printed—much of the credit creation by the central bank goes directly into raising healthcare costs.

Each year, as costs rise due to increased spending on healthcare, private insurance companies simply raise the costs of premiums so as to cover these increased expenditures they pay on our behalf. The more we spend, the higher are our premiums. But as prices rise, fewer people can afford premiums, and those paying premiums for others, such as employers, can't afford to cover as many treatments.[132] Just to

---

[132] People can't afford the premiums and smaller businesses can't afford to cover their employees. And since government does not cover everyone, and does not always cover all

prove that insurance companies are not simply raising their profits at our expense, as both individuals and politicians alike claim, consider their profits in **Figure 4.1**, which are lower than the average company. Profits—and costs—in the industry would be lower still if government did not restrict competition amongst insurance companies.

The Quality and Cost of Our Regulated Healthcare

With all this regulation and expensive healthcare, Americans receive only a mediocre quality of care. For instance, the U.S. is far from achieving the lowest world infant mortality and death rates; fatalities from incorrect healthcare treatment are the third-leading cause of death in the U.S., after heart disease and cancer; and over 225,000 people die each year from doctors' mistakes: 12,000 deaths occur each year due to unnecessary surgery; 7,000 deaths are due to medication errors in hospitals; 20,000 deaths are due to other hospital errors; 80,000 are due to infections in hospitals; and 106,000 due to the negative effects of drugs.[133]

And for this level of quality, we pay about $6,000 per person each year in the United States. How is it that we are unaware that we are paying this much? We don't see that amount subtracted from our checking accounts because individuals, on average, fund only about 20 percent of their annual healthcare costs with employers and governments paying the rest. But in truth, we all still pay the remaining amount, because all money eventually comes from individuals (or at least those who work and produce). The dollar amount of healthcare that employers pay on our behalf is in fact subtracted directly from our paychecks. Obviously, if companies did not have to pay healthcare costs, those monies would instead be paid to workers, or to machines that would increase the productivity and thus the paycheck of workers (as explained in Chapter 1). The dollar amount of healthcare that *government* pays for on our behalf is taken directly from our paychecks in the form of taxes and indirectly through inflation. Additionally, the Cato Institute estimates that the cost per household of medical providers' compliance with health

---

the costs incurred for those who need healthcare insurance, many are left out in the cold.

[133] Barbara Starfield, "Is U.S. Health Really the Best in the World?" *The Journal of the American Medical Association 284* (July 26, 2000).

services regulation was $1,546 in 2002. It also estimated that roughly one out of every six uninsured persons was uninsured because of the cost of regulations.[134] All of this regulation exists, yet most people still believe we have a free market in healthcare, and that that is the root of our problems.

On top of the two primary issues discussed above, doctors and hospitals are subjected to unbelievable amounts of burdensome oversight and enforcement agencies, bureaus and commissions. As Jones states: "Rules, regulations, and laws are duplicated, redundant, multiplied, magnified, and contradictory. Laws and regulations covering doctors and hospitals plus all the other parts of our healthcare system now account for over half of all the words, sentences, and paragraphs in our entire body of law."

Socialized Medicine

Socialists want us to turn to nationalized healthcare, where the state will pay for our healthcare (as though we will not still be paying for it). But this will not work either.[135] When medical care is free, people consume more of it. The costs would continually rise, as they currently do in the United States. Since national governments have limited budgets, governments with socialized medicine impose cost controls and limit spending to a particular amount. But since nothing limits individuals from going to the doctor, waiting lines grow longer and longer. At this point governments limit doctor visits or limit the types of procedures which can be done. For example a particular treatment might only be authorized given the existence of a particular set of other symptoms. Or surgery might be restricted to patients who are under a given age.

After getting sick, famed British record label owner, radio and TV presenter, nightclub owner, and journalist Tony Wilson (about whom the film 24 Hour Party People was made) faced death due to

---

[134] Robert Longley, "Cato Claims FDA Denies Health Coverage to Over 7 Million," http://usgovinfo.about.com/od/medicarehealthinsurance/a/fdacato.htm.

[135] The explanations in this section on nationalized healthcare are patterned after the explanation given by Professor George Reisman, "Papiere, Bitte (Papers, Please)," http://georgereisman.com/blog/2006_02_01_archive.html.

the fact that Britain's National Health System (NHS) refused to fund an expensive cancer drug he needed to stay alive. He stated "I've never paid for private health care because I'm a socialist. Now I find you can get tummy tucks and cosmetic surgery on the NHS but not the drugs I need to stay alive. It is a scandal." Wilson died not long after in 2007.[136]

In England's state-run system, the waiting list is nearly 800,000 people. This is in addition to those denied medical attention: 7,000 for hip replacements; between 4,000 and 20,000 for coronary bypass surgery; 10,000 to 15,000 for cancer chemotherapy.

Even with our current screwed up system, one can get treatment if they, or their friends or charities, can pay the price. Under socialized medicine, where many are prevented by government from getting care, the socialist's "right" to healthcare certainly goes out the window.

Additionally, in countries with socialized medicine, physicians' and researchers' incomes are limited, thus taking away their incentive to compete or to be innovative with new forms of technology or treatments. Such is inherently the case under a government bureaucracy.[137] For these very reasons, Canada's healthcare system has taken the first step towards privatization, due to Quebec's lifting a ban on private health insurance. As the New York Times Stated:

> The Supreme Court decision ruled that long waits for various medical procedures in the province had violated patients' "life and personal security, inviolability and freedom," and that prohibition of private health insurance was unconstitutional when the public health system did not deliver "reasonable services."[138]

The quality of service also diminishes with reduced incentives. Soviet hospitals were characterized by widespread apathy and disregard for lives: AIDS was contracted in Russia primarily through dirty

---

[136] James McIntyre, "Tony Wilson, founder of 'Madchester', dies after battle with kidney cancer," *The Independent UK* (August 11, 2007).

[137] For an excellent exposition of this fact, see Ludwig von Mises, Bureaucracy (1944).

[138] Clifford Krauss, "Ruling Has Canada Planting Seeds of Private Health Care," *The New York Times* (February 20, 2006).

needles at state hospitals; patients had to pay bribes in order to receive minimal attention (anesthesia was often withheld until bribes were paid); patients were routinely taken from their deathbed and shoved out the door in order to improve success rate statistics; X-rays were denied in order to save the expensive film.

Socialists believe we have a "right" to healthcare. They simultaneously refuse to believe that having the right to something that is necessarily taken from others against their will constitutes theft; they believe that to associate "theft" with taxes is nutty, no matter how accurate it is in reality (see Chapter 7 for a detailed discussion). Suppose that you were one of the first settlers of this country, at Plymouth Rock, for example, where a majority of the settlers starved to death because the leaders had implemented communism.[139] When the settlers were spending their day working the land with the few tools they had, exactly what healthcare did they have a right to? Did they have a *right* to take their neighbors bandages? Did they have a *right* to take their neighbor's alcohol to poor on their wounds? Real healthcare did not exist then and there. It was later *created and produced* in this country. If we all believe we have a right to have as much as we want of the limited amount of healthcare available, from whom will we take it? And do we also have a *right* to food? The first settlers at Plymouth Rock indeed relied on each other to produce food for them, thus producing little themselves. The food was put into a common pile where everyone came to take what they wanted. Soon, the food was gone and the settlers were starving. A system based on positive "rights" leads to poverty.

Only Free Markets Can Solve the Healthcare Crisis

Every election cycle, we hear politicians talk only of cost controls, electronic medical records, and preventing lawsuits in order to solve our medical crisis. We do not hear from them discussions of the real problems of government-paid insurance and the third-party payer system, and of medical boards. Some pundits argue that technology

---

[139] On this, see: Richard J. Maybury, "The Great Thanksgiving Hoax," http://mises.org/daily/336, and Gary Galles, "Property and the First Thanksgiving," http://mises.org/daily/1678.

increases medical costs. Though technology lowers costs in other industries, people think that it somehow increases costs in the healthcare industry. Indeed, Paul Krugman claims that healthcare costs rise simply "because of medical progress."[140] With these kinds of backwards notions, our "leaders" set out to implement yet more regulation and price controls, which will only exacerbate the problem.

What we need are truly free markets in healthcare, which would bring about an increased supply of doctors and healthcare facilities, and drastically lower costs. By bringing free market profits to the industry, the quality of care would improve due to providers competing to make the most money by trying to please the most consumers. Healthcare costs used to represent 5 percent of national income, now it's 17 percent.[141] Each year, due to increased demand paid for by companies and the government, a greater proportion of our incomes are funneled into healthcare expenditures, and a smaller proportion into other goods. Under free markets, healthcare prices would fall in real terms (if not also nominal terms), and the cost of staying in a hospital would approximate the costs of staying in a hotel plus the additional marginal costs of the labor services of nurses and doctors, and the costs of the use of the tools and technology. If we all paid for our own healthcare, instead of having others pay, it would be mathematically impossible for costs to be at a level above what each of us could afford; doctors and hospitals could not make as much money if they charged more than people could afford to pay. This is why we can afford things in other industries—because goods are priced at a level commensurate with our incomes. The key is to pay for our own healthcare as needed. Costs of healthcare would be affordable to everyone in the same way that food, televisions, and tools at Home Depot are; they would be just another average cost that we pay.

For those who still doubt such an argument, think seriously about whether the supposed high costs that would occur in a free market would really outweigh the costs we incur today where healthcare costs rise at two to three times the rate of inflation. And

---

[140] Paul Krugman, "Bad Medicine," *The New York Times* (March 19, 2002).

[141] As an aside, those same statistics are even more dramatic for the financial services industry.

consider whether the supposed physical harm that would occur would outweigh the deaths and physical suffering that occur today due to the fact that millions can't afford access to healthcare. Additionally, if licensing is so important in order to guarantee competent and qualified service providers, shouldn't we, in the same vein, require all politicians to go through years of training in the areas of philosophy, history, economics (including free market economics), industrial production, accounting, and management before they are permitted to pass laws that affect the economy and our lives? Shouldn't they be licensed?

Regulation of Local Government Services

The following posting contains an email to ABC News' John Stossel in response to a report Stossel did on regulation. The email speaks for itself:

> I own a private, non-emergency ambulance service in Northwest Arkansas. On 01/01/09, private ambulance services [were] no longer allowed to transport patients in one of the cities we have served for over 25 years. The city of Fayetteville, along with eight smaller cities, has formed an ambulance authority that [now has] exclusive rights to all emergency and non-emergency transfers within the nine cities. ... Essentially, the Fayetteville City Council has decided to eliminate any competition and charge whatever it wants. My service currently has contracts with two hospitals in Fayetteville and charges the minimum amount allowed by Medicare ($195.67 + $6.87 per mile) for any transports for these facilities. We have competed directly with the government-owned service for 25 years, and, quite frankly, run circles around them. In response, they had taxpayers pay $100,000 for a bogus study that recommended, lo and behold, that they be the only provider in town. [Now] transports in Fayetteville will cost patients $523.34 + $10.74 per mile. That is at least 2.64 times what they pay private services today. Health care facilities affected by the enormous price increase are upset,

but they have made little progress in eliminating this government monopoly.[142]

Regulation of the Airline Industry

From the beginning of the airline industry until 1978, the Civil Aeronautics Board (CAB) controlled an artificial cartelization of the airline industry. It limited competition, kept fares far above the free-market price, and allowed politically favored airlines to obtain profitable routes. Competitors were prevented from entering the industry or literally put out of business when the CAB prevented their operations from continuing. In 1978 the government abolished the CAB and allowed airlines to more freely compete, after which, new airlines cropped up, and inefficient ones left the industry. The result was fares that were 40 percent lower, a 50 percent increase in flights, and a 112 percent increase in passenger boardings over the next 20 years.[143]

But in place of the CAB we now have the FAA controlling much of the industry. Instead of allowing free-market prices to dictate the cost of "slot" fees (takeoff and landing spots on runways), which would equate supply with demand, the FAA rations slots, and charges a below-the-free-market-price that causes congestion on airport runways. A free-market pricing system (whereby prices are determined based on competitors buying and selling) would raise prices during peak hours, limiting flight privileges to those who could most afford it, such as large airlines carrying business travelers. Most smaller corporate jets and delivery service jets would then not take up runway space during rush hour. The FAA, absent competition and the need for profits, has no incentive to keep traffic flowing efficiently.

Air traffic control is a monopoly run by the FAA. While the number of flights was increased through the years, the number of air traffic controllers has not kept pace. Even though private industry builds and operates the planes, the government supposes that private industry should not run traffic control services. But there is no reason

---

[142] 4029TV.com, "Private Ambulance Services Upset With New Change," http://www.4029tv.com/news/18396977/detail.html.

[143] Carolyn Lochhead, "Small airlines—and a few politicians—try to again put Washington behind the ticket counter," *Reason Magazine* (July 1998).

why it shouldn't. Privatized air traffic control and runway slot control would increase the number of flights per hour and reduce the overcrowding and shortages of runways, preventing planes circling for hours waiting to land (or, waiting on the tarmac—an occurrence the media blames on airlines, who are simply following FAA rules).

Another problem with airline service is that every single commercial airport in this country is owned and operated by local governments (except for two airports run by the federal government), who don't have the incentive, or the skill, to provide the services needed for smooth operations. Worse, airport security is handled by the federal government. Is it any wonder, therefore, that we stand in line for hours sometimes to check in or to go through security? The Feds are also responsible for baggage handling. Do you think as many bags would be mishandled and lost by profit-seeking companies? More importantly, local governments don't build enough gates, runways, and even airports to satisfy demand. Thus, airports often selectively assign a limited number of gates to politically favored airlines. In many cities, the arrival of new and competing airlines is prevented due to economically powerful airlines that hold sway over local city councils preventing gates from being made available to competitors.

Anyone who is not aware of the previous facts should still have known that the airline industry is highly regulated because they don't' see foreign airlines compete with domestic ones. Foreign carriers are allowed to fly into and out of a particular destination in the U.S., but not from city to city. Were Lufthansa, for example, allowed to fly from, say, Salt Lake City to Nashville, competition would intensify and prices would fall.

One reason this has not taken place, besides the fact that our government attempts to protect domestic carriers from competition, is that here again, government economists, have their feeble theories about how capital should be efficiently allocated in the industry. It is argued that due to the high fixed costs of operating, it is more efficient to allow only a few carriers manage the load. Such irrationality, or more specifically, political wrangling, probably does not need to be addressed at this point—there are many companies and would-be companies ready and willing to compete. We should let them.

With all the protection, government control, and regulation in the airline industry, taking even an hour's flight is a stressful, exhausting, four-hour challenge. And inefficient, loss-making airlines need taxpayer bailouts every decade. We should demand of our government that it privatize the entire industry and abolish all regulation. Lines would disappear, costs would decline, quality would improve, and safety would increase.

Regulation of the Oil Industry

On the supply side, it's simple: we don't produce enough oil in the U.S. because the government prevents it. Because of extensive regulation, mostly environmental regulation, it is simply too expensive to explore, refine, and produce oil at a faster pace than we do currently. Additionally, the government maintains a monopoly ownership of land that has large oil deposits (for example, the government owns over 87 percent of land in Alaska). Because of environmental regulations, there has not been a new oil refinery built in the United States in more than 30 years, and the number of refiners has been cut in half in the last 15 years. Saudi Arabia has even offered to build two new refineries in the U.S., but only if "someone else obtains all the necessary environmental permits first."[144] They would produce oil for us in the U.S. but environmental laws prevent them from doing so.

America's invasion of Iraq, a former large oil producer, has also served to reduce the world supply of oil. And to the small extent that OPEC influences oil prices, we can blame government intervention in those countries, since OPEC is comprised largely of state-owned companies. Privately competing firms in Iran or Nigeria would have no incentive to withhold oil from the market, and competition would prevent these private firms from raising prices.

American consumers are also unable to consume as much oil as they would otherwise because stiff taxes make the price artificially high. Taxes vary by state, but they comprise about 50 cents of every gallon of gas, on average. Gasoline tax is just another method of extracting money from tax payers because one of the many

---

[144] Charles Featherstone, "The Myth of 'Peak Oil'," http://mises.org/daily/1717.

other forms of tax money (state & local income tax, etc.) was spent on wealth redistribution instead of roads and highways. Of course, high taxes are also used as an incentive to make us drive less, since the government does not build enough roads with all the tax money it confiscates.

On the demand side of gasoline prices, we've already seen in Chapter 3 that prices rise mostly because of the printing presses of world governments. While speculators are *usually* blamed by governments (and even economists) for dramatic price changes (especially currency collapses), they are almost always caused by the government itself. But speculators (and investors in general) cannot just run a price up for no reason. They cannot control the entire world market for oil. For every trading position they open, they must close another. Therefore, their speculation must be correct or they will suffer losses. World governments dramatically reduced their rates of printing money in 2006 and 2007. As a result of this, and the recessions that action brought about, we saw world demand, and therefore prices, collapse in 2008. Any speculators betting that prices were going to rise in mid-2008 got slaughtered by betting incorrectly. Yet no one asks why the speculators supposedly decided to suddenly drive oil prices lower. Do they no longer want to make profits?

Analogously, though OPEC and oil companies were being blamed for manipulating oil prices, no one asked why they had decided not to manipulate prices as they were falling from the mid 1980s until the late 1990s, when oil prices ended up at $12 per barrel. OPEC produces only 30 million of the 80 million barrels produced each day;[145] plus, they still face consumers who will purchase less oil if prices rise too much. Not to mention that individual countries within the cartel regularly cheat on their quotas. In sum, OPEC thus has little pricing power. Along the same lines, the size of American oil companies pales in comparison to the sum of all other oil producers in the world. Therefore, it's impossible for American firms to control oil prices. Still, a recent poll shows that 69 percent of the American

---

[145] Featherstone, "Peak Oil."

people "can see the president making gasoline prices go up or down [manipulating prices]."[146]

It is true, however, as commonly stated, that America consumes much more energy than other countries. Yet this is a wonderful fact, not one to deplore. America's level of oil consumption reveals the amount of capital we have in our possession and reflects the amount of goods we are able to produce. It reveals, and is the reason for, the advanced technological state of our country. It reveals that our standard of living is that much higher than most other countries.

More importantly, we should consume *more*, not less! We need to consume energy—mainly in the form of oil, for now—in order to advance and progress economically. There is plenty of oil in the world to do this with, and as technology advances we'll find more. If we don't find more, so what? Given the price of oil that will exist when oil stocks are becoming depleted, the cost of producing oil will exceed the cost of alternative fuels, and we will then switch our production to those alternatives. While socialists claim that oil companies prevent the switch from taking place now, the truth is that oil companies, or any other entrepreneurs, will use their capital to produce *any* type of energy that's possible at prices consumers are willing to pay. Currently, consumers are not willing to pay two or three times as much for energy. And government subsidies aimed at making alternative energy "affordable" do the opposite. Subsidies deduct money from our wages so that they can then be used to purchase alternative energy we would not choose to pay for on our own. This destroys wealth, as well as making us pay more for energy than we have to, leaving less money for other parts of our lives. It is simply not yet economically feasible to use most alternative energies.

Therefore, let's use oil and use a lot of it. The more we use, the more prosperous we will be. At today's rate of world consumption, there are enough oil reserves for 40 more years. That amount will likely increase, as it always has. The only reason, besides environmentalism, that we have a mindset of needing to conserve energy is that our government(s) does not provide enough of it. If we got government

---

[146] Nancy Benac and Trevor Thompson, "With 'Change' in Mind, Voters Voice Expectations for the Next President," *Associated Press* (January 12, 2008).

out of the way and allowed the free market to produce energy, we would have an abundance of energy and at lower prices.

Hurricane Katrina

Thanks to the media and the leftists, it is now folklore that Hurricane Katrina was the reason New Orleans was flooded and partially destroyed. Few people seem to know or care to remember that hours after the hurricane passed, New Orleans was relatively calm and unscathed. It was *after* the hurricane that the levies broke. The levies were a crucial part of the New Orleans infrastructure—built, owned, and managed by the government. The levies had not been kept up properly for years. Had they instead been in private hands, run by a profit-seeking entity, they would have likely been newer and stronger, and capable of withstanding foreseeable stresses.[147]

In any case, New Orleans should not even have become a major city, but instead remained a small port. Had the government not been involved, New Orleans would not have grown to the size it was. This is because, due to hurricanes and flooding, most people would not have chosen to live there because the risk of having their property damaged or destroyed was too great. Because of the high risks, property would have been either prohibitively expensive or uninsurable all together. But instead, both state and federal governments subsidized flood insurance and other disaster insurance.[148] In other words, homeowners and businesses were encouraged to build in dangerous places they otherwise wouldn't have because the rest of the nation paid for their losses or potential losses. Now, due to problems which have arisen from this, congress is actually considering *increasing* the subsidies.[149] Additionally, people who don't have insurance can increasingly rely on retroactive government emergency aid money to bail

---

[147] Yes, the marketplace could figure out a way for a company to price the service and earn revenues for such an investment.

[148] The Ayn Rand Center for Individual Rights, "How Government Makes Disasters More Disastrous," http://www.aynrand.org/site/News2?page=NewsArticle &id=17647 &news_iv_ctrl=1021.

[149] Matt A. Meyer, "Hurricane Insurance: Forcing All to Subsidize the Few," http://www.heritage.org/Research/Homelandsecurity/wm1972.cfm.

them out. This is yet another example of wealth redistribution and the destruction of wealth.

Abolish All Regulation

Though there is not enough space here to list all examples of government regulation in all industries, the same types of cause-and-effect with negative outcomes explained above apply to almost every industry and government agency. Regulations related to even those areas where people strongly believe government should have sole power to keep us safe can be shown to be detrimental to our lives. For example, the FDA delays (often for decades) in approving, or prevents us from having, life-saving drugs and technologies that are available in other countries. Conversely, it approves dangerous food, drugs, and products. Free-market consumer agencies—whose success depends on getting it right—could serve the public's interest much more effectively, with many fewer deaths involved.

Virtually all regulation is politically-based, and merely enables one group to benefit at the expense of another. Regulation does not, as most people believe, help and protect all of society. Contradictory as it may sound, only the free market can regulate the marketplace. Intense competition among multiple parties, all seeking profits, ensures that products will be as safe as possible, that prices will be as low as possible, that quality will be as high as possible, and that consumers will always have alternatives. It is laws and the court system that protect us; regulation, on the other hand, often forces citizens to deal with monopolies or other inefficient entities that lack the incentive to do the right thing. Government can't help us, but the self-regulating free market can.

PART THREE

Government Control Versus Free Markets

Chapter 5:

The Evil Corporation

Many of us who live in relatively free countries take our standards of living for granted. We don't give much thought to how food constantly appears on store shelves, always available for us as we "run by" in our automobiles to pick something up on the way to our warm, safe, and lighted homes. It's easy for us to pay several days' salary to fly in an airplane across the Atlantic, while sipping wine, watching movies, and selecting among various meals, to visit countries that would have been impossible for the average person to reach just over a hundred years ago. We accept almost as given the ability to walk down the street speaking with friends or family 3,000 miles away using little boxes in our hands that cost only several hours' worth of work to buy.

These luxuries that have never before been obtainable in the history of the world were brought to us by capitalism—the economic system whereby people are left free to produce and exchange as they choose, so long as they bring no physical harm to others or their property. A salient feature of modern capitalism is the large corporation,[150] which often has a presence in every state and country and is the

---

[150] Though the first publicly held corporation is thought to be that of the Stora Kopparberg mine in 1288.

dominant firm in its industry. Such successful corporations are seen to wield great economic and political power unfairly.

This chapter addresses the accusations commonly leveled against big corporations and the myths as well as the realities that lie behind these accusations. My purpose in this chapter is to show that in markets genuinely free of government interference, successful companies, no matter how large or powerful, cannot defraud, exploit, oppress, or in any way harm consumers or employees. I will show why we should not only embrace large companies (or any company for that matter), but should even campaign to protect companies from government requirements and restrictions on production and from government protections and privileges granted to some companies at the expense of others.

Capitalism's Good Deeds

Ancient Greece marked the most culturally and economically advanced and developed state of Western civilization since the first modern humans of approximately 200,000 years ago. Yet in this glorious state, homes had no heat, and most had no running water; people regularly relieved themselves in public streets. Their homes had no chimneys, so fireplaces and oil lamps filled their rooms with smoke and soot.

Life in Europe during the Middle Ages was not much more comfortable. Dwellings, generally built of wood, mud, grass, and leaves, usually consisted of one room with no formal ceiling or floor, and often housed not only entire families but their animals as well. There was no running water or sanitation. Bread and drink consisted primarily of rye and oats. Livelihoods were precarious and consisted of alternating periods of plenty and starvation. Droughts, famines, crime, and violence were common, as were scurvy, leprosy, typhoid diseases, wars, pestilences and plagues. Famine persisted until the last two hundred years in the now capitalist societies; in non-capitalist societies famine continues. Famines, traditionally prominent, feared, and dreaded, have killed tens of millions of people throughout history. One writer compiled a detailed summary of 22 famines on the British Isles in the 13th century alone. Tens of thousands of people in London died during large famines, and they often resorted to eating horseflesh, bark from trees, and grass.[151] As recently as the 19th century, deaths from lack of food occurred en masse: 800,000 died in India in 1838; 1,000,000 died in Bengal and western India in 1866; 1,500,000 in India in 1869; 5,000,000 died in India between 1876 and 1878; 9,500,000 died in China between 1877 and 1878; 1,000,000 died in India in 1897. Today, however, in a world in which more people live than the total number who have ever previously existed, the preponderance of people (except those in countries without any semblance of free markets) have plenty of food and nutrition.

There are also more modern countries in the twentieth century that have suffered starvation, but these are primarily in the category of communist (i.e., non-capitalistic) countries, which became "modern" only through previous periods of relative capitalism (e.g., China and Russia). It was the economic policies implemented by the communist leaders that led to the lack of food. For example, more than 20 million people died in the Soviet Union in the 1920s and 1930s, shortly after the Bolshevik revolution; more than 20 million also died in Maoist China; it's estimated that 600,000 died in North Korea in the mid to late 1990s.

Capitalism has prevented starvation, eradicated diseases, led to the development of sanitation systems and products, made us stronger, healthier, and longer-living, built cities with all the modern conveniences and luxuries we enjoy, and continues to do so to this day. Nevertheless, many people have the audacity to call this system immoral and unworkable. They say it has negative, rather than positive results. They say that those entities that bring to us all the things that make our lives better—businesses—are evil. Instead of acknowledging the many ways that they and the rest of society benefit from these companies, these people maintain that the primary production generated by businesses is wealth for their rich owners and managers, and further, that their gain comes at the expense of the rest of society—especially of the poor.

---

[151] Cornelius Walford, "The Famines of the World," *Journal of the Royal Statistical Society* (March 19, 1878).

It would be fine if this type of ignorance were restricted to the pretentious group of academics and politicians from whence it originates, but these "experts" convince the rest of society to believe their lies, which then become common public perception. With the public believing it's in their interest for government to protect them with taxes and regulations on business, they begin supporting policies that not only actually fail to protect them, but harm them.

As an example, oil production disruptions in the United States following a hurricane in fall 2008 left many gas stations in southern states without gas for over a week, resulting in cars idling in hour-long lines, and many running out of gas on the road. Meanwhile, neighboring states had plenty of gas, much of which could have been diverted to those states that needed more. Had prices in states that needed gas been allowed to rise to a higher level than in non-needy states, it would have been profitable to truck gasoline the extra 300 or 500 miles and sell to the needy stations that were offering to pay premium prices. But state legislatures in the needy states had implemented anti-price gouging laws (to protect consumers and show that they were "doing something"), which prevented gas stations from raising prices above normal market prices for fear of being fined the stated $10,000 to $25,000 penalties. Thus, the "benefits" of this regulation were reduced business incomes for small business owners (the gas stations) and a shortage of gas for consumers. The price gouging law could not help consumers under any circumstance because there is no such thing as price gouging in competitive markets. With competition between gas stations causing each one to try and undercut the other's price to increase their sales, prices can never rise very far above costs.

Companies cannot hurt us if they have competition, which, as we saw, sometimes consists only of the *threat of* competition. But regulation usually *allows* companies to take advantage of us by preventing competition.

Do Businesses Gain At Our Expense?

In a free market, companies can survive only by pleasing their customers. If enough customers like what a business is selling, they will buy enough of it at a high enough price to bring a profit. If they don't, the company will suffer a loss and fail. Its resources will then be transferred to another company to use in its more profitable operations. The imperative of pleasing customers applies as well to goods that we "must have." If a provider of bandages has better-sticking, better-feeling, better-priced bandages, this provider will gain more market share. Many gas stations have gone out of business during recent times despite being able to charge high prices for an important good that we all "must have" simply because they did not, for example, offer auto-pay credit card machines or aesthetically pleasing and modern gas pumps and convenience stores.

Capitalism is the ultimate democratic force because consumers, by voting with their dollars, decide what and how much gets produced. If people begin spending more on SUVs, carmakers rush to make more of them in all kinds of shapes and sizes. If consumer trends turn to "green" cars, manufacturers rush to produce automobiles that run on fuel cells, batteries, biodiesel, natural gas, and the like. If consumers spend more on, say, pet food, prices rise in that industry, bringing about high profits, causing other entrepreneurs to chase those profits and increase the supply of pet food. The result is in line with consumers' desires, as communicated through their spending patterns. If they *want* more pet food available, they get it! Further, the bigger the business, the more it is *the masses* who are being served. As the great economist Ludwig von Mises put it: *"Those underlings who in all the preceding ages of history had formed the herds of slaves and serfs, of paupers and beggars, became the buying public for whose favor the businesspeople canvass. They are the customers who are 'always right.'"*[152]

The price system—the prices of everything in an economy as determined by consumer choices—directs the production of consumer goods to keep them in line with consumer desires. The production of capital goods, the goods that produce consumer goods, is in turn directed by the spending of the companies producing consumer goods. After all, every single capital good produced in this world—concrete, factories, hammers, generators, tankers, commercial aircraft, etc.—is made ultimately to produce things for consumers; these

---

[152] *The Anti-Capitalistic Mentality*, p. 2.

are the goods that create the goods that we buy. Every consumer on Main Street, simply by choosing to buy particular goods or services, directs the production processes of the entire world economy. This is what free market economists call "consumer sovereignty." This equilibrating production process, as directed by prices and profits, are what Adam Smith referred to as the "invisible hand" of the market.

Are Profits Bad?

Since profits are awarded only to those who please consumers, then it must follow that profits are good, not bad. Profits result from companies having created something that is valuable enough that customers would rather have *it* than the money they exchange for it. If they thought they would be better off with their money than the product, they would have instead kept the money.

Profits also mean that a particular amount of physical resources (which are combined and assembled to make products) sell for more than the cost of the amount of resources that went into making them.[153] *Profits mean we add to the stock of real wealth in our economy. Conversely, losses, or negative profits, mean that value of the resources consumed in making the product is greater than the value of the product itself. Losses thus result in a destruction of real wealth.*

Yet many consumers despise profitable companies while they pity unprofitable ones. The government, with our tax money, subsidizes those companies destroying wealth (those with losses) while it imposes higher taxes on companies that create wealth (those with profits). We the public, therefore, suffer, because anything we tax, we get less of. During the 2008 presidential debates, vice-presidential nominee Sarah Palin, who claimed to support free markets, was proud that she had imposed "windfall profits" taxes on oil companies in Alaska (for their evil big profits). But by taxing them, she reduced the companies' output and hurt consumers. Yet these actions are somehow seen as good and right by most people in society. Conversely, unprofitable companies such as Delta and other airlines received a $15 billion government bailout in 2001. They now once again need a new bailout.

---

[153] Because producing for a loss means that more resources are being consumed in the production process than the production process is creating in new wealth.

Both pragmatism and logic dictate that we should allow unprofitable businesses to go under so that their people, tools, and machinery can be used more profitably somewhere else where they are creating wealth and pleasing consumers.

Simply to survive, and especially to gain wealth, companies must find ways to satisfy the public with new products or lower costs. But as soon as they do, competition arrives to steal the profits. Companies can never sit back and relax with their profits; they must constantly innovate, or at least adapt others' innovations, or they will cease to exist from lack of profits (or, they can convince Congress to give them special favors in the form of regulation which harms competitors).

Profits Benefit Buyers and Regulate Companies

As this discussion and the detailed explanation of profits in Chapter 1, as well as the discussion on monopolies in Chapter 4 make clear, profits in any industry can never remain large (percentage-wise) for very long. Higher profits bring more competition and lower selling prices. To ward off competition, companies keep selling prices as low as possible, and try to achieve even lower prices by becoming more efficient. The opposite occurs with wages: competition forces companies to pay the highest wages they can. The same concept applies to quality and safety of products: low quality and unsafe products will result in a loss of revenues and profits. Competition and *basic* laws regulate companies; additional thousands of pages of government regulations do the opposite.

Clearly, consumers benefit from companies seeking profits, which is precisely why every industry should be for-profit. Many people say that the healthcare industry, for example, should not be for-profit as it leads to healthcare providers focusing on making money rather than taking care of people. But the truth is quite the opposite. In free markets, providers can make good money only if they provide high-quality services at low prices in order to please customers so much that they will choose them over their competitors. In today's regulated markets, providers have all the clients they can possibly handle; they don't have to compete for them or try to please any given customer.

Haven't you noticed how your doctor rushes you in and out, after having made you wait hours? Compare that experience to one in a relatively free industry: in taking your automobile to be repaired, at a dealer or private mechanic, they usually receive your car the day you call, have it finished that afternoon, and often offer you transportation to and from their shop. They also spend plenty of time showing and explaining the problems, and usually charging less to repair $40,000 automobiles than your doctor charges to fix you—all while making normal (low) profit margins. Additionally, inefficiency from lack of competition and regulatory burdens raises costs.

Should Profits Be Shared?

It has been argued that companies don't share their profits with local economies, or with anyone else at all. Likewise, it has been said that greedy company executives live like fat cats from the large profits their companies bring in. But these arguments fail to consider what profits actually are and how they work. It should be understood that profits are not pocketed by executives but instead are distributed to shareholders or invested in the company's future production, production which helps all communities through the supply of more goods at lower costs.

Profits belong to the owners of the company, the shareholders, who consist of thousands or even millions of people, in the case of large corporations. For example, we hear constantly that ExxonMobil made a whopping $40 billion in profits in 2007. But this, on its own, means nothing; it has to be put in perspective. The $40 billion represented a 10 percent profit[154] (up from only 4.3 percent in 1999[155])—an average rate of profit in other industries[156]—and much smaller than

---

[154] ExxonMobil, 2007 Summary Annual Report, http://thomson.mobular.net/thomson/7/2675/3201/.

[155] ExxonMobil, 1999 Consolidated Statement of Income, http://www.exxonmobil.com/Corporate/Newsroom/Publications/shareholder_publications/c_fo_99/page_16.pdf.

[156] Here we are discussing the rate of profit on revenues. The notion of a uniform rate of profit applies to the rate of return on capital invested. This is another reason why income statement profits—those usually reported in the media—are not a reliable source of true profitability. As an example, the grocery store industry, with regular profits of "only" 2–3 percent do much better in terms of return on capital invested.

in many, such as those for financial services firms.[157] And profits don't come cheaply: the company did have to fork out $334 billion in order to achieve sales revenues of $404 billion, and they had to pay $29 billion in taxes. The remaining $40 billion profit is then spread over the company's thousands of shareholders, some of whom own many millions of shares and some of whom own two or three shares. Either way, the profit each shareholder made still equaled a rate of profit of 10 percent on their wealth. But whatever amount of money shareholders made represents new wealth. With that new wealth, they can spend in ways that make their lives better, or put the wealth in the bank where it will be used as capital to make *everyone's* lives better. Depending on the scenario (i.e., whether the new wealth is spent or reinvested), either some or all of society is better off, and no one has lost out in the process.

Instead of complaining that ExxonMobil's profits were as high as $40 billion, we should all be complaining that they are not as high as $400 billion! If they had been, that would mean ExxonMobil had produced about ten times the amount of oil (and paid out approximately ten times the amount of wages). In that case, we would all have more oil available at lower prices. And of course, had ExxonMobil not had to pay $29 billion in taxes, they would have produced that much more oil for consumers, or they would have that much more funding available with which to discover new oil, including the payment of additional wages. The same concept applies to every company in every industry. But instead of having more and higher wages and more, lower-priced goods by not having companies pay high taxes, most voters instead choose to have companies pay the high taxes, a situation that results in those very people ending up with lower incomes and fewer goods at higher prices!

Second, most profits are not usually paid out to shareholders, but instead are reinvested in the company's operations. The reinvested profits are used to pay for the costs the company has to incur in making

---

[157] Since the financial services industry is far from a free market, it usually has high profits due to government regulation which allows these companies to gain from the central banks' printing of money. This is why the size of the industry relative to the size of the overall economy has continued to grow over the decades.

next year's products. The more that is reinvested, the more salaries that can be paid and the more output the company can produce.

Third, what observers should be concerned with are not profits, but costs/expenditures. Profits are only a small part of any financial statement. If a company has a 10 percent profit, they have spent 90 percent of the amount of their sales revenues in paying salaries and paying for capital goods. Both of these expenditures benefit society. The salaries are obviously income for workers. The capital goods help workers produce more and thus get paid more, and they produce the company's product, which consumers will then have available. In other words, *it is society, not executives (and not even the rich and the capitalists themselves), who benefit most from a company's capital.*

True, executives may be paid *dramatically* more than workers, but they bring in *dramatically more* revenues to the company than do the workers (and *dramatically* more wealth to consumers in the form of more goods and services), as we have already learned. They are also paid, ultimately, for making sure that all of a company's employees have continued employment at the company— good decisions mean continued jobs, bad decisions mean everyone is out of work. Executives should be compensated the going market wage for the work they do, and should *not* be compensated well, if at all, for incurring losses. *But, their compensation should be decided amongst the shareholders (and their board of directors), since they own the company.* Neither the government nor we citizens (unless we are direct shareholders) should have any input; this should be negotiated between the two private parties. It's neither our company nor our money (until we steal it from shareholders and executives through taxes); it's theirs!

There are cases in which the largest shareholders are also the executives running the company. This situation might well result in executives paying themselves too much while running an inefficient company that does not make profits.[158] But even in these cases, minority shareholders can *choose* not to own the company shares (for publicly traded companies, they can sell them any minute of the day, literally within three seconds, on stock exchanges) and workers can *choose* not to work there. But the compensation and management

---

[158] I used to work for such a company.

decisions should be made between the private parties involved; government and society should have nothing to do with it.

More Capitalism Means Lower Profits

We have explained that large profits exist where there are new and innovative products or new methods of production, both of which bring about improvements in quality or cost for things consumers are buying. Yet some might still emotionally describe these temporarily large profits as obscene. But these detractors fail to grasp that it is the prospect of large profits that brings about the new or improved products and services. They enjoy their iPods, stylish shoes, and beverages, but deride the incentive—profits—that brought these products into existence to begin with. In countries or regions where there is no prospect of profiting from developing these products, they are simply not developed. They are not created at all if the creators cannot reap the benefits of their hard work, risk, and opportunity costs. Additionally, for each person who becomes rich from seeking large profits, there are about five who lose a lot of money (often their life's savings) because they failed to succeed. And many of those who become rich later become poor due to subsequent risks not paying off. Socialists do not consider the years of hard work, dedication, risk of failure, risk of career, risk of smaller fortunes that it takes to bring about large profits. They close their eyes to these things and pretend that without any effort at all, these evil businesspeople become instant millionaires overnight. Of course, should a homeless person win the lottery—becoming an instant millionaire overnight—socialists would likely celebrate this event (as would I), even though the homeless person truly put no effort into earning his millions.

Further, if socialists deride large profits as obscene, they should also deride the incomes of artists, self-employed writers, independent fishermen, and psychologists. This is because these people make a much higher percentage of profits than do even corporations with new products making temporarily large profits. For as we have seen, they are not paid *wages*—wages arise only with the existence of capitalists who pay workers *before* the product is produced. Without capitalists, the only form of income is *profits*, not wages.[159] The profits this group earns has few costs in the form of materials and supplies subtracted from the revenues they earn. Suppose a farmer produces his own tools and pays only for seeds. If he sells his produce in the market for $30,000, his deduction from the revenues that go towards paying for the seeds might be $2,000. This leaves a 93 percent profit. If the farmer buys new and improved tools from others, he might have to deduct $5,000 (in addition to the $2,000) from the $30,000 in revenues, leaving a 76 percent profit[160]. Both of these theoretical profits are larger than the average 10 percent or so profits corporations make. Profits, therefore, don't necessarily mean a lot.

It is larger companies, primarily, who pay *wages*. Larger companies pay much more of their profits to the so-called *factors of production* (labor and machines)—if the average corporation makes a 10 percent profit, then 90 percent of their revenues are spent on the factors of production. Even a company with a new product that is making large profits of 50 percent still has smaller profits than our farmer, artist, or small fisherman, who usually has to deduct much less than 40 percent of revenues for supplies. A psychologist would have to deduct nothing but the cost of their note pads and pens, and their office and furniture (the latter, due to accounting guidelines, has its costs spread across many years).[161]

It should be clear from this example that large companies have much smaller profits because they have much greater expenditures on the means of production. We have fewer people remaining as sole proprietors in our society today because greater efficiencies can be had in most industries by having fewer producers in an industry making and producing a greater volume than could be produced with more numerous producers. Thus, most people work for a business that has devised means of producing more efficiently because workers can earn more in this way than producing on their own (their

---

[159] A unique insight by economist George Reisman.

[160] In reality, these costs would be spread across multiple years, making his profit each year even larger.

[161] Non-business-related costs such as education are not included on business income statements. Any personal costs, for the artists or the rich CEO, are just that—personal costs.

wages are more than the dollar amount of the high percentage profits they could earn on their own). The business owner spends most of the company's revenues to purchase machines and labor. The greater our level of capitalism—in this case, the paying for machines and labor—the greater our productivity (and real incomes). More capitalism means more would-be profits are instead used to pay labor and machines. Thus, if socialists want companies to earn lower profits, they should support capitalism.

Still, a good socialist would argue that though the small farmer or psychologist might be earning a higher *rate* of profit, the absolute dollar amount of their profit is much smaller and much less obscene. The argument is valid, but it does not mean the large profits are bad. It means that the small producers are not able to offer as much of a supply of goods to society. That is, unless, you add them all together. In that case, if we add the millions of sole proprietors together and come up with profits in the billions, how is that better than if we grouped all the sole proprietors in each industry into a company where, with economies of scale, they could produce more in total, and where they would have higher incomes from doing so?

Imagine that you bought a bracelet at an arts and crafts street fair that you really liked. Suppose the producer and seller of that bracelet sold 30 of the bracelets that year. Had the artist instead sold 3,000 bracelets, consider how many people would be as happy as you, how many people thought the bracelet was preferable to the money they gave up in exchange. But if the small-time artist was in fact so successful at selling bracelets that the street fair table grew in size and became a large company—with the help of employees who would have new jobs—selling thousands of the same bracelets at the same rate of profit, that artist would then be derided as an evil profiteer.

Do Some Gain at the Expense of Others?

But if someone is making a profit, does that mean someone else is incurring a loss? Yes and no, mainly no. *Other companies* might incur a loss if they are not competitive enough. In that case, capital (i.e., production capabilities) is transferred from those who cannot please consumers and create wealth to those who can; capital moves into the hands of the most capable. **But business profits do *not* come at the expense of workers, consumers, or society as a whole.** Profits, we learned, are compensation to capitalists for providing companies with the capital used in producing products and for going without the money that is instead used to produce goods and services. As part of the production of goods and services, capital pays for the tools used in the production process and for the labor. Thus, capital—money owned and unconsumed by individuals—pays our wages and creates the things we need. Capital also funds the creation of new companies. *Everyone gains* in this process, even those business owners who were not previously competitive enough to maintain their capital and profits, since they will instead have new alternative opportunities for employment as well as lower retail prices on which to spend their new wages. Workers gain by being paid wages with which they can purchase the very goods they produce, while committing nothing but time and energy to the process. Consumers gain by having more goods available at lower prices. Further, both the exchange of labor for *wages paid by companies* (in the case of workers), and the exchange of money for *goods produced by companies* (in the case of consumers) are done *voluntarily*, without coercion or force of any kind.

The more wealth the rich capitalists acquire and transfer into production processes, the more companies produce and the lower are prices (in real terms, excluding inflation). Further, the more capital employed per worker, the more each worker can produce, and the more their real wages rise.

Are Businesspeople Evil?

Again, yes and no. On a personal level, there are many decent and honest businesspeople, and there are also those who are just bad people. The business world can indeed be political and cut-throat, but mainly internally, not towards consumers. Many employees do get screwed over and treated badly, but usually by co-workers or their immediate managers, not by top executives (except for those working directly under top executives). The ones treating others badly are just as often women as men. These are everyday people you talk to at parties, or your best friends. Humans are humans. Though there are negative aspects to business operations, the overall outcome is usually pretty favorable for most workers. And I doubt very much that workers get significantly screwed over more than several times in their entire careers. In reality, it happens to all of us workers to some degree, periodically, but in the long run we usually all benefit—just as in life itself.

Additionally, businesspeople care very little, if at all, about workers under (or above) them. But because the marketplace is competitive, they have an incentive to take care of workers as best they can and make sure they are happy. Otherwise, their own performance and paychecks will suffer. This is why there are regular perks, parties, recognition and awards, spot bonuses, and even such benefits as health club memberships, transportation services, and company-paid off-site meetings in vacation destinations—all are deductions from profits.

But on a business level, executives are out to make profits, make higher salaries, and further their careers. Most do this legally, but as in the rest of society, there are unfortunately those who cheat (for which they should be held accountable—by those harmed, not by the government). There is no doubt that most businesspeople would like to exploit both workers and consumers alike. They would, if possible, underpay workers and overcharge consumers. But as we have learned and will continue to learn, competition prevents this from happening. Governments, however, by giving special privileges to companies, can and do allow workers and consumers to be harmed.

Surprisingly, about half of the businesspeople in the United States are politically left-leaning, in part because, ironically, they believe regulation and government force are needed to protect society (these are their views apart from their lives as businesspeople). They also believe that wealth redistribution will help the poor. Most of the other half, though not *officially* left-leaning, still believe we need *some* level of government control. Businesspeople often know very little about economics; if they do, it's likely not free-market (real) economics. For the most part, they don't need to know economics to run a business.

But the lack of economic knowledge is what causes businesspeople as individual members of society to believe as naively as do non-businesspeople that things such as taxing, regulating, redistribution, and price controls can somehow help society, and especially the poor. One CEO of a medium-sized company who told me that he thought that the government programs of the Great Depression that paid people to dig ditches or canals that would never be used actually benefited the economy. In fact, they were simply destroying wealth. That same CEO told me that the 1997 Florida Marlins cheated in winning the World Series because they "bought" the best players. But that's exactly how businesses prosper—by paying for the best people (and it's what the CEO tries to do as a manager). An intelligent business consultant who advises Fortune 500 companies, when told that the housing boom was a bubble sure to end in falling prices, hotly argued to the contrary, saying that falling house prices were in fact impossible, because the housing boom was based on population growth. Another experienced business consultant once asked me rhetorically, "But don't we have free markets?" And part of her job deals precisely with addressing regulatory issues businesses face! Finally, the most shocking example of businesspeople knowing nothing about economics comes from a discussion with a co-worker who once managed investment funds for a large multinational company (who therefore should understand the financial system), and who actually taught college economics courses. When I mentioned the process by which our central bank prints money, he adamantly and emotionally assured me that it was not true that government creates money.[162] But, in fact, the money creation process is described not only in virtually every macroeconomic 101 textbook used in any university, but also on the website of the Federal Reserve Bank of New York itself, where every step of the process by which they create money from thin air is outlined in detail.[163] Had he understood what the money-creation process really is, he would have understood that that's the only way the investments that he used to manage increased in value.

---

[162] He also asserted that F.H. Hayek did not win the Nobel prize. In fact, he won it in 1974 for his work on the business cycle, which was presented in Chapter 3.

[163] The explanation has now been moved to an "off-site" web site: The U.S. Federal Reserve, "The Principle of Multiple Deposit Creation," http://www.federalreserveeducation.org/fed101_html/policy/frtoday_depositCreation.pdf, and The U.S. Federal Reserve, "How does The Fed Create Money?" http://www.federalreserveeducation.org/fed101/policy/money.htm.

Naiveté about economics generates the proposals and actions of left-leaning successful businesspeople such as Bill Gates, Warren Buffett, and Michael Bloomberg, who all propose that the rich should give their money away in one form or another. Bloomberg actually redistributes wealth and regulates in his role as mayor. Bill Gates gives his money to the needy in Africa and elsewhere. Warren Buffet (along with former Treasury secretary and Citigroup executive Robert Rubin) believes that society as a whole should receive the inheritance of wealthy parents who die, instead of their own children. The problem with these notions, besides the moral implications, is that if the wealth is given away, it is consumed. If it is kept with the rich owners or their children as savings, most of it will be invested in one way or another to support the production of more goods and services, *which are self-funding and repeatable.* If it were not true that the rich keep most of their wealth instead of spend it, we would not have millionaires and billionaires actually holding millions and billions. We would also not have capital and machines, because very little of those things are purchased with the combined small savings of the average person—most are purchased for our benefit (and their profits) by the rich.

Society would be helped by Buffet's money much more if it were given in the form of factories and equipment than if it were just all handed out once in cash to the poor to be spent a single time on consumer goods, in which case it is then gone forever. Gates's scenario is a little different: If his money, instead of being handed out to citizens of various African countries, were used to protest dictatorships, to support capitalistic, or at least anti-socialist uprisings, or to bribe leaders to allow their citizens to 1) have freedom to own their own property; 2) keep their earnings; 3) trade freely with others; and 4) borrow capital from abroad (maybe Gates's own money), some of the oppressed poor in those African countries might then be able to accumulate wealth and create prosperity *perpetually.* A one-time handout to fight diseases will save lives that one time. Having the production capability to continuously increase cleanliness, healthiness, and availability of food resulting from material well-being will not only save lives, but keep them saved year after year.

Big Businesses Start Small

A small business can become big only by pleasing a tremendous number of people. Most big companies started out as family businesses. So many people wanted what the family businesses had to offer that the businesses grew rapidly over the years, eventually becoming corporations. Just because small businesses are eventually bought out by larger ones or go public on their own (sell ownership in the business to the public) does not mean they suddenly become evil and terrible with the intention of ripping off customers. Even if they try, they cannot—assuming that they are operating in a free market.

Socialists praise small, independent companies and disdain large ones. One would have to wonder what their threshold for "large" is. What if a mom and pop store opens another location across town? What if they open several more? What if they expand across a larger 5- or 25-state region? What if they sell partial ownership to outsiders in order to raise cash? What if they sell the entire company to a larger company? What if the larger company is a multinational corporation owned primarily by one family? In which of these cases is a company big and evil vs. small and innocent?

Recently, I was talking to a manager at a local Asian restaurant who denounced a rival chain, PF Chang's, as a "corporate operation." Yet his own firm is owned not only by two partners who founded the firm, but also by two other outside equity partners (tantamount to shareholders), and it also has five locations in three states. Though it is owned by four individuals instead of a thousand, it still gets capital invested for its operations via these shareholders, and probably also via loans from banks, which would be equivalent to bond holders. Is this restaurant a corporate entity? Perhaps not in the legal sense, but it has shareholders and it is a chain. Has it become evil yet? Only socialists can judge.

Just because a business is large does not mean that it is somehow more harmful. One might object by saying that it does harm because wealthy corporations can "buy" their way into what they want and then defraud or otherwise harm others, but given free markets, corporations can do no such thing as they would not be intertwined with the government—government would not have the power to help them. In the manipulated markets we have today, large corporations are more likely to engage in lobbying, taking tax breaks, and buying what they need through "contributions" because they are more relentlessly targeted by society, government, unions, and socialists of all colors. Thus, they use the political means available in order to reduce the weight of government on their back. This argument in no way condones these underhanded actions, but simply acknowledges the current reality. Large companies in today's markets are, however, 100 percent guilty of using their size to keep out small competitors by asking government to impose costly regulations that their smaller competitors cannot afford to take on. By definition, free markets would dictate that corporations have no engagement whatsoever with government and vice versa. It is because government intervenes in the free market, imposing itself on companies, that companies have to "work" with and "negotiate" with government.

Large corporations simply serve society on a larger scale than smaller companies. They obtain increased efficiencies by achieving economies of scale and can therefore produce a greater quantity of goods for us at lower prices (and hire more workers) than could 10 different firms one-tenth their size. Remember that their large size or lack of actual competitors does not allow them to take advantage of us.

Corporate Social Responsibility: A Sham

Corporate Social Responsibility (CSR) is defined in Wikipedia as follows:

> a concept whereby organizations consider the interests of society by taking responsibility for the impact of their activities on customers, suppliers, employees, shareholders, communities and other stakeholders, as well as the environment. This obligation is seen to extend beyond the statutory obligation to comply with legislation and sees organizations voluntarily taking further steps to improve the quality of life for employees and their families as well as for the local community and society at large.[164]

---

[164] Wikipedia, "Corporate Social Responsibility," http://en.wikipedia.org/wiki/Corporate_social_responsibility.

This definition tells us that companies are not only to obey the law, but that they are supposed to make decisions, at least in part, based on everyone and everything outside of their business. In other words, business is expected to exist to benefit society. Separate from the fact that businesses already benefit society in every way, the idea of CSR is utter nonsense and is simply an attempt by socialists to gain some control over supposedly evil and greedy corporations that harm them and the "community." An entire book could be written on this topic alone. But since there's not the space for such material here, let's take a broad view of the sham called corporate social responsibility.

As we have learned, absent regulation, companies cannot harm us citizens, except by breaking the established laws and the rules governing capitalism (engaging in physical harm, theft, or fraud). Unless these rules are broken, corporations cannot steal, defraud, or physically harm members of their community. Corporations provide goods to society, jobs to employees, and an increased standard of living to all, while taking nothing in return by force, but only through voluntary exchange.

Companies have a responsibility to their owners (shareholders) *only*—not to any so-called stakeholders, such as suppliers, customers, and the "community." It might well be, and likely is, in a company's *interest* to treat these groups well, but such good treatment should be done only for the sake of making profits. It should already be seen that in the effort to make profits, the well-being of all of these groups will naturally be in the best interest of businesses.

But CSR advocates want companies to go *beyond* what they would do on their own, and intentionally benefit society more than they already do; their end goal is to simply have companies hand out money. For example, CSR advocates cite Shell Oil's involvement in South Africa's *Flower Valley*, a "botanical treasure...[that influences]... bio-diversity and community empowerment...by promoting ways in which *fynbos* [which means natural shrubland] resources can be sustainably utilized,"[165] where learning centers are set up for children. A common CSR approach, they state, is to give aid to impoverished

165 The GivenGain Group, "About GivenGain," http://www.givengain.com/cgi-bin/giga.cgi?cmd=about.

communities in developing countries. So what this really means is that since these countries have failed to support property rights, free markets, and capitalism—which would have resulted in the eradication of poverty and which would have provided the needed education and training—shareholders of multinational corporations are instead supposed to subsidize and support the starving people of the world. It is not, CSR advocates implicitly argue, individual citizens of the developed world who should sacrifice with their own money for these failed nations. It is *other people and their money* that is invested in companies who are supposed to.

Were corporations forced to carry out CSR on the scale proposed by its socialist advocates, the result would be lower profits. Lower profits would mean the laying off of workers and the reduction of output. And since the rate of return (profit) would be lower, companies would lose investor capital and thus decline. The minimum damage would be fewer workers, fewer goods produced for society at higher prices, and even less money available to give away to others. The maximum damage would be that the company would go out of business, and all its employees would be left without work. Either way, real wealth is destroyed.

One might naively retort that there are "proven" business cases stating that CSR is profitable to businesses. If there truly are, it is only in the context mentioned above—that businesses contribute to society to the extent that it helps their profits. But the point being made above is that if businesses are pushed to "invest" in society more than is profitable, not only is it unprofitable, but it is destructive to them (and society). It is in a company's public interest to do something such as to support a charity or sponsor a marathon run against a disease. But with the public's being suckered into CSR propaganda, companies are being prodded to spend more and more of their profits in CSR-type marketing and sponsorships because, if they don't, they will lose customers, who mistakenly believe CSR schemes will have a net benefit on society and that corporations are only non-evil if they give money away. These consumers don't realize that the long-term result of either morally or socially imposed CSR is not only a decreased standard of living for themselves, but also for those they are intending to help.

Businesses, in seeking profits, help the so-called community in multiple ways. Any further "community" help that particular members of society desire and promote under the guise of CSR should instead be funded from their own pockets. If we as consumers are all concerned about cause X or Y, then we have the freedom to dig into our own pockets and give to the cause. Instead, those who advocate CSR spend relatively little of their own money and instead pressure others to pay for their causes. CSR is no less than a wealth redistribution scheme that impoverishes society as a whole.

Businesses are the Hands That Feed Us

In case you have not realized it, it is businesses that have given us every physical thing we have. Look around you right now. You probably see a computer, a desk, a chair, carpet, windows, a house or an office, pens, papers, calculators, a television, a copy machine, lights, air conditioning, clothes, pictures, radios, food, or many other possible goods that make your life more enjoyable or less challenging. All of these were made by people seeking to obtain some type of profit; most of these things were made by businesses of some type, and most were probably made by large corporations. Likewise, most of us work for businesses seeking profits. Or we sell the goods we produce to people who have money paid to them as wages by a business. Or we work for a non-profit or state agency that is wholly funded and supported by for-profit corporations either directly or indirectly. *Nearly all of the wealth we citizens have came about from businesses seeking profits.*

Instead of biting this hand that feeds us, we would all be better off feeding *it* and doing everything we can to get out of its way. For the more we tax it, regulate it, penalize it, restrict its output, force it to lose money by paying too-high wages or by selling products for too low a price, or otherwise suppress it in any of the myriad ways we currently suppress our businesses, the more we reduce our own economic (and social) well-being.

Walmart:
The Quintessential Evil Corporation

Since Walmart is the poster child for the evil corporation, let's address some of the complaints against Walmart specifically, in light of arguments set forth thus far about businesses. At the outset it should be understood that the negative campaigns against Walmart are mostly led by two groups. The first are the extreme left-wing socialists. Their lack of knowledge of economics leads them to rail against anything capitalistic and to fear economic freedom. As socialists, they are moved by emotional impressions about what helps or hurts society, and they are unaware of how capital, profits, and businesspeople help workers, consumers, and all of society.

The second group that is a primary driver of anti-Walmart propaganda is labor unions, primarily the United Food and Commercial Workers Union (UFCW). Since unions have learned that they haven't historically gotten very far with the use of strikes, fear and intimidation tactics, destruction of company property, and physically assaulting non-union workers, they often opt for what is called "corporate campaigns" in the labor union literature.[166] These propaganda tactics have the goal of coaxing Walmart's non-union workers into forming or joining a union. They come at it from the angle of trying to convince the public that Walmart is evil and harmful, so that Walmart will give in and sign a union contract. With such a gullible, economically illiterate public, their tactics are making progress.

Unions do what they can to sink Walmart into their union abyss because their livelihood is at stake. Unions raise costs in the companies they infiltrate, causing them to pay higher wages and benefits, and preventing the companies from advancing technologically (because they have the mistaken belief that technology causes unemployment), thereby lowering their levels of productivity. The result is inefficient, high cost, low-quality and bad-service companies that can't compete with non-union companies. With the increasing threat that efficient non-union companies will take away market share, and therefore jobs, from the unions' own crippled firms, unions try to

---

[166] Thomas J. DiLorenzo, "The Union Conspiracy Against Walmart Workers," http://mises.org/daily/2016.

even the playing field with the business equivalent of beating non-union companies in the knee with a bat (whereas they historically physically beat people with bats).

Destroying the "Mom and Pops"

An old charge against Walmart is that it puts "mom and pop" stores out of business. This might be true, but change is inevitable, and new businesses often cause the demise of old ones, as Joseph Schumpeter explained in his theory of Creative Destruction.[167] Computer manufacturers put typewriter makers out of business; airlines put passenger trains out of business; grocery stores put street markets out of business. Though some workers are unfortunately displaced in the short-run, this is how societies progress.

The fact that Walmart took business away from other stores (including K-Mart, JC Penney, Sears, Woolworth's, TG&Y, Ben Franklin, etc.) means that consumers preferred Walmart's offerings to those of the other stores. Sam Walton's first small family-owned store was successful because he marked-up items less than competitors (he benefitted consumers). Had the mom and pops innovated and expanded so as to give consumers a larger variety of products at lower prices, they could still be in business as well (and some are). A primary way in which Walmart was able to offer large variety at low prices was that it gained economies of scale as it grew. Had the mom and pops grown their business—offering customers larger variety at lower prices—as Walmart did (which began as a mom and pop store), or formed consortiums with others in order to achieve bulk discounts or other efficiencies, they could have more easily competed. In my home town, one of the most popular grocery stores is a mom and pop that joined the IGA consortium, and has thrived for over a half century, unchanged for the last four decades, while larger chains have come and gone.

But, one might argue, adopting and growing too large might change the character and quaintness of mom and pop stores. This is likely true. But consumers (i.e., society at large) have voted with their

---

[167] Joseph Schumpeter, *Capitalism, Socialism, and Democracy* (1992).

wallets and shown that they prefer large selection and low prices to charm and cuteness, in most cases. In other cases, small and charming stores still exist and thrive. So blame your neighbors for change, not the local Walmart.

The lower prices Walmart offers mean an absolute lower *cost* of living for all consumers who shop at the store, thereby delivering to them a higher *standard* of living. Any temporary hardship that mom and pops face from losing their stores and jobs is more than offset by lower prices for everyone else (those who think in terms of "the greater good" should appreciate this fact). The temporary hardships mom and pop owners might face from losing their businesses can also be more easily dealt with by them, given both Walmart's lower prices as well overall lower prices throughout the economy (arising from increased supply from Walmart) for the goods they need.

Walmart's Receiving of Government Subsidies

Anti-Walmart activists complain that the company partially lives off taxpayers because Walmart sometimes receives tax breaks, free or low-cost land, low-cost financing, and outright grants by state and local governments. These accusations partly consist of truth, and partly of the twisting of the truth, hypocrisy, and the unfortunate consequences of a lack of free markets. So let's look carefully and clearly at this murky issue.

In true free markets, there would be no corporatism. No companies would receive any special favor from government. But we don't have free markets. Our current markets, which are hampered by constant government intervention in the marketplace, result in various groups (companies, industries, unions, environmentalists, exporters, retired persons/AARP, etc.) competing with each other by soliciting special privileges from the government. Companies and industries in particular seek special privileges *in part*[168] to loosen the shackles already imposed on them by government, a situation that denies them the freedom to operate and compete as they wish. Unfortunately, Walmart has become involved in this so-called "rent-seeking." The

---

[168] The other part is that they do in fact compete unfairly, because our current system allows them to.

company used to mind its own business and compete fairly, but now it does not. However, as has been pointed out,[169] it is highly possible that Walmart was caught in a situation wherein if they did not engage in lobbying and government favor-seeking, their competition certainly would, which would leave Walmart at a disadvantage.

Though Walmart is wrong to seek special government privileges such as subsidies, it must be pointed out that in isolation, or, considering that this is how a *government-regulated* economy currently works, there is nothing wrong with Walmart's taking advantage of tax incentives to invest in particular locations. After all subsidies and loopholes, Walmart still paid 33.6 percent of its income to the government in taxes in 2007.[170] Thus, they are still by far a net tax *payer*, not receiver. Walmart, like the rest of us tax payers, is coerced by the government to hand over part of its income, most of which is transferred directly to other people or groups (and mostly to the socioeconomic class to which most of Walmart's "poor" employees and customers belong—thus, they are supporting this class in multiple ways). Therefore, they should take advantage of any opportunity that would allow them to have some of their tax money *returned to them* (i.e., "government subsidy"); they do no physical or *monetary* harm to anyone in the process.[171] The same concept applies to any of us net tax *payers* (as opposed to net tax *recipients*—those who pay no tax and instead *receive* money from us taxpayers). Did you complain that you were receiving a subsidy when you took advantage of your so-called tax rebate in 2008?

On that point, what is most disturbing about those who complain about Walmart's subsidies is that they are not against subsidies in general, only if it is specifically Walmart or another perceived evil capitalistic company receiving them (regardless of the amount of money these companies pay in total). These people would have no problem with a mom and pop bookstore, coffee shop, or movie theater, or a union-destroyed automobile company receiving subsidies. Nor would

---

[169] Skip Olivia, in response to Jeffrey Tucker, "Is Walmart Illegitimate?" http://blog.mises.org/archives/002038.asp.

[170] WalMart, 2007 Annual Report to Investors, http://walmartstores.com/Media/Investors/2007_annual_report.pdf.

[171] Unless one counts the returning of stolen money to its original owner as harming the thief who first stole it.

they protest Walmart's being assessed *additional* taxes for no reason. They also likely don't oppose "innocent" homeowners getting government subsidies to stay in the homes they bought but could not afford. And they strongly promote subsidies to farmers and to supposed green businesses, subsidies that constitute a net destruction of wealth and net loss of jobs and lower wages throughout society. These critics think subsidies are ill-advised or unfair if they do not benefit the critics' own favored interest groups, but thoroughly justified if they do. If, instead of pursuing these arbitrary intrusive policies of favoring some industries and not others, we kept government out of the marketplace altogether, nobody would get hurt—and we would all benefit.

Walmart Anti-Unionism

The discussion about unions in Chapter 1 should largely serve as a defense of Walmart's anti-union stance. Because unions are so destructive, because unions feed like leeches, sucking money out of companies, and because unions weaken and often destroy businesses, Walmart's union position should be celebrated, not attacked. For Walmart workers to desire unionization means for them to want to steal from Walmart by reneging on their previous agreement to work for a particular wage, and instead demand a higher wage (which, with government supported force—current laws regarding unions—they would obtain).

Low Wages

It is often asserted that Walmart pays lows wages. This accusation implies that Walmart arbitrarily just picks a low wage it wants to pay and that's that. If this is in fact the case, why wouldn't it pick wage rates that are half of what it is currently paying? Or a quarter? Why would they pay anything at all? In reality, Walmart *has* to pay wages that are market rates for the level of experience and the quality of the workers it hires. If it doesn't pay the market rate, it will not obtain the workers it needs, as other firms will outbid it. And the more Walmart expands, and the more it thus requires workers, the higher the wages it will have to offer in order to compete for the limited amount of qualified workers. Companies are not caretakers of their employees; they are purchasers of the labor services employees are offering.

Walmart employees work at Walmart because they have not found a *better* opportunity, or else they would instead have taken it. They feel that the wage is beneficial for them, or they would not exchange their time and labor for that amount of pay. And they do this voluntarily—they are free to leave at any time. Walmart needs mostly low-skilled laborers for the operations it performs. This means that it is a large employer of low-skilled labor force that would have a hard time finding work other places; Walmart prevents these workers from having *no* job, or lower-paying ones. If the workers wish to become skilled laborers, they can spend their free time in the public libraries on the weekend gaining knowledge (one could obtain the equivalent knowledge of an M.B.A from one's local library). They could also take free government money to go to a college or a university and obtain a degree. These types of accomplishments would earn workers higher wages. Naturally, many Walmart employees learn on the job and move up the ladder as time passes.

And it seems that there are plenty who think the market wage Walmart offers is a pretty good deal. There was overwhelming demand for employment at the new Walmart which recently opened near this author's home. *The Atlanta Journal Constitution* reported that *"In just two days, and with virtually no advertising or even any signs, a staggering 7,500 people filled out applications for one of the 350 to 400 available jobs."* According to *ChicagoBusiness.com,* the turnout was much higher for a store there. It reports that *"The new Walmart Stores Inc. location opening Friday in suburban Evergreen Park received a record 25,000 applications for 325 positions, the highest for any one location in the retailer's history."*[172] As free-market commentator Sean Corrigan pointed out, "thousands demand to be exploited." Walmart's wages are on par with Target and other "big-box" retailers, and are higher than most mom and pop wages. Yet few complain about Walmart's competitors (although Target is beginning to hit the socialist radar screen).

Paul Krugman claims that Walmart puts people out of work because the companies it drives out of business have to lay off employees. Besides the fact that Walmart simply *moves* most of the jobs from

---

[172] Schruti Date Singh, "Walmart gets 25,000 applications for Evergreen Park store," *Chicago Business* (January 25, 2006).

their previous employer to Walmart, this view assumes that what is important is jobs per se. But what brings an improvement in our standard of living is not *having* jobs, but increased productivity in our various jobs, which results in fewer workers needed to produce the same amount. One result of this productivity is that over time most of us have to move to another job. But with more wealth having been created from the same process that causes us to have to switch jobs, average real wages across all jobs become higher. Walmart, with its vast technology, does an outstanding job of increasing productivity. And its ability to progressively produce the same amount with fewer workers ultimately means that more stores can be created which will require *additional* workers (unless unions and leftists get their way).

An area in which Walmart should legitimately be blamed for doing the wrong thing is that of the minimum wage. Beginning in 2005, Walmart actively supported an increase in the minimum wage. It was praised in the media for having such a good social conscience. But its intentions were not good. Walmart paid between $8.23 and $9.68 per hour (Walmart claimed a higher rate of over $10.00) versus the then–minimum wage of $5.15. If the minimum wage increased (which it did), most of Walmart's competitors, being less efficient, would be put at a disadvantage, since they could not as easily afford to pay higher wages and remain as profitable. This was a great way for Walmart to weaken those who threatened it. Companies learned long ago that they could use government power to prevent competition. As Lew Rockwell states:

> This is how child labor legislation, mandated pensions, labor union impositions, health and safety regulations, and the entire panoply of business regimentation came about. It was pushed by big businesses that had already absorbed the costs of these practices into their profit margins so as to burden smaller businesses that did not have these practices. Regulation is thus a violent method of competition.[173]

Absent this regulation, there would be more free market competition, resulting in more jobs and more output that would bring about lower prices and thus higher *real* wages.

---

[173] Llewellyn H. Rockwell, "Walmart Warms to the State," http://mises.org/daily/1950.

Executive Pay far Exceeds Worker Pay

Though this issue has been addressed in various places already, several new points must be made. Walmart CEO Lee Scott (2000-2009) earned millions of dollars, and he deserved it. He brought in *billions* to Walmart owners, who were thus glad to pay him "only" millions. They would like to have paid him less, but CEOs have market prices just like us workers. Scott was the son of a gas station owner in Kansas. He joined Walmart after proving his talents at a small trucking company after college. He worked his way up in the company—all other co-workers had the same opportunity. His arrival in the CEO position means Walmart believed he was the best candidate to steer the company. His success or failure meant Walmart's progress or its demise. If he continued to succeed, the result was the enrichment of shareholders, workers, and all of Walmart's customers. *This* is why he was paid so much more than a check-out clerk .

Society is under the very dangerous impression that companies operate in order to pay wages as charity to employees. Instead, the company exists to produce the service of providing products to millions of people at low prices. It is not a charity. If socialist commentators believe Walmart (and other companies) should pay wages mostly to support the poor, why don't they start their own corporations that do just that? The reason they don't is that they cannot think of a product or service they would produce that 1) will enable their business to grow from a small one to a large one so that millions can be hired, and 2) will be profitable, enabling them to *stay* in business. If they could, and they did start a business, they could not pay higher-than-market wages very long or they would go out of business.[174] I would argue that since socialists abhor profits and do not care if a company incurs losses, they should tolerate their socialist company incurring losses in the name of the poor—they themselves should incur financial losses so that others—the workers—will incur financial gain. But they will not do this. Why? Because they are not willing to lose *their own* wealth in order to pay higher wages—they instead want *others* (businesses' shareholders) to lose theirs.

---

[174] Socialism promoter and U2 frontman, Bono, learned this when he started a clothing line and had to pay himself wages. See Thomas J. Lorenzo and Vedran Vuk, "Bono the Capitalist Exploiter," http://mises.org/daily/2529.

Walmart Sells Cheap Products from Red China

And what of the accusation that Walmart sells cheap things from a communist country? It should first be understood that low-cost does not necessarily mean cheap. Walmart offers most of the same things as do many other stores that don't elicit the same negative attention, but they do so by offering lower prices than other stores can achieve.

I once heard an anti-Walmart accusation that Walmart chose, indiscriminately, not to do business with a particular jeans company, thus causing it to go out of business. Upon researching the matter, I learned the real story. This particular company's jeans were indeed rejected by Walmart because their costs resulted in a price point that was too expensive for Walmart's customers. The jeans company did not, however, go out of business. They went back and found ways to reduce their operating costs in order to lower the cost of manufacturing the jeans, after which Walmart indeed took them on as a supplier. The jeans company CEO later stated that the high quality and low-price threshold Walmart demands has made his company more efficient and competitive, and that he was thankful for that.

As for the fact that many goods come from China, so what? Many of our goods in this country come from China, whether purchased from Walmart or from other stores. There is nothing wrong with this. Trade is a positive thing and benefits every country involved in it (as long as trade is not manipulated by governments with restrictions, tariffs, subsidies, etc., so as to make its costs greater than its benefits). It is to our advantage to buy from China.

The fact that China is officially communist means nothing, because they *act* more capitalistic than communistic. Similarly, the west is supposed to be capitalistic, but we are in reality far from it, and we inch down the spectrum towards the other end where communism lies with every year that passes. We will soon meet China in the middle of that spectrum, and they will likely pass us to become more capitalistic than we are. Actually, since China is clearly advancing economically, since they are creating more capital than is being destroyed or deteriorated, and we are not, they must in fact already be more capitalistic than we are. Engaging in trade with China helps it realize the benefits from trade and from capitalism, and helps slide them up that spectrum towards freedom. From the trade that results, we both become wealthier.

Walmart's Lacking Healthcare Coverage

It is no secret that Walmart does not provide as extensive a healthcare program as do many other companies. For example, *Wake-upwalmart.com*, an anti-Walmart site, states that Walmart's insurance covers only 43 percent of its employees, while the average large company (over 200 people) covers 66 percent of employees. Essentially, from every angle, Walmart's healthcare is lacking.

Once again, the primary mistake is the assumption that Walmart exists in order to take care of its employees. It does not; and if it tried to, it would be out of business and the employees would be on the street. For various reasons, companies have many government incentives to provide healthcare (covering on average 76 percent of healthcare costs) for their employees. Many firms take advantage of the incentives to different degrees. One employer might offer a particular pay and benefits package; another might offer a different one. For whatever reason, Walmart has determined that it can be more competitive by offering less in the area of healthcare (which allows them to hire more workers, among other things). This is their right. It is not a right of employees—of any company—to have others pay their expenses.

More importantly, the complaints against Walmart's not handing out more healthcare money miss the bigger healthcare point. That is that healthcare is such a burden on our lives to begin with, not because of companies, but because of socialized markets, as we saw in Chapter 4. If we had a free market in healthcare, we would not need to make companies and the richer taxpayers pay our bills; healthcare costs would be just another service we would pay reasonable prices for out of our paychecks. We need to place blame at the root of the problem, not at the various ways people or companies *react* to the problems caused by our politicians.

Walmart Is Too Big and Powerful

Walmart's critics are obsessed with the idea of "corporate greed," and they have made Walmart their poster child. When they look at the amount of combined wealth that a large business has in comparison to individuals, they shudder. They believe that Walmart uses this wealth immorally to benefit itself at the expense of the rest of society. They do not realize that Walmart's wealth, or any company's wealth, is either in its operations, through which it is supplying goods and services to consumers and paying wages to employees, or that the wealth has been partially returned to its owners (having been paid out in dividends), most of whom are normal individuals like you and me, and who are spending the money in their communities.

As supposedly big and powerful as Walmart is, it could be broken tomorrow should we Walmart customers learn that there is a better alternative. Kmart started the very same year as Walmart, but has been less successful in providing a quality product at good prices. It therefore shrank, closed stores, went bankrupt, and was eventually acquired by Sears. Woolworth's, one of the largest department stores in the world for most of the last century, failed to compete effectively and went out of business in the U.S.[175] The very same thing can happen to Walmart if it doesn't continue staying ahead of the value curve. Walmart's competitors are trying daily to overtake it; one day they probably will. Even if Walmart were the only discount store, we would have nothing to fear as long as competitors were not prevented by governments from entering the industry. If Walmart's prices rose or if its quality diminished, other firms or private entrepreneurs would enter the industry to take away its revenues. It is competition that keeps Walmart both successful and benign. Regardless of its size, the company has no way of harming us; instead, it is we consumers who could harm it (given relatively free markets in the retail industry).

In other countries, the most successful and popular firms in their industries are often criticized just as Walmart is here. In Greece, for example, a successful retail store called Hondos Center is hated by some for the fact that it drives out competitors and pays low wages. People everywhere mistake the pleasing of consumers and the employment of workers for the manipulation of consumers, sabotaging of competitors, and the exploitation of workers—often intentionally.

---

[175] For all practical purposes.

What's surprising about the "big and powerful" argument is that those who fear Walmart do not instead fear the government. While Walmart has many competitors, the government is a monopoly, and one that has the power to prevent others from competing with it. While Walmart has no ability to use physical force over employees or customers, the government does, and it actively takes advantage of this ability. Walmart can only charge at or below market prices, while the government charges virtually whatever prices it wants to (taxes, fees, inflation, etc.). It physically forces us to pay for what we did not choose to buy (if we fail to pay, police will show up at our door with guns and handcuffs). The government literally steals from us and forces us to do what it wants. The government arbitrarily sets the rules of the game. Yet most in society want the government to "protect" us against companies that cannot harm us in any way, and that have competition biting at their heels, restraining them from charging us too much or paying workers too little. Society chooses monopolies and coercion over competitive markets and freedom.

Survival of the Fittest or Unfittest?

The companies that operate most efficiently and provide the greatest value to their customers are the ones most hated by the leftists (and many rightists, too). They are hated precisely because of the fact that they have grown large—and supposedly powerful—by being successful in bringing to society the highest quality products at the lowest prices. They are hated because a majority of people like what these companies offer them. What is to be hated about this? Nothing! But the socialist critics—including left-wing economists—can't stand to see that capitalism is successful because they simply feel on some emotional level that socialism is somehow the morally right choice.

What the critics of capitalism fail to understand are the true relations of economic cause and effect in free markets and how they result in helping every single group in society, especially the poor. Economic science is complicated and poorly understood by most people. Therefore, when propagandists use (fallacious) economics as a tool to give them the cloak of credibility, most everyday people fall for the propaganda.

As Paul Kirklin writes:[176]

> The...critics' understanding of economics isn't much better than could be expected of a small child. They are incapable of seeing anything except the most direct effects of an action or policy in the short-term. If a child sees something he wants, he takes it, and so do...critics. Never mind if this causes destruction and decline in the long-term for the economic system as a whole and unemployment and impoverishment for those they are allegedly trying to help.

This also leaves wealth-creating executives faced not only with the tough job of running a large company in a very competitive marketplace, but also simultaneously having to fight rear-guard actions against armies of saboteurs and their naïve followers.

The result of the saboteurs' efforts is precisely to bring about the very conditions they are supposedly trying to prevent. The policies they promote to fight unemployment actually *cause* unemployment. The ways they seek to prevent the wage earner from being impoverished lowers wages instead of raising them. The tactics they use to prevent companies from harming society are instead what allow them to do just that.

In sum, only by acting with a correct understanding of what conditions facilitate profitable relations among companies, workers, and society—i.e., by limiting, and preferably eliminating, government intrusions into markets—can we avoid economic stagnation and decline that currently menace us in every sector of the economy. We must understand that corporations are not evil, but instead are the true benefactors of the general public, even if their actions are only self-serving. Their innovation, commitment, and investment in capital and time, have brought us—all of us—the myriad conveniences and pleasures of modern life, and will continue to do so to an even greater extent in the future if we let them. But government regulations and other ill-conceived intrusions into the marketplace have diminished, and risk disabling irreversibly, this marvelous engine of progress.

---

[176] Paul Kirklin, "The Ultimate pro-WalMart Article," http://mises.org/daily/2219#13.

Chapter 6:

When Capitalism Is Taken Away

The last chapter discussed, in part, how the economy functions in direct accordance with consumers' desires: production is based on what consumers signal that they want, as determined by their purchases. These desires are transmitted through prices they pay and the costs and profits associated with those prices. Profits and the price system lead to a smoothly functioning economy where most things desired exist,[177] but shortages don't.

We have also seen that when government intervenes in this system by means such as imposing price controls, mandating production in ways different than would otherwise take place, preventing the ownership of the production processes, preventing money from flowing to or from an industry or country, printing new money (inflation), or heavily taxing production and wealth, the market does not function efficiently. Slight government interventions will result in a little less production of wealth; significant interventions will result in economic stagnation (which is what we're near today); heavy intervention or a complete takeover of the price and production system will result in economic decline and impoverishment.

---

[177] The desired thing exists as long as it's technologically feasible, or as long as there is enough demand for it that it is profitable to make.

This chapter reviews several historical scenarios where different large-scale acts of government intervention in the marketplace led to reductions in economic growth in some instances and outright destruction of the entire economy in others. The first is the Great Depression of the 1930s, the second is the rise and fall of the Roman Empire, and the third is the twentieth century development of communism in selected countries. The chapter will conclude with a comparison of the different levels of economic freedom between various countries, showing that those which are the freest generally have higher standards of living.

The Great Depression: Government's Creation

Most people's impression of what happened during the Great Depression goes something like this: because of greedy businesspeople and investors, and because of the free-market policies of President Hoover (Republican), the stock market crashed and plunged us into a depression resulting in millions of people being unemployed and suffering. It was then that Franklin Delano Roosevelt came along with ingenious policies of social protection, wealth redistribution, and regulation that got us out of the depression. Believing this story is like believing that black is white or that up is down. Let's quickly review the years of the Great Depression, and observe economic cause and effect.

What Created the Onset of the Depression?

As is the case today, it was in fact the government's central bank, not the stock market crash itself, that *started* the economic problems of the 1930s. As we have seen, when the central bank pumps money into the economy, it causes not only inflation, but it ultimately also causes a large-scale misallocation of capital, financial losses among companies, bank losses, and a contraction of the money supply, all of which result in reduced production, bankruptcies, layoffs, and increased unemployment, not to mention stock market booms and busts.

It was precisely this sequence of events that caused not the Great Depression itself, but the initial economic downturn. The U.S. central bank, the Federal Reserve, expanded the money supply by about 60 percent between 1921 and 1929.[178] Official inflation rates were low, primarily due to extraordinary technology-based productivity increases. But the fact that prices rose at all, instead of falling, during this time of high productivity, reveals that *real* inflation (i.e., increases in the money supply) was high. The large amounts of money being inserted into the economy, along with, to a *lesser* degree, gold (real money at the time) flowing in from WWI debtor countries, started a large economic boom that caused this period to be called the "roaring 20s." But when the Fed shut off the money valve and thus reduced its rate of printing money (interest rates rose from 3.5 percent to 6 percent between 1928 and 1929), the boom came to a crashing halt.

The reduction in money supply, which fell by 30 percent over the next three years, caused the economy to collapse and the stock market to fall. Up until that point in our nation's history, the government mostly did not attempt to manage and intervene in response to recessions (some more than others) and most recessions lasted less than two years. The 1930s "depression" too would have been an ordinary recession had the government refrained from intervening. Natural market forces would have corrected the economic imbalances: the price system would have moved labor and capital back to where they were most effective, and losses would have been realized. But the market was not allowed to "clear" (supply and demand stayed misaligned)—as is the case today. Our politicians prevented the free market from working.

The Economy Under Hoover

Once the recession began, Hoover engaged in unprecedented interference in the economy in order to try and "help it." He was rightly accused by his 1932 presidential opponent Franklin Roosevelt of taxing and spending too much, boosting the national debt, choking off trade, putting millions on the dole, and trying to centralize economic turmoil in Washington. Hoover's administration created 30 new government departments and hired 3,000 new bureaucrats.

---

[178] Murray Rothbard, *America's Great Depression* (2000).

John Nance Garner, Roosevelt's running mate, stated that Hoover was "leading the country down the path of socialism."[179]

In 1930, Hoover, ignoring the pleas of many economists, signed the Smoot-Hawley Tariff, virtually preventing foreign goods from entering the country. This act increased tariff rates on various imports by between 20 percent and 60 percent, on average. Production processes that used inputs imported from abroad were thus hit with higher costs, resulting in unemployment. For example, most of the 60,000 employees of plants making cheap clothing from imported wool rags became unemployed after the tariff on wool rags rose by 14 percent.[180] Hoover and Congress thought that by raising trade barriers they would cause more citizens to buy *American* goods, thereby reducing unemployment. But they didn't consider that tariffs, besides raising costs to consumers, would cause unemployment in those sectors making goods to be exported to other countries.

Once foreigners became less able to sell their goods in the American market, they became concomitantly less able to buy American goods. American agriculture was hit the hardest. Thanks to their politicians, farmers immediately lost a third of their market, causing (along with a declining money supply) agricultural prices to plummet and tens of thousands of farmers to go bankrupt. (Keep in mind that during this time, almost 30 percent of the population was involved in farming.)[181]

Losses from farming and other industries caused losses for banks, since their loans were not repaid. Over 9,000 banks went out of business between 1930 and 1933. The stock market, as measured by the Dow Jones, fell by almost 90 percent by summer 1932. It would take 25 years for the market to reach once again its 1929 peak (and 35–40 years when adjusting for inflation).

---

[179] Otto Friedrich, Hays Gorey, and Ruth Mehrtens Galvin, "FDR's Disputed Legacy," *Time* (February 1, 1982).

[180] Lawrence W. Reed, "Great Myths of the Great Depression," http://www.mackinac.org/archives/1998/sp1998-01.pdf. A majority of the information in this section is derived from Reed's paper.

[181] Ibid.

Since falling prices were hurting farmers, the government attempted to raise farm prices by reducing agricultural production. Thus, the government, with public tax money, paid farmers *not* to work, *not to* grow food, and *not* to grow livestock, which also implicitly means it paid them *not* to hire farm workers. Not only were they directed not to produce, they were directed actually to destroy crops and animals. Federal agents sanctioned the plowing under of fields of cotton, wheat, and corn—mules had to be retrained to walk on the crops, since they had previously been trained not to. Healthy sheep, pigs (including six million baby pigs), and cattle were slaughtered and buried in mass graves. While much of the rest of the country was desperate for food, the government was destroying it in order to *attempt* to benefit a single political group. Roosevelt, in his administration, not only continued these policies, but accelerated them.

Some farmers also took matters into their own hands. One farm union, led by a preacher, tried to force all farmers, against their will, not to produce food.[182] To ensure that independent farmers did not increase supply, the farm unions in several midwest states created an embargo that prevented food from being exported from those states— even threatening fellow farmers and the public with guns in enforcing their blockade. The governor of Minnesota went so far as to *assist* the union by offering to use the state militia to prevent innocent citizens from engaging in the trade of crops.

Farmers were also aided by the senate, which directed the FTC to investigate the supposedly too-low export prices being paid to grain farmers.[183] Congress, in doing its part, helped farmers to threaten the meatpacking industry. Farmers had always complained that the meatpackers paid them too little for livestock (while consumers, of course, complained that the meatpackers charged too much at retail). Since meatpackers were not a big voting block, congress, under the pretense of a war emergency, threatened to authorize the president to take over and manage their operations. The meatpackers were eventually forced to curtail many of their (harmless) operations and to

---

[182] Murray Rothbard, *America's Great Depression* (1990).
[183] Ibid.

accept regulation by the Secretary of Agriculture. Thus, farmers were allowed to benefit at the expense of the meatpackers and the public.

With economy-wide consumer prices falling, wages rates needed to fall as well. But Hoover single-handedly came up with the idea to keep wages high.[184] His notion was that high wages bring wealth, although in fact, as we have seen, it's savings and productivity that bring high wages. He thought that by restoring wages to what they had been, he would restore wealth.[185] He thus forced businesses to keep wages high. Shockingly, many business leaders—not just unions—were at first on board with this idea, because they, too, thought it would help the economy, and eventually, the plan became broader and mandatory. But since companies' *revenues* were falling—due to deflation—in order for businesses to be profitable, *costs*, including wages, needed to fall as well. During the period in which consumer prices (business selling prices) fell by 25 percent from 1929 through 1933, wages decreased by only 15 percent. This represented a relative *increase* in wage rates and thus in business costs. The result, obviously, was widespread unemployment. Had wage rates been allowed to fall to the market price, production would still have been profitable for businesses, and they would still have needed the workers—there would still have been a demand for business products either by other businesses or by consumers, who would still have had jobs, and would have kept spending. The only difference in terms of total production, employment, and wages by businesses would have been the *change in prices* of goods and labor (except that a change would have needed to occur in the distribution of labor and production: many people would have needed to *switch* jobs, given that the change in the flow of money from the central bank had caused a change in the demand for consumer goods relative to capital goods industries). The Great Depression wage experiment proved that wage rates are a result of economic environments, not the creator of them.

As often is the case, businesses were all too happy to cozy up to government in cases where they could benefit. Gerard Swope, the

---

[184] Ibid.

[185] The low prices, remember, were brought about by previous government policies of inflation, which naturally ends with deflation.

head of General Electric, called for the cartelization of American business. This regulation, where the Federal Government would "coordinate production and consumption" was welcomed by much of the business world, including the U.S. Chamber of Commerce.[186] Why? Because such (socialist) planning would result in restricting production in order to increase selling prices, an outcome that could not be accomplished without government regulation. In free markets, companies could not achieve a cartel because the various members would ignore cartel rules and increase supply by more than they are supposed to in order to gain extra profits. Plus, there would always be new outside competition.

Because of the widespread unemployment, Hoover dramatically increased government spending on subsidies and relief schemes. The government's share of GNP increased from 16.4 percent to 21.5 percent over a single one-year period between 1930 and 1931. Since farmers had been hurt by Hoover's previous policies, he handed out to them hundreds of millions of dollars paid for by other taxpayers. Billions more were given out to other businesses and individuals suffering from prior government actions.

Similar to the politicians of today, Hoover blamed the crisis on a lack of credit stemming from free-market failures, without identifying exactly what caused that lack of credit.[187] Hoover wanted to loosen bankruptcy laws so as to make lenders, instead of consumers, suffer from the lack of being able to pay debts (just as our politicians today have done with consumer mortgages and credit cards).

As though the previous policies of high tariffs, large subsidies, and a deflationary monetary policy were not enough, congress then passed, and Hoover signed, the Revenue Act of 1932, which resulted in the largest tax increase in peacetime history. This act *doubled* the income tax, raising the normal rate from a range of 1.5–5 percent, to a range of 4–8 percent.[188] The top tax bracket increased to a marginal rate of 63 percent! Additionally, exemptions were lowered, corporate and

---

[186] Murray Rothbard, *America's Great Depression* (1990).

[187] Today, our politicians blame the lack of credit on the housing market bust, without identifying what caused the housing bust (the central bank's printing of money).

[188] Murray Rothbard, *America's Great Depression* (1990).

estate taxes were raised, new gift, gasoline, and automobile taxes were imposed, and even the writing of checks became taxed (just as some in congress today want to tax each and every stock trade). Not only were people made poorer by these tax increases, but their savings, particularly those of the rich, were desperately needed in the private sector in order to produce goods and to pay wages. By 1933, the results of these policies resulted in one quarter of the population being unemployed. Some states saw as much as 40 percent unemployment and some cities reached 80 percent.[189]

The Economy Under Roosevelt

Unlike Hoover, Roosevelt blamed the depression on "unscrupulous money changers," just as our politicians today blame "predatory" lenders for the housing bust and speculators for high oil prices. And like Hoover (or Obama), he placed no blame on the central bank or the previous government policies which had brought about the problems at hand.

FDR won the 1932 election on the promise of a 25 percent reduction in federal spending, a balanced budget, a sound currency based on gold, an end to the "extravagance" of Hoover's farm programs, and the elimination of government from areas that "belonged more appropriately to private enterprise."

But Roosevelt delivered on none of these promises. He used the very same economic manipulation tactics as Hoover, and simply magnified their intensity. As Murray Rothbard stated, Hoover and Roosevelt were ideological twins. Rexford Guy Tugwell, Roosevelt's close advisor and a great admirer of Stalin and socialist central planning, stated that "We didn't admit it at the time, but practically the whole New Deal was extrapolated from programs Hoover started."[190]

During the first year of the New Deal, though government revenues were only $3 billion, Roosevelt proposed spending $10 billion

---

[189] Lawrence W. Reed, (Great Myths of the Great Depression), http://www.mackinac.org/archives/1998/sp1998-01.pdf.

[190] Paul Johnson, *A History of the American People* (1997), p. 740.

(equivalent to $16 trillion today). Federal expenditures would rise 83 percent in the three years between 1933 and 1936.[191]

As is the case with our crisis today, banking regulation in the 1920s not only caused the Great Depression, but made it worse. Almost all of the banks that went under during the Great Depression were those in states with unit banking laws—i.e., laws prohibiting branch banking that allows banks to diversify their assets and reduce their risks.[192] Canada, which allowed unit banking, had not one bank failure, while in the U.S., 9,000 banks failed.[193] Further, Canada did not have a central bank "saving the economy" during the worst part of the Great Depression.[194]

Roosevelt, who promised during his elections to take care of the nation's money, instead stole it. Upon being given the power by congress, he seized citizens' private gold holdings, taking away the only *real* money citizens had, forcing them to hold only paper bills instead. After doing this, Roosevelt devalued the dollar by 40 percent, causing citizens to lose 40 percent of their wealth in global terms. It was one morning over breakfast that Roosevelt decided to change the ratio between gold and paper bills, arbitrarily settling on a 21-cent price hike, because it was a lucky number.[195] When Roosevelt ultimately made holding gold illegal, he caused the government to renege on its previous promise to convert citizens' paper bills to actual gold and silver—into real wealth.

The largest of the many New Deal government agencies was the Works Progress Administration (WPA), which employed millions of Americans to build highways, bridges, public buildings, canals, dams, and sidewalks, as well as to engage in artistic projects such as the production of paintings, theatrical and musical performances (about 4,000 a month). In contrast to most of these other government

---

[191] Lawrence W. Reed, (Great Myths of the Great Depression), http://www.mackinac. org/archives/1998/sp1998-01.pdf.

[192] Jim Powell, *FDR's Folly: How Roosevelt and His New Deal Prolonged the Great Depression* (New York: Crown Forum, 2003), p. 32.

[193] Ibid.

[194] David Beckworth, "What many of the Great Depression Comparisons Miss," http:// macromarketmusings.blogspot.com/2008/03/what-many-of-great-depression.html.

[195] Lawrence W. Reed, (Great Myths of the Great Depression), http://www.mackinac. org/archives/1998/sp1998-01.pdf.

works projects, it could be argued that infrastructure projects truly contributed to economic growth and did have economic value. But most of the construction did not consist of work that directly benefited the production of goods and services. The myriad projects such as bridges, canals, and roads that were seldom or never used were a complete waste, not only of funds that paid workers' wages, but also of physical resources that could have been used elsewhere to produce goods consumers needed more urgently.

Similarly, even those projects that were conducive to economic growth still mostly resulted in a decreased standard of living. This is because the labor, materials, and machines employed, for example, to pave a road, could instead have been used to produce household goods or other capital goods. The real importance and the need of one type of investment (such as highways) relative to another type (such as bread and sugar) can be determined only by consumers and businesses through the price system. It is highly likely that had government allowed a free market, suffering consumers would have first chosen to have more food and clothing during the decade of the 1930s, and settled for postponing new sidewalks and public buildings until more immediate needs were satisfied.

Perhaps the most dramatic regulation enacted under Roosevelt was the totalitarian-style National Industrial Recovery Act (NRA). Passed in 1933, the NRA suddenly forced most manufacturing industries into government-mandated cartels—and forced businesses to finance them with newly assessed taxes (throwing yet more workers on the street). The mammoth bureaucracy created under the act was given unprecedented powers that would have made Italian dictator Benito Mussolini proud. General Hugh "Iron Pants" Johnson, who ran the NRA, and who was an admirer of Mussolini, proclaimed: "May Almighty God have mercy on anyone who attempts to interfere" with his agency.[196] And he personally threatened to publicly boycott or "punch in the nose" anyone who refused to comply with the NRA.

The NRA developed more than 500 codes that regulated prices and terms of sale of individual products, transforming American

---

[196] Lawrence W. Reed, (Great Myths of the Great Depression), http://www.mackinac. org/archives/1998/sp1998-01.pdf.

industry into a fascist operation. The codes, which spanned a slew of manufacturing categories, covered more than 2 million employers and 22 million workers. As Lawrence W. Reed states:

> There were codes for the production of hair tonic, dog leashes, and even musical comedies. A New Jersey tailor named Jack Magid was arrested and sent to jail for the "crime" of pressing a suit of clothes for 35 cents rather than the NRA-inspired "Tailor's Code" of 40 cents.

The NRA had its own enforcement police who would enter factories, send out the owner and confiscate their books, and line up the employees to interrogate them. These enforcers would storm through the clothing district at night knocking down doors with axes to look for those who were committing the terrible crime of sewing clothes. For such NRA accomplishments as these, *Time* Magazine named Hugh Johnson the New Dealer Man of the Year in 1933.[197]

In the five months prior to the act's passage, the economy was finally showing some signs of recovery, with factory payrolls having increased by 35 percent and employment by 23 percent. But six months after the implementation of NRA rules that raised business costs, taxed production, limited the hours worked, and raised wage rates, industrial production fell by 25 percent. The Supreme Court judged the NRA unconstitutional in 1935.

Not only did Roosevelt raise minimum wage laws that threw an estimated 500,000 blacks out of work,[198] but he further increased taxes, insuring that fewer jobs would be created, and likely more destroyed. Naturally, like politicians today, he increased taxes on the evil rich, and introduced a five-percent withholding tax on corporate dividends. After several rounds of tax hikes, he eventually achieved a top marginal tax rate of 90 percent.[199] He was accused by Senator Arthur Vandenberg of Michigan of doing what virtually every politician does today, namely, following the socialist notion that America

---

[197] "Person of the Year: Hugh S. Johnson," *Time Magazine* (January 1, 1934).

[198] Lawrence W. Reed, (Great Myths of the Great Depression), http://www.mackinac.org/archives/1998/sp1998-01.pdf.

[199] Brookings Institution Tax Policy Institute, Historical Top Tax Rates, http://www.tax-policycenter.org/taxfacts/displayafact.cfm?Docid=213.

could "lift the lower one-third up" by pulling "the upper two-thirds down"[200] (today, however, we try to lift the bottom nine-tenths up by pulling the top one-tenth down). In 1941, he even attempted to have a 99.5 percent marginal tax rate imposed on incomes over $100,000. When an advisor asked him why, Roosevelt replied, "Why Not?" He also issued an executive order to tax all income over $25,000 at 100 percent—to take every bit of income anyone earned that was in excess of $25,000! Soon after, congress rescinded the order.

Dramatic legislation supposedly intended to aid workers directly was also passed during the depths of the depression. For example, the Wagner Act in 1935 removed labor disputes from courts and placed them under the National Labor Relations Board, which was full of union sympathizers who distorted the law and shunned equality under the law. Most employer resistance to labor unions was crushed. Anything businesses did to defend themselves against unions that were destroying them was deemed to be an "unfair labor practice" punishable by the board. The NLRB ultimately made it illegal to resist the demands of labor union leaders, leaving businesses forced to "negotiate" with them. Naturally, with these kinds of laws, union membership more than doubled, and boycotts, strikes, seizures of plants, and violence increased strongly, causing sharp reductions in productivity and sharp increases in unemployment. Due to union coercion, wages increased by 14 percent in 1937 alone, meaning that fewer people could be employed.

Roosevelt, in being anti-business, was then necessarily anti-economy, and therefore anti-prosperity. He blamed businesses for blocking the recovery and for not hiring and not producing, even though it was he and congress—unbeknownst to them—that were responsible for the continued depression. Instead of freeing the economy and allowing business to be more profitable, Roosevelt punished businesses further, therefore also punishing workers and consumers. He imposed new restrictions on the stock market and assessed a new tax on corporate retained earnings (profits not paid out as dividends). He increased the capital gains tax from 12.5 percent in 1933 to 39 percent in 1937.[201]

---

[200] C. David Tompkins, *Senator Arthur H. Vandenberg: The Evolution of a Modern Republican, 1884-1945* (1970), p. 157.

[201] Citizens for Tax Justice, Historical Tax Rates, http://www.huppi.com/kangaroo/TaxTimeline.htm.

He tried his best to extract all possible wealth from investors responsible for providing capital for companies to operate with. The result was a depletion of capital, and investors who were too scared, for fear of confiscation, to fund business operations.

While very modest economic improvement had been occurring in the mid 1930s, these additional anti-business policies, along with a sudden reduction of a previously high pace of money creation, caused a second round of economic suffering. From spring 1937 to spring 1938, the stock market fell by almost 50 percent. Unemployment, at 17 percent in 1936, rose to almost 20 percent in 1938. Bad economic policies generated a recession within a recession.

Overall, the economy did not improve until World War II came along. For on the eve of the war in 1939, GNP per capita was lower than in 1929. Similarly, unemployment, which was 3.2 percent in 1929, was still over 17 percent in 1939.

But contrary to popular opinion, it was not the economic stimulus of the war which improved the economy, as production of bombs and tanks—instead of bread and houses—make an economy weaker, not stronger. As **Figure 6.1** reveals, unemployment declined because the value of what workers could produce was no longer below the cost of employing those workers (there was increasingly less payment of wage rates above and beyond the value of what businesses were getting in return for those wage rates). Wage rates became more profitable primarily because of the wage and price controls government instituted at the start of the war. The wage controls prevented wage rates from increasing, while high inflation rates raised business selling prices.[202] The mix of price controls and inflation is not, however, a productive way to have full employment: citizens were still relatively impoverished during WWII because they earned wages, but had few goods available to purchase. The unemployment rate also improved from the fact that we sent 16 million of our youngest and least skilled workers off to war, thus reducing the number of those out of work.

---

[202] An insight obtained from Reisman.

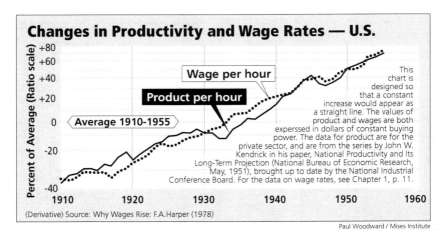

Figure 6.1: Why wages rise

As is usually the case with government spending and government "help," the actions taken during the Great Depression were based more on politics than on truly helping those in need. Economists Couch and Shughart, upon statistically analyzing New Deal government spending, concluded that "The weight of this evidence thus points to a political explanation for New Deal spending patterns: other things being the same, more federal aid was allocated to states which had supported FDR most solidly in 1932 and which were crucial to the president's 1936 Electoral College strategy."[203] They also assert that the more economically devastated south, which was already mostly democratic, received disproportionately little new deal spending since it did not need to be encouraged to vote for Roosevelt.

New Deal money intended for economic aid was misused in many areas in order to win votes. Republican government workers in Kentucky were told that they would have to change their party affiliation if they wanted to keep their jobs, as were Pennsylvania WPA workers, many of whom were fired for refusing. Tennessee WPA workers were instructed to contribute 2 percent of their salaries to the Democratic Party as a condition of receiving their wages. In Cook county Illinois, 450 men were directed by the WPA to

---

[203] Jim F. Couch and William F. Shughart II, *The Political Economy of the New Deal* (1998).

canvass for Democratic votes in 1938. The men were all laid off the day after the election.[204]

The Roman Empire: From Economic Triumph to Economic Disintegration[205]

In the earlier and middle stages of the Roman Republic and Roman Empire, from about 600 B.C. to 200 A.D., the period in which continuous economic development occurred, there was little political or social (for many) freedom. But rulers, such as Augustus and Tiberius, did encourage economic freedom, as they favored private enterprise, private property, free trade, and reduced burdens of taxation. Importantly, during the first century B.C., the significant reduction in wars led to increased trade and commerce. With only a modest custom duty of 5 percent, there was mostly free trade throughout the empire. Thus, there existed a high degree of economic prosperity, which was enabled by the freedom of individuals to produce and exchange as they saw fit.[206]

Taxes were modest in the earliest days of the Republic; they were applied to all forms of personal wealth at a rate of .01 percent ($^1/_{100}$ of a percent), but periodically rose to .03 percent to pay for wars. Taxes first came about largely due to an expansion of social welfare in the form of free grains (and during some periods, free oil, pork, wine, salt, and in Constantinople, even houses) which were formally paid for solely by the emperor. Like today, politicians bought the public's goodwill by giving them free things by taking them from others. One politician, Claudius, ran for tribune on a free-wheat platform.[207] The more the dole was expanded, the more of an influx of people there was into Rome to receive such subsidies.

---

[204] Thomas J. DiLorenzo, "The Truth about the Great Depression" (lecture), http://mises.org/multimedia/mp3/DiLorenzo/DiLorenzo-9.mp3.

[205] A majority of this section on the Roman Empire was take from: 1) Bruce Bartlett, "How Excessive Government Killed Ancient Rome," http://www.cato.org/pubs/journal/cjv14n2-7.html; 2) Michel Rostovzeff, *The Social and Economic History of the Roman Empire* (1926); and 3) Ludwig von Mises, *Human Action* (1963).

[206] Except in Egypt, which remained largely government-controlled.

[207] Henry Hazlitt, *The Conquest of Poverty* (1973).

But taxes eventually rose along with the expansion of the empire. In the first century B.C., under Augustus, the wealth tax reached one percent, and a poll tax was implemented. The flat tax, unlike the previous tax system where individual tax collectors colluded with the state to extract as much wealth from high-income individuals as possible, gave greater incentives to individuals to produce, since it was less progressive.

Rome's pro-growth policies of moderate taxes, a stable currency (lack of inflation), and a common market (the entire Mediterranean), are shown by empirical historical research to have had a positive effect on trade, namely that of the sharp increase in the number of shipwrecks during the time of the late republic and early Empire.[208] The assumption, of course, is that an increase in shipwrecks arose from an increase in shipping. Social and economic historian Michael Rostovtzeff asserted that both foreign and regional trade were the primary sources of wealth in the Roman Empire.[209] There were many other indices of prosperity as well: it has been estimated that money supply grew in line with production, pointing to a lack of inflation; an array of technologies such as heated pools and concrete were invented; large, magnificent buildings and homes were built; government revenues were very abundant, and the state took on many massive infrastructure projects (including roads, bridges, and water and sewage systems) that facilitated trade. Prosperity was increasing and the world had never before seen such a high standard of living (for those who were not slaves).

Once the empire stopped expanding in the second century, there were no new sources of tax revenue, and the imperial functions had to be funded completely internally. The demand for government revenue soon began to undermine the growth of the Roman economy. As the growing government bureaucracy and increasing costs of the army stretched the government coffers, emperors, beginning with Nero, resorted to debasing the currency (diluting or diminishing the amount of real gold and silver in each coin so as to pocket

---

[208] K. Hopkins, "Taxes and Trade in the Roman Empire (200 B.C-AD. 400)," *Journal of Roman Studies 70* (1980), 101-25.

[209] Michael Ivanovich Rostovtzeff, *The Social and Economic History of the Roman Empire* (1926), p. 172.

the difference by creating more coins with the stolen wealth). Various emperors debased their coins by anywhere from 15 percent to 95 percent. Inflation therefore began to appear.

The devaluation of the currency, however, did not help the government finances in the long run because citizens, in trying to prevent the government from stealing their wealth, hoarded the older, more valuable coins, and paid taxes with the less valuable ones. The more the government inflated, the greater was its demand for revenues, but the fewer taxes it collected relative to the rising prices. Thus, the emperors resorted to trumped-up charges to confiscate the property of the wealthy. They would also invent excuses for tax donations, such as the accession of a new emperor or a military victory. The wealthy bore the brunt of the tax increases, which later included taxes on inheritance and the freeing of slaves. Some less immoral leaders, such as Pertinax (193 A.D.) reduced taxes. He stated "that he was better satisfied to administer a poor republic with innocence, than to acquire riches by the ways of tyranny and dishonor."[210]

But most emperors continued to confiscate or drive away private wealth. This policy resulted in economic growth slowing to a standstill. And when the wealthy were no longer able to support the state, the state turned to the middle and lower classes. As Rostovtzeff states: "The heavier the pressure of the state on the upper classes, the more intolerable became the condition of the lower."[211]

In the third century A.D., due to high inflation and taxation, the money economy finally collapsed. But funds were still needed for the army to fight off invaders, and, additionally, to keep the emperor in power. Thus, the army needed to be maintained at all costs, even to the detriment of the people. Without a money economy, the government began taxing citizens by physically taking their wealth (which, technically, is no different from taxes): they would confiscate food, cattle, and other items produced by citizens.

---

[210] Bruce Bartlett, "How Excessive Government Killed Ancient Rome," http://www.cato.org/pubs/journal/cjv14n2-7.html.

[211] Michael Ivanovich Rostovtzeff, *The Social and Economic History of the Roman Empire* (1926), p. 430.

The result was complete physical control of the population by the imperial government. Workers were forced to remain working and producing in their particular place of employment. As under communism, farmers and their descendents were required by the government to remain farmers, and even soldiers and their children were forced to remain soldiers. The rich were forced to work for the government, and anyone who acquired wealth hid it and acted and appeared as poor as possible.

The early centuries of the Roman Empire saw such an advanced state of economic achievement that there was a complete division of labor. In this state, citizens became wealthier by focusing their production on what they were best at, trading with others for what they needed. They forewent the attempt to be self-sufficient. Those in the cities produced various goods, and traded their production for agricultural products and raw materials from the countryside. More and more citizens moved into Rome to work in industries in the city. All regions were inter-dependent—i.e., the state in which prosperity is achieved.

But in the later part of the empire, from the late 200s until the late 400s A.D., the encroachment of the state and the breakdown of the economy led to increased feudalization and an erosion of the division of labor. Since trade was deteriorating due to a barter economy in which it's difficult to exchange one's particular production for that of another (there is no medium of exchange in the form of money), people fled to the country to take up subsistence farming.

By the end of the third century, Rome was no longer able to obtain the physical wealth needed to support the army and other government "services," and resorted to more intense debasement of the currency to bring in revenues, bringing inflation rates to 15,000 percent. Since the very existence of the state was threatened, Diocletian (284-305 A.D.) attempted to solve the previous government-created problems at hand with yet more government intervention. Believing, as do politicians today, that economic crises are caused by citizens (including companies) instead of by the government itself, he imposed price controls on many goods and services. These were, as always, a failure, even though the penalty for buying and selling at the real market price was death. Some price controls were repealed after prices continued to rise even though many citizens had been murdered by the state for the crime of exchanging goods. But price controls on grains and other staples remained, as it was deemed immoral to ask more than customary prices for these important goods, and officials, like today, were quick to punish those who were seen as profiteering. The result was an inefficient wholesale trade in these commodities that led to effective nationalization. The government set the price too low, making it unprofitable to produce these important staples; thus shortages remained permanent.

Workers and businesses were eventually organized into organizations controlled by the state, wherein the government directed production of the economy—unsuccessfully. Individuals then began abandoning the land they were working on and fleeing the city. Industry moved to the country, leaving Rome an empty economic shell that produced nothing. The government also provided nothing for its people but still demanded their wealth for the sake of giving it to others.

Later emperors such as Julian (361-63 A.D.) and Valens (364-78 A.D.) continued debasing the currency and imposing price controls. With prices rising but selling prices kept artificially low, production was paralyzed. The masses could not obtain food and other needed products. Commerce in grain and other necessities ceased.

Within fifty years after Diocletian, taxes approximately doubled, making it impossible for farmers to live on their production. This led to the final breakdown of the economy. The number of tax recipients exceeded the number of taxpayers. With so much of the farmers' land and resources taken to pay taxes, they too abandoned their land, leaving it to become forest. Still, tax rates kept rising even though tax revenues continued to fall, as burdened citizens became more adept at evading taxes, eventually withdrawing from society all together.

Large, powerful landowners, who were able to both legally and illegally (bribery) avoid taxes organized around themselves small, private, communities, or villae. Small landowners, bankrupted by taxes, when lucky, were able to offer themselves as tenants or slaves (who paid no taxes) in order to have access to food. The turning of one's self into a slave was so widespread and so harmful to the state's revenue

Source: Pictures from the Mercati e Foro di Traiano museum, Rome, Italy

Figure 6.2: Rome both in her glory days and after her fall.

collection that in 386 A.D. Emperor Valens declared it illegal to give up liberty to become a slave.

At the end of the empire, there was no trade, no construction, no building of anything. There was only subsistence farming. There was also no money left with which to pay the army. Because of declining funding, the empire had been shrinking for 200 years.

Though the Roman state had defended itself from invaders for centuries, its ability to do so was reduced as time passed and the empire lost economic strength. The invaders had not become stronger; the empire had become weaker. Though the fall of the empire is a major event in the history books, it was rather anti-climactic at the time, as the way of life of most Romans had already been reduced to nothingness. In fact, many citizens welcomed the barbarians because they removed the source of oppressive taxation. There was nothing for the barbarians to steal or to control—all wealth and civilization was already destroyed. **Figure 6.2** gives an idea of Rome's development during the existence of capitalism and then after.

Both the Great Depression and the decline of the Roman Empire were results of the state's intervening in the private marketplace and its seeking of power and control. But for the most part, in both cases, individual citizens had no way of knowing that their problems were caused by the very entity they relied on to solve their problems. Most people don't understand that if there is a lack of production of goods or a lack of increasing real wages it is because government is preventing progress by taxing, regulating, or otherwise confiscating capital.

Most people do not see that if there are some people (or many) unemployed, even though there is always more work to be done than there are people to do it, it can only be that something is preventing workers from being hired. And as is the case currently, citizens don't see that the economy and the financial system cannot just collapse on their own, but that the collapse is the result of government manipulation of the marketplace.

As should be understood from these historical examples, government's intervention on behalf of those supposedly underprivileged or exploited workers and consumers results in diminishing, not enhancing, the standard of living of these groups. This will be even clearer in the following section on communism.

Communism: Equality at Its Finest

The driving force of the desire for and implementation of communism is capitalism's supposed immorality, its supposed exploitation of workers, and its inequality. As we have seen, the accusation of exploitation is diametrically opposite to reality. Morality will be discussed in the following chapter, but for the time being, as you read, be thinking about which *outcomes* and *means to achieving particular outcomes* are moral and which are immoral.

Inequality, specifically, is probably the primary objection people have to capitalism (and indeed, under true capitalism, there is inequality). Therefore, as you absorb the following information, also consider what is better: 1) rising standards of living for *everyone*, even though some become much wealthier than others, or 2) equality for all, but at a true subsistence level of existence. And remember that anything in between the two (i.e., the "third way," or, capitalism that's "managed" or "tamed" by government) results mostly in a static economic state.

For clarity of perspective, keep in mind that communism is in fact socialism's most extreme form—it is in fact socialism. Socialism, in the formal sense, is a state where government *fully controls* the means of production (factories, shops, machines, etc.). This can be done directly or indirectly. For example, the Nazis, who most associate with the extreme right, were in fact socialists: NAZI stood for *Nationalsozialistische Deutsche Arbeiterpartei,* or the *National Socialist German Worker Party.*

The Nazis controlled every aspect of the German economy. Though businesses were privately owned, it was in name only, since business-people produced exactly what the state directed. The movie *Schindler's List* offers a good depiction of this arrangement. It should also be noted that the Nazis had an elaborate program of wealth redistribution which included the abolition of all "unearned income," "the nationalization of all trusts [large companies]," and land expropriation without compensa-tion.[212] Thus, even far right dictators are also socialists when they control a nation's economy, which is the case most of the time.

Throughout this book, I label those who promote even limited socialism as socialists because they in fact want *some* government control of the economy, and because *some* always inevitably leads to *more* and *more*. This is not only due to the continued existence of the "moral" reasons for which the initial few social policies were initiated, but also because their effects always lead to more economic problems which must be addressed, and which are almost always addressed with yet more government control of the economy (in other words, as time progresses, there's no such thing as only a *little* socialism), as is the case in the U.S. today. It should not be forgotten that government control, under socialism, is always for the supposed benefit of society as a whole, thus the name *social*-ism. Communism is simply the full and complete state of socialism, wherein government controls every aspect of the economy by claiming ownership over every part of it in the name of making society better off by ridding it of the immorality and inequities of capitalism.

Socialists Can't Calculate

There are two fundamental problems with communism. The first has to do with the lack of incentives; since no individual can per-sonally benefit from inventing, creating, building or doing in any way anything above and beyond what is ordered, there is no incentive for them to do so. People therefore don't take the risks necessary to offer new products or create new companies, not only because they are not allowed, but because even if they were, they could not increase their own standard of living in doing so. The second problem with

---

[212] David Gordon, "Nazi Economic Policy," http://mises.org/daily/3274.

communism is that, since there is no price and profit system, no one knows exactly what or how much to produce. They also don't know whether they are creating or destroying wealth in the process. Without a market and associated market prices driven by consumer spending, they can't calculate profits and losses, which are the sole means of determining what and how much should be produced. In free markets, by contrast, production is always in accordance with consumers' wishes; businesses and consumers have their interests aligned.

Additionally, in a free market, it is millions of individuals interpreting the signals given by prices and profits, and using this information to take their own initiative to act in a way that is best for themselves. These millions of individuals then engage with others, to design, produce, market, distribute, trade, and sell the resources they have at their disposal.

Under communism, in contrast, a group of men sit around a table and attempt to coordinate an economy consisting of millions of individuals, machines, and tools, tens of thousands of mines, farms, factories, transportation equipment, warehouses, and stores. Under capitalism, those who specialize in particular trades or intimately deal with particular resources or pieces of equipment best know the subject matter in which they engage. They are, therefore, more than anyone else, experts at deciding how much of each input should be used, which particular combination of limited resources should be used, where new products or services are most needed, and what means are best for achieving particular goals. There is no way that a group of planners—even at an industry level—can issue mandates for businesses and individuals to follow which result in greater efficiency and effectiveness at producing goods and services than can millions of individuals working independently (yet together as a whole) through the guiding direction of free market signals.

Consider, as just one example of millions of goods, the production of sofas. They can be produced in various styles, with various materials; by hand or by machine or a combination of both. They can be produced in the mountains, by the sea, in warm or cold places. There can be a few or many, given that everyone already has a sofa. How many will need to be produced for replacement purposes or for additional rooms in homes? How will these different production considerations be resolved?

These questions are important because the answers will affect the rest of the economy. If the couch is made of leather, how much leather should be used to make couches versus making shoes, car seats, purses, belts, or baseball gloves? Should the sofa frame be made of wood or metal? If wood should be used, how will the wood that is taken to produce couches affect the amount available to produce desks, chairs, houses, and book shelves? If the sofa cushions are stuffed with foam, how much foam should be allocated to sofa cushions versus beds and pillows? And would it be more efficient to use the petroleum that goes into producing the foam in the production of gasoline, natural gas, lubricants, wax, asphalt, or other chemicals instead? What is the most efficient mix of the use of these scarce resources? How can a small group of economic planners not only determine how much of which resource should be used where, but whether or not the result of the millions of different combinations of these groups of resources in the various places across the thousands of cities, thousands of companies, hundreds of industries, and in millions of products will result in increased wealth and not a net waste of resources? How can a small group of people contain the knowledge, insight, and skills equal to that of millions of individuals and orchestrate a comparable outcome as those thinking for themselves? They can't.

Communism Results in Suffering

In fact, no communist regime has been successful at coordinating production to a level that results in even a subsistence standard of living. Communist countries survived only because they received help from capitalistic countries in the form of donations of food and the building of factories. Before Russia became communist, it was a large exporter of wheat, rye, barley, and oats. Under communism it could not grow enough of these items to feed its people, eventually becoming the largest importer of grain, as the United States and other countries either donated grain or guaranteed the loans that enabled grain to be imported from other countries. Similarly, the U.S. and its allies are keeping North Korea communist today by continually sending them food and other aid, without which they would implode. Aid to the Soviet Union took place only after government leaders finally agreed to the imports; under Lenin, the intellectuals that arranged for foreign aid were arrested and sent to death on Lenin's orders.[213]

There were several periods of starvation in Soviet Russia simply because the lack of profits and incentives led to the lack of food production. As one example, after communism first took hold in Russia, Lenin assured peasants that they owned their own land, but they were forced to sell their production to the state for ultra-low prices. When they refused to sell for such low prices, the state eventually took their production by force—including seed grain needed to prepare the next year's crops. The result was widespread famine where more than 7 million eventually starved to death, and millions more died in concentration camps in Siberia—punishment for complaining about such acts of oppression.[214]

Communist China under Mao and his "Great Leap Forward" was no better. Mao also expropriated farms, a process begun by shooting the richer peasants who were accused of exploiting the poorer ones. When the once fruitful lands could not achieve enough production under government control to feed the population, widespread famine took hold. Starvation was so tortuous that families swapped children in order to eat them.[215] Eventually tens of millions of Chinese starved to death, and tens of millions were either executed or held in concentration camps. This is why, for example, my good Chinese friend Maurice says he's shorter and smaller: because he was malnourished at the time he was growing up in a land lacking food. The suffering ended only as the Chinese government allowed freer markets to exist beginning in the 1970s; the freer the markets became, the more food and consumer goods Chinese citizens produced and consumed.

---

[213] At least in the specific case referenced, they were offered the reprieve of being exiled. See Stéphane Courtois, Nicolas Werth, Jean-Louis Panné, Andrzej Paczkowski, Karel Bartosek, Jean-Louis Margolin, Stephane Courtois, Mark Kramer, with Jonathan Murphy (Translator), *The Black Book of Communism: Crimes, Terror, Repression* (1999).

[214] Bryan Caplan, "The Museum of Capitalism FAQ," http://www.gmu.edu/departments/economics/bcaplan/museum/faqframe.htm.

[215] Llewellyn H. Rockwell, "The Death Camp of Communist China," http://mises.org/daily/2652.

The lack of private property, incentives, and profits results in chaos. The Soviet Union claimed to be building plants and factories for decades, yet never achieved a wide-scale production of consumer goods. Grocery store shelves were usually mostly empty (as exemplified in **Figure 6.3**), and people had to wait in long lines just to obtain basic necessities, of which there was only a limited supply often accessible only by using "ration cards." People often had to wait ten years to obtain a telephone, and once they got it, it often never worked, as was also the case with electricity.

The inability to coordinate production resulted in tooth brushes without bristles, machinery without replacement parts, and buildings without window panes. Scientists often had to make their own tools because they could not rely on their being available. Because of the unreliability of suppliers, most *factories* attempted to be self-sufficient, thus failing to integrate into a division of labor and making the economy less efficient and poorer.

In 2007, it was reported that a Polish man woke up from a 19-year coma surprised to see how much better life had become under freer markets.[216] He stated that "the world is prettier now" and that he was shocked to see the vibrant streets and the shops in the town. He remembered shelves filled only with mustard and vinegar.

Upon a visit to Warsaw in 1996, while sitting at a warm café sipping tea, I was told by a local couple I was visiting with that such a thing was a new experience for them. Under communism restaurants and cafes as they have today did not exist—only several dingy government-run restaurants. Further, they said, most people did not go out much at night because it was dark due to a lack of street lights, and because there was nowhere to go and nothing to do.

Life under communism is dull and grey because no one is trying to figure out how to please others. The lack of the ability to get rich from using private property and capital to fulfill the desires of consumers who want to improve their lives results in the absence of most things people would like to have. *Socialism is not an actual economic*

---

[216] Associated Press, "Polish man emerges from 19-year coma," *USA Today* (June 3, 2007).

Figure 6.3: A picture from Soviet Russia showing a meat store with little meat available.

system of any sort that encompasses a plan to produce and create; it's simply the abolition of individuals working and acting in their best interest. It results in an outcome that is therefore *contrary* to what individuals would desire in order to improve their lives. Similarly, in my view, capitalism is not a "system" (or ideology) per se; it has no design or *formal* organization. Capitalism is simply what occurs if all people are left free to live life the way they choose (harming others being prohibited). Though capitalism does not entail planning in terms of designing its operations, it fully consists, effectively, of planning every moment of the day. Individuals plan how they can better their lives by pleasing others. And they are usually successful at it, because if they fail, they suffer losses.

Social and Economic Restrictions Under Socialism

Under full socialism, the state declares all property its own. Its property can be used only as the state specifically directs, and for nothing more. Therefore, citizens of a communist country end up being complete slaves to the state. They are not allowed to travel beyond certain regions or to move to cities they choose. They are prevented from farming or selling for their own profit. In the U.S.S.R., the penalty for renting out a room in your home for profit was to have one's home taken away. A *New York Times* magazine article recently touched on this point in regards to Cuba. The writer was documenting her trip with her mother and aunt to Cuba to visit her mother's childhood friend. The friend's neighbors had reported her for having houseguests, suspecting that she was renting rooms to tourists. Eventually the writer and her family, after waiting for hours in a government office, had to pay $200 to the government to stay at their friend's home! After the writer expressed frustration at having to pay such a cost, her mother's friend stated in all seriousness to her and her family that if they did not pay, she would "hang."[217]

Even those who did nothing "wrong" were not safe from state punishment under communism. When the Soviet Union made a half-hearted attempt at private ownership in the 1980s, government bureaucrats simply found a new way to extract money from citizens; for as soon as someone started a business, they would be shut down until bribes were paid to the local party members.[218] A person who was head of a large manufacturing business had one enemy in the government who accused him of accounting dishonesty. Instead of paying a bribe to settle the matter, the man proclaimed his innocence. Therefore, he soon found a team of government accountants who pored over his books for weeks until they found a very minor and accidental mistake. For this he was threatened with eight years in prison until he decided to pay off the prosecutors, judge, and bureaucrats. The judge still gave him a one-year suspended sentence.[219]

Another young man who heard that market activity was legal raised a pig, hoping to sell it for a profit. After months of carefully growing the pig, he took it to market where the health inspector immediately chopped off a third of the pig claiming that he was

---

[217] Rachel Kushner, "The Cuban Way," *The New York Times Magazine* (October 19, 2008), p. 70. It was not known exactly what "hang" meant in this context. It must be noted that the Cubans are not as well known for murders of individual citizens.

[218] As explained by Yuri N. Maltsev, "The Decline and Fall of Gorbachev and the Soviet State," http://mises.org/daily/3105. This phenomenon is also common in third-world countries that are much less economically free.

[219] Ibid.

looking for worms. Then the police came and took the best pieces for themselves, without even a thank you. He then had to a pay a bribe to the market officials in order to receive a space in which to sell what was left of the pig. By the end of the day, he earned only enough to buy the bottle of Vodka with which he needed to drown his sorrows.[220]

Just like our half-socialist governments in the west, communist governments take additional wealth from their citizens through inflation.[221] Communist leaders then respond to price rises in the same way as do our leaders: with price controls. But price controls lead to unprofitable production, which leads to a need on the part of citizens to evade the price controls. Thus, black markets develop. The government responds with harsh penalties for selling at these true market prices, instead of the artificial government-dictated prices. This leads to government spies, who cause the black market to become even more secretive. Thus, officials begin to rely on the citizens to become informers, and to rat out those selling or producing illegally (like the neighbor in Cuba above). But since it is difficult for people to convict their fellow citizens and send them to jail for several years for selling shirts or potatoes above a certain price, the government instead relies on tribunals consisting of government officials.[222] Since the state owns everything, anyone who does act in a way that is not in accordance with what is dictated by the state is accused of "stealing from the state" or sabotaging the national plan. Punishment can range from several years in prison, to exile, to slave labor in Siberia, to firing squads.

Rule by Terror

Knowing that citizens are outraged at the way they are handled like animals, the state keeps its citizens highly repressed, so that they don't have a chance to stand up for themselves. They are not allowed to speak or write their thoughts, and if they do, they are often killed.

---

[220] As explained by Yuri N. Maltsev, "The Decline and Fall of Gorbachev and the Soviet State," http://mises.org/daily/3105.

[221] George Reisman, "Why Nazism Was Socialism and Why Socialism is Totalitarianism," http://mises.org/daily/1937.

[222] Ibid.

But they are in danger of this regardless because leaders are often not sure who might turn against them, and therefore have to kill entire groups of people in order to make sure they purge all dissenters. One is no safer as a member of the government. In order to stay in power, communist rulers have to rule with an iron first, and everyone is a possible enemy and target.

When the citizens of Ukraine rebelled against Stalin's forcing them to be part of the Soviet Union, Stalin cut off food supplies. The starving who went to farm fields to take grain were shot dead on the spot. It became commonplace to see people lying dead from starvation on the sidewalks. Many were buried alive. Cannibalism became so widespread that the government printed posters which read, "Eating your children is an act of barbarism."[223] Eventually, seven million people, or one quarter of the population died.

Yet all of the terror and repression under full socialism is still claimed to be in the name of taking care of the people. Communist (as well as less socialistic) states usually call themselves a "people's democracy" or "people's republic" as though it exists to serve the people, even though the "people" have no choices or say-so whatsoever. The "common good," in reality, ends up being only the "leaders' good." The individual is simply a means to the state's ends. Indeed, the results are as good as can be expected under a system in which the government controls everything and the individual controls nothing, including his own daily life.

On a somewhat similar note, government ownership of companies in a non-communist society should be addressed here. Socialist commentators, such as Bill Maher of HBO's *Real Time with Bill Maher,* ask what the problem is with state ownership of companies, since it means that *everyone* owns the companies. The discussion thus far should give the answer: if the state owns something, citizens get either less or absolutely nothing from it.

---

[223] Stéphane Courtois, Nicolas Werth, Jean-Louis Panné, Andrzej Paczkowski, Karel Bartosek, Jean-Louis Margolin, Stephane Courtois, Mark Kramer, with Jonathan Murphy (Translator), *The Black Book of Communism: Crimes, Terror, Repression* (1999).

The Audacity of Defending Communism

I will not indulge in questioning why there are still individuals living in relatively free societies such as the U.S. and Western Europe who promote communism, and even go to the trouble to advertise their desires with such things as Che Guevara t-shirts. Though most of these people will claim communism has never been done correctly, in their ignorance they fail to see that it is impossible for it to be done without the very outcomes seen in every communist country. But what I believe should be discussed briefly are some general academic defenses of socialism.

More specifically, I would like to address some public responses which were made by anti-capitalistic commentators regarding the publishing of the book *The Black Book of Communism: Crimes, Terror, Repression* (abbreviated as BBOC henceforth) by Stéphane Courtois and other European researchers.[224] The comments in question are those listed in the "criticism" section of the book's Wikipedia entry.[225] I believe the response to these comments will clarify common misconceptions many have of the supposed ills of capitalism.

Why would one bother to put themselves out in the public to defend communism? Barring those who live in the middle of the Amazon forest, any person living and breathing who has engaged in even slight research on communism is well aware of the death and destruction it caused, no matter what its supposed moral aim. Thus, I ask rhetorically, what agendas one would have in attempting a defense of it?

A recurrent argument throughout the criticism section is that many of the deaths under communism were unintentional. This is, shockingly, stated as though it actually makes a difference. Granted, shooting people in the head or torturing them to death is more evil than preventing them from being able to save their own lives from starvation, freezing cold, or incompetence (as when government officials

---

[224] Stéphane Courtois, Nicolas Werth, Jean-Louis Panné, Andrzej Paczkowski, Karel Bartosek, Jean-Louis Margolin, Stephane Courtois, Mark Kramer, with Jonathan Murphy (Translator), *The Black Book of Communism: Crimes, Terror, Repression* (1999).

[225] Wikipedia, "The Big Black Book of Communism," http://en.wikipedia.org/wiki/Black_Book_of_Communism.

accepted bribes from food vendors to permit them to declare their product radiation-free after the Chernobyl nuclear accident[226]). But this in no way diminishes the fact that allowing people to die, to forcibly prevent them from doing what is needed in order *not to die*, is itself evil. This is especially true considering that deaths were (and still are) occurring for decades under communism, although it had long been clear that preventing citizens from being free was what caused the deaths, in numerous ways. Especially after leaders learn the negative effects of their own actions, to continue with those same deathly policies is almost as brutally sinister as is murder. Defending communism by attempting to distinguish between the intentional deaths of millions and the "accidental" death of millions, both which result from aggression against citizens by their government, is sinister as well.

The fundamental cause of both the direct and indirect deaths under communism is the prevention of people to be free to act as they wish, as long as they observe the rights of others. With this in mind, we can immediately identify the flaw in another of the criticisms of the BBOC, namely, that many of the crimes, terror, and repression discussed in the book did not take place in actual communist countries, but under other types of regimes. It should be clear at this point that the title of a regime matters none—it is the actions which count. Though the United States is held to be a free country, government takes more control of the economy and people by the year. At the point that famines and *overt* murders of citizens by the U.S. government take place in an America where the state controls all personal production and exchange, it too should then be classified under full socialism, even if our flag of "freedom" is still waving. What constitutes the level of socialism is not a name; it's the extent to which government has in fact socialized the country in question. Any famines which occur in today's modern world can only be found to have taken place in a socialistic country—whether it calls itself socialist or not—where citizens are not able to produce, sell, or import food. This is true because a free market would have prevented such famine.

---

[226] Yuri N. Maltsev, "The Decline and Fall of Gorbachev and the Soviet State," http://mises.org/daily/3105.

The most important criticism to address in the Wikipedia entry, made by socialist academic Noam Chomsky and others, is that the book fails to account for deaths made by capitalistic countries. In his ignorance, Chomsky audaciously identifies India as a capitalistic country. First, there is in fact NO capitalistic country in the world. Not one. There are those that are more and less capitalistic only. Every single country has some degree of government intervention in the economy. Every country, to some degree, prints money, confiscates incomes, regulates industry, subsidizes companies, prevents competition, or imposes price controls, tariffs, or quotas. Most countries, including the U.S., do all of these things to some degree.

According to The Heritage Foundation's 2007 Index of Economic Freedom, India, overall, is 56 percent free, which means it is 44 percent socialistic (and that's after many years of increasing economic freedom). The United States, in contrast, is 82 percent free. (These rankings will be discussed in detail in the next section.) Clearly India is not a capitalistic country—it is one in which some aspects of the market are free to function, but others are not. Not only is much of the Indian parliament made up of socialist and communist parties, but its constitution states that it is a "socialist secular democratic republic."[227] India, in fact, is a sort of poster child for many free-market economists; it is often referred to as an example of how an economy can stagnate and its people can suffer due to a lack of free markets.

After the 2009 Indian elections, a news report read, "The left-of-center Congress, … has long tried to balance free market reforms with a vow to protect the downtrodden in this country of 1.2 billion people."[228] As is the case in the U.S. and other countries, most people will gloss over the part of the statement which says free markets were *balanced with protection of the poor* (a thing they've not been too successful with). They will pretend that this government intervention does not exist and does not have any impact whatsoever, and retain in their mind only the statement about free markets. They and the media, and leftists such as Chomsky, will simply call India (and America) a

[227] The Indian Embassy, Extracts from The Constitution of India, http://www.indianembassy.org/dydemo/constitution.htm

[228] See The Associated Press, "Indian Prime Minister Claims Victory, 'Massive Mandate' in Elections," *Fox News* (May 16, 2009).

free-market, capitalist country. The fact is that the "balancing" is much more than even balancing, it is tantamount to handcuffs being placed on the marketplace.

But to the critic's point, indeed, tens of millions of deaths have occurred in India. But these are the results of socialism, not capitalism. For it is the socialist part of the economy—that which prevents the market from working—to which we can attribute almost all of the deaths (to the extent that the deaths occurred as, say, a result of one businessman choosing to kill another or a citizen, it is due to the failure to adhere to free market principles). Similarly, deaths that occur in America from, for example, an absence of available healthcare due to the prevention of a free healthcare market, or in other countries from a war that our presidents initiate, can also be attributed only to socialism (i.e., government control), not capitalism. For under free markets, as we've seen, needed goods would be produced, and starvation would not occur, and diseases would be rare. Also, government would not have the ability to kill people or to prohibit, e.g., free exchange like healthcare services from being rendered. These things can only happen after a country's citizens allow their governments to engage in harmful actions.

Similar to the comment about India being capitalistic, one critic argues that capitalism should be blamed for causing poverty in the world today. The argument is that millions have died (somehow) because of inequality which arises from capitalism.[229] Though capitalism indeed brings inequality, the kind of inequality that separates the rich west from those starving in the dirt in Chad or Angola occurs because capitalism lifts nations up while socialism drags them down. Otherwise, the less equal poor in Chad and Angola would live, at a minimum, more like the "poor"[230] in America. True poverty cannot occur under capitalism. Blaming world poverty on capitalism is like blaming a plane crash on the fact that planes have the ability to fly—the plane crashed precisely because it didn't fly.

---

[229] Daniel Singer, "Exploiting a Tragedy, or Le Rouge en Noir," *The Nation* (November 25, 1999).

[230] To be discussed in the next chapter.

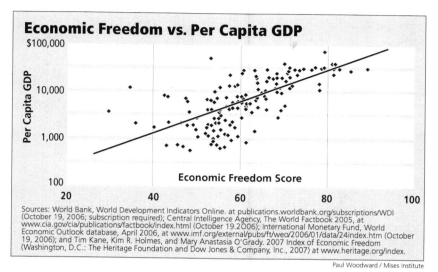

Sources: World Bank, World Development Indicators Online. at publications.worldbank.org/subscriptions/WDI (October 19, 2006; subscription required); Central Intelligence Agency, The World Factbook 2005, at www.cia.gov/cia/publications/factbook/index.html (October 19.2006); International Monetary Fund, World Economic Outlook database, April 2006, at www.imf.org/external/pubs/ft/weo/2006/01/data/24index.htm (October 19, 2006); and Tim Kane, Kim R. Holmes, and Mary Anastasia O'Grady. 2007 Index of Economic Freedom (Washington, D.C.: The Heritage Foundation and Dow Jones & Company, Inc., 2007) at www.heritage.org/index.

Paul Woodward / Mises Institute

Figure 6.4: Economic Freedom and Prosperity.
Source: The Heritage Foundation and Dow Jones & Company

Economic Freedom in Various Countries

This chapter's purpose has been to show the difference in how economies function with and without capitalism. In some cases we have seen where economies thrived because freer markets existed, and in others we have seen how economies collapsed when free markets were prevented. As a departure from examining economies in transition, it should be useful to compare economies that are freer with those that are less free, as they exist today, and have existed in recent years. To do this we will look at the relationship between economic freedom and standards of living among countries.

Two sources of information will be used for this purpose. The first is the *Economic Freedom of the World Index*, published by the Frasier Institute, and the *Index of Economic Freedom*, published by the Heritage Foundation and the Wall Street Journal. Both indexes, using 2007 data, assess the extent to which countries are economically free, as measured by variables such as the size of government, strength of the legal system, security of property rights, extent of inflation, freedom to trade, burdens of business and labor market regulation, and levels of corruption. Both indexes obtain statistics for each of these categories,

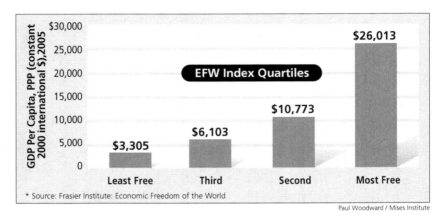

Figure 6.5: Purchasing Power for Countries Grouped by Quartile.
Source: Heritage Foundation: Economic Freedom of the World.

listing them on a scale from lowest to highest, and then aggregate the individual statistics for each country so as to form an overall score.

First, let's look at the overall picture. **Figure 6.4** shows the general relationship between economic freedom and prosperity. It reveals that, on average, the greater the economic freedom, the more prosperous countries are. Similarly, **Figure 6.5** reveals the level of economic prosperity for different groups of countries. Specifically, it shows that those countries which fall into the top quartile of economic freedom have average incomes (purchasing power) of $26,013 while those countries in the bottom quartile have average incomes of $3,305.

The ten freest countries are as follows:

Economic Freedom of the World	Index of Economic Freedom
1 Hong Kong	1 Hong Kong
2 Singapore	2 Singapore
3 New Zealand	3 Australia
4 Switzerland	4 United States
5 United States (tied for 5th-7th)	5 New Zealand
6 United Kingdom (tied for 5th-7th)	6 United Kingdom
7 Canada (tied for 5th-7th)	7 Ireland
8 Estonia (tied for 8th-9th)	8 Luxembourg
9 Ireland (tied for 8th-9th)	9 Switzerland
10 Australia	10 Canada

The ten least-free countries are as follows:[231]

Economic Freedom of the World	Index of Economic Freedom
1 Zimbabwe	1 North Korea
2 Myanmar	2 Cuba
3 Democratic Republic of Congo	3 Libya
4 Angola	4 Zimbabwe
5 Republic of Congo	5 Burma (Myanmar)
6 Central African Republic	6 Turkmenistan
7 Venezuela	7 Republic of Congo
8 Burundi	8 Iran
9 Togo	9 Angola
10 Niger	10 Guinea-Bissau

There is obviously not enough space here to show the detailed results of each country in the indexes, but it should be helpful to see some examples of sample countries in the top, middle, and bottom of the economic freedom rankings.

The freest country in the world is Hong Kong, which comes in at 89 percent free in both indexes. Its top marginal tax rate is 20 percent (up from 15 percent in 1980); government spending as a percent of GDP is 18.3 percent; the government prints money at a pace of 5 percent per year; it has almost completely free ability to trade internationally; and it has moderate regulations on employing workers and operating a business (86 percent free from regulation). Hong Kong's unemployment rate over the last 10 years has been 5.1 percent, and its GDP per capita is $42,000 (by comparison, the U.S. is $45,800).[232] Hong Kong is known as a nation of stability. It was a British territory that was allowed to be a free trade port, and grew rapidly after WWII, based on policies of mostly free trade—one of the premier historical episodes of a country growing from poor to rich through engaging in capitalism. In the 1960s and 1970s, it was "Made in Hong Kong" (instead of India or China) that was stamped on so many American

---

[231] Listings and rankings will differ considerably. This is because data is difficult to obtain in order to provide a ranking in some cases. Thus, one index might rank using partial data, while the other might not attempt to rank at all.

[232] U.S. Central Intelligence Agency, Country Comparison: GDP Per Capita, https://www.cia.gov/library/publications/the-world-factbook/rankorder/2004rank.html.

imports. As the country became more developed, it evolved into a ser-vices-based economy.

An example of a country which is halfway free is Argentina, which ranks 54 percent free on one index and 57 percent free on the other. Its economic profile is as follows: government spending as a percent of GDP is 20.9 percent; the top marginal tax rate is 35 per-cent (but 46 percent for payroll tax); it has a less than trustworthy legal system (46 percent free); money supply growth is 33 percent per year (33 percent free); international trade freedom is less than 60 percent; and freedom from business regulation averages less than 50 percent. In 2007 the country had an unemployment rate of 16 percent and a GDP per capita of $13,100.[233]

Argentina was one of the richest countries in the world at the turn of last century. Through the years the country grew into a wel-fare state, which, along with direct government intervention in the economy, caused it to decline. Argentina has been one of the famous "Banana Republics," even though it is one of the more developed Latin American countries. It has had constant bouts of hyperinflation since the 1970s. Of its many economic collapses, the most recent was in 2002 when the government's printing of money crashed the econ-omy and caused the entire banking system to collapse.

Towards the bottom of the list of economic freedom is The Democratic Republic of Congo (formerly known as Zaire), which is ranked 29 percent free and 36 percent free. It is 53 percent free in terms of the size of government; marginal tax rates are 50 percent; there are virtually no property rights or reliable legal system; money supply grows at 2,290 percent per year; and businesses are 67 percent controlled by the state. The resulting unemployment rate cannot be determined due to a lack of reliable government figures, but is likely similar to that of Zimbabwe or Liberia, which have unemployment rates of 80 percent and 85 percent, respectively, and which have simi-lar GDP figures and comparable economies in general. GDP per cap-ita in the Congo is $300 per person.

---

[233] U.S. Central Intelligence Agency, Country Comparison: GDP Per Capita, https://www.cia.gov/library/publications/the-world-factbook/rankorder/2004rank.html.

From 1965 until 1997 the country was run by a dictator, Mobutu Sese Seko, who, like many dictators, gained power through a CIA-sponsored coup. He confiscated all property of foreign firms, often redistributing it to family members and friends. That, and the act of confiscating property from his own citizens both directly and through printing money, allowed Mobutu to build a wealth of $5 billion, the same as the national debt.[234] The economy has retrogressed every year since 1989. The infrastructure is in shambles and industry represents less than 2 percent of GDP. According to the UN, less than 15 percent of the population has access to clean water, and malnutrition is widespread.[235] Yet President Bush called Mobutu "our best friend in Africa," and the Carter administration financially supported him in fighting off political rebellions aimed at removing him from power.

The Congo, like Argentina, is packed with natural resources, and should be one of the wealthiest countries in the world. But what counts is whether a country's resources are managed profitably. Conversely, a country lacking resources would not be prevented from becoming wealthy. Japan, for example, with very few natural resources, became wealthy by importing various materials and assembling them into final products with its (then) cheap labor. Most of the newly developed Asian countries—not to mention Switzerland—also have few natural resources. But any country, no matter what resources, capital, or education levels it has, can become a prosperous country if allowed the freedom to become so. If citizens are given the right to own their property and are insured that it will not be taken by the state, they will find ways to produce and exchange for profit. A newly-free country starting with nothing can exchange its labor for foreign capital and for foreign knowledge of production techniques.

Most people think that a formal education is the key to prosperity, but it is not. Knowledge of literature, plays, geography, history, and the arts is useful, but does not produce goods. Too many countries have learned that throwing more and more money at traditional education is insufficient in itself. The important education—the one that

---

[234] See Brief Biographies, Mobutu Sese Seko, http://biography.jrank.org/pages/2974/Seko-Mobutu-Sese.html. However, many suspect he was never a billionaire at all.

[235] Library of Congress Country Studies, Zaire: Sanitation and Nutrition, http://lcweb2.loc.gov/cgi-bin/query/r?frd/cstdy:@field(DOCID+zr0102).

creates an increase in prosperity—takes place in the factories and the fields. If a country is allowed the freedom, in time, knowledge, productivity, capital, savings, and wealth will all increase. Poverty, hunger, disease, insecurity, fear, and suffering will all decrease.

Some who read these words will accuse me of being naïve and of indulging in narrow ideological fantasy. I would argue that it's the other way around. The United States, the U.N., IMF, World Bank, etc.—in other words, taxpayers—have spent hundreds of billions for decades to educate poor countries and to them give money, knowledge of production, and even to buy them factories, tools, and machines. We have had our best and brightest Harvard and Yale economists design and plan their economies. We have instructed their leaders as to exactly what must be done. It has all failed—in just about every single instance. On the other hand, there is not one example of a country whose people were allowed to be free—truly free—that still failed. Shouldn't we try capitalism in third world countries once? Just once? Nothing else has worked for these poor countries, what could be the harm in letting them own property and run their businesses freely? If American politicians insist upon using government force to control other countries, they should at least use it in the way it was largely used in Japan, Hong Kong, and West Germany after WWII— by imposing freedom and free markets, not some bogus "democracy" that really consists of total government control. Iraq would be a great place to start.

Similarly, it is only freedom and free markets which will solve the problems that we face today in the U.S. It should be clear that government intervention in the economy does not work, but in fact multiplies problems—problems caused by previous intervention. Just as the Roman Empire slowly retrogressed over time, so could the United States. As we continue to tax and inflate away our wealth, and prevent our people and businesses from producing and selling as they see fit, we will surely continue to see lower real incomes (incomes not keeping up with inflation). As we destroy our capital and our productive capabilities, we will have fewer goods and innovations each year. It is highly possible that in 100 years from now we will live just as we did 100 years ago.

In contrast, imagine what life would be like today had the Roman Empire continued its economic growth with its advanced engineering. It was on the verge of an industrial revolution like the one which began in 16th century England. Had Rome experienced such an industrial revolution in say, 500 A.D., the world could have lived just as we do today—with automobiles, airplanes, washing machines, and cell phones—in 900 A.D. Instead, the world was in the middle of the dark ages. If the world was similar to today's world in 900 A.D. or 1000 A.D., imagine what life would be like for us today. We would have an unimaginable standard of living! We would have to work $1/100$ as long or hard to achieve 100 times our current standard of living. Currently, we expect our descendants to live 100 times better than we do in the years 2500 or 3000. But if we continually have less wealth in future years with which to build fewer factories and machines, our children's children could wind up as our ancestors did after the Fall of Rome.

PART FOUR

Special Topics
and
Considerations

Chapter 7:

The Morality of Capitalism

I have demonstrated throughout the previous chapters that capitalism results in prosperity while socialism results in poverty, destruction, and suffering. But since capitalism is clearly superior to socialism and benefits everyone who lives under it, why do so many people still support socialism, or some slightly attenuated form of it (American Democrats, social democrats, labor parties, etc.)? Obvious answers include ignorance and politics.

But another driving force in the advocating of socialism, especially among people who are thoughtful about moral issues, is the notion that capitalism is morally corrupt, while socialism is morally good. Their assumption is that capitalism is selfish because individuals are first and mostly concerned about themselves and profit instead of about their fellow man. But 1) are most people, including socialists, really concerned with others before themselves? And 2) even if people are concerned with themselves before others, does that mean that others necessarily suffer as a result? Let's explore these moral accusations in detail.

Do Socialists Really Care About Others First?

But socialists and the supposed disenfranchised people—the interest groups that socialists seek to protect from abuse—themselves exhibit self-interest as much as anyone: it is because of their own self-interest that left-leaning unions want higher pay for themselves at the expense of the rest of society. It is due to self-interest that our supposedly high-minded political leaders, particularly Democrats in this case, who get votes by promising to help others, often engage in illegally receiving funds, gifts, or favors, or failing to pay income taxes.[236]

Self-interest is why so many homeowners support proposed legislation allowing the government to bail them out at the expense of other taxpayers; they are concerned with their own mortgages, not the mortgages of their neighbors. Those same homeowners, many of whom are Democrats or harder-core socialists, want to get wealthy through increasing home values, and don't want prices to fall, even though it is precisely falling home prices that would help poorer families to be able to own homes. It is left-wing environmentalists who want government to prevent production and progress just so that they can get their green world at society's expense and detriment. This is pure selfishness.

As another example: although socialists would not admit it publicly, they usually put time and effort into seeking a new job or a pay raise for themselves before helping others do the same—but, of course, they don't mind voting for government to take money from the rich to help their fellow men in the meantime—and they don't usually care about other people in general, just other "disenfranchised" people.

I live in an extraordinarily socialist part of my city, and the supposedly morally concerned citizens here are selfish enough to litter and leave dog droppings on public grass and sidewalks, to complain that neighbors in their condo building are "stealing" air conditioning

---

[236] For myriad examples, see Wikipedia, "Political Scandals of the United States," http://en.wikipedia.org/wiki/Political_scandals_of_the_United_States. Also simply read recent articles about many of the officials Obama put in charge of the treasury department.

by keeping their hallway door open, and to demand that the local zoning board prevent new apartment buildings from being built next to them so that they will not have to share the roads with more cars, lose the views from their living room windows, and have their property values threatened.[237]

Socialists despise self-interested entrepreneurs or other business-people because they see them getting rich. Probably, then, it is a kind of envy that makes them want to compel the rich to be interested in others in that they (the rich) are forced by government to give the socialists or socialists' interest group their money.

Socialists should accept the fact that, absent exceptional circumstances, we all care about ourselves and our families first, and others second. But most importantly, socialists should recognize that *under free markets, in pursuing our own self interests, we inevitably help everyone else.* Under a government manipulated economy, as the examples from the last chapter show, this is not the case. Knowing that those who are successful in getting rich do so by providing needed goods, services, and jobs, and lower prices to others in the process tells us that what socialists should be concerned with are *outcomes*, not the *means of achieving the outcomes*. If so-called "greed" results in lifting up all of society, but the "concern for the common good" does the opposite, should we not accept the seeming paradox that greed is good?

Capitalists Are Not Greedy, You Are

The term greed is used by socialists to deride people or companies for both 1) becoming wealthy in free markets wherein wealth could not have been gained without having created much *more* wealth for the rest of society, and 2) causing the economic problems that are in reality caused by the government leaders the socialists voted for. The word greed is used in the former case merely to express jealousy for actions which involve nothing negative or shameful, and in the latter case to assign blame to those who socialists *wish were guilty*, even though they have no idea who is really at fault.

---

[237] Zoning boards: yet another example that government exists so that one group can gain at the expense of others.

Both greed and wealth are relative terms. The word greed, defined by Merriam-Webster dictionary as *"a selfish and excessive desire for more of something (like money) than is needed,"* shouldn't even be part of our vocabulary for the most part. Who is to say how much is "needed"? People usually argue that a rich businessman does not "need" billions of dollars, or does not "need" millions of times more wealth than the average person has. But why not? After all, the average person today has millions of times more wealth than the poor in many countries. *Those* poor would look at us and say that we don't "need" mp3 players, trips to Disney World, three bedroom homes instead of two, or two family cars (or even one). Three hundred years ago no one had such things. Why do we have and need them now? But had you been a commoner back then, you would have said that the King did not "need" all his wealth; but most today live better than did kings back then, even if we don't have as many physical possessions. When future generations live like millionaires do today, they will say that those who have a trillion dollars (instead of tens of billions that the richest have today), do not "need" it, but will defend their own "need" for living like a millionaire does today. It's all relative.

The fact is that most of us largely rational human beings are never wholly satisfied. Given the opportunity, we would all like to have more food, more clothing, more or bigger homes, more vacations, a nicer or more elegant automobile, or more dinners and drinks out with friends. My mother has said, as so many people do, that she has everything she needs. She does not want a bigger house or a boat or a newer car. Yet she decided not to travel to Europe last year because of the falling dollar, not to redecorate her out-of-date home, not to buy a separate utility vehicle for running errands—all because these things are too expensive. Though she claims she doesn't need more wealth, it's clear that she would enjoy her life more if she had certain things that wealth could buy. We should therefore understand why Donald Trump "needs" five houses, Paris Hilton "needs" a $500,000 clubbing budget, and I "need" an apartment in Paris. These things make our lives more enjoyable.

This is not at all to discount the happiness that comes from spiritual, emotional and cultural experiences; but such things are outside the scope of this book, the subject of which is economic. Although money does not *always* buy happiness, it often does. It may not solve all our problems, but it sure can solve many of them. It can definitely buy us safety and security for the most part. And once we have our basic needs, money can buy us relaxation, pleasure, entertainment, and a focus away from our worries. It can even get us out of prison in a third-world country (via bribes) after partying too hard and being arrested for drunken tirades towards police officers. Whatever other problems we have in our lives, money can make things better. The more money we have, the more we can enjoy ourselves.

What about corporate "greed"? Again there is no such thing: don't confuse greed with theft or mismanagement. The actions of Bernie Madoff, Jeffrey Skilling, Ken Lay and the like are actions of thieves —like those of a burglar, scam artist, or mugger. These are actions which are against the laws of capitalism.

Materialism and Money

People are always claiming that the world is too materialistic, and that capitalism promotes this materialism. Yet, enjoying material goods is not a bad thing—it's a fantastic thing! Indeed, we care about material things because they enrich our lives by either making each day on earth less challenging or more entertaining. But that does not mean that society cares more about, say, new clothes from Dolce and Gabbana or a nifty gardening tool from Home Depot than it does about spiritual beliefs or the well-being of other people. Besides, material goods can make better off our family or others in society we care about. A family member might benefit from a new medical device or new shingles for their leaking roof; a poor family could certainly benefit from new shoes or a new home (and the more we build, the more affordable these things are).

Socialists in particular are hypocritical when they say that people or society in general are too focused on both money and material things. They state that they need only so much, and the rest of us should need only so much as well. But as much as they want to help the poor, we seldom see them willingly giving up considerable amounts of their own money to send to others around the world who are poorer than they.

There are signs all around us that prove people want more "money." The constant call for better working conditions in some countries, or more and better homes in others reflects the need for more capital, or money. And the fact that even though we live better today than previous generations, most people still want higher wages relative to the "rich," shows that human wants are practically unlimited, and that we can always make further improvements.

Obviously, then, we want more money in order to have more things. Money is the medium of exchange we use to obtain the quality of life we desire. Money buys beer, mattresses, dental floss, medicine, movies, toothbrushes, computers and software, and trips home for Christmas with family.

To have more of these things we need to earn more money. But socialists believe making high incomes is wrong, if "high" means considerably higher than others make (and only socialists can truly tell us how much of an income is too high). But according to their own altruistic beliefs, they should see that high incomes are good: higher incomes only come about from providing more things to others that they need. The greater a man's income, the greater has been his service to others. Therefore, were one to take a lower, more modest job and income because *they believe* it's wrong to take a higher one, they are acting selfishly, and not serving their fellow man by providing him things he would like to have (remember that salaries are in accordance with the value of what one produces).

Even if socialists truly want to have fewer things, they have no right to make everyone else in society have fewer things by employing government force for these purposes, as they currently do through regulation, taxation, and other intervention. So then who should decide how much we work and how many things we produce? We all should, individually. Our own actions will reveal how much we want to consume and therefore how much should be produced. For all the complaints that Americans do not have as many government-mandated holidays that force companies to give employees more time off, the fact is that people can choose to work fewer hours and settle for having fewer material goods if they want to.

If we choose to consume less, market prices will reveal this, and production will therefore also decrease. Also, the price of labor corresponding to various amounts of production—the level of salaries being paid—will in turn help us determine how much we want or need to work. High wages might give us incentives to work more and earn more money, or they might give us incentives to work less, since we can maintain a particular lifestyle by working fewer hours in order to achieve it. We will each decide which case applies to us individually.

The Immorality of Democratic Voting

Businesspeople, if they are successfully "greedy," become rich by providing their fellow citizens (i.e., consumer) with things that make them better off. In other words, they have to earn it. But many who espouse that people don't need more than a basic level of existence, in their *own* greed, constantly vote for politicians who will take money from others and give it to them. They, just like the businessman, want more than they currently have. But instead of earning it as the businessman or capitalist does, the socialists steal it from those who have more. The businesspeople's actions are moral (unless they earned their money by theft or by being given privileges by government), while theirs are not.

The sad fact is that this is exactly what our political system—democracy—is all about. It is a system where the masses, those with less money than the minority group that has great wealth, vote for politicians who offer to take money from the wealthy minority and redistribute it to them in return for giving the politician their votes. Voting wealth out of the pockets of those who have it is socialism, because it is for done the "common good," for the benefit of helping that part of society which earns less. This is why Democracy has been likened to two wolves and a sheep voting on what to have for dinner. This is also what is known as "social justice." Politicians are simply people who learn to be good actors in order to win your vote. They ultimately care little about real progress for the country or the lives of individuals; they care about their political careers.

Wealth redistribution, therefore, is theft. It is the taking by force from one group in order to give to another. Force is involved because anyone who fails to pay assessed taxes—confiscatory taxes that mostly go directly into someone else's pockets—will be put in prison. People from whom money is taken have not usually voted for this action,[238] but those who wanted to receive others' money usually have voted to take it from them. Many socialists will dispute this and argue that *most* people want to pay the amount of taxes they pay. This implies, for example, that when the government doubled the tax rate during the great depression, people, coincidentally, simultaneously wanted to voluntarily pay double the amount of income tax. It implies that when marginal tax rates reached 90 percent, people truly wanted to work and hand over 90 percent of their marginal earnings. The argument is too weak to take seriously. Besides, if most people want to pay all the taxes they pay, socialists will have no problem switching the payment of taxes from being required by law to being *voluntary*.[239]

Wealth redistribution does not involve only social programs such as welfare, Medicaid, and Medicare. It involves any occurrence of one party receiving money, physical goods, or services, that they did not pay the full cost of, but that another party did, on their behalf. For example, public transportation involves wealth redistribution because most who use it did not pay for the bulk of the cost. Even though they contribute by purchasing their tickets, the ticket is highly subsidized because wealthier taxpayers fund most of the cost. Similarly, National Public Radio is a wealth redistribution program (mostly from the rich to the middle class). Many who listen to it paid taxes towards it, but many of those who do not listen also pay for it, and often pay *more*. If NPR is a viable business that would have enough people wanting to use it, it would be profitable on its own without government funding. If NPR could not survive without the government, it is a loss-making enterprise that is consuming wealth. That

---

[238] Many of the rich, misguidedly, do vote for their money to be redistributed, but most people do not, and do not want it taken from them. If you think I'm wrong, then you would surely not oppose making taxation voluntary, or letting the rich choose their own marginal tax rate, since if people want to give their money away, they in fact will. The mere existence of tax havens and tax evasion, both of which are highly moral, proves that rich people do not always want to willingly give up their money.

[239] As occurred under Queen Elizabeth I, resulting in a more prosperous economy. Also, it is precisely because most people will not voluntarily pay the amount of tax they are currently paying that socialists have to use force in order to make people hand their money over.

wealth could instead be used for profitable ventures, which would better serve society. We can see from this last example that only by having profit and loss statements can we determine whether a product or service is something consumers really want to have. There are never any profit and loss statements associated with anything the government operates, so we do not know which services are really beneficial in economic terms.[240]

Most of the taxes paid in the U.S. (and most countries) are paid by a small group of people, the rich. In 2005, 53.7 percent of all income taxes in the United States were paid by those earning over $200,000. Those earning between $100,000 and $200,000 paid 28.3 percent of all taxes. This means that 82 percent of all taxes were paid by those earning over $100,000.[241] Those with incomes below $40,000, in total, paid no income tax: their tax liability was more than offset by the tax rebates from the Earned Income Tax Credit. In other words, many receive money (from the rich) "returned" to them for taxes that were never paid.

Further, most taxes do not go towards essential government services such as road infrastructure, parks, education, the legal system, or police and fire departments—they go directly into other people's pockets. No more than 10 percent of the 2009 Federal Government Budget goes towards these essential government services (and most of these services are taken care of with separate state and local taxes). More than 65 percent of the budget goes towards social programs or some other type of income support or assistance. (Most of the remaining portion goes to fund our wars, or, "national defense" as it's called.)

Many claim, without an understanding of what's really happening, that somehow the rich take money from the poor. The facts show it is quite the other way around, considering the following numbers.

---

[240] A budget is not a profit and loss statement, and the revenues on a government budget are revenues expropriated from taxpayers, not voluntary purchases of the product or service being provided.

[241] Bruce Bartlett, "Tax Facts," http://www.creators.com/opinion/bruce-bartlett/tax-facts.html .

According to a detailed report[242] by the Tax Foundation,[243] in 2004, the bottom 20 percent of all income earners received $8.21 in government spending for every $1.00 in total[244] taxes they paid (and $14.76 for every dollar of federal taxes paid). The middle 20 percent received $1.30 for every $1 in taxes paid. But the top 20 percent of income earners received only $0.41 for every dollar of taxes paid. (Though they don't give the figures for the top 5 percent of taxpayers, who pay almost 60 percent of all taxes,[245] their receipt of government spending, by logical deduction, must be below $0.05 or less for every dollar they pay.)

In dollar amounts, households in the lowest-earning quintile in 2004 received about $31,185 *more* in government spending than they paid in taxes, while the middle quintile received $6,424 more than they paid. The top quintiles, however, *paid* $48,449 more in taxes than they received in government spending. In the aggregate, the top 40 percent of income-earning households paid roughly $1.03 trillion more in total taxes than they received in government spending, while the bottom 60 percent received $1.53 trillion more in government spending than they paid in taxes (the difference being the amount spent by government in excess of what it brought in—an excess mostly financed by the *future* top income earners). This is wealth redistribution.

We can see from these statistics how absurd is the phrase "tax breaks for the rich." The rich do indeed benefit most from tax breaks because of the fact that they *pay* most taxes. Tax breaks are the giving back to the rich some of the money that was previously taken from them. Yet socialists call this redistribution from the poor to the wealthy! In other words, if the poor aren't allowed to receive *as much* of others' incomes as before, and the rich are allowed to keep more of their income, then, in the eyes of socialists, the rich are *taking* from the poor. This is like saying that a thief who must return a woman's

---

[242] Andrew Chamberlain, "Who Pays Taxes and Who Receives Government Spending? An Analysis of Federal, State and Local Tax and Spending Distributions, 1991-2004," http://www.taxfoundation.org/publications/show/2282.html.

[243] The Tax Foundation, http://www.taxfoundation.org/.

[244] The Tax Foundation, "Who Pays America's Tax Burden, and Who Gets the Most Government Spending?" http://www.taxfoundation.org/files/sr151.pdf.

[245] Will Wilkinson, "All Tax Plans Are Wealth Redistribution," http://www.cato.org/pub_display.php?pub_id=9739.

purse after getting caught stealing it is redistributing money from himself to her.

When the government imposes taxes on the rich or less rich for the purposes of giving the money to another it is no different than taking his car, house, farm, or individual possessions. It is often the case that people who inherit property from deceased family members, even property that has been in their family for generations, have to sell the property just to pay the taxes. They really do lose their physical property. Even when taxes are taken straight out of people's salary, the monetary income taken could instead have been spent to buy physical goods or assets. It is family property that will never exist but would have otherwise.

What is the morality of forcing wealth from those who have it to those who have less? How is it that people are outraged when a CEO steals from his company, or a street thug steals a car, but they are not upset with themselves and their poorer neighbors for stealing from those who rightfully earned more money than they? Indeed they actively support such theft and vote for more of it! I conclude that society does not really care about morals. They care about what's best for them, defining terms in different ways in different situations, to fit their own personal or ideological agenda. Socialists condemn the businessman who becomes rich by pleasing others and providing jobs for workers and who harmed no one else in the process. But socialists claim that workers (and non-workers) who were paid the full value of their work by the businessman but still choose government force to make him pay more, are innocent, righteous, and *deserve* "social justice."

As a reminder of why businesspeople take nothing from others but simply benefit from creating wealth for them, consider the fishing net example from Chapter 1. If an island businessman creates a fishing net, he is able to reap the reward of more fish (more wealth). If he sells the net to others, he becomes wealthy by exchanging fishing nets for money (which exchanges for wealth). With others having a net, too, *they* can have more fish at lower prices (fewer hours of labor). Plus, those who help the fisherman make nets get paid wages in the process. The businessman creates wealth for everyone without taking from anyone in the process. *Everyone* benefits!

When people elect politicians who make campaign promises to interfere with the marketplace, they implicitly instruct government to take control of private companies. Businesses of all sizes, whose owners voluntarily went into business to bring us goods and services in order to make a profit then become slaves to society because the government, representing the people, dictates to companies how much to produce, what it *must* produce, what is not allowed to do, what prices it must sell above or below, what materials it is allowed or forced to use in production, and how much of its income must be sent to other people or companies.

Suppose your family decided to start a business. You invest time, sweat, money, and opportunity costs in creating a new product or service. Your company's product did not previously exist, but you made it available for others, without harming or forcing anyone to exchange their income for the product. After some years, your product becomes so popular that your family has now become wealthy through voluntary exchange. Others, who engage in forceful, not voluntary, exchange, in their jealousy, use the government to regulate you. They force you to sell part of your company to your competitors (anti-trust legislation) who are not able to compete as efficiently and effectively; they force you to pay your workers more than you can afford (union legislation); they force you to sell your product for a lower price than the market demands and for a lower price than you would like (price controls); they force you to produce in a way that pollutes less but raises your costs and reduces your output (EPA legislation); they then impose a "windfall profits tax" because they *think* you're earning too much money *this* year. Your company started out being your private property that benefited society, but then society— through government regulation—took control of it and sucked it dry. Now your family earns less, your workers earn less, and less of your product is available to consumers, and at a higher price. The consumers got what they voted for. Voting for the government to improve one's life almost always results in the opposite.

In 2008, congresswoman Maxine Waters threatened, on behalf of "society," to nationalize (i.e., to steal) the privately owned companies in the oil industry[246] due to the "large" profits they were making, since oil was at the highest price in years. But Congress itself brought about the high profits by 1) sanctioning the printing of money by the Fed (increased demand) and 2) preventing new oil drilling and refining (reduced supply). One hundred fifty years ago, oil was a worthless substance. Companies voluntarily extracted and refined it, and made it useful, significantly improving our lives in the process. But by threatening nationalization, the government now threatens to take away the property of the millions of individuals who own these companies, by force, against their will. Americans should have been shocked and aghast that this government threat could happen in their own "free" country; instead, most agreed with her sentiments. If this is moral, then virtually anything could be argued as being moral.

The Delusion That There is Need for Wealth Redistribution

While many socialists think there should be some particular way to "distribute" "society's" wealth, there is no such thing as a stock of ownerless goods that need to be divided. Goods and services come into existence as somebody's property. If they are to be distributed, one must first confiscate them from their rightful owners.[247]

Most people incorrectly believe that there is a limited and unchanging amount of wealth in the world. Based on this, they fear that the rich somehow steal too much of it for themselves, and that government should be used so as to redistribute part of the wealth to those who "deserve" it. But there is not a definite and unchanging amount of wealth. There was originally no wealth in the world. When the first cave men created the first clothes, set up the first cave homes, and collected the first food to eat, wealth was first created. As time passed, and men built homes, transportation, tools, food, and other necessities, along with goods for pleasure, more wealth was created. Today, our wealth is produced in (and partially consists of) factories, mills, mines, and workshops. We literally create more every year

---

[246] Fox News, "Maxine Waters threatens to nationalize U.S. oil industries" (YouTube excerpt) http://www.youtube.com/watch?v=PUaY3LhJ-IQ&feature=related.

[247] As originally stated by Ludwig von Mises.

(or did until recently). Those who invent, design, direct, fund, and risk their savings and careers to produce this wealth are the ones who naturally get compensated for doing so. In the process, these people appropriately compensate workers for the amount they produce. But the incomes the rich receive in this process are earned by them by having created something that did not previously exist; *they created their own wealth, they did not take it from someone else.* Thus, in free markets, the rich can never, ever gain at the expense of anyone else.[248]

There is, therefore, no need for a societal question of "how to distribute the wealth," as socialists claim. Under free markets, the wealth is allocated efficiently to each of us in proportion to how much of a role we had in creating it. Some workers, such as programmers, marketing executives, inventors, and entrepreneurs, have skills and knowledge that allow them to produce many times what others are able to produce, and are in higher demand. Lower skilled workers, such as manual laborers, clerical staff, operators of industrial machines, and repairmen, are greater in number, and have fewer skills and knowledge; thus, they contribute less to wealth production. They are, however, due to market forces, paid for every bit of the value that they help produce, and they constantly have more wealth created for them.

Because some are capable of producing more than others, they are compensated more than others. But since what everyone is engaged in is increasing the supply of goods, *everyone's* wealth is increasing (or at least it would under free markets), since almost all prices are then falling in real terms, and even in nominal terms when inflation does not exist. In fact, even those who produce nothing gain from this process because things they buy cost less each year (in actual prices if money is not being printed, and in real terms if it is being printed). Businessmen make even the non-workers better off!

And without the rich—the businesspeople, entrepreneurs, and capitalists—workers would have no work to do or salaries to earn.

---

[248] Even taking away business revenues from other companies does not actually involve taking something from them, as other businesses never took the revenue; consumers simply decided to give the revenues to the more successful firm.

Wealth creation is a partnership between the "poor" and "rich," between the workers and businesspeople.[249]

Imagine what would happen if all businesspeople and rich capitalists ceased to exist tomorrow. Workers would have no offices, factories, or distribution centers to go to for work, as they would all be gone since they are the property of the capitalists. These workers would also have no more salaries. There would be no way to produce anything, except by self-producing at home and trading with neighbors. With the rich and their capital gone, standards of living would plummet.

No matter how hard workers might try to replicate the offices and factories the businesspeople and capitalists had previously built, they would not be as successful because if they were as successful as were the previous-existing rich individuals, they would have already out-competed the rich to begin with. The rich give us poor and middle class our wealth—they don't take, they give.

If we will agree to let the wealthy earn many more times than the less wealthy, since they create many more times more wealth, we will still have their factories, offices, and tools—their capital—with which to keep producing. The more wealth we let them keep, the more of it we can use in order to produce for ourselves. For this, we only have to allow them to receive interest payments, in the form of profit, interest, dividends, and draw. Most of the wealth of the rich is always distributed among workers; the rich simply retain formal ownership.

The Flawed Notion of "Giving Back to Society"

We hear constantly about the need to give back to society. But it does not seem that people think through what they are advocating when they propose this idea. The concept is naturally aimed predominantly at successful people; and the rich in general. But the rich should not feel obligated to "give back" anything, since they already give the most. They are the ones who pay the most taxes, and are therefore

---

[249] And wealth destruction is what happens in the cases of "public/private partnerships."

the ones who mostly provide society with roads, schools, colleges and universities, public parks, libraries, museums, armed forces, police, fire departments, football stadiums, public transportation, welfare, Medicare, Medicaid, and other government institutions and services. They are the ones who give massive amounts of donations to charities, universities, and other private institutions, separately from the amount they give through forced taxation. They do all this in addition to funding our jobs and producing our goods and services. How, then, can it be that they need to give *back*? It is the rest of society who should give back to the rich.

Who is society anyway? Isn't it you and me, all of our friends and family...and the "rich"? Aren't we all society? If we are, then don't we *all* make success possible? Therefore, shouldn't we all keep our money since we all contributed? If our taxes are to be paid to society, then who exactly comprises society that will receive it? We all do. So why should we pay ourselves to compensate ourselves for making it possible for ourselves to be successful?

And the rich should not pay *more* in giving back to society because it was *not* society (i.e., the non-rich, as it is implied) that made it possible for the rich to have *more* success than the rest of us. This weak argument basically reduces to the unfair belief that simply because one is rich, one has to "give back" (i.e., "give") to "society." And somehow, the rich are not members of "society." The notion that the rich should pay disproportionately more in taxes presupposes that even though we each had the opportunities to succeed, those who are more successful should pay the rest of us who were less successful even though the successful ones made success possible just as much as the rest of us made it possible? Obviously, the whole thing boils down to having those who were not as good at creating wealth for themselves and for society wanting to take from those who were better at doing so. The rich, along with the rest of us, should give charity and donations to those in need, but it should be done voluntarily, not by government force.

Obviously "society" (the non-rich, as it's implied by socialists) does not provide the opportunity for success since it does not fund the federal, state, and local government institutions listed above. Society, for the most part, provides neither our wages nor goods available for our purchase. The rich entrepreneurs, investors, businesspeople, and capitalists provide those things. What *does* "society" provide? Members of "society" are net *receivers* of wealth and government services which are paid for by the rich. The only thing "society" provides is the relative freedom (relative to not being free at all) to produce and exchange and operate a business as one pleases, based on society's voting to elect rulers who allow this relative freedom. Without this freedom, no riches could be had (except, of course, what the king, dictator, or commissar, who would otherwise rule society, would take for himself through forced labor).

How Anti-Inequality and Anti-Poverty Policies Cause Inequality

The desire to create equality is itself a major cause of rising inequality. The expansion of credit by the central bank, the primary purpose of which is to fund government spending on wealth redistribution,[250] is a primary driver of sharply rising income disparities between the income classes.

In a free market, those who save would increase their wealth more rapidly than those who don't, because they would be earning a rate of return on their saved incomes. But their increased incomes, on average, could only be in line with the going rate of economy-wide profit (about 5–10 percent per year). There could not be a class of people who pull away from the rest of society by such a large degree as exists today.

But the incomes of rich savers rise disproportionately today due to the central bank's credit expansion. As the Fed prints new money, a significant amount flows into the financial markets, pushing the prices of stocks, bonds, and real estate, among other assets, higher and higher. Because of changes in the financial system structure, this disproportionate increase in incomes from investments in financial assets (as opposed to income from wages) exists to a larger degree in the last

---

[250] Since most government spending and government deficits in fact fund such wealth redistribution.

twenty, and especially ten, years.[251] The rise in the value of these assets has far outpaced the rise in wages paid to workers since more money, proportionately, has flowed into pushing asset prices higher than has flowed into the real economy to push wages higher. Since most people on the wealthier end of the spectrum hold a substantial portion of their wealth in these assets, their total incomes rise faster than those of average wage earners, who hold much less of their wealth in financial assets. Thus, this asset inflation created by the central bank makes the incomes of the rich outpace the rest of society.

CEO salaries rise for similar reasons—newly existing money pushes them higher. Companies borrowing newly created money have increased buying power with which to bid a higher price for a new CEO or to keep their current CEO from going to another company that is looking to pay higher CEO wages with *their* new money from the central bank.

While incomes of the rich continue to rise, workers' wages are increasingly reduced by salary deductions employers are forced by government to withhold. Costs such as social security contributions that are deducted from paychecks have increased through the years, lessening workers' take-home pay. The same phenomenon applies to other costs imposed on companies, some voluntary, but most of which are mandated by government. Costs for such things as workplace gyms, health insurance, daycare services, family leave benefits, OSHA requirements, environmental regulations, workers compensation, licenses, permits, and all other regulatory costs constitute costs deducted from wages. Since there is only so much money a company has to spend, any amount spent on costs other than capital goods and labor are amounts deducted from what is spent on capital goods and labor. Business spending still increases through time along with increases in the money supply, but less of the spending makes it into the take-home pay of workers.

---

[251] This is also why price inflation has not been significant over this period, a period in which an unprecedented amount of money has been created. Most of the new money flowed into the financial system and remained there. It did not leak very much into the real economy and push up consumer prices. For an excellent exposition on this topic, see Peter Warburton, *Debt and Delusion: Central Bank Follies That Threaten Economic Disaster* (1999).

Spending on government social programs and any other redistribution schemes also lowers wages. Any money that is taken from businesses—directly through business taxes, or indirectly through personal and inheritance taxes—is money that would otherwise mostly go specifically to paying wages (along with purchases of factories and machines) during the same time period (and if the money were paid out as wages instead of as free money for individuals to consume, the payments would be *repeatable*). Taxes do *not* come out of profits—companies will make sure to maintain their rate of profit or else they cannot afford to stay in business. Thus, taxes come out of productive expenditures, or, the money that companies would otherwise spend on wages and capital goods.

A last point is that minimum wage and pro-union legislation cause inequality in a slightly different manner. Those who are knocked out of the work force due to these laws obviously receive no wage income, but those who remain employed share all of the income that is available to be paid out in wages by companies. The salaries of the employed are elevated because were it not for the unemployed being so, the unemployed would receive part of the wages being paid out to those who are not unemployed.

The Poor

Socialists commonly cite the existence of the poor as a reason for socialism, and they claim that their concern for the poor shows compassion and morality. Since the topic of poverty is a key battleground in the war of socialism versus capitalism, it is relevant to examine what poverty is, how much of it exists in the U.S., and how we can truly eliminate it.

Who Are The Poor?

When we hear of the poor, we envision a massive group of people without food and shelter. In reality, most of the poor in capitalistic countries such as the U.S. are not in such a state. Data from the most recent census reveals that of the official "poor":[252]

---

[252] Robert E. Rector and Kirk A. Johnson, "Understanding Poverty and Economic Inequality in the United States," http://www.heritage.org/research/welfare/bg1796.cfm.

- 76 percent have air conditioning

- 66 percent have more than two rooms of living space per person

- 97 percent own at least one color television

- 62 percent have either cable or satellite television

- Almost 75 percent of households own a car (30 percent own two or more)

- 73 percent own microwave ovens

- More than 50 percent have stereos

- 33 percent have automatic dishwashers

- 99 percent have refrigerators

- Virtually none lack running water or flushing toilets

- 46 percent own their own home, the average of which is a three bedroom house with 1.5 baths, that has a carport and porch or patio, and the average value of which is 70 percent of the median American home

If we observe our presumably poorest citizens on our public transportation systems we see that they have cell phones, adequate clothing, personal audio devices, and are generally clean and free of disease and deformities. They also have the comfort of using a heated and air-conditioned transportation car that has carpet and flat-panel televisions for their amusement (paid for primarily by the wealthy, of course).

If you were to compare these American poor to the poor in Bolivia, Honduras, Cambodia, or India (or even to many of the poor in Mexico, Romania, Thailand, and Russia), you would see a stark difference. The poor in these countries often literally live in open-air huts with large leaves for roofs and stacked bricks that serve as a shared stove for multiple families. For the poor of the third world countries, there is, for the most part, no money, no exchange of goods—just basic survival by subsistence farming or by hunting or fishing for food. To these people, American street sweepers and factory workers live a life of luxury.

The difference between the "wealthy poor" in capitalist countries and the "deprived and desolate poor" in non-capitalist countries is no coincidence. The freedom that exists in capitalistic countries results in more invested capital per worker. This means that workers can produce far more wealth for themselves and for the rest of society. In non-capitalist countries today (and in the days before capitalism first appeared) poverty really means that no work is available; there is no means by which to improve one's state of being, or even to maintain it. Under capitalism, as we see, there is almost no question of poverty existing in this sense. Anyone who is not mentally or physically disabled can perform work and earn an income if they choose (except when prevented by the setting of minimum wages by government). Today, any poverty in the world is caused by an absence of capitalism, not the existence of capitalism.

Though the poor in this country have continuously seen their standard of living rise by capitalism, anti-capitalists continually point to the poor as evidence of a need for wealth redistribution (i.e., less capitalism), just because the poor earn *less* than do the rich. But there will always be a bottom 10 percent or 20 percent of the population in income in any society no matter how wealthy we all become. Thus, politicians and socialists always have a group to point to that are always in need of "assistance."

But even if we focus on the bottom 10 percent or 20 percent of Americans, it would still be difficult to identify who the poor are, because the composition of this group changes constantly. The "disadvantaged," the group that is supposedly made poor by the rich, are not a static, defined group. A study by Michael Cox and Richard Alm of the Federal Reserve Bank of Dallas showed that of the bottom fifth of income earners in 1975, only 5 percent were still poor 16 years later. Less than 1 percent remained in the bottom fifth for the entire 16 years. Thirty percent rose from the bottom fifth to the top fifth. In sum, few people remain at subsistence level. There are ways out of poverty for most.

Not to diminish the pains and difficulties of poverty, but in terms of the ability to achieve an absolute level of health and strength, the "poor" are usually in the same shape as the average person. Poor children take in virtually the same amount of protein, vitamins, and minerals as middle-class children; and they actually consume more meat. Most poor children grow to be larger, stronger, and healthier than the average WWII soldier. Though some poor families have temporary challenges with hunger, 89 percent of the poor report that their families have "enough" to eat; only 2 percent say they "often" do not have enough food.[253]

Further, the poor are not as poor as government statistics intentionally misrepresent. For example the ratio of "incomes"—the primary measurement used by government—of the top fifth to the bottom fifth of income earners is 15 to 1, but the ratio of their *consumption* is 4 to 1. This is because the poor usually have access to money that does not fall under taxable income, including government handouts. Their assets and wealth are not considered at all. The census bureau previously stated that people it deems "poor" typically spend $2.24 for every $1.00 in [government] reported income.[254]

Though there are indeed people who are in dire straits and need immediate help, most of the people we generally call "poor" are not as poor as anti-capitalists make them out to be. Depending on whom they are compared to, the poor can appear to be outright rich. Socialists make it appear as though there are many more poor people than there really are, so as to justify stealing more money from the rich to try and "equal out" society. When we speak of the poor, we should only speak of those who are physically unable to work and provide for themselves, not the entire bottom 20 percent of income earners who represent tens of millions of people.

More on the Minimum Wage

It was explained in Chapter 1 that the minimum wage raises labor costs to the point where companies cannot afford to hire all the workers they previously did, since they have a limited amount of funds available with which to hire workers.

---

[253] Information in this paragraph obtained from Robert E. Rector and Kirk A. Johnson, "Understanding Poverty and Economic Inequality in the United States," http://www.heritage.org/research/welfare/bg1796.cfm.

[254] Thomas DiLorenzo, "Reinventing America's Poor," http://mises.org/freemarket_detail.aspx?control=289.

Even ACORN, the organization that claims to help the poor by, among other means, promoting a "living wage," learned this first hand.[255] ACORN sued the state of California in 1995 for exemption from state labor laws, in order to avoid having to pay the minimum wage to its own employees. The organization argued before the court that "the more that ACORN must pay each individual outreach worker—either because of minimum wage or overtime require-ments—the fewer outreach workers it will be able to hire."[256] (As a comparable example, esteemed minimum wage advocate Nancy Pelosi also refused to pay minimum wage to her own workers.[257])

But besides the fact that the minimum wage cannot truly help low-skilled workers earn higher salaries, it's not needed in order for them to do so anyway. Low-end wages, just like high-end wages, will increase through time as increased capital accumulation brings about increased productivity, and especially as workers improve their skills. For example, wage rates for minimum wage employees grew at more than five times the rate for those earning above minimum wage between 1998 and 2002. Nearly 66 percent of all minimum wage employees who remain employed earn more than the minimum wage after one year of employment.

Since most of the low income earners are newer workers start-ing out and acquiring skills that will enable them to eventually earn more money, over 97 percent of all employees in the U.S. earn more than the minimum wage by age 30. Those who do not achieve this rate of pay do not acquire the needed skills for one reason or another; the explanation likely has to do with mental illness or personal moti-vation. Just about all workers can progress by remaining employed

---

[255] A majority of the information on minimum wage in this chapter was obtained from Shawn Ritenour, "What You Need to Know About the Minimum Wage," http://mises.org/daily/1603.

[256] Association of Community Organizations for Reform Now vs. State of California, Department of Industrial Relations, Divison of Labor Standards Enforcement, Case No. AO 69744, Appellant's Opening Brief, in the Court of Appeal of California, First Appel-late District, Division Five, August, 1995, cited in Employment Policies Institute, Q & A: Minimum Wage Employee Profile, (May 1997).

[257] Pelosi's Double Standard on the Minimum Wage, YouTube excerpt from inter-view with House Speaker Nancy Pelosi, http://www.youtube.com/watch?v=8pFC3 LKMIQo.

and gaining experience. But those who are forced into unemployment by the minimum wage often never get the opportunity.

And contrary to what ACORN, our politicians, and other social-ists would have you believe, it is not usually the case that minimum wage earners are single mothers raising children. The 1995 Current Population Survey showed that of all workers earning the minimum wage immediately prior to President Clinton's 1996 increase of that wage, 37.6 percent were teenagers living with their parents, 17.1 per-cent were single adults living by themselves, and 21.5 percent were adults married to a spouse who was also employed. Only 5.5 percent of workers earning minimum wage were single parents, and only 7.8 percent were married but still the sole family wage earner.[258]

The Failure of Anti-Poverty and Wealth Redistribution Schemes

Our government has been "fighting poverty" for most of the last century. Tens of trillions of dollars have been spent. Yet success never comes. When it becomes apparent that "poverty" is not being eradi-cated, our politicians throw yet more money at the supposed prob-lem. The increased money comes from our increased taxes (including the inflation tax).

Original tax rates in this country were 0 percent. The first official income tax appeared in 1913 with the passing of the Sixteenth Amend-ment.[259] It was a rate of 0.4 percent—a rate that Congress deemed "fair." The original marginal tax rate on the super rich was 7 percent. It eventually reached a peace-time high of 92 percent (Sweden reached an unbelievable 102%). Once our effective tax rates reach 100 percent, we will effectively be a communist country.[260] Year by year, working persons have had to pay a higher proportion of their incomes for their own compulsory "insurance," or to support other people. But year by

[258] Employment Policies Institute, *Q & A: Minimum Wage Employee Profile*, May 1997.

[259] Though our constitution states that such a thing is illegal unless distributed equally among all citizens. For 137 years until this time, tariffs paid for the needs of the country.

[260] In fact, since the government can actually print all the money it needs, the goal of tax-ation is, as stated by socialists themselves, "to leave less in the hands of the taxpayer," as pointed out by Ludwig von Mises, *Human Action: A Treatise on Economics* (1963), p. 807.

year there are still more people in need of government support. This is partially because as more people understand that incomes can be had without working for them, more people position themselves as poor so that they can receive benefits. No matter how much money is thrown at the problem, there will always be both the government-defined poor as well as the natural non-disability poor; there will always be people who *choose* not to better themselves, due to various psychological or mental desires to remain in their current state.

Yet any attempt to equalize people by redistributing wealth must result in a destruction of capital and of the ability to create jobs and prosperity, and thus reduced incomes. Even Leonid Brezhnev, First Secretary of the Soviet Communist Party, stated that "One can only distribute and consume what has been produced; this is an elementary truth."[261] What he failed to learn, as history shows, was that only the protection of private property and free markets can bring about the coordination of people and physical resources in a way which increases the production of wealth, while government economic planning and forced redistribution reduces production.

But besides the fact that so-called poverty will never be eliminated simply because at least one person will always be poorer than all others, politicians have a vested interest in *preventing* the alleviation of poverty. If Americans are fully employed and earning continually increasing wages, who needs the thousands of welfare bureaucrats in Washington? Though socialists believe that these bureaucrats (at least the Democrats) are truly benevolent individuals concerned about the well-being of others, in reality they are there to gain power, live off of taxpayer money, and advance their careers. Why else, for example, would Congress vote to repeatedly give itself wage increases—along with lifetime pensions in the millions[262]—that far outpace the consumer price index and the wages of workers.[263]

---

[261] Clyde H. Farnsworth, "Connally Tells Bankers U.S. Will Defend Dollar" *The New York Times* (May 29, 1971).

[262] See Peter J. Sepp, "Congressional Perks: How the Trappings of Office Trap Taxpayers," http://www.ntu.org/main/press.php?PressID=343 and Washington Windfall, http://www.fa-ir.org/alabama/corrupt/Congressional%20Retirement%20Benefits.htm.

[263] See: Victor Sperandeo, *Trader Vic II – Principles of Professional Speculation* (1998), p. 257 and Steven Moore, "Congress vs. America: How Congress Raises Its Own Pay," http://

Thus, politicians will always claim that masses of poor people need their assistance. This is why they continually re-define poverty and raise the income threshold for the "poverty line." In this way they can instantly have more poor people who need help from more tax-payer money and more bureaucrats. Our welfare and redistribution system sustains an industry of tens of millions of both public and pri-vate "aid" workers. Actual facts and outcomes of this industry's work demonstrate that its goal is not to eliminate poverty, but to expand government dependence through increased taxing, spending, and regulation.

Why do voters not see that the welfare policies of the last hun-dred years have failed to alleviate "poverty" and that something differ-ent should be done? Many do, but too many other people benefit (or so they think) from the current system by having money redistributed to them; they thus keep voting for it. Also, many of the people are socialists with socialist ideals detached from reality. I suppose the rest of the well-intentioned voters are simply naïve.

Real Solutions to Poverty

Very few people examine why the poor are poor. We generally give our and others' money to "the poor" because we blindly believe that they can't help the situation they're in and that they would oth-erwise starve or freeze to death. But if we really delve into their past and look at the decisions they have made, we would find that *most* of the ongoing poor are poor largely because they have, through their own actions and inactions, chosen to be. Many people think it is immoral to "judge" them and to consider the notion that they might have brought it on themselves. We don't question why we observe many of the poor visibly doing nothing day by day while we are at our offices working to support them.

Similarly, many of us workers see even co-workers who are not nearly as hard-working and who clearly just show up to collect a pay-check between nine and five without putting a lot of thought and care into their work. We don't like to admit that these work habits could

---

www.heritage.org/Research/GovernmentReform/bg744.cfm, and Chris Edwards, "Fed-eral Pay Outpaces Private-Sector Pay," http://www.cato.org/pubs/tbb/tbb-0605-35.pdf.

be related to why these workers do not earn as much as others who work much harder.

As another example, most of us have family or extended family members who do not have much wealth because they have lived well beyond their means and have made poor personal and career decisions. We have family members that chose not to continue their education—education that is free to the poor—and chose not to work hard to have a career (granted, it's not obligatory to have a "career," but it is in fact what usually brings in more money). We ignore these things and pretend that each and every poor person achieved their current state by being held down by the exploitative actions of others. We thus vote over and over to hand over money, not mostly from ourselves, but mainly from the rich, to the poor. The more we give the poor, the more incentive they have to rely on what we give them instead of earning more for themselves, an act which would require time, effort, and hardship on their part.

Redistributing wealth from the rich to the poor only reduces the wealth of both groups, but particularly of the poor. Every country that has ever made a serious attempt to equalize its citizens has gone to ruin, because forced equality reduces the incentive the rich have to invest capital and instead encourages the consumption of it, since it is likely to be taken from them. Additionally, as more and more people choose to become receivers instead of givers, there is not enough wealth being created by those who produce to support both themselves and the rest of society. The system breaks down and poverty for all arises.

Socialism and communism always falsely parade as systems of equality and liberty of all citizens, but they have always resulted in economic retrogression for all (except the rulers). Partial socialism, as we have today, has always resulted in stagnant or slowly retrogressing economic performance, as we have today. The general public does not understand that taking money from the rich has a very real and *negative* economic cause and effect; they imagine some economic vacuum in which there is no real change in the amount of capital per worker and their corresponding wages. They think that government, not businesses, creates wealth and provides for them. They see government as a spender, not as the taker that it is. As Ludwig von Mises stated, "spending and unbalanced budgets are merely synonyms for capital consumption."[264] The only real way to improve the lot of the poor is to replace their payments from government with payments from companies, in the form of wages.

The first and easiest step to increase the incomes of the poor would be to eliminate all laws that fix the price of labor above the market price. This alone would create full employment. The average poor family with children is supported by only 800 hours of work each year. This is equivalent to 16 hours of work per week. If the average poor family was able to increase the hours worked to 2,000 hours each year (i.e., one adult family member working a full 40 hour week), nearly 75 percent of poor children would be lifted out of poverty. This could be achieved by eliminating labor laws that require potential employers to pay workers wages higher than the market price they would otherwise pay. If poor workers were able (and willing) to work as many hours as a lot of middle and upper class workers do—50, 60, or even 70 hours per week—they could afford to live on minimum wage and below, especially if they had few or no children (the government currently gives them the incentive to have children by paying them for each child).

The second step towards helping the poor would be to cease all redistribution payments. This would cause workers' real wages to increase because the money that was previously consumed by being redistributed through antipoverty programs would be used by companies to purchase more capital goods and pay more wages, resulting in increased productivity and thus more consumer goods, resulting in lower prices relative to wages. This is true even if we take into account that the government might still be printing money, causing all prices to rise. In this case, all prices will rise, but the price of labor—our wages—would rise faster, because the supply of labor would not be increasing as fast as the supply of goods; in other words, inflation would not push prices of goods higher as fast as it pushes prices of wages higher. Changes in *real* wages always follow changes in productivity. When real wages don't keep up with inflation (such as right now), the explanation is almost certainly that real productivity is not

---

[264] Ludwig von Mises, *Human Action: A Treatise on Economics* (1963), p. 850.

increasing.[265] This is ultimately because we are consuming capital as fast or faster than we are replacing it.

Real wealth is created only through production. Thus, the only possible way to help the poor is to provide jobs that are *profitable*. Providing jobs without the corresponding creation of more goods—such as unprofitable, government-created "green jobs"—does not help anyone. These, and other government-created jobs involving public works projects result mostly in the destruction of capital and wealth. The few government jobs that involve improving roads, ports, and railways do allow us to produce more goods, but these projects could be performed more cheaply and efficiently by individual firms. More importantly, government does not use market prices to determine which projects need to be undertaken when; instead, the decisions are made based on politics. The result is too much of one good or service and too little of another. This is why, for example, we have too few roads and therefore "too much traffic."

Government works projects are usually taken on during bad economic times when unemployment is high. Politicians "create" these jobs in addition to the ones that already existed to serve the same purpose. But what is needed is not new jobs to perform inefficient, wealth-consuming work, but jobs in private industry to create real wealth. Government works projects hire workers that, had they not been prevented from doing so by previous government regulation and intervention, would otherwise be working for individual companies and contributing to the production of real wealth.

Real wealth-producing jobs that contribute to increasing real wages can come about only by allowing companies the freedom to produce as they see fit, and by allowing capital to work for us instead of being consumed in redistribution. Poverty can be solved *only* with profitable wage payments and lower costs of living arising from increasing productivity. As long as we are producing and as long as there are not regulations preventing employment, there will always be jobs for everyone.

---

[265] Don't measure productivity by the official productivity numbers the government calculates. These numbers, as will be explained in the next chapter, mostly reflect inflation, not actual productivity.

Living on an Income Lower than that of a "Living Wage"

Those opposing free markets usually support minimum wage legislation and wealth redistribution because, they state, no one could live on the basic wages employers would offer those unskilled and unknowledgeable workers. Remember, this level of worker has no more than a high school education (and possibly not a real one of those), even if he or she officially graduated or obtained a GED. Otherwise, with even basic skills and knowledge, most workers would likely start off in life with a much higher salary than minimum wage. One could ask why such unskilled and unknowledgeable workers exist when they have free government education,[266] free college education (there is always a grant available for one who is poor, but worst case, there are guaranteed school loans that one can actually get away with not having to pay back), and free government libraries where they can learn all day long. But we will ignore this valid question and assume that there are those who are just in this state for no reason, and especially at no fault of their own.

Let's see how one could live while earning $6 per hour, which is considerably less than the current minimum wage of $7.25 per hour, and a wage that would likely be paid in a free market. We will consider the costs of a single person with no children—a typical profile of minimum wage earners (single parents with children on minimum wage is a rarity).[267]

Figure 7.1 shows how a single individual earning minimum wage can afford to live, using average nationwide costs as an example, and assuming a 60-hour work week. Many variations of this model could exist: A less expensive apartment rented; public transportation could replace having a car; more medical care could be had by spending less on movies and going out; one could work even more hours by working weekends too, etc. It might seem inhumane to socialists that minimum wage earners might have to work 60 hours per week

---

[266] Which among other things, are supposed to teach students how life works and how to prepare for the future.

[267] Also, one would think that if someone could not afford to have children, they would not do so until they earned more (unless they were enticed to by the government's offering to give money for each child birthed, as is the case currently).

	Monthly	Annually
Income		
Salary	1,560	18,720
After Tax Total	1,279	15,350
Expenses		
Rent	475	5,700
Utilities	40	480
Phone	30	360
Car/insurance	140	1,680
Gas	50	600
Furniture	20	240
Clothes	50	600
Food/Groceries	275	3,300
Fast food/café/movies	60	720
Medical	75	900
Miscellaneous	60	720
Total Expenses	**1,275**	**15,300**

Comments / assumptions:

1. **Hourly Wage** of $6/hr.; 60 hr. work week
2. **Rent:** Equals 63 percent of median national rent of $760 per month
3. **Car:** assumes purchase of a $4,000 used car financed over 48 months @ 10 percent interest
4. **Gas:** assumes car is mostly driven only for work
5. **Furniture:** assumes rental of bed, couch, and table
6. **Medical:** assumes no health insurance through employer; also assumes the need of less healthcare than average since minimum wage worker is likely younger and healthier

Figure 7.1: Incomes and Expenditures of a Minimum Wage Salary

to get by, even though the rest of us often work that much and more. But since these workers possess very low productivity due to a lack of skills and knowledge, they have to make up for it by working more hours, just as all Americans did 150 years ago when our national productivity was so low.

One could object that the model presented here is not realistic because it does not include travel, Christmas presents, or visits to the zoo. But there are in fact many things people would have to go without if they are poor—at least until they improve their productivity. This should be a primary incentive to try and earn more money. Also, if needed, a minimum wage earner could take on debt by way of loans or credit cards, and they could pay off the debt within a few years, since earning minimum wage would be temporary. However, many remain on low salaries because they choose not to do the things that would earn them more. They thus *choose* lower wages over working harder.

The model in **Figure 7.1**, which is based on our current mixed economy, would be improved under capitalism. If income taxes were lowered or abolished, the worker would have a higher take-home wage. If corporate income taxes were lowered or abolished, all workers, besides higher salaries, would have higher productivity, which means that all of the costs in the model would decline, and houses and shoes and most other goods would cost significantly less. If regulations were reduced or repealed, money that employers spend on regulation would instead be paid to workers and machines, raising both nominal and real incomes.

Helping the "Real" Poor

If we did not pretend that one fifth of our society was poor, and if we instead focused only on the true poor people—those who are truly unable to help themselves because of mental or physical disabilities—we could afford to provide a true safety net through charities and voluntary giving. Most of us care tremendously about these people and would gladly spend part of our incomes helping them. The numbers of people truly in need are relatively so few that we would be able to support them with a fraction of what we currently pay in taxes to support the much larger number of people we currently support. For example, were government to provide this true safety net—which would not be the recommended route for multiple reasons beyond the scope of this book—it could certainly do so with less than a 1 percent tax rate. We could actually eliminate most current federal taxes and use our current state income taxes or state sales taxes to provide such a safety net. This is because most state and local taxes, currently funding *local* wealth redistribution programs, could be given only to those in true need (and the rest could be spent on infrastructure and the like, as they are supposed to be).

Under a free market, our tax rates and our costs of living would be drastically lower; our real incomes would thus be drastically higher. We could therefore afford to give more real charity. Whereas today, even though we give millions to charity and to government programs, our low level of real incomes cannot fully support the large number of people who are supposedly in need of help. Since we classify so many people as poor who are not, there are tens of millions of people who siphon money away from those who really need it. The selfishness of the "fake poor" (including many middle class citizens), creates a monetary shortfall for the "real poor" which leaves them with terrible, suffering lives.

We can afford to help those who are truly unable help themselves solely with the funding from charity; and we do not need forced taxation. It is often argued that we must have government to provide for the truly needy because individuals are too selfish to care about these people. This is an offense. Most of us positively want to help those truly in need. And it is already proven that people will give: on top of the trillions already taken from them, people willingly gave over $300 billion to charity in 2007.[268] If we assume that as many as one out of every two hundred people (half of one percent of the population) are mentally or physically incapacitated and unable to earn an income during any given year, and if we assume that of all charity, only half goes for the sole purpose of helping incapacitated people get along in life and have an income, that leaves $100,000 in income per year per incapacitated person (($300 billion × 1/2) / (300 million Americans × .5 percent)). This compares to the median income per family currently in the U.S. of $48,000. Additionally, most of these people will have family or even friends who will take care of them physically and financially, including a working spouse, in many cases. Not to mention, in a free market, people who were not previously incapacitated would have insurance that covers them both temporarily and for life in case they became incapacitated.

Those who can usually provide for themselves but who might face sudden hardships for whatever reason would have true unemployment insurance provided by private insurance companies that would fill the gap. The premiums would be affordable because the likelihood that something would prevent them from being able to work, and that it would not be a temporary inability to work, would be unlikely. But if such a calamity were to occur, they would be taken care of.

In free markets, people have jobs and high enough salaries to buy goods they need. The unemployable would be protected by both

---

[268] Vinnee Tong, "Record $300B Given to Charity," *Deseret News* (June 25, 2007).

charity and insurance (on top of help from friends and family). Considering all the points above, you can see why there is no reason why anyone would not have enough employment and money, or insurance, to live without suffering.

It's Never Enough

Still, even the situation described above would not satisfy the real socialists. They do not ultimately support freedom and prosperity for all; socialists support having everyone live as *they* see best according to *their* moral views. As Victor Sperandeo put it: "The essence of the communist's, socialist's, collectivist's, and liberal democrat's goal is the ethics of altruism, which is not the policy of being kind or nice to people in need, but rather the view that sacrifice for whatever cause sounds necessary is 'the good,' and living for your own self-interest is 'the bad.'[269]

Most religious organizations also promote an anti-capitalist mentality, even though most biblical passages, regardless of what most people think, absolutely promote capitalism and accumulating wealth.[270] In his Christmas Day speech of 2009, Pope Benedict XVI warned that the world was headed toward ruin if selfishness prevailed over solidarity during tough economic times for rich and poor nations. He stated, in similar manner to how the Catholic Church[271] supported early Italian Fascism in the 1930s, that "If people look only to their own interests, our world will certainly fall apart." This is absolutely false. Unbeknownst to him, the full range of economic problems in the world today, including war and starvation, is caused by governments seeking control of both society and national economies. The Pope does not understand that the economic problems we have are a direct result of actions already taken based on the moral philosophy he preaches. If the pope would mind his own business and let self interest take place, the very issues he wants us to pray about would

---

[269] Victor Sperandeo, *Methods of a Wall Street Master* (1993).

[270] This topic is beyond the scope of this book, but interested readers can find many volumes of work on the topic at www.garynorth.com.

[271] I'm not targeting Catholics in particular; Jewish, Protestant, and Orthodox religions, as well as non-Christian religions do the same.

not exist. Alternatively, if he learned how prosperity and economic (as well as physical) security are created, instead of preaching false prophecies, he would instead promote capitalism and save lives instead of ruining them.

Another example of this mentality, again by Victor Sperandeo, is best presented in its original form:

> Today's political mentality is best summed up by the chairman of the House Ways and Means Committee Dan Rostenkowski, Democrat of Illinois, who said, "I'll do anything to go after the pocketbooks of those who have been enjoying themselves for the last decade." Contrast this with James Madison, the fourth president of the United States and the man called "Father of the Constitution," who wrote, "[The] chief object [of government is] to protect the separate and unequal faculties of acquiring prosperity," and you can see more than a slight change in the government's view of moral and political beliefs since 1913.

We have so long believed that we must give and give in order both to help the poor and punish the rich that the average person now pays roughly 50 percent of their income to the government, in one form or another. Most of what we pay simply goes towards building the socialist dream of having the government control citizens dependent on it, instead of the traditional dream of having citizens control a government dependent on them. We as a society have voted for this situation because we are under the false belief that it will make us better protected and financially secure. It should be seen by now that it does the opposite.

An Unsustainable Economy

While our means of producing are sustainable, the current structure and path of our economy are not. This is because we continually engage in less production. This fact is proven by observing that our wages no longer keep pace with inflation. The cause of our economic stagnation is our "progressive" social structure which prevents a truly progressive economic structure because it consumes more wealth than it creates.

In sum, "progressivism" helps no one. Both the poor and the average person would have their economic state significantly improved by allowing others to keep their own property. Counter-intuitive as it might seem, letting the rich stay rich will bring more jobs, money, and wealth to everyone. Preventing envy from getting the best of us is the only way to eliminate poverty as well as to act in a morally correct fashion.

While capitalism harms no one and has the chief goal of protecting people and their property, socialism harms everyone and has the primary purpose of taking property from one group to give to another. Though socialists make use of the terms "freedom" and "liberty," in truth, so-called "liberal" policies take away liberties. Capitalists are the true liberals, both socially and economically. Capitalism is moral while socialism is immoral.

Chapter 8:

War and Patriotism

War is anti-capitalistic. Indeed, it threatens to destroy capitalism. When nations engage in war, liberties are dismantled and government control of the economy increases; standards of living decline as resources are redirected from the production of goods and services to the production of guns, bullets, and tanks; and the possibility of losing a war threatens the very existence of the nation. Not to mention that engaging in foreign conflicts for any reason besides immediate and urgent self-defense impoverishes other nations, creates enemies, manipulates for the worse the various economic engines of the world, and weakens our own defenses here at home. All of these factors undermine capitalism. Most important, wars claim the lives and property of mostly innocent people.

This chapter will reveal that war is politically and economically unnecessary, that there is usually not a legitimate reason for war. Since most people believe our politicians' claims that we are constantly threatened by evil forces lurking outside our borders, this chapter will show, in contrast, that most wars are intentionally created by politicians who invent threats, because they benefit from war or because they believe that a nation needs war in order to succeed.

180 million people were killed in wars during the twentieth century, far more than in any previous century.[272] This is equivalent to almost 5,000 people killed per day. Most of the dead were civilians, often women and children.[273] This number does not include those merely wounded, tortured, mutilated, dislocated, raped, diseased, or impoverished. Between the moment "peace" was declared after WWII in 1945 and the time of the Israel/Palestine "Peace Accord" in 1993, more than 150 wars were fought throughout the world.[274] These wars were not started by individuals or businesses, but by "legitimate" government forces—or by "revolutionary forces" seeking government power. Thus the root cause of war is almost always the nation state system, or those attempting to control the nation state. We should, therefore, discourage state control and consolidation of power.

Socialists often claim that capitalists start wars in order to further their interests and make higher profits. But it is rather the nation state, pursuing the interests of its leaders, that starts wars. It is common, though, that powerful businessmen, essentially in collusion with politicians, use the government to gain at the expense of all those victims of wars. To the extent that war is driven by businesses (by way of influencing politicians), the problem stems from the ability of the government to 1) have the power to centrally control all economic activity and intervene in industry and to 2) have unlimited power to tax, especially to create money (i.e., steal money) in order to fund as many wars as desired. Without these powers, the government could only engage in conflicts for which the people *voluntarily*, or at least by direct voting, allowed it to collect taxes; *citizens* would decide how much and how often they needed protection (and would probably agree to pay 80+ percent tax rates if needed to fund an immediate threat to their property). Under this structure, government would have to fully organize its wars as a *customer* or *trading partner* of industry, not as a controller of industry.

---

[272] For the details, see Matthew White, "Source List and Detailed Death Tolls for the Twentieth Century Hemoclysm," http://users.erols.com/mwhite28/warstat1.htm.

[273] In the 18th and 19th centuries, war was between the various rulers and their armies, and civilians were, as far as possible, left alone. These laws of war allowed warring parties to target each other's forces and governments, not individual citizens.

[274] Alvin and Heidi Toffler, *War and Anti-War: Survival at the Dawn of the 21st Century* (1993).

Under capitalism, partnerships between the government and military suppliers—including banks—would be both prohibited and impossible. Under mostly free markets in a system of a limited government restricted to 1) providing only basic infrastructure services, 2) upholding laws to fully protect private property and individual freedom, and 3) defending interests *at home,* there would be no opportunities for politicians to engage in military actions for economic reasons. Government would not be intertwined with businesses as it is in today's political structure, since it could not intervene in the economy. Any supposed economic problem would be solved by the marketplace.

In fact, under true capitalism, wars would exist only when the capitalist country was attacked by an outside force. Any "anticipatory reaction strikes," "defensive" actions on behalf of other states being attacked, or the carrying out of foreign "regime changes" for the purpose of imposing supposed democracy, such as the U.S. engages in today, would constitute aggression and be illegal.

Though our school history books and most of our historians tell us that America's wars have been fought for the high and necessary goal of defending our country and our freedom, the truth is otherwise. The real causes of wars are rarely what we are told by official sources. As is commonly noted, truth is the first casualty of war. Since most citizens instinctively oppose war and death, their leaders often have to develop propaganda that instills a hatred for the enemy and reveals a supposed threat to the people that justifies the sacrifices they want the people to make. Historians of the winning side then write accounts substantially relaying the official story leaders tell.

Many important facts and circumstances surrounding the onset of wars are not shared with individual citizens, who usually do not bother digging into publicly available reports to piece together the real story, either at the time or after the event. Americans in particular are usually led to believe that an evil force—communism, terrorists, religious fanatics, a new Hitler (every run of the mill dictator is labeled the next Hitler), etc.—is lurking on the horizon, poised to strike at any moment. Therefore, it's necessary to strike first. We are also told that it is only those dangerous foreigners who are provocative, that we ourselves do nothing to stoke the fire—we are as innocent as can be. In fact, however, we often push our way to the front of the line to get on the stage of war.

Since this book is focused primarily on American leaders and their management of the nation, it will be instructive to look briefly at some past wars and smaller conflicts America has been involved in so as to understand the difference between the official stories and reality. This will be done using particular (true) information that is rarely revealed to the public,[275] enabling readers/voters to better understand real history. A review of several instances of America's foreign policy will show that the U.S. doesn't simply play the role of kind protectorate for others' countries—or even our own.

Obviously, the United States—one of the freest countries in the history of the world—is not the sole bad actor. Our enemies are surely as bad or worse than we are, and other countries in our position would no doubt carry out the same or worse actions. Nevertheless, there is in our case a disparity between the high morality of our claimed purposes and the reality of our undertakings.

While the goal of this chapter is to present this hard-to-find but nevertheless public information, there will not be space to fully support the claims, other than referencing sources. Much of the information below will be shocking and may strike readers as incredible. Readers are therefore encouraged to consult the sources listed in the footnotes on their own, and to do other research. Local bookstores are probably not the best places to seek this information: many vested interests with an incentive to maintain the current system would prefer that the information not become common knowledge. Indeed, much of the information in this chapter would not have surfaced were it not for the Freedom of Information Act. There are, in any case, numerous sources of documentation about the following topics released from the U.S. and other world governments.[276]

---

[275] Just as economic cause and effect is rarely revealed to the public.

[276] Even public (government) broadcasting has confirmed many accusations in this chapter: in 2009 Georgia Public Broadcasting aired "Behind Closed Doors," which confirms many of my claims about Roosevelt and Churchill. Similar confirmations can be found from the Smithsonian Institute (see references), and Wikipedia, which I hold as *generally* reliable because of the fact that each topic has multiple contributors from various schools of thought, instead of a single source with its own political or ideological

The Civil War[277]

To kick off our set of brief examples of the real details of actual wars showing that conflicts do not take place exactly as we are told, *and that they need not have taken place*, let's start with the Civil War. Although many assume that the Civil War in the U.S. was fought for the high moral purpose of freeing the slaves, the truth is otherwise. Government power, economics, and ideology were the driving factors.[278] Slavery played into these issues, inasmuch as how slaves being counted as citizens in terms of the census would affect control of the government and the balance of power between the North and South. Had slavery alone been the issue, it could have been abolished in the same way as in every other country in the Western hemisphere, namely by compensating slaveholders.

The South wanted to secede from the Union mainly because of economic exploitation by the North, particularly as it related to punitive import tariffs: 75 percent of the tariffs were imposed on the South's ports, but the overwhelming bulk of tariff revenues were spent in the North. In essence, money was being redistributed from the South to the North. The South wanted free trade with no tariffs and consequently felt compelled to secede in order to control its own economic future.

Though slavery is clearly morally reprehensible, we should remember that it was in fact legal in the US at the beginning of the Civil War.[279] The only formal question regarding slavery at the time was whether the North should return escaped slaves, and whether the newly created states should hold slaves. Nor were secessionist movements restricted to the southern states. Many northern states, such

---

agenda (though none of the information relayed here is based on Wikipedia as a primary source).

[277] Most information in this section is derived from John V. Denson, *A Century of War: Lincoln, Wilson & Roosevelt* (2006).

[278] Evangelical religion, which will not be discussed here, was a dominant factor driving the statist ideology.

[279] Not only were blacks slaves, but some whites were as well (criminals from Britain). Also, there were black slave owners who owned black slaves, many, who owned over 100 slaves: Robert M Grooms, "Dixie's Censored Subject: Black Slaveowners," http://americancivilwar.com/authors/black_slaveowners.htm.

as Maryland, Connecticut, and most New England States, had themselves tried to secede, as did New York City during the war. [280]

Indeed even Lincoln's Republicans and many northern states opposed emancipation due to the labor competition freedom would create.[281] Republicans protested the expansion of slavery, not for moral reasons, but because of the change in balance of government power that would represent.[282] And Lincoln's eventual Emancipation Proclamation issued during the war did not free all slaves—only ones in the states the North did not control. Slavery still existed in "loyal" border states and in Washington, D.C., itself.

Lincoln had previously declared, as indeed had our nation's founders, that the right to shake off an existing government and to form one that better suits a people is a most "valuable" and "sacred" right.[283] Therefore if America's war of independence from Britain was just, so was the South's. Further, Lincoln had denied any intention to interfere with the South's slavery and had no legal right to do so.

The South wanted only secession, but Lincoln, in calling for a blockade of southern ports,[284] in fact initiated the war, maneuvering the South into firing first (killing no one), so that he could engage in war against it. Even some Northern newspapers saw though this charade and questioned Lincoln's intentions. Besides wanting the South to fund most of his budget, for ideological and religious reasons, Lincoln sought a centralized government with increased power.

Over 600,000 people died during the Civil War. Many of those wounded or killed were civilians targeted by Lincoln's forces[285]—both black and white women and children were robbed, brutalized,

---

[280] See David Gordon, ed., *Secession, State and Liberty* (1998), which shows that both the North and South had promoted the "right" to secession and had both threatened such actions on numerous occasions before the Civil War.

[281] Stephan Kinsella, *Tariffs, Blockades, and Inflation: The Economics of the Civil War* (book review), http://mises.org/journals/jls/18_4/18_4_3.pdf.

[282] Ibid.

[283] John Shipley Tilley, *Lincoln Takes Command* (1991).

[284] James G. Randall, *Constitutional Problems Under Lincoln* (1951), p. 50.

[285] Burke Davis, "The Price in Blood! Casualties in the Civil War," http://www.civilwarhome.com/casualties.htm.

tortured, raped, and left homeless. Southern blacks were regularly beaten, tortured, or killed by their northern liberators.[286]

Others merely lost their freedoms during the war: Lincoln suspended habeas corpus, arrested judges who declared his actions illegal, suspended state legislatures on the suspicion that they might vote for secession, confiscated railroads and "disloyal" newspapers,[287] and arrested thirteen thousand people without cause or warrants for protesting his war. He also used American soldiers to slaughter Indians who were in the path of his friends' desired railroad tracks.

The United States Supreme Court later stated that the war had two starting points before the firing at Fort Sumter, both initiated by President Lincoln in calling for a blockade of Southern ports.[288] Thus, through the use of force, Lincoln transformed America from a confederation of states to a consolidated warfare-welfare state, thereby creating American nationalism, which, like all nationalism is both jingoistic and fascistic.

Is Secession A Bad Thing?[289]

We saw above that the Civil War would not have taken place had Lincoln allowed the South to secede. And secession is seen by most as a terrible thing that tears countries apart; whenever the possibility of secession is mentioned in today's world, the concept is viewed as something only lunatics would support. "How could anyone dare promote changing the borders of these United States of America!" But there is nothing sacred about national borders as they stand. They are arbitrary lines, imposed by centralized governments, separating people. Plus, no borders are permanent; the U.S. did not have its current borders 100—and especially 150—years ago and will likely have different ones 100 years from now.

---

[286] Walter Brian Cisco, *War Crimes Against Southern Civilians* (2007).

[287] Mark E. Nealy, *The Fate of Liberty: Abraham Lincoln and Civil Liberties* (1992), pp. 10, 23

[288] James G. Randall, *Constitutional Problems Under Lincoln* (1951), p.50.

[289] Most of the information in this and the next section are taken, quite directly, from the section, "The Nationalities Question," by Murray Rothbard, from the book *The Irrepressible Rothbard: The Rothbard-Rockwell Report Essays of Murray N. Rothbard* (2000).

Minority secession movements are seen as violating democratic majority rule. But the crucial and always unanswered question is: democratic rule over what geographical area? Most people assert that there should be a single, overriding government agency with a monopoly force to settle disputes by coercion. Fine, but if that's the case, then by the very same logic, shouldn't all nation-states be replaced by a one-world monopoly government? After all, don't we currently have "international anarchy" ("anarchy" is defined as a lack of overall government control, not a state of chaos)? Most people rightly protest a one world government for fear that world taxation, socialization, control, and a lack of local freedom would totally and irreversibly suppress the liberty and property of Americans. Even American Democrats hate the idea of a one-world government (unless they can be assured of controlling it).

In the U.S. and Europe, the individual geographical regions that were consolidated into today's nation states used to consist of individual monarchies (in Europe) and of smaller autonomous cities and states (in the United States), where people lived much more prosperously and safely (there was no income tax, no inflation, low crime, strong economic growth). Though a centralized world government is not promoted by most people, the historical trend, as far as government action is concerned, has been to combine smaller regions into larger centralized areas, but not the reverse.

Yet individual groups of the world in some of these larger regions often want self-rule, such as the Kurds in Turkey, the Basques of Northern Spain, French Canadians, the Chiapas in Mexico, the lower Saxons and Bavarians of Germany, the Padania region of Italy, Northern Ireland, etc. If we've combined ourselves into larger centrally-planned nation-states, what's wrong with undoing that and reverting to smaller autonomous regions, for those who want them?

Exactly what should national boundaries be based upon? What national boundaries are considered as just? In the first place, it must be recognized that there are no just national boundaries per se. Real justice can be founded only on the property rights of individuals. If fifty people decided voluntarily to set up an organization for common services or self-defense of their properties and themselves in a certain geographical area (as happened in California in the 1800s before the state government took over), then the boundaries of that area, based on the just property rights of the members, would also be just.

National boundaries are just only when based on voluntary consent and the property rights of their members or citizens. The only way to have national boundaries as just as possible is to preserve and cherish the right of secession, the right of different regions, groups, or ethnic nationalities to leave the larger entity and set up their own independent nation. If the natural right of secession is not permitted, if people cannot live how they please, there is no true freedom. As Murray Rothbard said:

> There is no nation; there are only individuals. The nation is a collectivist and therefore pernicious concept. The concept of 'national self-determination' is fallacious, since only the individual has a 'self.' Since the nation and the State are both collective concepts, both are pernicious and should be combated.[290]

Given that nation-states do exist, they should (a) never exercise their power beyond their territorial area (a foreign policy of "isolationism"), and (b) maintain the right of secession of groups or entities within their territorial area. The right of secession, if strongly upheld, implies also the right of one or more villages to secede even from its own ethnic nation, or, even the right of a single individual to secede.

Respecting the Borders of Other Countries

It is the fact that nation-states exercise power beyond their borders and fail to allow "self-determination" in countries in which they interfere that many of the problems of the 20th century developed. This was the case particularly with respect to British, French, and American foreign policy, where these countries carved up pieces of Europe and the Middle East, arbitrarily assigning borders in order to break countries apart (Germany, Poland, Austria-Hungary, Palestine, etc.) or to assemble them by force (Czechoslovakia, Syria, Iraq, Jordan etc.).[291] The Allied forces, due to politics, recognized and protected

---

[290] Murray Rothbard, *The irrepressible Rothbard: The Rothbard-Rockwell report essays of Murray N. Rothbard* (2000).

[291] Churchill used to brag that he created Jordan in an afternoon.

existing borders when it benefited them (saving Poland and Hungary from the Nazis and the Soviets in 1939), and refused to recognize existing borders when it did not (failing to save Czechoslovakia from the Nazis in 1938 or the Baltic States from the Soviets in 1940). In creating countries in the name of "self-determination," the Allies made some ethnicities more equal than others, by forcing the "bad" ethnic groups to be ruled by our friends, the "good" ethnic groups.

Due to politicians seeking power and alliances in 20th century Europe, border changes created minorities and international conflicts, regional and civil wars, and were often accompanied by violence and ethnic cleansing. People were not free to live as they wished, but only as rulers, although democratically elected, physically forced them to.

Our democratic, freedom-seeking leaders also intervene or don't intervene in domestic affairs within other nation's borders, such as when the U.S., paying "allies" to join them, invaded Iraq to save its people—particularly its gassed Kurdish minority—from a ruthless thug and to stop the Iraqis from accessing the same weapons that we have and use. Yet, when it came to the on-going genocide in Rwanda (resulting from one group trying to force another to live a particular way within defined borders), the U.S. apparently decided that those people were not worth saving, or that there were no strategic reasons for doing so. So much for saving human lives being a primary objective.

The inconsistencies are clear to those who take time to think about them. As *Newsweek* stated with respect to foreign policy in 1991:

> What is sacrosanct about existing borders, given that many ethnic groups have plausible claims to their traditional land? Bush seems to agree in the case of the Palestinians—but not the Kurds, or Yugoslavia's Croats and Slovenes. And some threats to international order stem from violence or political repression within the borders of a single country. Doesn't "order" depend to some extent on the spread of democracy? Bush seems to think so in Cuba, but not in China. The president sometimes professes ambivalence about interfering in other countries' internal matters (the clash between Mos-

cow and Lithuania, for example). But he has plunged into the affairs of Kuwait, Iraq and Panama.[292]

(Panama, incidentally, is a prime example of how the U.S. does not practice what it preaches concerning democracy. After we invaded that sovereign country to depose Noriega merely because he quit taking orders from the U.S. government, Panamanian citizens cried for free elections. Instead, the U.S. swore in its hand-picked Endara regime on a U.S. military base hours after the invasion.)

Sanctifying status quo boundaries has been the basis of U.S. foreign policy since the establishment of the League of Nations and its successor the United Nations, all based on the incoherent and disastrous concept of "collective security against aggression."

This logic underlay U.S. intervention in World Wars I and II, and in the Korean War: first we determine (often incorrectly) which is the "aggressor state," and then all nation-states are supposed to band together to combat, repel, and punish the aggressor.

A major flaw in this concept, as hinted at in the *Newsweek* quote above, is that when an individual aggresses upon another person, there is usually clarity, based on property rights, as to who is the aggressor and who is the victim. But what happens when nation-state A aggresses against the border of nation-state B, often claiming that the border is unjust and the result of a previous aggression against State A decades before? How can we be certain that State A is the aggressor and that we must dismiss its claims out of hand?

When nation-states arbitrarily claim individual property as belonging to their borders, and other nation-states want the land instead, or, those who rightfully own the land want to unshackle themselves from the current nation-state who holds them, troubles necessarily arise.

---

[292] Charles Lane, "Haiti: Why the Coup Matters," *Newsweek* (October 14, 1991), p. 34., http://www.newsweek.com/id/127115.

World War I [293]

Turning now to the first World War, we find that there was no need for America to enter the war, and above all, that there was no need for war, period. The Great War started as a narrowly European conflict begun by Serbia, in which America had no reason to engage.

Due to the Europeans' complicated web of alliances and need to fight multiple countries in multiple places, the Germans, once their borders were threatened, chose to pass through neutral Belgium in order to quickly prevent France from attacking first. The British, incorrectly interpreting these actions as an economic threat to their own empire, though it had no legal responsibility to assist Belgium, stepped in to fight Germany, thereby turning a regional conflict into a world war. Though most British cabinet ministers were initially hesitant to wage war, Britain's foreign minister, Edward Grey, the country's primary proponent of war, succeeded in persuading the majority of the people to support the move, just as George W. Bush somehow persuaded American politicians and citizens into war against all odds in 2003.

Ironically, not only did Germany's military actions not endanger Britain, but Germany's Kaiser would likely have honored his commitment (on the eve of the war) to guarantee French and Belgian territorial integrity in exchange for Britain's neutrality. The Bolsheviks, upon taking power in Russia, released documents proving that Germany went to great lengths to avoid the war. All countries were guilty, but had Britain left the warring countries to fight amongst themselves, millions of deaths and the destruction of hundreds of cities would have been prevented.

German and British soldiers spent Christmas Eve 1914 together under a voluntary cease-fire, helping each other bury their dead, playing soccer, exchanging chocolates and cigarettes, celebrating Christmas, and discussing the various pieces of war propaganda appearing in their respective country's newspapers.[294] One of the British soldiers,

---

[293] Most information in this section is derived from Niall Ferguson's *The Pity of War* (1998) and Mises Institute lectures and papers on the war, predominately those by Ralph Raico and Murray Rothbard.

[294] John V. Denson, *A Century of War: Lincoln, Wilson, and Roosevelt* (2006), p. 189.

years later as a Cabinet Minister, explained to the House of Commons that "if we had been left by ourselves there would never have been another shot fired... it was only the fact that we were being controlled by others that made it necessary for us to start trying to shoot one another again."[295] The soldiers from each side realized they had no idea what they were fighting about, which was mostly for their politicians' careers.

Had Britain, who pulled America into the war, stayed out of the war, there likely would have been a quick and easy German victory, with some territorial changes in Eastern Europe, but probably no mass destruction and death. Russia would not have been destroyed and seen its government collapse. Therefore, there would have been no Bolshevik Revolution, no Lenin, and no Stalin (and possibly no Mao in China). Had the small German victories been the extent of the war, there would have been no Versailles Treaty, and therefore no Hitler (see below), and therefore no World War II and Cold War. Overwhelming evidence suggests that the Germans had no plans for massive expansion in Europe.

In this latter scenario, not only would most of the 20 million deaths of WWI have been avoided, but also the 50 million deaths of WWII—mostly civilians—not to mention the hundreds of millions killed under the communist regimes that sprang up on the back of Russia's WWI collapse. Additionally, without the weakened and impoverished immune systems of the people of the world during WWI, the Spanish Flu, which killed more than 20 million worldwide starting in the last year of the war, would likely not have been able to spread like wildfire as it did.

Other nations can be belligerent if they must; but there is no need for America to get involved.

The Politicians' Need for War

Today, politicians go to war largely to increase their power, but this power is achieved at the expense of the power and freedom of the

---

[295] Sir Kingsley Wood made the statement, as quoted by John V. Denson, *A Century of War: Lincoln, Wilson & Roosevelt* (2006).

people. Since war is an instrument used to aggrandize state power, most of the losses of individual freedoms occur during times of war.

During WWI for example, the Sabotage and Seditions act was passed, allowing the federal government to punish anyone with an opinion that was "disloyal, profane, scurrilous, or abusive."[296] This act prevented the post office at one point from delivering mail that was "antiwar." And we have all seen the freedoms taken from us by the Patriot Act. Wilson and the war also gave America the Federal Reserve and the (permanent) income tax, along with the Federal Trade Commission, the League of Nations, and the Versailles Treaty, which directly led to World War II. The German language was made illegal, and in some states only English was legal. Citizens were asked to report those selling goods for less than the government-stated price. The injustices were numerous, and many last to this day.

There are, however, many advantages for politicians who go to war. They gain substantially increased "wartime" powers; they unite a country which comes together to support the glorious "war effort"; they gain fame and admiration for "heroically" leading a country through the difficult challenge of "defending freedom." But only governments go to war, not people. The people of various countries usually get along fine and would never fight were it not for their government's telling them to or putting them in positions where they feel compelled, and, were it not for their thinking that they somehow need politicians to "lead them."

It might be argued that the soldiers of the Christmas truce of WWI who would not have continued fighting on their own might grow up into businessmen who would want to fight for each other's profits. But without a national government to do their fighting for them, they would have been constrained to stick with business, i.e., merely exchanging money for resources, and competing with their products and their prices instead of with machine guns and bombs.

I've traveled to many countries which do not like the United States. But the people are very warm to me. This is because, as they

---

[296] Douglas Carey, (Wartime's Lost Liberties), http://mises.org/story/844.

state, they dislike my government, not the people (even though it's the people, in democracies, who support the government by voting for it).

Democratic House member Charlie Rangel proposed in 2007 that the U.S. force all young men to serve in the military so that politicians would be less likely to start wars, since their own sons might have to fight. A more humane option would be a law requiring the president, his staff, and all members of congress to go to the front lines and fight during war instead of allowing them to stay at a safe distance in their leather chairs and marble buildings.

The Economic "Need" for War

In absence of politicians managing an economy, what would be left would be individuals living, working, and trading with each other all around the world. There would be little need to fight for land or resources; what resources were needed could be obtained through free exchange. One could buy all the land and oil they need; there are millions of entities willing to sell these items. (Often, though, resources in today's government-run economy can be unavailable because government misuses, hoards or controls them to a degree that they are not available for exchange on the market. An example would be African countries whose dictators don't allow the economic investments needed to take their natural resources out of the ground. Or the nationalized steel and oil companies, whose assets are not for sale at any price.) After all, Japan became much more successful economically by laboring and buying resources after World War II than it was in stealing them from Korea and China before that.

There is also no need to "find a distant market." It would be ideal if other countries were involved in world production and exchange, but if they are not, so be it; they should be left alone. If a country can't find export markets because there are no trading countries, it can exchange and consume all of its production in the home country, since there could never be a satiation of goods at home. But since ignorant government officials and businessmen who fund their campaigns feel a need to somehow find foreign markets, wars ensue. Industry can find foreign markets by itself; governments usually intervene to try and *force* foreign markets into becoming "democracies" and trading partners. This is unneeded and immoral.

We don't need to impose democracy. Even if countries want to become full communists, let them; they won't survive anyway. As we learned from Chapter 6, communism cannot survive on its own. Had the Soviet Union taken over Europe, America, or the world, it wouldn't have lasted long. Communism was no real threat, but hundreds of millions of people in hundreds of countries suffered under brutal regimes or died in the name of keeping communism at a distance. They would probably have been better off under communism.

We don't need the world to be democratic or even capitalistic in order to prosper. It's true, we will prosper much more with capitalism existing in more countries, but it's not a necessity. And it should be clear by now that Democracy is usually mutually exclusive from Capitalism and freedom. The last century has been filled with democracies starting wars, suppressing citizens, and preventing economic progress. And we have seen already that wars themselves do not help grow an economy.

There is also no need to be economically or militarily "powerful." There certainly is no need for power in order to progress economically—quite the opposite. There also cannot be such thing as a country being an economic "power"[297] under capitalism, because private enterprises produce and exchange goods—they do not physically compete. Under capitalism, a strong economy can only come about due to voluntary and peaceful exchange, not by force.

There is no need for any type of "economic control," nationally or internationally, especially at the cost of millions of lives and the loss of freedom, which is what has been the result of democratic socialist countries seeking this control. We should heed the words of George Washington:

> The Great rule of conduct for us, in regard to foreign Nations
> is in extending our commercial relations to have with them as

---

[297] There is also no such thing as an "engine of growth" for the world. Just because one country can produce goods rapidly and advance, this action does not cause another nation to grow. Just becoming wealthy and being able to purchase goods from a poor country does not increase the amount of goods a poor country can create.

little political connection as possible.... 'Tis our true policy to steer clear of permanent Alliances, with any portion of the foreign world.[298]

World War II[299]

As in the Civil War and World War I, we find more evidence of unnecessary belligerence and deceit leading to WWII. After WWI ended, the British continued their naval blockade of Germany, thereby causing 800,000 civilian deaths through starvation and, driving Germany to agree to sign the vindictive and punitive Versailles Treaty.[300] This treaty not only imposed reparations beyond what the German economy could endure, but also distributed portions of the country to Poland (which was set up by the U.S. as a client state in order to keep Germany and Russia in check), Czechoslovakia, and Austria, denying self-determination to millions of Germans, despite President Wilson's assurances to the contrary. Hitler, later, was *democratically* voted into power on the promise to fight communism and end the Versailles Treaty. After the Allies rejected numerous offers of renegotiations from Hitler—except for an approval for Germany to reclaim some of Czechoslovakia—including a 25-year non-aggression pact [301] and returning to the Allies' originally-promised treaty terms, and after the allies essentially canceled Poland and Germany's 1934 non-aggression pact, Germany, *in cooperation with the Soviet Union*, invaded Czechoslovakia, Austria and Poland in order to reclaim their land and people (and probably to acquire additional land). Hitler had not expected the Allies to fight over a treaty they themselves declared unfair. The Allies claimed to have entered the war specifically to defend Poland, but they mostly refused to help Poland in any real way. In fact, Poland was ultimately "saved" by being carved up by Roosevelt, Churchill, and their ally Stalin to suffer yet more death and torture under the Soviet Union.

---

[298] W.B. Allen, ed., *George Washington: A Collection* (1988).

[299] Most information in this section is derived from John V. Denson's book *A Century of War: Lincoln, Wilson & Roosevelt* (2006).

[300] Caroll Quigley, *Tragedy and Hope: A History of the World in Our Time* (1974), p. 950.

[301] A. J. P. Taylor, *The Origins of the Second World War* (1996), p.100.

After the war started, though British citizens did not want war, Churchill engaged in bombing raids on German cities, contrary to the usual story that Hitler—who wanted no fight with Britain, and allowed allied forces to escape Dunkirk—bombed first. And though American citizens also wanted to stay out of the war, Roosevelt did everything possible to get them in, by trying to have the "enemy" fire the first shot. He had destroyers chase and provoke Nazi subs and taunt Japanese war ships in hopes that they would fire back (with the approval of "losing one or two cruisers"), sent 50 destroyers to aid Britain, cut off the Japanese oil supply, etc. After one German sub finally shot back, Roosevelt declared: *"In the long run...all that will matter is who fired the last shot. America has been attacked."*

When the Japanese tried to negotiate, Roosevelt refused, as he did with Hitler. Knowing they would be attacked, the Japanese—who were guilty of invading and slaughtering the Chinese at the time—decided to strike first (protective reaction strike), at Pearl Harbor. Roosevelt knew of the impending attack both from the Peruvian ambassador[302] and from intercepted radio transmissions from Japanese carriers and battleships en route to Hawaii (though the usual story is that the Japanese maintained radio silence).[303] Except for reporting the ambassador's information as rumors, Roosevelt withheld most intelligence from Pearl Harbor commanders,[304] but he did direct commanders to leave their oldest ships in Pearl Harbor and to send twenty-one of the newest and most modern ships away from the path of the oncoming Japanese fleet.[305] In 1999, the U.S. Senate concluded that the previous scapegoats, Pearl Harbor officers, "were not provided necessary and critical intelligence that was available, that foretold of war with Japan, that warned of imminent attack, and that would have alerted them to prepare for the attack."[306]

---

[302] John V. Denson, *A Century of War: Lincoln, Wilson & Roosevelt* (2006).

[303] See Robert B. Stinnett, *Day of Deceit: The Truth about FDR and Pearl Harbor* (2000), p. 144–45, 152 and 154.

[304] John V. Denson, *A Century of War: Lincoln, Wilson & Roosevelt* (2006).

[305] Robert B. Stinnett, *Day of Deceit: The Truth about FDR and Pearl Harbor* (2000).

[306] See Roth Amendment No. 388 to the Defense Authorization Act passed by the United States Senate for the 106th Congress, First Session May 25, 1999, and the Senate Congressional Record for May 24, 1999, Sec. 582, p. S 5879.

The War ended with atomic bombs being dropped on Japanese citizens, even though the Japanese had been trying to surrender for months, and though its army was on its last leg. Roosevelt would not allow them to because their one condition was that they keep their emperor. But once the war ended, America insisted that Japan keep its emperor anyway, even shielding the imperial family from charges of war crimes, though they were surely guilty of such.

America's World Dominance

We often hear that America is the "world police" or that it is "imperialistic," but do we really know what this means? Have most people really looked into the facts? Probably not. So let's take a brief look at the role the United States plays in affecting people throughout the world.

For well over 50 years now, the U.S. government has attempted to, and been largely successful at, controlling much of the world.[307] It has attempted, and usually accomplished, the overthrow of over 40 foreign governments and the smashing of more than 30 rebellion movements fighting against oppressive regimes.[308] It spends hundreds of billions of dollars a year of our tax money maintaining its overseas operations: over 325,000 military personnel and more than 700 military bases in over 130 countries. These operations are not in place to protect us from aggressors; they are there to make sure other countries do exactly what the U.S. wants them to, for the U.S. to maintain dominance.

In addition to using tools such as the United Nations and NATO to control other countries, the U.S. has very often, and continues to, either directly or indirectly engage in torture, murder, genocide, use of chemical and biological weapons, terrorism, famine, starvation, bombing, ethnic cleansing, drug trafficking, invasions, sanctions, embargoes, assassinations, perverting elections, deposing democratically elected leaders, propaganda, blackmail, and extortion (yet today, people are obsessed over "mere" water-boarding, and water-boarding only). These actions take place largely through policies carried out by dictators that America sets up in countries throughout the world. William

---

[307] Much of the facts and discussion in this section are from William Blum, *Rogue State: A Guide to the World's Only Superpower* (2006).
[308] Ibid.

Blum, in his book *Rogue State: A Guide to the World's Only Superpower,* compiles a list (which is far from complete) of many of these interventions. They are listed in **Figure 8.1**.

Let's look at a few brief examples of these foreign interventions to get the idea of America's actions. Many of the following descriptions are from Blum's book.

Indonesia, 1965

The U.S. helped oust Sukarno, who had communist leanings, and replaced him with General Suharto and the Indonesian military. Suharto oversaw a purge of all people who were or might possibly be suspected of communist ties or sympathies. The *New York Times* called it "one of the most savage mass slayings in modern political history."[309] It is estimated that within a few years between a half million and a million or more people were killed. The Clinton administration later called Suharto "our kind of guy."[310]

It was learned afterward that the U.S. embassy had compiled lists of names it turned over to the Indonesian army so that these individuals could be hunted down and killed. One U.S. diplomat stated, "They probably killed a lot of people, and I probably have a lot of blood on my hands. But that's not all bad. There's a time when you have to strike hard at a decisive moment."[311]

Cambodia, 1970s

Notorious general Pol Pot and his Khmer Rouge, after ousting the U.S.-supported regime of Lon Nol, engaged in mass murders reminiscent of Nazi genocide. Four years later, Vietnam overthrew Pol Pot. But since the U.S. hated the Vietnamese government, it secretly financed Pol Pot and coordinated with him. The American funds helped to support Pol Pot's killing of villagers and would undoubtedly have led to many more mass murders, tortures, and continued communism had the Khmer Rouge returned to power.

---

[309] William Blum, *Rogue State: A Guide to the World's Only Superpower* (2006) p. 141.

[310] Ibid, p. 147

[311] Ibid, p. 147

U.S. interventions abroad, 1945-2009

China, 1945-51	The Congo/Zaire, 1960-65, 1977-78	Chad, 1981-82
France, 1947	France/Algeria, 1960s	Grenada, 1979-83
Marshall Islands, 1946-58	Brazil, 1961-64	Suriname, 1982-84
Italy, 1947-1970s	Peru, 1965	Libya, 1981-89
Greece, 1947-49	Dominican Republic, 1963-65	Fiji, 1987
Philippines, 1945-53	Cuba, 1959 to present	Panama, 1989
Korea, 1945-53	Indonesia, 1965	Afghanistan, 1979-92
Albania, 1949-53	Ghana, 1966	El Salvador, 1980-92
Eastern Europe, 1948-56	Uruguay, 1969-72	Haiti, 1987-94
Germany 1950s	Chile, 1964-73	Bulgaria, 1990-91
Iran, 1953	Greece, 1967-74	Albania, 1991-92
Guatemala, 1953-1990s	South Africa, 1960s-1980s	Somalia, 1993
Costa Rica, mid-1950s, 1970-71	Bolivia, 1964-75	Iraq, 1990s
Middle East, 1956-58	Australia, 1972-75	Peru, 1990s-present
Indonesia, 1957-58	Iraq, 1972-75	Mexico, 1990s-present
Haiti, 1959	Portugal, 1974-76	Columbia, 1990s-present
Western Europe, 1950s-1960s	East Timor, 1975-79Angola, 1975-1980s	Yugoslavia, 1995-99
British Guina/Guyana, 1953-64	Jamaica, 1976	Afghanistan, 2001-present*
Iraq, 1958-63	Honduras, 1980s	Iraq, 2003-present*
Soviet Union, 1940s-1960s	Nicaragua, 1978-90	Yemen, 2003*
Vietnam, 1945-73	Philippines, 1970s-1990s	Georgia, 2003*
Cambodia, 1955-73	Seychelles, 1979-81	Pakistan, 2006*
Laos, 1957-73	South Yemen, 1979-84	South Ossetia, Georgia, 2008*
Thailand, 1965-73	South Korea, 1980	Pakistan, 2009*
Ecuador, 1960-63		*Compiled by the author

Source: William Blum, *Rogue State: A Guide to the World's Only Superpower*

Figure 8.1

Europe, post WWII

The CIA created secret civilian armies that it controlled all over Europe, especially in Germany, after WWII. The operations were rolled into NATO after its creation. The civilian armies engaged in

354   The Case for Legalizing Capitalism | Kelly

random acts of terrorism which were orchestrated so as to appear to have been carried out by leftists; the goal was to make people fearful of the Soviets and disinclined to vote for leftist communist parties. An example of the terrorist acts was the bombing of the Bologna railway station in 1980, claiming 86 lives.[312]

Afghanistan, 1979-92

Since the country had a Marxist president supported by the Soviet Union, the U.S. wanted to oust it. It teamed up with the Taliban Islamic fundamentalists to intentionally induce the Soviets to respond. President Carter's national security advisor Zbigniew Brzezinski stated that "the secret operation was an excellent idea...it had the idea of drawing the Russians into a trap...giving the U.S.S.R. its Vietnam war." America's guys, the Mujadeen, engaged in torture that even U.S. government officials called "indescribable horror."[313] Half of the population was horribly affected: 1 million died, 3 million became disabled, 5 million became refuges.

Yugoslavia

The U.S. government supports breakaway provinces (such as Taiwan) when it's in the U.S.'s interests, but opposes them when they're not. President Clinton, in reference to Chechnya's attempted secession from Russia, stated, "we once had a Civil War in our country... over the proposition that Abraham Lincoln gave his life for, that no State had a right to withdraw from our Union."[314] Three years later, President Clinton opposed Serbian president Slobodan Milosevic preventing Kosovo from withdrawing from the Federal Republic of Yugoslavia. Clinton, who promised to be an anti-war president, breaking international law, and under the guise of NATO, bombed Yugoslavia for 40 days, destroying much of the country.

Clinton cited a "moral imperative" for his bombings; but at the same time, America's ally, Turkey, had for fifteen years been carrying

---

[312] William Blum, *Rogue State: A Guide to the World's Only Superpower* (2006), p. 130.

[313] Ibid., p. 5.

[314] U.S. Government Printing Office, *Public Papers of the Presidents of the United States* (1996), vol. I, p. 614.

out many of the same abuses against the Kurds as Serbia was against Kosovo. Nor did Clinton spy a moral imperative to stop the genocide in Rwanda a few years earlier. NATO bombings gave rise to most of the deaths in Yugoslavia, provoked most of the Serbian atrocities, created an environmental disaster, and left numerous unexploded uranium and cluster bombs. This bombing, like most, involved the firm expectation by American military planners that many innocent civilians would be killed. Additionally, several hundred thousand were left homeless.[315]

Palestine

The British promised Palestine to Arabs while simultaneously promising it to Jews for their "National Home." It allowed Jewish settlers to acquire land (often by bribing government officials) from Britain which it and Turkey had taken from Arab peasants who had traditionally occupied the land, and threw the Palestinians off their land.

Disgusted with trying to manage the conflicting desires of both Jews and Arabs, the British finally withdrew from the region after WWII and left the mess up to the United Nations, where the U.S. exerted a tremendous amount of pressure to partition Palestine, which the U.N. reluctantly acted on. The Partition granted the Jews almost half of Palestine, even though they represented a very small fraction of the population. Afterward, the conditions of this partition were ignored and largely disregarded by Israel, and it began forcefully to acquire much of the rest of Palestine, instigating violence against those in its path. Most of the original Palestinians were eventually driven from their homes and bank accounts. Now they fight to get them back.

Jews and Arabs lived peacefully in the Middle East for hundreds of years. Today, they are constantly at war. The United States helps fund the forces of both Israel and Palestine, but gives Israel over 20 times more.[316] It is commonly explained by politicians and the media that Israel is simply defending itself from unfair attacks, and that the Palestinians are no-good terrorists. When Iran (and Arab states) says

---

[315] William Blum, *Rogue State: A Guide to the World's Only Superpower* (2006).

[316] IfAmericansKnew.org, "U.S. Military Aid and the Israel/Palestine Conflict," http://www.ifamericansknew.org/stats/usaid.html.

that Israel has no right to exist and that it should be wiped off the earth, the media and politicians portray these words as nuclear threats (knowing the public will fall for it), when actual translations reveal that Iran is primarily saying that Israel is an illegitimate state illegally occupying Palestinian land, and should therefore cease to exist, at least in that spot.

It is very true and very sad that Jews have been unfairly persecuted for centuries. It would be nice for them to have a safe place of their own (although many ethnic and religious groups are persecuted and do not have the luxury of their own homeland), and I would personally help them to defend themselves from any aggressors. But regardless of the agonizing unfair abuse they've endured through the centuries, their homeland should have been acquired fairly. Jews could have acquired the land legitimately through purchase from the rightful owners. In this way, they would be entitled to all the land they could afford, even if they bought all of Palestine and changed the name to Israel! Additionally, if the U.S. was going to give away land, instead of giving others' land, it would have been better to give away its own uninhabited (and geographically comparable) land in the western United States.

The Middle East Today

This friction between Israel and the Arab world is the root issue of many, if not most, of the problems in the Middle East today (and many of our terrorist threats). And the U.S. constantly intervenes to keep an artificially structured middle east artificial. But almost everything it does simply causes more problems. For example, our current problems in Iraq are of our own doings. The CIA helped bring Saddam Hussein to power, and we funded his war against Iran. He then used those weapons to invade Kuwait, only after the U.S. explicitly gave him the green light to do so. He gassed his people with chemical and biological weapons supplied by the U.S. After helping him, we then felt compelled to attack him because he was a supposed threat to us.

Likewise, we intervened in Iran for years, we knocked off their elected leaders and inserted our own, we bombed their ships, and shot down their passenger planes. Iranians finally overthrew the Shah America imposed on them, and kidnapped its embassy workers.

Iran recently celebrated its 30th anniversary of the ouster of their American imposed Shah. It was also the anniversary of the seizure of the American embassy in Tehran. On that anniversary Iran's supreme leader Ayatollah Ali Khamenei proclaimed that "hatred towards the US government is deep-seated because of its plots against the Iranian people over the past 50 years…[b]esides, they have not apologised yet and rather keep on their arrogant attitude."[317] He proposed to the new Obama administration that "If you change your attitude, we will change our attitude."[318]

Hugo Chavez indicated similar sentiments to Obama at the Summit of the Americas by giving him a book, "The Open Veins of Latin America: Five Centuries of the Pillage of a Continent," which chronicles western economic and political intervention on his continent (though their own leaders have done far more damage in the last century).

Now that we have ravaged Afghanistan and killed more than a million Iraqis (of course the media, and Americans in general, only care about the body count of U.S. soldiers, as though Iraqis are not real human beings who are just as valuable), we need a new war. So Iran is now once again being made the new poster child for the supposed threat to the world. We have screwed with them for decades, but we call them the ones who are threatening harm.

They are no threat; we are the threat, and they are rightly scared of us. But the U.S. intentionally makes them out to be the menace because it needs a new war, a new reason for the public to "come together" and support our benevolent government who wants to bomb the world in order to keep us safe—perpetual war for perpetual peace. Even though, surprisingly, the American public retrospectively saw that the invasion of Iraq was a sham, they shockingly returned

---

[317] Agence France-Presse, "Iran's Khamenei sees no easing of hatred for US," (October 29, 2008), http://afp.google.com/article/ALeqM5iXsm0qMrnC8bDCjkshC7tu2mvxyA.

[318] Agence France-Presse, "Iran can change if US leads: Khamenei," (March 21, 2009), http://news.theage.com.au/breaking-news-world/iran-can-change-if-us-leads-khamenei-20090321-94z5.html.

their head to the sand once George W. Bush moved to his next desired war, the one against Iran. Had he stayed in office long enough he probably would have been allowed by the American people to get away with attacking Iran. But what's also scary is that President Obama and Secretary of State Hillary Clinton are now continuing the fake tough talk and are implying that Iran is somehow a threat.

With respect to foreign countries and terrorists, we have to ask: If we didn't bother them, what possible beef could they have with a country keeping to itself half-way around the world? Would they want to invade us and take our buildings and homes and ship them to their own country? Do they want to steal our bank accounts (in which case massive amounts of dollar bills flowing into Iran would only raise prices, and dilute the effects of their new wealth)? Do they want to reside in Virginia and Oklahoma instead of their native lands? What do they actually gain? They really don't have a reason to bother us except for the fact that we make their lives difficult. Moreover, in case a country did attack, doesn't it make sense that our country would be safer with our forces at home instead of abroad?

President Obama has already decided to send tens of thousands of troops back to Afghanistan. Since almost every president, Democrat or Republican, eventually goes down the war-mongering path, it would not be surprising of Obama to eventually deliver his (contrived) case to the American public, stating how Iran is now the new threat to world safety and must be dealt with immediately…in the name of freedom and security, of course. Oh yeah, and "patriotism" too.

How to Start a War

The politician's best excuse to get a country into war is an imminent threat of attack by a madman dictator holding "weapons of mass destruction." This worked quite easily to get America into Iraq in 2003. It is America's best chance to start a war with Iran or North Korea. Of course, there are currently 29 nations holding weapons of mass destruction.

There are no military threats 99 percent of the time. "Threats" usually consist of either 1) a country building up arms simply because the other is doing so and because each side is afraid the first side will attack or 2) a country being fearful of a military attack only because of the fact that their previous hostile actions have either intentionally or unintentionally brought the threat about. Both of these cases applied to countries on both sides of the Iron curtain during the cold war (after all, the U.S. and its allies did invade Russia in 1918),[319] and the former case specifically applies to current U.S. fears of a military buildup in China, and vice versa. Neither case should be a reality to countries which remained neutral and isolationist. As should be apparent from the information in this chapter, isolationism saves many more lives than does "defending" other countries that are aggressed upon.

A solid general tool politicians apply is that of "national interest," which is simply and cunningly defined to cover every ill and grievance under the sun. Any two groups fighting, anyone starving or anyone with a hate thought anywhere in the world, and especially, any nation not a "democracy" as we define it is a threat to our "national interest."

Aggression usually starts with sanctions. This allows a step-by-step escalation of intervention, since immediate bombing or invasion does not go over well for most Americans. Our government first needs to cut off supplies to a country, starving its citizens.[320] Then, we impose "unconditional" surrender or "unconditional" compliance with our demands. Knowing our extreme and outrageous demands will not be met, we can then claim that they are not being peace-making and are still a threat. Then, we can bomb and invade. Troops are usually sent first as "humanitarian aid, with a gun in one hand and a food packet in another." When the locals reject our benevolent help and start firing at us, then we go in with orders to kill. When there is no need to make an affair public, funding an opposing group or taking out the current leaders of the country in question via secret operations can do the trick.

Since most countries don't measure up to America's high moral demands upon them, there are usually plenty of dirty countries for us

---

[319] During the cold war, the Soviets were truly scared that they would be attacked by America at any moment. America made no effort to let them think otherwise and to therefore work towards peace.

[320] Both former ambassadors to the U.N., Madeleine Albright, and Bill Richardson, both Democrats, are on record as stating that the cost of half a million dead children in Iraq was worth the high price. They, of course, did not have to be the one paying the price.

to clean up. With bombs and tanks we can impose "human rights," "multiculturalism," "freedom," "free trade," and "democracy."

The Need for War and the Terrorist Threat

Once the cold war ended in 1990, our massive defense program, which consumes one-fourth of all government spending, needed a new excuse in order to retain its unbelievably bloated size. The defense department needs a justification to exist. It needs a reason to "protect" citizens and to keep its extraordinary power. Allowing peace to exist would mean that many of our politicians and military personnel, all of whom are simply government workers, would have to be workers in the real world producing wealth instead of destroying it.

For well over 40 years, the U.S. was always fighting the supposed communist threat. Now, the excuses are terrorists, a Hitler-like madman (or even just a really offensive guy), or the war on drugs (ignoring our partners' own drug trafficking).

A common excuse for military buildup is the likelihood of an imminent attack from North Korea. This supposed threat has been trumped up for decades, and its heightened intensity usually corresponds with either the annual Congressional debates on defense appropriations or talks between the secretary of defense and South Korean defense officials. We sometimes hear that troops are amassing on the border just north of Seoul. But more than 75 percent of North Korean troops have been "massed" on the border of South Korea since the late 1970s, in response to new and threatening U.S. nuclear strategies.

Terrorism is the best excuse, because it can be pointed to anywhere and everywhere: secessionists are fighting with the only tools they have with which to gain independence—with car bombs and the like—against a massive, highly-armed state? Terrorism! Nationals are fighting to stop the U.S. from overthrowing their government? Terrorism! A government official was murdered as a protest to a CIA assassination or an arrest of a rebel leader fighting to end U.S.-backed suppression? Terrorism! When Middle Easterners attack the West as revenge or protest for U.S. government actions, we call it terrorism. When the CIA operatives or its client states terrorize others, or when

America bombs a country for days on end, it's called fighting for freedom or fighting the war on terror. Blum shows in his book that most well known terrorist attacks can be traced back to the groups the U.S. trained in Afghanistan against the Russians.

Osama bin Laden himself has stated that his beef with America and the West is based on our previous actions in trying to manipulate the world. He even suggested reading Blum's book. Similarly, six of eight Muslim men found guilty in 2008 of plotting to bomb multiple airliners claimed in video tapes that their attacks served as revenge for Western actions. One bomber said, "This is revenge for the actions of the USA in the Muslim lands and their accomplices such as the British and the Jews."[321] Another said that "Osama [Bin Laden] has warned you many times to leave our lands or you will be destroyed, and now the time has come for you to be destroyed."[322] A third one stated, "If you want to kill our women and children then the same thing will happen to you. This is not a joke. If you think you can go into our land and do what you are doing in Iraq, Afghanistan and Palestine and keep on supporting those that are fighting against the Muslims and think it will not come back on to your doorstep then you have another thing coming."[323] It does appear as though Al Qaeda doesn't seem to attack countries or peoples who do not appear to aggress upon them: Switzerland and Norway, for example *almost completely* stay out of international political and especially military efforts, and are not targets for terrorists.

Blum also shows that America itself literally harbors terrorists. Many of those involved in terrorist acts in Latin America, under the direction of the CIA, now live safely in America, protected by America. Blum particularly cites Cuban exiles in Florida who regularly engage in terrorist attacks in and around Cuba.

---

[321] The Associated Press, "Jury watches 'martyr' video in airline bomb plot," (April 10, 2008), http://www.msnbc.msn.com/id/24051411/.

[322] The Associated Press, "Plotters made martyrdom videos," (April 4, 2008), http://news.bbc.co.uk/2/hi/uk_news/7330330.stm.

[323] David Breyers, "British Muslim praises bin Laden in 'airline terror plot martyrdom video,'" *The Times Online* (April 10, 2008), http://www.timesonline.co.uk/tol/news/uk/crime/article3721351.ece.

Why Not Stop Our Part of the Terrorism?

In the mean time, the West and the terrorists continue to play the silly game of attacking each other because the other attacked them. Why don't we just stop playing and see what happens? The best thing President Obama could do is to bring home our troops from around the world, apologize for any unfairness or wrongdoings (I know: that doesn't sound tough enough, and we have to save face for some reason), and strongly state that the U.S. will engage in absolutely no military operations unless the U.S. is attacked after this point. If there's an attack after that, we can tear apart those responsible. But why not see if much of the world violence, and threats against the U.S., might stop if we quit perpetuating the cyclical game of tag?

It is interesting that right-wingers hold Germany to be the sole guilty party of WWI, when it did not start the war, and when it was compelled to attack—after its southern border had already been threatened by Serbia—before it was itself attacked. They do not consider the imminent threats that forced Germany into action. Yet, these same people call daily for the U.S. to take action against soon-to-be-aggressors, namely terrorists. They refuse to recognize that Germany's actions were linked to a pending threat, but constantly use threats to justify America's military actions around the world. And just as these people refuse to acknowledge any political or military actions that could have caused Germany to become engaged in either of the world wars, they refuse to recognize any previous political or military actions by America that could cause terrorists to hate the U.S. and want to attack us today. We must come to grips with the fact that actions have consequences; that cause has effect.

There do appear to be a group of Muslim fundamentalists who are just nuts and want to do harm to those who aren't of their religious persuasion or don't share their ideological beliefs. But I think we can handle them if we're attacked, and they will likely be less aggressive if they are not aggressed upon by the West. The notion that we've got to go get them before they get us, while it sounds all macho and even almost logical, does not consider the laws of unintended consequences. Just as protecting (supposed) neutral and innocent countries such as Poland and Belgium caused those countries (and ours) to suffer more drastically than they would have otherwise, attacking those we think (usually knowingly falsely) will attack us, will likely lead to much more death and destruction, on both sides, than we anticipate ahead of time. And just as throwing money at social and economic problems does not and cannot bring about improvements, so the United States government cannot cure all the ills of mankind.

This chapter (and author) is not intended to be anti-American, anti-Semite, pro-Nazi, or pro-terrorism. It is not desired that these statements express support for any side, as all sides are highly guilty in multiple ways. It's just to say that we have to call a spade a spade and be honest with ourselves regarding our own role in having created the current world (dis)order. We have to understand that we bring most of our national security troubles on ourselves, just as we do with our economic problems.

There are many who defend most of the numerous conflicts America has been involved in, claiming that in each of these cases, we really did need to get involved with the private affairs of other countries. They claim that many countries would have been taken over and millions would have been killed. But thanks to warmongers and rulers—many of whom America creates—who don't respect property rights, countries are constantly taken over and millions are killed— *even though we do police the world.* My argument has been that America actively makes things worse by getting involved, causing many conflicts and more deaths than would occur otherwise. Before confidently refuting my assertions, one should ask themselves whether 180 million deaths last century, and hundreds of millions more physically injured or dislocated, was really the *optimal* outcome? Do we really believe that had America not intervened in the world wars and private conflicts that there would have instead been 250 million, 500 million, or 1 billion people killed? Was 180 million dead really, truly the best we could have hoped for?

As H.L. Mencken wrote:

> When after many battles past,
> Both, tired with blows, make peace at last,
> What is it, after all, the people get?
> Why, taxes, widows, wooden legs, and debt.

Patriotism

Having learned that the government acts in ways detrimental to its citizens economically, and by causing wars, we should ask exactly why we support our politicians, why we support most of our military operations, and why we support our very national identity. In short, we should ask ourselves why we are patriotic.

What is patriotism? What exactly are we supporting when we are patriotic? If the answer is "our country," does that mean a geographical region which our government has artificially and arbitrarily identified as its own? If so, does our patriotism change when the boundaries change? Should we not have been patriotic toward the southwestern states before we stole them from Mexico? Should the residents there have been patriotic towards the U.S. once they were forced to be citizens? Should the citizens of the various countries of the Soviet Republic have been patriotic to the U.S.S.R after they were forced at gunpoint to be countrymen? Should the citizens of Czechoslovakia—who were forced together by Wilson—have been patriotic towards the Czech Republic or to Slovakia after the nation split up? Geographical borders are only imaginary, temporary, lines.

Is patriotism instead the act of being loyal to the land itself, specifically the land upon which one grew up? If so, should someone who grows up in Nevada but moves to Connecticut for their career be patriotic towards Nevada or Connecticut? One might reply that the answer is both, since one lived in and identified with both regions. If that's the case, what if one grew up in the U.S., but had a career overseas in South Korea teaching school or working for a multinational corporation? Is it bad if such a person is also patriotic towards South Korea? What if I have lived in France and learned to love the people and the land and actually prefer France to the U.S.? To whom should I be patriotic, to France or to the U.S.? Am I unpatriotic to favor France? If so, were our forefathers unpatriotic to want independence from their native Britain and make America their new home? We Americans don't seem to think so now. But if the Latinos of Miami wanted to make Miami their own new Cuba by seceding, or if the southwestern states wanted to secede from the nation as a separate country or once again become part of Mexico, we would call them traitors.

Or is patriotism based on a connection to the people of a nation, to our fellow citizens? If so, should I be loyal to Americans because they are my compatriots? Why should I? It is my very patriotic neighbors who democratically vote to take my property and give it to someone else against my will. It is my neighbors who vote for regulation and government intervention that makes my life worse. It is my fellow citizens who vote for politicians that create wars and send millions of their own citizens to die.

Naturally, our government leaders call stealing from our neighbors patriotic. In 2008, Joe Biden said, "it's time [for the rich] to be patriotic...time to jump in...time to be part of the deal...time to get America out of the rut."[324] Many people in fact do believe that the rich need to pitch in and help us innocent workers who are in this rut—a rut created by Biden and other government officials by their policies of printing money, spending more than they can steal from citizens, and in many other ways destroying our wealth and bringing on economic crises. It is a rut which was created because we voted yet again for the same bad policies of the last 100 years. Biden implicitly says the wealthy are using too much of their money to provide us with goods and jobs. They should instead turn their assets into cash and give it to us to consume. Thus, according to Biden, it's unpatriotic to provide the things which improve our lives. Conversely, it's patriotic to squander all our wealth. If this is patriotism, we should all be anti-American. Most Americans support these terrible ideas and support terrible politicians like Biden who cause this harm. The same applies to politicians and citizens in every country. Why should one be loyal to such people?

The people of Argentina—and other Latin American countries—face massive economic crises caused by their thieving politicians every decade, crises that involve hyperinflation that wipes out their life's savings, creates banking crises, mass unemployment, massive national debt, and general suffering. They have endured human rights abuses, political persecution, subservient judiciaries, lack of accountability, widespread corruption, virulent demagoguery, social upheaval, and the absence of individual economic rights for centuries. Yet Argentineans

---

[324] ABC News, Clip of Vice President Joseph Biden, http://www.youtube.com/watch?v=UCqgNWRjmAc&feature=PlayList&p=A30979D65E3F316F&index=0&playnext=1.

are incredibly patriotic and proud of their nation. Citizens of Mexico and Cuba risk life and limb to escape to the United States in order to find work and survival, since their fellow citizens and government offer them few opportunities at home for prosperity. Yet both of these peoples proudly display their native flags while in exile. Citizens of Germany and Austria have been led into war over and over with millions of fathers and brothers killed, yet they are historically always patriotic and ready for the next war (though since WWII they have been largely antiwar). Why should any of these people be patriotic? Exactly what are they supporting by being devoted to their country?

Patriotism is an abstract notion with no real substance. It means nothing; it's just a façade, a fake, imaginary glue that keeps a people naively devoted to causes, countries, governments, and neighbors who usually bring them harm (the phrase "come together" is similarly ambiguous and empty). National borders mean nothing. They would not exist without government force, and they are usually laid out for reasons of politics and power, not in accordance with the religions, identities, culture, or preferences of individuals. Time and again, decade after decade, borders change. The people on each side of a new border are supposed to be loyal to people within their new border, and to the new government forced upon them. They often resist and want their previous identities back. It is for this reason, and for reasons of freedom and self-rule, that regions such as Chechnya, Georgia, Palestine, Quebec, Northern Tibet, Taiwan, Sri Lanka and Kosovo, among many others, often fight for independence. More often than not, those who fight for freedom (and for socialism, incidentally) are called freedom fighters, but they are labeled terrorists by those who oppose their separation. In today's America, patriotism, effectively, is the act of aggressing upon other nations; it is the act of stealing from our fellow man in the name of furthering our prosperity, while in fact destroying our prosperity. It is under the name of patriotism and supposed freedom that it is justifiable for the U.S. to attack citizens of any country, including its own.

Patriotism is usually the *cause* of many of our problems, not the solution to them. And as time passes, we become more obsessed with it. Now, a government official, or even football players and referees, cannot appear in public without an American flag on their lapel or

Life Magazine

Figure 8.2: German Citizens Supporting Adolf Hitler and his national cause.

jersey. Soon, it will be required that each of our cars have the yellow or red, white, and blue ribbon sticker plastered on it (for the few that don't already)—and such things have certainly happened in this country previously. We must all show that we are, as Biden said, "part of the deal." It is reminiscent of Nazism, where all citizens swore allegiance to their ruler and proudly saluted and waved the Nazi flag in the name of nationalism; they lived and died for the glorious fatherland (**Figure 8.2**). We are only several steps behind them.

The right-wing radio hosts further this cause by obsessing about why we need to protect ourselves from aggressors and terrorists and fight for our freedom. In truth, there would be little to no protection needed if we would just leave the rest of the world alone. And not only do Republicans not offer us freedom through the economic and social policies they propose, but they cause us to lose freedom at rapid rates during times of the wars they sucker us into. The patriotism charade is now at the point that these talk show hosts tell each caller (that they agree with) that they "are great Americans," and each caller, in return, tells the host that he, too, "is a great American." One wonders how they don't feel just a bit silly with such melodramatic antics.

And when all of "our boys," our "heroes," are at war, willingly taking money to go and kill other people around the world, many of us blindly "support our troops." It does not matter whether our troops are actually helping or harming us, or saving people or destroying them: since they are *American* troops, we should support them... just as the German people blindly supported their Nazi troops simply because they were German.

Patriotism leads people in each country to think that *their* country is superior to others, and that their country must survive and prosper at all costs—even if it means death to people in other countries. Patriotism breeds an "us versus them" attitude. Without the notion of patriotism and national borders, people would live wherever and however they prefer, practice religions they want, marry whomever they desire, and produce, exchange, and prosper in whatever way they see fit. (There does need to be, and there would be, a governing body, just not a single one with monopoly powers of enforcement and control.) We would not see ourselves so much as members of particular groups (nationalities), but as various people of the world. And yet we are forced by law to "celebrate" diversity in our government-controlled world. In absence of government borders, people would more easily mix and mingle in the world and not look at each other as "those other people" but instead naturally look at them as their neighbors. Those who wanted to be racist or simply to keep to their own kind would be able to do that, too, on as much property as they could peacefully acquire through exchange.

People could quickly rush to judge me as unthankful. They could say that I should be grateful that my country has permitted me the level of freedom that it has, which is in fact far in excess of most countries, even if it diminishes by the month. Indeed, I am grateful to be lucky enough to live in a place that offers relative freedom. But this is not a reason to be loyal. If it were, we could also argue that a wife who gets beaten up periodically by her husband who threatens to bring much greater harm to her if she tries to leave him, but is otherwise treated well and quasi-lovingly by him, should also be loyal to him. She should in this case be thankful that he allows her a relatively normal life, even if he threatens to use force against her and periodically does. This thinking is wrong. No one should be loyal and patriotic to someone who allows them to be *mostly* free but still treats them unfairly. Freedom from harm and coercion should be a natural right, not something granted by those good enough not to kill us or keep us as slaves. This is why, for example, it is still illegal and unacceptable to forcefully hold women against their will or to strike a fellow man as an initiating aggressive act. Aggression is aggression, even in a free society.

The Ills of Democracy and Political Parties

Political parties in every country have their "schticks," and each one usually entails some form of socialism. In the U.S., the Republicans' agenda consists of imposing their hypocritical and extreme religious beliefs on our country and causing wars, killing, and setting up dictators in other countries. The Democrats' agenda involves deliberately trying to destroy our means of increasing our standards of living, and trying to equalize everyone by dragging us all down to the lowest economic common denominator. These issues are the things each party merely *focuses on*; but, in fact, both parties promote most of the same policies. Both of these groups, along with every other form of government, engage in the use of force to make people live and act differently from what they would otherwise choose, and to make them hand over much of their personal property once it's been fairly earned. Regardless of the fact that Republicans (and Democrats to a lesser degree) claim to be about free markets and capitalism, they are not. Republicans are socialist and totalitarian just like the Democrats. Individuals fervently support their respective Republican and Democratic parties, and see the other party, which they detest, as supporting reprehensible views. In the bigger picture, Republicans and Democrats are virtually side by side on the political spectrum that runs from Communism (full socialism) on one side, to free market capitalism (complete freedom) on the other. Both parties, for example, recently had their respective plans for government bailouts, and for nationalizing our healthcare system.

Our society is always proud to support "democracy" as though it automatically equates to freedom. But freedom is not necessarily related to democracy and may or may not coincide with it. A dictator, such as Pinochet in Chile, can create largely free markets, and a democracy can create near or complete totalitarianism, as was the case with the democratic election of Adolf Hitler and more recently with that of Hugo Chavez. Democracy can really be reduced simply to a method of voting, one which allows the expropriation of the property of others—"the tyranny of the majority."

Though it is socialists of one stripe or another, be they Fascists, dictators, Communists, or Democrats who have begun every war in the last century, killing hundreds of millions, who have strictly and often violently controlled and directed individuals in their respective countries, and who have caused starvation, unemployment, and suffering of millions for decades, it is socialism that most people in the world cling to as something that will help them. Mild socialists (your average Democrat or environmentalist), curiously, think that extreme socialists (communists) are bad, even though communism is just an advanced state of the policies socialists adamantly support.

After World War II our economists and government officials were impressed with the socialist system that destroyed Germany's economy, and they wanted to replicate it for the economy of the new West Germany. Thankfully, West German leaders, aware of this, and aware of the destruction that Nazi economic policies had caused, through twists and turns, set up a system of relatively free markets which brought dramatic economic growth for the next thirty years (overcoming the negative effects of the Marshall Plan[325]). People support the evil of socialism because, ironically, they fear that individual companies—which have rarely, if ever, had anyone killed, and which, absent government regulation, have never taken anything forcefully from anyone, and could not only not bring harm, but provide improvements for our lives—can somehow hurt them. All because they don't understand what capitalism is and how it works.

The Patriotism of Politicians

While politicians claim to be patriotic and to do what's best for America, they do the opposite. How could they know what would truly help or hurt American citizens? Have they spent years studying

[325] To understand the myth of the Marshall Plan, see: Jeffrey Tucker, "The Marshall Plan Myth," http://mises.org/freemarket_detail.aspx?control=120.

economic cause and effect? Have they learned production techniques that could result in greater output? Have they read numerous books on organizational behavior, so that they can "plan" the economy? Of course not! They have spent their days kissing babies, polling to find out what voters want, learning to be actors, and making emotional, passionate speeches that appeal to the masses who will be suckered into such antics. In short, politicians are equivalent to game show hosts. If they were really patriotic, they would spend their time figuring out how truly to help people, instead of simply figuring out how to win votes.

We naively believe politicians are there to "lead us." We believe that the president, in "running the country," has the toughest job on earth. This is partly because people who do not understand economics believe that a country cannot "run" on its own. But it can. It is the individual people and businesses that progress our lives. The president does not get up in the morning and turn on the factory lights or start the machines. He does not determine how much should be produced that day. He does not decide who should work where. Individuals, capital, and market prices run the country. President Obama is not "leading" us through this crisis—he's simply manipulating the economy further than it was already manipulated. Had he not done so, the market (i.e., individuals) could have already fixed itself.

We have seen that the government's planning does not help an economy. We have seen that regulation does not protect citizens from companies, and that military actions do not protect citizens from foreign aggressors (except in special circumstances). Of course, some of the actions the president engages in involve setting or adjusting laws pertaining to protecting our legal rights and our legal property. But most of his actions involve just the opposite—taking our property or preventing our free will choices. For example, there are laws that prevent gangs from barging into our homes and kicking us out of them; but, at the same time, there are many more laws linked to how our homes will be taken from us by the government if we fail to pay one of the myriad taxes forced upon us—taxes that *legally* allow our property, our paychecks, to be given to others, including these very gangs, via wealth redistribution.

The same type of "work on behalf of the people" is done by all members of Congress and the Senate, and to a lesser degree by state and local government. The country would get along quite fine any given year if congress and the president ignored all of the "work" it would otherwise do, except for focusing on the 1 percent or so of the decisions that involve truly protecting citizens and providing basic services that we want and need. Most of the other 99 percent of their work involves imposing implied or actual government force for the purpose of benefiting one group at the expense of another. The government is simply an institution—an instrument—that is used to bring about these iniquitous actions.

Politicians' "work" involves doing what is needed to please their constituents. Their constituents, in turn, usually want government subsidies, regulation, wealth transfers, or some other government force imposed, so that they can benefit from the suppression of others when they otherwise could not. Almost everything we see government doing today consists of this: bankers, car companies, airlines, and steel companies are subsidized at the expense of taxpayers so that they don't have to go out of business; workers are protected from having to receive market wages; poor workers are protected with a minimum wage; companies are regulated so that they don't harm consumers; government forces the negation of contracts such that borrowers can benefit at the expense of lenders; inflation is generated so that more money can be taken from taxpayers and given to others; environmental legislation is imposed in order to let environmentalists "protect our environment" at the expense of the rest of us; one industry is prevented from producing a particular product so that another industry's profits will not be affected. The list literally goes on and on for tens of thousands of pages (in the national register).

Though all of these actions are detrimental to society, politicians don't care. What they care about is getting votes. They care about getting re-elected. They will therefore do what *appears* to help voters, even though their actions usually harm voters. The long-term health of the country is not in their interest; the short-term success of their career is. They do not know exactly what would help or what would harm, but they need not be concerned with such immaterial matters. This is why it is so vitally important for voters themselves to understand what helps and harms them. If voters would demand of politicians the things that would truly benefit them, politicians would give it to them, for they would pass or not pass whatever laws would get them votes.

If people demanded that government quit printing money, quit regulating businesses, quit taxing, and stopped stealing from the rich, the government would cease these operations. Then, all members of society would see a dramatic increase in their standards of living, with jobs available to everyone and prices falling by the day. But there is a catch: those of us who earn less than the average—those who are net beneficiaries of wealth redistribution—would have to clearly understand how they would benefit from refusing to vote for free money. They would have to understand that, instead of having money handed to them, they would instead earn money in the form of a salary. But this change in structure would result in significantly increased wealth for this group. This issue is likely the biggest challenge free markets face, for it is very difficult to convince someone that if they refuse free money they will be better off.

A Proposal to Divide Up a Nation

Since most Americans do not understand how prosperity is created, and since we have different views on how our rulers should rule us, we constantly group into political factions (Democrats, Republicans, Greens, Communists, Libertarians, etc.) and fight each other in order to get the kind of system each group wants by trying to take control of our one, single, monopoly government. The winning group gets much of what they want, but their gains are diluted because the winning politicians must keep in mind the wants of the opposing groups, since they consist of career-affecting voters. Politicians are constantly juggling the wants of these different groups.

This is, for example, why Iraq is in such a mess today. Saddam Hussein, for all his evils, was good at giving the different Iraqi interest groups many of the various things they wanted. Today, the U.S.-based regime leaves many of these groups alienated, causing them to rebel and terrorize. But like most countries, Iraq is one whose people are comprised of different religions, ethnicities, and desires, but currently forced to consolidate against their will under one umbrella. Therefore,

Iraq should be allowed to be broken up into different provinces, leaving its people to join the regions that they would prefer.

Since the United States, too, is comprised of different interest groups fighting for the kind of government and rule each group desires, instead of competing, why shouldn't we allow the United States to be divided into different provinces, where self-rule according to the desires of each province is permissible? It would really not be dissimilar from our original structure of having the individual states be mostly autonomous entities.

If we truly support freedom, why shouldn't we be able to live as we choose? The current answer is that we can't, because our neighbors would like to live differently from us. To solve this problem, why not let our neighbors live as they choose on their property (in their province), and let us live as we wish on our property (in our province)? The 50 states or even portions of states could be grouped into as many different provinces as needed, based on the number of different groups who wish to self-rule as they like. One region could be for communists, another for their cousins the socialists, and others for the greens and the free marketers. The overarching protocol would be absolute self-rule, free from any influence from a centralized federal government. The free market region, for example, would have its own monies that would be unrelated to the Federal Reserve's U.S. dollar; it would have its own laws, with absolutely no control whatsoever by the government of any other region; there would be no central government connecting all provinces, unless a province *chose* to join with another for centralized control.

Since each political group thinks that its way is the best way to run a country and believes its system leads to people being better off than under other types of systems, such a simultaneous experiment testing different economic/political models, starting from an equal base, would be an objective way of proving which system truly creates a better world for its citizens (though the division of East and West Germany already proved this).

There would naturally be some concerns over what it means to divide up a nation. In the first instance, there would be concern over resources. This is not a problem. The free market region needs none;

so those of us who would choose to live in that province would be happy taking the geographical area of fewest resources, and would even take the smallest piece of the pie. Give us the Arizona desert, for example! We will engage in trade for the resources we need, and within a few years, the Arizona desert will look like Beverly Hills. So that they can have better lives, we will also welcome the homeless, the poor, gays, minorities, the uneducated, Jews, Muslims, and, due to an open immigration policy, anyone else from anywhere in the world. The Communist region could try to be self-sufficient, as Communists would naturally choose. They could create scores of jobs by building automobile plants, steel mills, oil wells, mines, and power grids. The socialist region could have a mix of the free market and communist regions. The green region could take down the concrete and steel buildings and parking lots they often complain about and plant grass and trees and live off the land.

But what about the logistics of having millions uprooted and moving across the country to their desired region? Americans are already pretty mobile and rarely stay in the same place all their lives. Perhaps most would be very willing to move in order to live in the way in which they chose. Others could remain where they are and see how it goes (except that those in the communist region would not have a lot of time to decide, since the communist government would inevitably put up borders and take away passports to prevent people from leaving). There would still be people who would have to choose between moving against their will or living in a way they would otherwise reject. But acting and living in a way that is against their will is what most people have to do today under our current system. Otherwise, most details can likely be worked out.

Chapter 9:

Environmentalism
— At Any Cost

Going green...it's all the rage these days. If you're not into it, you're out of it. If you're against it, you're evil. But have all the masses who uncritically buy into environmentalism hook, line, and sinker done all their homework? Have they spent hours upon hours reading not only the research from environmentalists and other left-wingers, but from all sides? The so-called greens, by both request and by government dictate, are asking us to make drastic changes in the way we live our lives and to reduce the amount of goods and services available to us. We should therefore be very sure we know what damage is being done to the environment, what the effects are, and how it could both help or hurt us to alter our preferred ways of living in order to supposedly "save the planet."[326]

---

[326] A majority of the ideas in this chapter are obtained from two primary authors. The information relating to the current state of the environment can be largely attributed to Bjorn Lomborg, a former Greenpeace activist who learned through scientific research that the world was not quite in the terrible shape we are led to believe. The information relating to the economic effects of environmentalism and the threats to our standard of living which arise from them can be largely attributed to George Reisman.

This author's case for the use of two dominant sources of information can easily be defended. The goal of this chapter is not to present contrasting views of environmentalism and to compare them, as the dominant pro-environmentalist view is omnipresent. The intent here is to present the little-mentioned alternative views, which this author

This chapter will present views which are contrary to popular understandings of environmentalism. It will show that the state of the environment is not as bad as it's made out to be, and is in fact improving in most areas, not declining. Further, it will be shown that nothing should be done to prevent emissions of carbon dioxide in the name of stopping global warming. Not only would restricting emissions reduce our current standard of living at the least, and cause economic retrogression and even death at the most, but by continuing to grow our economy with current "dirty" methods, we can advance to a state where we develop cleaner methods of production which are as cost effective as our current means of production. It will also be shown that contrary to popular opinion, "greedy" profit seeking companies will in fact switch to cleaner and greener ways to operate without government regulation.

I do not pretend to be an environmental expert or even someone even remotely interested in environmental science. This chapter simply compiles the various anti-environmental arguments that others have developed so as to present an alternative case to the reader.

The Problem of Disinformation

Many of the environmentalist's claims are legitimate and important to address. But many others are illogical and misleading, if not outright deceptive. Much of their information is completely detached from reality and tantamount to propaganda. Being aware of this bias is important—not in order necessarily to refute any possible environmentalist claim that comes along, but to be skeptical about declarations until they are proven true. The environmentalist movement sweeping the world today is led by a small group of people who believe that nature has more value than do human beings or human well-being. These people, who favor socialism and the attendant lack of freedom it entails for humans, by contrast, want complete freedom for animals, even at the expense of human lives (and they do

---

strongly believes in. Since the alternative view can be found in robust form from two major sources, and since these two sources are a mirror representation of other sources of alternative views, efficiency of research material is the primary consideration. These two sources mostly fully encompass the anti-environmental concerns and subject matter, and are sufficient for presenting the alternative case to the public.

not remind us that 99 percent of all species that have existed on this earth became extinct on their own, due to conditions and events such as global cooling, astronomical episodes, volcanoes, genetic evolution, and food scarcity[327]). They even want to eradicate "footprints" of human existence, and perhaps the human species all together.

Sound extreme? Perhaps, but this notion is explicitly stated by many environmentalists, and implicitly endorsed in their demands for government force to be employed so that their goals will be achieved. For example, one Australian medical expert has called for a $5,000 tax on all children born, and an annual carbon tax of up to $800 per child, due to the supposed negative effect on the environment each person produces.[328] The environmental group The Voluntary Human Extinction Program, which has the slogan, "May we live long and die out," consists of volunteers who have made decisions to remain childless, so that other species can live instead.[329] The group's founder states, "As long as there's one breeding pair of homosapiens on the planet, there's too great a threat to the biosphere." Do you doubt that this group would support government action (government force) to advance their cause?[330] A University of Texas biology professor claims that humans must die for earth to live, and states that disease "will control the scourge of humanity. We're looking forward to a huge collapse."[331] These people certainly must be the life of the party at summer cookouts.

Most of the rest of society, unaware of the environmentalists' real goals and propaganda, and unaware of how their own lives would be affected should the environmentalists get their way, hear the *general* message about being good to the planet, not consuming

---

[327] Bruce Walsh, Extinction, http://nitro.biosci.arizona.edu/courses/EEB105/lectures/extinction/extinction.html.

[328] Jen Kelly, "Baby tax needed to save planet, claims expert," *The Advertiser* (December 10, 2007). Who would receive these funds? Probably the environmentalists and the poor.

[329] Chelsea Schilling, "Wanna help the planet? 'Let's all just die!'" http://worldnetdaily.com/index.php?fa=PAGE.view&pageId=63755.

[330] Michael Y. Park, "Anti-People Group Pushes for Man's Extinction," *Fox News* (July 29, 2001).

[331] The Associated Press, "Professor: Many Humans Have to Die for Earth to Live," *Fox News* (April 5, 2006).

all our natural resources, and keeping the earth in good shape for our children, and agree that this seems like the right and practical thing to do. They then effectively become environmentalists and, unknowingly, support actions and government laws which would degrade and diminish their own lives and those of their children.

Alarmism, and thus misinformation, has existed for many years—indeed, centuries—in the environmental debate. Environmentalist and economist Bjorn Lomborg points out in his book, *Cool It*,[332] that as Europe descended into the little Ice Age in the 1400s, the bad weather and resulting bad crops were blamed on witches. There was a high correlation between weather and witchcraft trials across Europe. As many as 12,000 "witches" were executed between 1500 and 1700, and are still being executed in Africa today. Also in Europe, in 1816, a very rainy summer which, in reality, was brought about by a volcanic eruption, was blamed at the time on the use of lightning conductors (which had, ironically, previously been blamed for droughts). Wet summers in the 1910s and 1920s were blamed on gunfire from WWI and on the initiation of transatlantic shortwave radio.

In a further irony, for most of the last 100 years, it was global cooling, not global warming, that was the climate problem, and credible publications were involved in relaying this tenuous information. In 1912 an article in the *Los Angeles Times* claimed that a fifth ice age was on the way. In 1923 a *Chicago Times* article declared that "A Scientist Says Arctic Ice Will Wipe Out Canada" along with large parts of Asia and Europe. Later, in the 1930s the concern became global warming, and the question arose as to whether CO_2 emissions could be the cause. A *New York Times* article stated in 1952 that "the world has been getting warmer in the last half century," and in 1959 another article proclaimed that the glaciers were melting and that the ice in the Arctic Ocean was about half as thick as it was the previous century.[333]

But by the 1940s, global mean temperatures were already falling again, which led to claims in the 1970s that the earth was in danger

---

[332] Bjørn Lomborg, *Cool It: The Skeptical Environmentalist's Guide to Global Warming* (2007).
[333] Ibid.

once again of an ice age. Some books explained that the exciting days of global warming were over and that advancing glaciers were endangering multiple countries, and that the cold weather could cause mass starvation by the year 2000. It was also said that global cooling had killed hundreds of thousands in the developing world, and that if action was not taken, world famine, world chaos, and world war would all come by the year 2000. Well-known newspapers and magazines claimed that pollution was causing global cooling and that droughts would be the result.

Another example of alarmism and misinformation was the scare of acid rain destroying lakes in the 1980s. While acid rain does exist (largely as a result of governmental requirements that smoke stacks be built at least two hundred feet tall), it was not responsible for the previously-claimed acidification of the lakes in question. The acidification was instead the result of the ending of logging operations near these lakes.[334] The alkaline runoff, a natural result of these types of operations, had made these naturally acidic lakes non-acidic for several generations. More importantly, according to the final report of the U.S. government's National Acid Precipitation Assessment Program, the primary reason for the acidity to begin with was one hundred and fifty million tons a year of bird droppings.

Similarly, in the 1980s, there was an asbestos scare in the U.S. It turns out that asbestos was a danger, virtually exclusively, only to those who worked directly with friable (easily crushed with hand pressure) asbestos in places like mines and shipbuilding facilities. When people are not directly exposed to friable asbestos, as when they are simply located in a building that contains Asbestos Containing Material (ACM), their odds of being affected by it are zero to nil. In fact, according to the January 8, 1990 issue of *Forbes* magazine, in the forms in which it was commonly used in the U.S., asbestos is one-third as likely to be the cause of death as being struck by lightning.[335]

Environmentalists lead us to believe that most man-made chemicals are bad for us. But they don't regularly reveal such facts as that carcinogens, poisons, and radiation all exist in nature. At least half of the

[334] George Reisman, *Capitalism: A Treatise on Economics* (1996).
[335] Ibid.

chemicals in nature are carcinogenic when fed to animals in massive quantities, which is the same proportion that applies to man-made chemicals when fed in massive quantities.[336] In the same vein, these groups, who *always* propose socialism, don't reveal to us the massive and dramatic environmental degradation which takes place in communist countries where no one owns the land and thus no one has incentives to take care of it.

The Politics of the Environmental Movement

These environmentalists' claims are legitimized by government response. Politicians welcome any opportunity which creates a state of affairs wherein citizens will allow the government to impose itself more into their lives and take away more of their freedoms. Just as we learned in Chapter 8 that times of war are the most opportune for this power grab to take place, environmentalist movements are not far behind. Citizens believe that if they don't allow the government to set rules and regulations and intervene more in the economy, businesses will ruin the earth. Individuals don't even consider the possibility that these interventions could cost them dearly. But the government's actions do affect its citizens. I've shown throughout this book how the chain of events resulting from government actions does not reveal to individuals that it is government intervention which imposed burdens on them, since they are not able to visually observe the real relationships of cause and effect occurring before them. When their standards of living decline, it is then businesses that are blamed. Thus, governments get a green light, so to speak, from everyone.

Just as they do with wars or threats of war, governments do their best to convince people they are in danger from environmental damage unless the government takes actions. This is reflected in the goings-on of the apparent leading world authority on climate change, the United Nation's Intergovernmental Panel on Climate Change (IPCC). The IPCC is a commission set up by the World Meteorological Organization and the United Nations Environment Programme (UNPE) "to assess the scientific, technical, and socio-economic information relevant

---

[336] Ibid.

for the understanding of the risk of human-induced climate change."[337] It is a government organization assembled by various nations. Their natural incentive would be to find evidence supporting global warming, and to dismiss others' hypotheses as uncertain. Yet the IPCC is not without its critics. Individuals such as Lord Nigel Lawson, the former chancellor of the exchequer of the United Kingdom, Vaclav Klaus, president of the Czech Republic, famous scientists such as Freeman Dyson, and members of the IPCC itself, among many other respected scientists and economists have criticized the IPCC as producing biased and flawed results, and of being ignorant of economics.[338] The IPCC has also been accused by others of consisting of people driven by political agendas rather than by impartial scientists. As but one small example, *Der Spiegel Magazine*, among other sources, reported on the tedious debates that occurred behind the scenes regarding the 2007 IPCC Climate Report, where Americans absolutely insisted that the text "will likely happen" be changed to "will happen," leaving European delegates "outraged" (as usual, the Americans won out).

The Heartland Institute held a conference consisting of world renowned scientists and physicists in the spring of 2009 to publicly make its complete scientific case that global warming "facts" are not in any way proven.[339]

A little time spent on Google will reveal to anyone that there is far from a consensus on the issue of global warming, contrary to what the IPCC continues to claim. Many surveys can be found showing far less than a consensus. And one can easily review the blog comments associated with global warming articles appearing on mainstream news websites and see that individual Americans are far from being in agreement on global warming, contrary to what environmentalists tell us. There are also several petitions where scientists refute many

---

[337] The Intergovernmental Panel on Climate Change, IPCC Special Report on Emissions Scenarios, http://www.ipcc.ch/ipccreports/sres/emission/500.htm.

[338] Wikipedia, "Global Warming Controversy," http://en.wikipedia.org/wiki/Global_warming_controversy, and John Christy, "No consensus on IPCC's level of ignorance" (editorial), BBC News (November 13, 2007), and Uwe Buse, "Is the IPCC Doing Harm to Science?", *Spiegel* (May 3, 2007).

[339] The Heartland Institute, "Global Warming: Was it ever really a crisis?" http://www.heartland.org/events/NewYork09/index.html.

tenets of the global warming premise. Perhaps the most well known is the Oregon Petition, where more than 19,000 scientists and other qualified individuals stated that 1) limiting greenhouse gases would "harm the environment, hinder the advance of science and technology, and damage the health and welfare of mankind," 2) there is no convincing evidence that human-produced greenhouse gases are or will "cause catastrophic heating of the Earth's atmosphere and disruption of the Earth's climate," and 3) that increases in atmospheric carbon dioxide could produce many beneficial effects for plants and animals on Earth.

Neither political hacks nor environmentalists will hear opposing views or seriously consider other research besides that which supports their case. And since government ultimately funds most of the research being done on the environment, the incentives are there to produce compelling research outcomes that would benefit the government in its desire to have citizens think there are scientific reasons for why it should have more power. Richard Lindzen, a respected but skeptical climate scientist from MIT points out that

> Scientists who dissent from the alarmism have seen their grant funds disappear, their work derided, and themselves labeled as industry stooges, scientific hacks or worse. Consequently, lies about climate change gain credence even when they fly in the face of the science that supposedly is their basis.[340]

Even scientists and others who propose scientific solutions to global warming, as opposed to solutions which clamp down on our industrial output and quality of life, are ignored by the environmentalists. For example, atmospheric physicist John Latham suggested in 2006 that we could increase the reflectivity of low-flying clouds by creating more salt droplets from the ocean, which might, among other things, stabilize temperatures.[341] But the environmental groups were strangely dismissive and stated that they didn't know if it would be worth the time and energy to look into it. But shouldn't they be interested in at least partially assessing a new proposal if it could possibly offer a solution to a major world problem at a very low cost? The

---

[340] Lomborg, *Cool It* (2007).
[341] Ibid.

likely true answer was revealed when Greenpeace stated that they wouldn't be interested because they were looking for reductions in fossil fuels instead. They are far from the first to reveal that they are ultimately after the single goal of stopping human progress. Many environmentalists have stated that regardless of whether we have proof of man being a major factor in producing a climate problem, they want to reduce CO_2 production NOW!

At the same time that environmentalists don't want to hear opposing views, they are downright adamant about the world accepting theirs. Mark Lynas, author of a book revealing "the truth about our climate crisis," says that climate denial is equal to Holocaust denial and he would like to see similar trials where those who denied global warming would be put on trial for murder.[342] Similarly, David Roberts of the environmental magazine *Grist* talks about having "war crimes trials for these bastards—some sort of climate Nuremberg."[343] Even former French President Jacques Chirac wants to use force against the nonbelievers: he has led efforts to make non-compliance with emissions caps an international crime.

Environmental Issues and What to Do About Them

Environmentalists have a point in that there are some issues that should be addressed (which we'll discuss below). But they generally see environmentalism as a way to beat up on all those willingly producing and exchanging in the marketplace. They see the market and free enterprise as the cause of the problem and the government as the solution. For them, the supposed damage to nature caused by man will end when the market is eradicated. Given the gravity of the issue, it would behoove us to take a look at what the state of the environment is, what the problems are and are not, and what should or should not be done to address them. Let's take a brief look at some of the more popular issues.

---

[342] Ibid.
[343] Ibid.

Forests

It has been claimed that we are continuing to destroy our forests at an alarming rate, and that if we don't act now, we will lose them. This argument is unfounded. Lomborg points out that as of 2001, we have destroyed about 20 percent of all the forests that ever existed on earth. However, the developed world has destroyed about 50 percent of its forests. The poster child of deforestation, the Amazon forest, has seen a net deforestation of about 17 percent, meaning that about 83 percent of that jungle still exists as of 2006 (and for various reasons, it is estimated that it will not see a reduction in the future that takes it past the mark where 70 percent of it is still remaining)[344] (**Figure 9.1**).

Since World War II, depending on which studies are cited, we have experienced world net deforestation of somewhere between 0.85 percent (a net increase) and –0.44 percent (a net decrease). In other words the balance of forests is virtually unchanged. We have not had continued decreases in our forests because we plant new forests at about the same rate as we destroy them.

It could still be argued that we should not keep cutting trees at all. But it's important to remember that we use trees to support our quality of life—they help provide us with homes, furniture, paper, and commercial products. Could we use other materials instead? Yes, but depending on the relative price of trees versus other materials, it's cheaper and more efficient (i.e., it costs your family less, so that you can obtain other goods you need) to use wood.

Regardless, we still cut more down more trees in the world than needs to be the case. The primary reason for this excess cutting is that a majority of forest lands are not owned privately. If they were, the owners would have had incentives to take care of them. In places where property rights to forests are protected, forests are either stable or growing. The buffalo almost became extinct in the western United States because people freely hunted them on public land. But cows, which have been mostly privately owned, never faced extinction

---

[344] Wikipedia, The Amazon Rain Forest, http://en.wikipedia.org/wiki/Amazon_Rainforest. Though some environmental groups claim that 20 percent of the forest has been razed, see Rain-Tree.com,. Rainforest Facts, http://www.rain-tree.com/facts.htm.

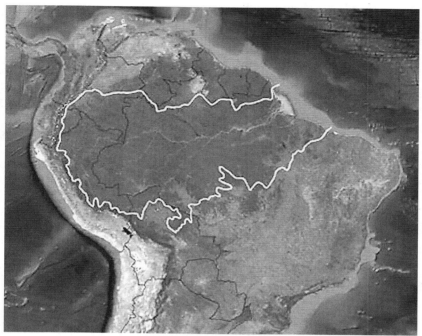

Source: NASA, via Wikipedia

Figure 9.1: A satellite view of the Amazon forest, which shows most of it still intact.

(except for cattle such as the Auroch, of Europe, which were hunted to death by noblemen hunting for sport, and who had no profit motive incentive to preserve them).[345]

Private ownership ensures that plants, animals, and other valued wildlife will thrive because owners can make more money by taking good care of their property rather than allowing it to disappear or deteriorate. In preserving these valuable assets, they can physically reproduce them for the purpose of repeat sales. For example, breeding and selling the cattle perpetually is more profitable than killing them all for a one-time sale. In the case of trees, landowners have an incentive to re-grow trees after they've cut them down.[346] One might ask: how do we know that tree owners would not sell all their property

---

[345] Wikipedia, Aurochs, http://en.wikipedia.org/wiki/Aurochs.

[346] For issues related to organisms and species being killed in the process, please read further in Lomborg's book.

to developers who might build a parking lot on the land? They would not, because if too many trees were cut down, the price of lumber would become very high, thereby making tree growing more profitable than parking lots or other alternative uses. Many trees are actually grown for the purposes of being made into paper. The amount of new forest growth exceeds by more than 20 times the amount of wood and paper that is consumed in the world every year.[347]

The re-growing of trees is in fact happening to a large degree in developed countries where the land is privately owned. For example, anyone who has driven down Interstate 75 through north and mid-Florida in the last 20 years will have noticed large numbers of tree farms which are growing taller and thicker by the year—even while lumber prices, until the last several years, have declined in real terms. The *New York Times* reported in April, 2008, that a new study by the National Academy of Sciences "confirms that reforestation has become a widespread pattern in well-off countries and also in a few that are not so well off." They note also that reforestation is linked to prosperity (and prosperity is linked to economic freedom).

Air Pollution

Air pollution is largely considered the most important environmental problem related to human health. What most people are not aware of is that air quality has improved dramatically through time in developed countries. That's right, improved. Think about what you know about the life in the past, from Hollywood movies if nothing else: the cities of early industrial Europe had no sewage or sanitation systems; their energy use consisted primarily of burning wood and coal; they did not have good waste disposal methods or services, etc. As a result, the air and the city streets were filthy and they stank. Lawrence Stone describes early modern London:[348]

> the city ditches, now often filled with stagnant water, were commonly used as latrines; butchers killed animals in their shops and threw the offal of the carcasses into the streets; dead animals were left to decay and fester where they

---

[347] Floy Lilly, "Three Myths about Trash," http://mises.org/story/3887.
[348] Lawrence Stone, *The Family, Sex and Marriage in England 1500-1800* (1979).

lay; latrine pits were dug close to wells, thus contaminating the water supply. Decomposing bodies of the rich in burial vaults beneath the church often stank out parson and congregation.[349]

Additionally, there were large amounts of both animal and human excrement left on the streets. Since households burned wood and then coal, the air was cloudy with dark smoke and ashes, and soot fell on houses, streets, and people.

Lomborg reveals that the city of London, which may serve as a proxy for developed nations' pollution levels, has seen a decrease in the two most dangerous forms of air pollution—particles (smoke and soot) and sulfur dioxide—of more than 90 percent each from their prior heights in the 1800s. And virtually all of this improvement came about before the existence of world government environmental protection agencies (the EPA, for example, began in the 1970s), as can be seen in **Figure 9.2**. Similarly, other important forms of more modern air pollution such as ozone, lead, nitrogen oxides, and carbon monoxide are now on the decline.

The EPA and other world government agencies smother the production of energy by imposing additional costs on consumers and businesses. The improvements mandated by government would naturally be achieved in time (due to competition between firms), and with lower costs, once technological progression made the changes cost effective. We all want a cleaner and safer environment, and the London pollution example shows that businesses will naturally find ways to produce in a cleaner fashion so as to please their customers, the consumers. Examples such as the creation of anti-lock brakes and airbags on cars show that companies will voluntarily make products safer in order to be more competitive. But if technology is not yet at the required state needed to solve current pollution, we may have to wait for its development before we can change our means of production (naturally, the lower the taxes, and thus the more capital available, the sooner technologies will advance). To use another car example to prove this point, consider that Ford first offered non-shatter glass in the 1930s, but then discontinued it until many years

---

[349] Lomborg, *Cool It* (2007).

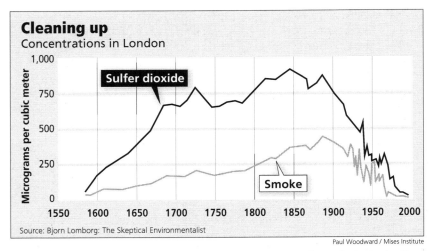

Figure 9.2: Historical Levels of the Two Most Damaging Forms of Air Pollution in the City of London.

later because consumers were not willing to pay the extra price for the product. When the cost of producing non-shatter glass became a fraction of what it had previously been, it was widely accepted.

Natural Resources and Sustainability

Sustainability is a common phrase which is now attached to virtually everything that takes place in the world. It is apparently imperative that we make sure that everything be sustainable. The current obsession with sustainability is not new; millennia ago people feared that the world was going to run out of natural resources. Thousands of years later, nothing has changed. Still, we are constantly reminded that we must conserve our natural resources or else we'll deplete them.

Nothing could be further from the truth. Consider that the entire earth is made of natural resources—from the upper reaches of the atmosphere to the core of the earth four thousand miles down.[350] The entire mass of the earth is comprised of chemical elements—oxygen, hydrogen, nitrogen, carbon, iron, nickel, etc. Man has literally only scraped the surface of the earth's resources, and has not even begun to

---

[350] George Reisman, *Capitalism: A Treatise on Economics* (1996).

obtain resources which lie two miles deep in the ocean, under its floor. As Reisman points out, even the sands of the Sahara Desert (which used to be moist and green and populated with people) are chemical elements that might one day be used for productive purposes. He also astutely notes that what is limited is natural resources *in usable form.* Virtually all natural resources we employ have to be altered by us, usually by being combined with other natural resources, to be in a state which serves a purpose for mankind (e.g., iron ore must be extracted from the ground and alloyed with various other metals and non-metals, mainly carbon and silicone, to form steel). Thus, what humans do in the passage of time is *expand* the supply of natural resources available. They do not destroy the environment but improve it. This will be obvious if you take a look out of your window right now and compare what you see to what was likely there in 1776 or 1200.

It could be asked, "but what about oil, since its supply is known to be limited?" We're not sure that's true, but even if it is, and if we run out, we'll move on to the next least expensive energy source. We have many of them, but most are not as economical as oil.

Energy itself is in extreme abundance in the world.[351] For example, a single thunderstorm produces more energy than the whole world currently produces in a year. The sun provides a constant supply of energy that is virtually never-ending. The Rocky Mountain states and Canada contain more liquid petroleum masses than do the liquid petroleum deposits in the Arab countries. Oil shale, which can be converted to oil, is in abundance in many countries, and is currently being extracted and used in Estonia, Brazil and China. Other countries such as Australia, the U.S., Canada, and Jordan had planned to start or restore shale oil production before oil prices fell.[352] Tar sands, which can also be converted to oil, are located in many countries, including the U.S., and two of them, Canada and Venezuela, have tar sands reserves approximately equal to the world's total reserves of conventional crude oil.[353] We can also harness energy from such uses as solar and wind power.

---

[351] George Reisman, *Capitalism: A Treatise on Economics* (1996).

[352] Wikipedia, "Oil Shale," http://en.wikipedia.org/wiki/Oil_shale.

[353] Wikipedia, "Tar Sand," http://en.wikipedia.org/wiki/Tar_sand.

So why don't we use all of these supposedly great sources, and particularly the clean ones? Because in most cases they're too expensive! Though resources are not limited, money is. Many will argue that costs do not matter; we need to save the earth now. But, in reality, we have to prioritize, as we have limited amounts of money (limited amounts of capital goods, consumer goods, and physical assets). If alternative energy sources that start up a car or heat a home are possible at a 50 percent increase in cost from what we currently pay, which fuel source do you think most people will choose? While hard core environmentalists *might* pay more, they would then necessarily have to reduce their expenditures on other things such as groceries, computers, travel, and houses (not to mention that the *price* of all these other goods will rise if wholesale adoption of more expensive energy production is employed).

Many people may think that we can use alternate energy sources with no additional costs. It's just not true. It will affect each and every one of us. But, if we will agree to keep burning cheaper fossil fuel for now, it will sustain us while our companies, in seeking profits, develop new technologies that will enable these alternative energy sources to become cost effective. At that point, *we will be able to quit using fossil fuels.*

Not only that, but the needed ability to dig ever further into the earth to locate new supplies of resources we currently use can only continue by creating newer and better capital goods and technologies which permit this obligatory advanced state of production. If our technological state came to a standstill, the human race would eventually die out because of a lack of means to produce more food for the growing population; we would certainly run out of *usable* resources. In the most benign case, we would revert to living off the land and trying to produce clothes and utensils for ourselves from nature; but without the needed capital goods and technologies, there would not be enough nature to go around, and starvation and fighting for limited resources would be widespread. This is why it's imperative to keep using fossil fuels to develop the tools needed, not only to survive now, but also to reach a state in which we don't have to rely on fossil fuels. Converting natural resources from the state in which we find them to the state in which we can use them takes time, resources, technology, and... fossil fuels, for now.

In the meantime, as oil continues to become more expensive relative to alternative energy sources, more and more investment and research—without government coercion—is going into developing these energy alternatives. Still, much of the ability to make these alternative sources available depends on our *general* level of economic development. As we progress technologically, we will be able to have cleaner and cleaner energy at lower prices.

Indeed, we would already have much lower current energy prices were it not for the fact that most world-wide ownership of oil and natural gas deposits, along with their refining and transformation into usable forms, has been in the hands of inefficient and wasteful government monopolies. Likewise, as we saw in Chapter 4, the environmental movement has prevented us from extracting and producing vast amounts of energy in this country. In supporting environmental causes for political reasons, the U.S. government has, in many ways, made it illegal to produce energy. Were it not for this, we might already be using clean energy.

There is, however, already a very cheap and clean source of energy available: nuclear power. There are two primary unjustified concerns which limit its use. The first is safety. Yet modern atomic facilities not only have multiple safeguards built in, but can withstand a direct hit by an airliner. The famous Three Mile Island accident in 1979 was proof of its safety, not of its dangers: no one died and no one who lived near the site has been found to have higher radiation levels than elsewhere. Similarly, the Chernobyl disaster is proof not so much of the inherent danger of nuclear power plants as of the incompetence in designing and managing them and the lack of regard for human life that exists under communism. The second concern is the dumping of nuclear waste. But there is plenty of land available for safe waste sites and there has yet to be proof of any overwhelming dangers of storing waste. Besides, we are already surrounded by these waste dumps. For example, as **Figure 9.3** displays, it has been estimated that over eight million tons of radioactive waste has been accumulated from nuclear fuel and weapons processing, and to a lesser degree from medical and industrial waste, and from the processing of oil, gas, coal, and some

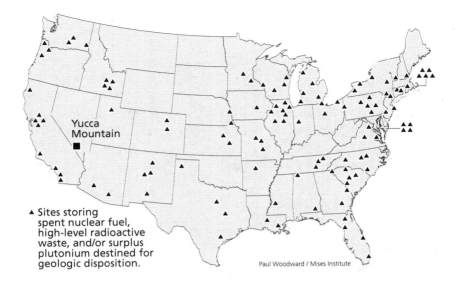

Yucca
Mountain

▲ Sites storing
spent nuclear fuel,
high-level radioactive
waste, and/or surplus
plutonium destined for
geologic disposition.

Paul Woodward / Mises Institute

Figure 9.3: Various nuclear waste dumps in the United States. Source: http://ocrwm.doe.
gov/info_library/newsroom/photos/photos_graphics.shtml.

minerals.[354] Additionally, there are already 104 nuclear plants operating in the U.S., and almost 200 in Europe!

Water

It is absolutely absurd that there should be any water shortage and a need to conserve water. Three fourths of the earth's surface is covered with water, and we should allow the free market to find efficient ways to convert it to potable water. Such conversions are already done on cruise ships, submarines, and for some entire towns. If the government would allow water services to be privately owned, competitive, and free of burdening regulation, we could have an abundance of water. By letting profit-seeking companies own water resources and produce water for us, in their quest to get rich, they will find ways to pump out plenty of fresh water for us all. Had water management been privatized all along, it is almost certain that the creation and use of desalination equipment would be widespread.

---

[354] Wikipedia, "Nuclear Waste," http://en.wikipedia.org/wiki/Nuclear_waste.

Its costs, like any other technology, would be a fraction of what it is today. We would therefore be siphoning water from world oceans at incredible rates (thus lowering world water levels). The United Nations World Water Council concluded in 2006 that the water crisis today is about how water is managed, not about having too little of it.[355] As for the quality of water in the developed countries, it is constantly improving—even the water in New York Harbor.[356]

It is worth noting here the response I received after stating these points about the water industry to a local government official I was speaking with. The politician first proclaimed that water was a limited resource (and we live in an area where there are water shortages), even though there is more of it on earth than we will probably ever need to use. After stating that she didn't believe my assertions about a free water industry and desalinization, the politician said that there would need to be a consensus before private companies were allowed to operate in the water industry.

It is this kind of government bureaucrat logic that prevents a smoothly functioning, progressing economy. The technology already exists for extracting water from the sea. It only needs to become cost effective. Though the politician knows from everyday life that televisions, computers, calculators, and all other technologies became cheaper and cost effective with widespread production, investment and use, she does not apply that logic and knowledge to the desalinization industry.

The politician, an environmentalist who was "tolerant" of my plea for freedom, was saying that companies should not be allowed to freely produce and compete in an industry unless they can prove ahead of time that they will be successful, and that until that time, a government monopoly must manage the industry—shortages, outages and all. Had the computer, refrigerator, automobile, airline, cell phone, steam engine, cruise ship and other industries had to prove their effectiveness ahead of time, we would likely not have many of those products. Had the telephone industry remained government

---

[355] Lomborg, *Cool It* (2007).

[356] For detailed analysis, see Bjørn Lomborg, *The Skeptical Environmentalist: Measuring the Real State of the World* (2001).

run (and cellular services prohibited) like the water industry, we would still have prohibitively expensive, low-quality service.

It is the fact that this mentality was largely shed in the sixteenth and seventeenth centuries that modern capitalism began and the world developed. It was when rulers let their subjects become free to live their own lives without being prohibited by government that man developed inventions, technologies, and tools that began providing needed supplies that improve our lives.[357] Oppressive governments have always existed, but economic prosperity did not occur until people were allowed to own and keep their own property, and to freely exchange it with others. This politician's mindset—that people should be prevented from acting in a way they choose until it is proven that they will produce good outcomes, and permitting actions only by a consensus of (usually uninformed) people—is one that will destroy human progress should it become pervasive.

It is also interesting that the politician would state that companies need to prove their effectiveness before being allowed to operate, when it is in fact government that operates without proving its effectiveness. Companies operate with a profit and loss statement. They have a pretty good idea of their success rate ahead of time. If they incur losses, they suffer and go bankrupt. Even if they fail, other companies buy the assets and turn the failures into successes. Government, however, "invests" in unprofitable industries almost 100 percent of the time, is not responsible for being accountable for losses, pours more money into bad projects to attempt to make previous bad investments better, and still fails at almost everything it does.

Population Growth

The 19th century economist Thomas Malthus claimed that the world would suffer from overpopulation because eventually there would not be enough farmland left to grow all the food required for the larger population. What he did not consider was that technology would improve so as to allow more and more food to be grown on the same amount of land. In fact, agriculture as a percentage of

---

[357] For an excellent summary of this progression, see Alvaro Vargas Llosa, *Liberty for Latin America* (2005), Chapter 4.

GDP has continually declined in most countries; we saw above that it has declined by over 80 percent in the U.S. over the last century. Given increased sophistication in farmland technologies, there is plenty of land in the U.S. and in the world for people, houses, and agriculture. Additionally, the existence of more people means there would be more of us who could contribute to economic production and more people with innovative ideas (seeking profits) to make our world a better place.

Recycling

It costs us more in time, energy, and money to recycle most items than it does to create them from scratch. Why should millions of us take time out of our day to clean, store, group, organize, and transport materials to the recycling dump when large machines operated by a handful of people can dig more of these materials out of the ground at a fraction of the cost? Recycling these materials involves a net consumption of time and capital which could be used to produce other important goods we need—recycling uses three times more resources than does throwing the waste in landfills. Some materials such as gold, silver, and aluminum should be recycled (and we should also be allowed by government to recycle nickels, as a nickel's contents are now worth more than the face value of the coin, thanks to government inflation). The determining factor should be the market price of the material in question; and the government should leave that decision to us individuals and our individual actions. There is no reason to take time to dig through garbage like paupers when we live in one of the richest countries in the world, in the most advanced era for human beings (San Francisco residents now face $100 fines for not separating food remnants from their paper and plastic). Similarly, our government should not be using taxpayer money to fund recycling programs, or mandating that companies must recycle or buy recycled material. Recycling constitutes a destruction of wealth and entails the reduction of our quality of life: the more money spent to subsidize recycling, the lower are wages and the higher are consumer prices. Forty percent of what we recycle ends up in the landfills anyway!

Many people express concerns over the growing landfills and the space they take up, yet most people have never even encountered a landfill. They take up so little space that they don't intrude into our daily lives. In fact, it is estimated that the total amount of waste the entire U.S. will produce this century can fit in an area of land 10 miles square.[358] With further technological progress, we will likely find ways within the next 100 years to make it so that our waste requires a fraction of that space. We might even find ways to make it virtually disappear.

Additionally, landfills are no longer a threat to the environment or public health.[359] All old landfills have been replaced with ones that do not leak hazardous materials. Not only that, landfills are a source of energy, as more and more of them are producing pipeline-quality natural gas.

A Category of its Own: Global Warming

Since global warming is the dominant environmental issue today, and the one which exerts the greatest potential social and political influence over our economic actions, we will look at the subject in detail. As with the other environmental issues, our goal here is to be hesitant to believe whatever emotional statements and manipulated statistics environmentalist throw out, but instead to try and get at the truth, and as part of this, to consider the contrarian and unconventional views of the topic. Also as above, I do not attempt to prove one particular scientific argument over another, but only to present these opposing ideas so as to give the reader a better framework within to make judgments for themselves. (I do, however, attempt to present a robust and compelling economic argument against the government-forced cessation of economic progress in the name of global warming.) The fact is, no one is really sure of anything when it comes to global warming. As David Holland, director of the Center for Atmosphere Ocean Science at New York University said about climate changes in Greenland: "This is like medical science in the 15th century. It's going to take a while to find out what's going on with the patient here."[360]

I will also not attempt to present a detailed and thorough display of all the myriad facts and figures which argue against the case that there is

---

[358] Floy Lilly, "Three Myths about Trash," http://mises.org/story/3887.

[359] Ibid.

[360] Karl Ritter, "Greenland's Melt Mystery Unfolds, at Glacial Pace," *The Associated Press* (September 10, 2009).

global warming. Since I personally don't know whether global warming exists, or whether it's man-made, I do not attempt to make a strong personal argument. What I seek to do is to offer counter arguments that are made by others, in order to give the "she said" to go along with the "he said" that is commonly presented in the media today.

To begin with, let's recall that a primary basis on which most arguments in favor of global warming are made relate to whether the earth is warming. In this vein, consider that 1998, not this year or last, was the year with the highest mean world temperature.[361] Additionally, the total extent of global warming since 1900 consists of a 1.25 degree Fahrenheit increase—hardly anything to get excited about, and the temperature could possibly sway towards the cooler side by the same amount in the next 100 years. And since the reason we are concerned about global warming is due to the greenhouse effect, it's important to know that, in general, emissions of greenhouse gases are good, since if these gases did not already exist in the atmosphere, the average temperature on earth would be about 59°F; the world would be too cold for life as we know it to exist.

Approximately every 100,000 years, the earth temporarily warms. The hottest period in human history occurred 4,000 to 7,500 years before humans created the Industrial Revolution. These warming periods, called interglacial periods, last 15,000 to 20,000 years. We are currently in the 18,000th year of our current interglacial period.[362] CO_2, the greenhouse gas accused of causing global warming, has been rising during these last 18,000 years along with temperatures. Yet global warming activists call recent CO_2 increases unnatural. Also, a minority of the green house effect is contributed by humans. Most of it is derived from 1) water vapor and 2) ocean biologic activity, volcanoes, decaying plants, and animal activity.[363] Lastly, many scientists argue that CO_2 increases do not lead to temperature rises, but lag them, possibly by hundreds of years.

[361] Annie Ogden, "Another warm year as Bali conference ends," http://www.eurekalert.org/pub_releases/2007-12/uoea-awy121207.php.

[362] Monte Hieb, "Global Warming: A Chilling Perspective," http://www.geocraft.com/WVFossils/ice_ages.html.

[363] Ibid.

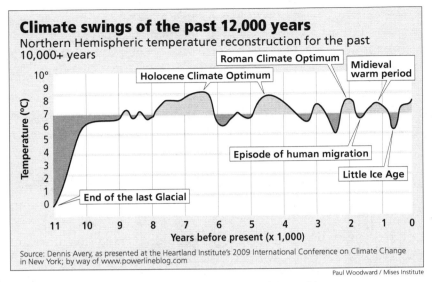

Figure 9.4: Historical swings of warming and cooling of the earth's temperatures.

It must be kept in mind that global temperatures have gone up and down several times in the last thousand years, as shown in **Figure 9.4** (the area on the far right is the most recent warming). Most recently, the earth experienced a warming period called the Medieval Warm Period between 900 and 1200. Warmer temperatures made possible human settlements in places like Greenland and Newfoundland that were previously uninhabitable. After that, global temperatures dropped during the Little Ice Age between the 1400s and 1600s. Millions died from extremely cold weather during this period. Since then, we have been warming again, and many scientists say we're now finishing the warming period.

The global temperature has been trending upwards at a steady trend of 0.5°C per century since the end of the Little Ice Age in the 1700s (when the Thames River would freeze over most winters).[364] The trend does not rise in a straight line however; it oscillates above

---

[364] These two paragraphs taken from Dr. David Evans, "Global Warming: A Classic Case of Alarmism," http://joannenova.com.au/2009/04/03/global-warming-a-classic-case-of-alarmism/.

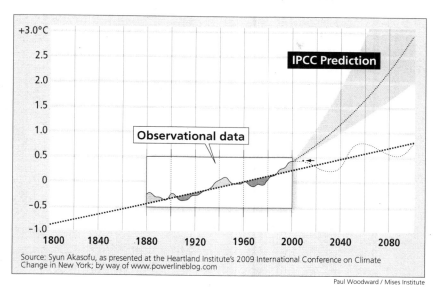

Source: Syun Akasofu, as presented at the Heartland Institute's 2009 International Conference on Climate Change in New York; by way of www.powerlineblog.com

Paul Woodward / Mises Institute

Figure 9.5: Historical swings of warming and cooling of the earth's temperatures.

and beyond the trend in increments lasting about thirty years in each direction:

1882 – 1910 Cooling	1910 – 1944 Warming
1944 – 1975 Cooling	1975 – 2001 Warming

Figure 9.5 reveals this trend. Here in 2009, we are at the point of the arrow, with temperature leveling off. The pattern suggests that the world has entered a period of slight cooling until about 2030.

As mentioned above, there was a cooling scare in the early 1970s at the end of the last cooling phase. The current global warming alarm is likely based on the last warming oscillation from 1975 to 2001. The IPCC warming predictions simply extrapolate the trend from the current warming in a way that assumes the current warming phase will continue at its current rate, while it is more likely that the trend will reverse.

Importantly, it must also be considered that data shows variations in sun activity to be proportional to variations in both CO_2 and temperature. The argument of many scientists is that the sun is the

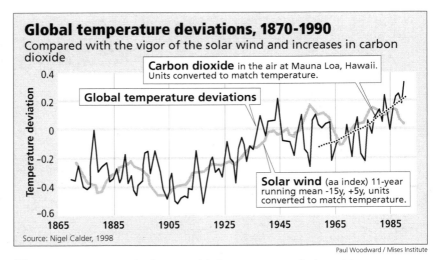

Figure 9.6: The relationship between global temperatures and solar activity.

primary cause of global warming (and other planets are warming as well). After all, 98 percent of the earth's warmth comes from the sun. British science writer Nigel Calder produced the chart in **Figure 9.6** showing the relationship between the sun (by measuring solar wind—the flow of charged particles) and global temperatures.[365] Similarly, Willie Soon, an astrophysicist at the Harvard-Smithsonian Center for Astrophysics, published a book called *The Maunder Minimum and the Variable Sun-Earth Connection,* which explains how solar cause and effect can influence the earth's climate.[366] There is also evidence that changes in the earth's core temperature cause temperature changes. At least one study shows that variations of core-generated magnetic intensity explain 79 percent of global average temperature changes.

The current "standard" forecasted scenario from the IPCC is that the temperature in 2100 will be 4.7°F higher than today (had the

---

[365] Nigel Calder, *The Carbon Dioxide Thermometer and the Cause of Global Warming* (lecture), SPRU (Science and Technology Policy Research) seminar, University of Sussex, Brighton, England (October 6, 1998). Solar wind is used here as a measure of sun intensity.

[366] Willie Wei-Hock Soon and Steven H. Yaskell, *The Maunder Minimum and the Variable Sun-Earth Connection* (2003).

Kyoto Protocol been adhered to, this 4.7°F increase would have been delayed by a scant five years, at the expense of a severe decrease in standards of living around the world). But that does not mean that every location on earth will be that much warmer. Global warming increases *cold* temperatures at a greater rate than warm temperatures, which means that night and winter temperatures will increase much more rapidly than will day and summer temperatures.[367] Thus, we should not think that just because average temperatures rise that we will have unbearable heat to contend with. Though more deaths from heat will unfortunately occur, deaths from cold will decline (something rarely mentioned by official climate reports).

Lomborg points out that while Al Gore scares people with myriad pictures of glaciers receding, the fact is that they have been advancing and receding regularly over the past ten thousand years, but are continuing to grow larger during each growth spurt than they were during previous growth spurts (additionally, many glaciers in the world are growing, and many locations are experiencing declining sea levels[368]). Over the last 10,000 years, some glaciers disappeared altogether, only to be reborn many times again later. Lomborg also notes that Mount Kilimanjaro has been losing ice since 1880, due to changing regional weather patterns.[369] Still, pictures of its diminishing ice have been used as examples of global warming even though that's not the cause of its decline. He also points out that the primary concern of local residents is not so much the dwindling ice, but economic conditions needed for prosperity, which are lacking.

An often-voiced effect related to global warming is rising sea levels. This concern is minimal, and is usually exaggerated in the media. The IPCC's latest report forecasts a mere one-foot increase in water levels over the next century—about the same that we've experienced since 1860. The number of feet of ocean level increase forecasted has been consistently reduced from the more than six feet forecasted by the EPA in the 1980s. Yet Al Gore still claims in his *An Inconvenient*

---

[367] Lomborg, *Cool It* (2007).

[368] Ice Age Now, "Glaciers are growing around the world, including the United States," http://www.iceagenow.com/Growing_Glaciers.htm.

[369] Lomborg, *Cool It* (2007).

Truth that water levels will rise twenty feet. He is using numbers from a very unrealistic hypothetical scenario in which Greenland collapses into the ocean. As a related point, the warmest decades in Greenland were in the 1930s and 1940s.[370] Another worst-case scenario sometimes mentioned is that of Antarctica falling into the ocean, resulting in a more than 100 foot increase in sea levels. But while the world media, in support of this notion, has been showing dramatic pictures of ice melting at the top of a thin, northerly peninsula on Antarctica due to warming, the other 96 percent of Antarctica has gotten colder.[371] The South Pole has been cooling since temperature measurements began in 1957. Antarctica is experiencing an increase in precipitation by the year, and is expected to gain more ice if global temperatures rise. This is because a warmer atmosphere means more precipitation, and since it will still be too cold for ice to melt in Antarctica, the ice will continue building up, likely *lowering* sea levels in the process. While it's uncertain as to whether Antarctica is currently gaining or losing ice, all scientific models project that it will gain ice this century.

Gore also claims that there is a "scientific consensus" that global warming is making hurricanes more powerful and more destructive. This has long been a factually incorrect conclusion. At the time of this writing, this falsehood is now hitting mainstream news headlines, along with the fact that warmer temperatures actually *reduce* hurricane activity.[372]

What Should Be Done About Global Warming?

Since it is the minority manmade CO_2 greenhouse gas emissions that are seen as the primary cause of global warming, environmentalists are demanding that these emissions be reduced by the use of government force. On the face of it, this seems like a harmless, if not healthy, solution. But the results of restricting the use of such things as

---

[370] Ibid.

[371] Ibid.

[372] Richard Black, "Hurricanes and global warming- a link?" *BBC* News (September 23, 2005).

solid and liquid fuels, carbon dioxide, methane, nitrous oxide, and CFCs would have a far-reaching, dramatic, and possibly catastrophic effect.

Most people seem to believe that if we reduce or stop using production methods which contain these polluting side effects, there would be little impact on their lives. This is a fatal mistake. Emitting these gases is a byproduct of the act of producing most things that make our lives enjoyable, and that even keep us alive. Food, beds, batteries, automobiles, operating tables, sanitation equipment, computers, backpacks, and medicine all require fossil fuels to be burned in their production, at least in the quality and quantity in which they currently exist. To be forced to emit less means a reduction in the quality and or quantity of virtually everything we use in our lives. Just as having the government regulate healthcare has caused rapidly rising healthcare costs and too few doctors, so will regulation of carbon emissions cause rapidly rising costs of everything we buy, while having too few goods available.

It might then be asked why we can't replace our methods of production with cleaner and greener methods. We can, but at a steep cost. We have, as consumers as a whole, revealed by the things we decide to purchase or not to purchase, that we are not yet willing to pay much more for these things (because we don't want to consume less of other things). For example, most people have not paid the considerably higher prices for solar power because they prefer to pay less for conventional sources. To force the production and use of alternative energy sources is to force people—in violation of their true desires and physical freedoms—to do without many of the necessities and luxuries they enjoy now. This is because the scarce materials, tools, and technology constituting the resources which produce these necessities and goods would instead have to be used for more expensive energy (again, because *more expensive* means that it takes more resources to produce). The same concept applies to businesses, which means companies will be providing fewer products at higher prices, and paying lower wages. In short, our standards of living will decline; and the poor will suffer the most. If people really want to stop companies from generating carbon emissions, they can do so, *willingly*, by not buying as many of the products that cause carbon to be emitted in their production process; there is no need for government force.

Environmentalists argue that people want their proposed changes. If this were true, there would be no need for government force to make us change our ways of living and producing. As we have seen previously, evil corporations will produce exactly what people want with resources they prefer.

But if we are allowed by government and environmentalists to continue producing with our current polluting methods, we will continue to advance technologically and reach a point where we can operate more cleanly at affordable costs. This will naturally occur through time—almost everything, as we have seen, becomes less expensive, in real terms, through time. What if the earth was indeed warming rapidly even without man's help? What would be more beneficial to us in adapting to and coping with coming changes? A more advanced society with tools and technology as we have today, or one like the Soviet Union or Cuba with their lack of or highly diminished capability to obtain these things? We could adapt to changing climates much better today—with our technologies, tools, refrigerators and air conditioners—than our ancestors could have 100 or 200 years ago. Clearly we need to progress, not retrogress, in order to not only withstand global warming, but to find ways to produce even more and better things than we have now, but with cleaner production methods.

The pollution that we currently create allows us to produce energy that lights, heats, and cools our homes, powers our cars, trucks, airplanes, ships, building cranes, and health facilities, and runs all of our refrigerators, toasters, televisions, and air conditioners, and provides power for our factories and plants that produce all the goods we use daily. Reducing pollution means reducing the availability of all the items we use to enjoy our standard of living.

It should also be understood that so-called "cap and trade," while held as a free-market process, is not so in the least. With cap and trade, government limits the amount of emissions that can be produced, and companies bid for the rights to the available quantity of emissions. Government-limited emissions trading in a "market" does not constitute free markets.

We must ask ourselves what we value most—cleaner air and cooler temperatures than might otherwise occur, or maintaining and improving our current level of civilization? The more we reduce our industrial base, the further back in time our standard of living will retrogress. We could easily place ourselves back to living life as they did in 1850, 1500, or during the time of ancient Greece. The average person today lives better than the richest rulers of two hundred years ago; for they did not have indoor plumbing, electricity, satellite TV with Tevo, unlimited quantities of food, or air conditioning; they did not travel on airplanes while enjoying movies and red wine; they did not have the ability to watch live video in countries on the other side of the world through the internet, or the ability to painlessly stop a decaying tooth from causing agony.

All of these things we have to aid our lives could cease or be drastically reduced with the implementation of regulation which restricts carbon emissions. Even the best scientific estimates of the "benefits" of the currently-proposed regulation show that we could only cool the earth by less than one-tenth of one degree Fahrenheit by 2050.[373]

Not only could this comfortable way of life diminish or vanish for us in developing countries because of environmental restrictions imposed before economies can profitably absorb them, but the result in the undeveloped world could be starvation, increased diseases, and the death of tens of millions of people. In fact, it's already been happening. As one example, consider the malaria-fighting chemical DDT. This pesticide had almost completely extinguished Malaria worldwide when it was outlawed in most countries (including the U.S.) for environmental reasons. Environmentalist Rachel Carson, an employee of the U.S. government's Fish and Wildlife Agency, wrote a famous and impactful book entitled *Silent Spring* in 1962, which argued that DDT was harming the environment and insects. After much laboratory testing, however, it was shown that there is no evidence that DDT had harmful effects on animals or humans. The World Health Organization has now re-approved its use decades later in 2006. In the years since it was banned in the early 1970s, over 500 million people have suffered from acute malaria each year, and over 1 million have died annually. Al Gore, who wrote an introduction to a later version

---

[373] For a summary, see Robert Murphy, "The Cost of Carbon Legislation," http://mises.org/story/3473.

of *Silent Spring*, failed to note the millions of lives DDT had saved or the millions who died because of its being banned.

Most people today would not consider not supporting environmentalism. It seems that all but a few evil, ignorant, illogical and earth-hating individuals are proudly supporting the cause. Virtually every business has green products or supposedly creates products in a way that is earth-friendly. Daily news articles are linked to environmentalism in every way—they either reveal how every news event was caused by global warming or they are consumer pieces instructing us on how we can change our lives to save the planet. This mass hysteria, again, is reminiscent of Nazism, where individuals and businesses rushed to market themselves as National Socialists. The majority of an entire country became supportive of this movement, and supported the isolation, labeling, and expulsion of Jews, minorities, homosexuals, and the like. Likewise, this majority supported the waging of war on the rest of Europe, and that majority is ultimately responsible for the deaths of over 50 million people, of which at least 6 million were brutally starved and tortured. Similarly, as we learned, tens of millions of people around the world blindly support the fallacious Marxist ideology which holds that laborers are somehow exploited by capitalists, leading to the support of socialist states that kill millions of their own citizens, either by force or by starvation. Deaths resulting from emotional ideologies, which ignore logical and factual realities, will occur tomorrow if environmentalists accomplish their goal of preventing economic progression.

There Are Better Ways to Fight Global Warming

Even if global warming is real, and even if it is man-made, instead of reducing our economic strength, we should use it to adjust to a changing climate. We should treat global warming as we do any other natural disaster or event, and adjust to it. As we learned previously, individuals, on the basis of their own profit and loss calculations, decide what actions to take in their lives that will serve them best. As long as we are not prevented by environmentalists and government laws, in the name of saving the planet, from making decisions from which we feel we benefit, each of us will do what's needed to adjust to changing conditions. We will decide where it is more advantageous, considering the perceived changes in the climate (which occur slowly), to live, work, and locate homes, farms and factories.

For example, if the Florida coast is going to lose some of its current shore lines, over time, houses will be taken down that are currently on the water and new beaches and homes will be built some distance inland. Orange grove owners in Florida might learn that they can make more money by selling their land for higher prices to those needing land for the purposes of relocating their home, and thus move their orange groves to Georgia where it's now warm enough to grow oranges on lower-cost land than they had in Florida.

Sound like a tremendous amount of trouble and expense? Remember that over time changes like this occur regardless of whether global warming exists. Over time, most of us naturally relocate, change jobs, build new factories in different locations, and develop new regions. And all physical items that we build deteriorate and need replacing or rebuilding. Similar changes occurred during the time we settled the western United States. During any period of economic development—such as when we switched from using horse and buggies to using automobiles—every business and individual in the economy had to calculate and adjust to changing conditions. The result was new roads, gas stations, convenience stores, shopping centers, and suburbs.

If temperatures rise (or fall), they will do so very slowly, leaving mankind many years to calculate, plan, and prepare. But such preparation should not be left to the government: we have learned how government central planning results in economic dis-coordination and a destruction of capital and wealth. Relying on governments to direct these changes would certainly result in starvation and death, as it has under every regime of central planning.

There are probably logical and rational ways to cool our planet by using the energy sources we currently have, as well as the greater and more improved energy sources we'll create in the future (if we're not stopped from progressing). Reisman suggests the possibility of setting off hydrogen bombs in uninhabited land north of 70° latitude. The idea is that particles released would float in the air at that latitude and block sunlight from reaching most of the Arctic's surface, thus maintaining a cold climate. Another idea is to pump water from the rising oceans through desalination plants and into the Sahara Desert and Australian deserts (which span most of that continent). This would help prevent rising waters while simultaneously making over 5 million miles of previously mostly uninhabitable areas livable. But to do this, we would need to keep improving our desalination technology—by producing with our current methods. These particular ideas may not be feasible, but there are likely many others which are. The point is that these are the ways in which we should be thinking, not in terms of stopping our economic progression and lowering our standard of living. We need progressive, not repressive solutions.

Warming climates, whether man-made or not, could in fact bring many benefits. Much of the barren land in northern Canada, northern Russia, and Greenland could become habitable, and warm enough to grow crops on. This could add to the world's food supplies while creating new and exciting cities. Similarly, more deaths from cold weather could be prevented. Deaths from warm weather can be reduced by increased production of air-conditioned buildings.

Today, even luxury hotels do not wash towels and change sheets daily, unless otherwise requested. Ugly, dim, energy-efficient light bulbs are replacing warmer, more pleasant ones. We are all asked to quit driving, or at least burden ourselves and reduce our hours of work and leisure so that we can take inconvenient (and loss-making) public transportation; we're asked to quit purchasing food and goods that require transportation from faraway places; we're asked to reduce our carbon footprint in every way possible. The next step is the forceful actions of government to make us live in a certain way. For example, traditional incandescent light bulbs are now illegal in Europe. People are forced to buy bulbs that are not as aesthetically pleasant, and cost 60 percent more.[374] Plus, they can't just be thrown away, they must be recycled because of the dangerous materials inside of them. Thus, a recycling tax is also added to the purchase price. The same laws are scheduled to start in the U.S. in 2012.

---

[374] "European countries phase out incandescent bulbs," *The Associated Press* (September 1, 2009).

This logic of constantly reducing our use of non-green materials ultimately leads us to do nothing but grow our own food and sew our own clothes, and have entertainment by sitting by the fire (which creates pollution) singing folk songs. In other words, we're asked to retrogress back to the dark ages. We should say no to this madness! We should enjoy our lives by doing the things that we feel benefit us. We have unlimited potential resources and increasing abilities to deal with whatever side effects come our way. We should move forward in our lives, not backward. We are a wealthy society—in developed countries, at least—and have progressed so that our lives can get better and easier, not more challenging and more difficult. We don't need to live like Robinson Crusoe. Say no to environmentalism. Say yes to life and to the future!

Most Environmental Problems Can Be Solved With Property Rights[375]

Though the state of the environment, as we have shown, is not nearly as bad as most believe, and as the environmentalists make it out to be, there are absolutely environmental problems which should be addressed. But the solution to most of these problems can be found in the protection of property rights, which would result in a much better economic outcome.

Air and water are in fact being polluted more than needed; oceans are being over-fished; land is being ravaged unnecessarily. Environmental issues such as these can be looked at as an interpersonal conflict. Two different parties want to use the same space for different purposes. If an oil company wants to drill on a particular piece of land that someone else wants to use as a nature preserve, how do we decide which party should win out? Were the land privately owned there would be no question about it—the parties which owned the land would do with it what they wanted. Naturally, land could then be sold for various purposes, and would go to the highest bidder. Oil drillers would outbid others for some land, and park providers/owners would outbid oil drillers and other parties for other pieces of land.

---

[375] A majority of the thoughts in this section came from the works of Loyola University economist Walter Block: http://walterblock.com/publications.

For very large pieces of land individuals wanted to protect, they could form partnerships or corporations and pool their money together to own and therefore preserve the land. In each case, those who owned the land would have the highest incentives to take care of it.

But how should we handle what economists call externalities—damage done to others' land which is not owned by the party causing the damage? Consider air pollution. In so far as a factory pollutes and causes damage to other property, it is an invasive act (a negative externality). The factory should bear the cost of this pollution. Originally, laws in this country that were brought over from the common law tradition in England formally protected private property rights. These laws were eventually overturned more than a century ago by progressive era courts that believed economic progress in the name of the common good should supersede individual rights. Before this time of diminished property rights protection, a person who had property damaged by air pollution could hold the polluter accountable, and be compensated by them (not by taxpayers).

If property rights included the air over one's property, one could pollute as long as the pollution did not affect neighboring properties. Since this is impossible, the polluter would be responsible for finding ways to prevent emissions from getting into the air. They might find ways of storing emissions in containers, or ways to convert it into water vapor, thus alleviating the problem.[376]

We all experience what is called "The Tragedy of the Commons."[377] This means that we tend not to take care of public property, which is available for all to use, as well as we do our own property. Thus we tend to destroy it. For example, people tend to litter on public streets but not on their own front yard.

Instead of protecting private property, environmentalists propose taxing us in different ways to get us to act the way they want, or to have trading of limited emissions rights between companies. These strategies, which all involve government regulation and distort

---

[376] This specific example came from Andrew Pack, "Environmental Preservation: A Matter of Property," http://mises.org/story/2136.
[377] Termed by biologist Garrett Hardin in his 1968 article.

our economic system, still do not compensate those who have been harmed by environmental damage. All kinds of government calculations are done to try to come up with the most effective penalties, with the aim of "maximizing the social value of resource usage." But values are subjective, and can only be accurately assessed by individuals from their own view of what's best for them. This means that social costs and social benefits do not exist as either measurable or even theoretical concepts.[378]

It sounds extreme at first blush, but all air, water, and land should be privately owned, not socialized. And we would still have nature reserves, beautiful mountains, and green fields. This is because owners would be able to make profits by offering these things (at lower costs than we pay in taxes to have them now). It is naturally difficult to initially comprehend how ownership of things like oceans, streams, and air space would be privately owned. But there has been much research and analysis performed to show how this type of ownership could exist.[379] In today's world of GPS technology, it would be easier than ever to have clear property lines in the air and oceans.

Environmental Degradation Worst in Places with Weakest Property Rights

Corporations are often accused of ruining the environment for the sake of profits. Free markets are seen as incompatible with environmental preservation; it is thus assumed that government regulation is required.[380] But if it were true that profit-seeking companies are the main cause of pollution, we would expect to find that socialist countries such as the Soviet Union, the former communist countries

---

[378] As stated by Roy Cordato, "An Austrian Theory of Environmental Economics," http://mises.org/story/1760.

[379] To begin with, reference Walter Block, "Coase and Demsetz on Private Property Rights." *Journal of Libertarian Studies* 1 (2) 1977; Israel Kirzner, "Welfare Economics: A Modern Austrian Perspective." in *Man, Economy, and Liberty: Essays in Honor of Murray N. Rothbard* (1988); and Murray Rothbard, "Law, Property Rights, and Air Pollution," *Cato Journal* 2 (1) (1982).

[380] Most of the ideas and information in this section come from Thomas J. DiLorenzo's "Why Socialism Causes Pollution" (1992), *The Freeman: Ideas on Liberty – The Foundation for Economic Education,* http://www.fee.org/publications/the-freeman/article. asp?aid=1909.

of Eastern Europe, China, and North Korea have the cleanest environments. This is not the case. In 2006, the most polluted places in the world were in countries that have the weakest property rights:[381]

1. Chernobyl, Ukraine
2. Dzerzhinsk, Russia
3. Haina, Dominican Republic
4. Kabwe, Zambia
5. La Oroya, Peru
6. Linfen, China
7. Maiuu Suu, Kyrgyzstan
8. Norilsk, Russia
9. Ranipet, India
10. Rudnaya Pristan/Dalnegorsk, Russia

The Soviet Union had extensive environmental laws and regulations to protect the public interest. Yet the environment suffered terribly under communism because of the tragedy of the commons. The empire not only poisoned its air and waters, but also its people. Soviet lakes, streams, and seas were a regular dumping ground for chemical waste. Thomas J. DiLorenzo describes one case:[382]

> A typical example of the environmental damage caused by the Soviet economic system is the exploitation of the Black Sea. To comply with five-year plans for housing and building construction, gravel, sand, and trees around the beaches were used for decades as construction materials. Because there is no private property, no value is attached to the gravel along the seashore. Since, in effect, it is free, the contractors haul it away. This practice caused massive beach erosion which reduced the Black Sea coast by 50 percent between 1920 and 1960. Eventually, hotels, hospitals, and of all things, a military sanitarium collapsed into the sea as the shore line gave way. Frequent landslides—as many as 300 per year—have been reported.

Many lakes and seas have almost dried up, with sea creatures dying off left and right. Lake Baikal, twice the size of Lake Superior, could

---

[381] According to the Technical Advisory Board of the Blacksmith Institute, an environmental NGO based in New York.

[382] Thomas J. DiLorenzo, "Why Socialism Causes Pollution," http://www.fee.org/publications/the-freeman/article.asp?aid=1909.

be observed with alkaline sewage clumps as large as 18 miles long and three miles wide.[383] Investor and world traveler Jim Rogers remarked after his 1991 motorcycle ride across Russia that all communist cars leak oil; he even experienced a crash due to an oil slick on the road.[384]

A similar environmental state can be found in China and the former communist countries of Eastern Europe. Years ago, the Worldwatch Institute stated that more than 90 percent of the trees in the pine forests in China's Sichuan province had died because of air pollution.[385] Similarly, near Chungking, the biggest city in southwest China, a 4,500-acre forest was reduced in half, as of the early 1990s.[386] In Poland, after the fall of communism, it was stated by the Polish Academy of Sciences that "a third of the nation's 38 million people live in areas of ecological disaster."[387]

Obviously, government does not do a good job of taking care of "the people's" property. The same is true of our government in the United States, as government agencies are among the worst polluters. The Department of Defense generates over 750,000 tons of hazardous waste each year—more than the top three chemical companies combined. Yet the agency remains largely free from compliance with federal and state Environmental Protection Agency laws.[388] In 2001, the EPA estimated that the total liability for the cleanup of toxic military sites would exceed $350 billion.

The Army's Rocky Mountain Arsenal, 27 square miles of "toxic horror" six miles north of Denver, as of the mid-1990s and before a taxpayer-funded cleanup began, was known as "the most polluted piece of ground in America."[389] Nerve gas, mustard shells, the

---

[383] Ibid.

[384] Jim Rogers, *On the Road with Jim Rogers: Investment Biker* (1994).

[385] Thomas J. DiLorenzo, "Why Socialism Causes Pollution," http://www.fee.org/publications/the-freeman/article.asp?aid=1909.

[386] Ibid.

[387] Ibid.

[388] Jeffrey St. Clair and Joshua Frank, "The Pentagon's Toxic Legacy," http://www.counterpunch.org/stclair05122008.html.

[389] Matthew Greene, "The Rocky Mountain Arsenal: States' Rights and the Cleanup of Hazardous Waste," http://www.colorado.edu/conflict/full_text_search/AllCRC Docs/94-58.htm.

anti-crop spray TX, and incendiary devices were dumped into this area for over 40 years.[390]

Government-owned power plants are a large source of sulfur dioxide emissions. The Tennessee Valley Authority, a government owned entity, operates 11 fossil plants with 59 coal-burning units.[391] It fought with state governments for years for the ability not to have to comply with state environmental regulations. Finally, the Supreme Court ruled that it could be exempt from meeting standards within which the private sector and local government power plants have to operate.[392]

State and local governments across the United States, in badly managing our infrastructure, cause more than 900 billion gallons of waste to flow out of leaking and dilapidated sewer pipes into rivers, lakes, and oceans.

United States agriculture policy has also created large amounts of pollution. Agriculture policies are set by Congress every five years or so in a package of laws and programs called the "farm bill." These policies not only provide taxpayer funded subsidies, which result in more farmers and farmland than we need, but also encourage over-utilization of land and erosion.[393] Additionally, powerful farm lobbies have protected themselves from having to comply with regulation imposed on other industries.

Choose Life, Not Environmentalism

It is probably clear at this point that environmentalists have a very biased agenda, and it's not in our interest. While the free market is the best means to protect the environment, it is also our only means of producing more, and in a greener way. Any other alternative will result in either lower standards of living or more pollution. Not only

---

[390] Thomas J. DiLorenzo, "Why Socialism Causes Pollution," http://www.fee.org/publications/the-freeman/article.asp?aid=1909.

[391] http://www.tva.gov/environment/air/tri_faq.htm.

[392] Thomas J. DiLorenzo, (Why Socialism Causes Pollution), http://www.fee.org/publications/the-freeman/article.asp?aid=1909.

[393] Ibid.

is the free market our only source of life and well-being, it is our only means to future prosperity.

By buying into environmental fallacies and scare tactics, the only outcome we can expect is a decline in our well-being and the failure to ever be able to produce without polluting. Until then polluting means progression, and environmentalism means retrogression.

PART FIVE

Putting it All Together

Chapter 10:

Socialist/Government Economic Policies

I t was asserted in Chapter 8 that politicians have very little interest in or knowledge of how an economy works. It was also explained that they have no incentive to do the right thing even if they knew what that was. Still, they make decisions and pass laws every day that affect our economic lives. This chapter will highlight popular and formal economic actions undertaken by our rulers, based on advice from their "advisors," in order to try and manage and control the economy, and, it will analyze the economic merit of these so-called macroeconomic policies. It will also attempt to explain why these policies are so popular and why better policies are not implemented instead. Most importantly, it will show that though these policies of economic manipulation are believed by government economists to arrive at a better outcome than can the free market, they in fact cannot. The importance of this chapter is that in disproving socialist macroeconomic theory, I will make null and void the rationale for why government must manipulate the broader economy instead of allowing the free market to work.

In order to fully examine these advanced economic theories and dismiss them as not having merit, I must go into some quite technical detail. The intended outcome is to show that government bureaucrats not only cannot improve our state of affairs, but 1) the free market can, and 2) government bureaucrats can only make things worse.

Planning Our Economy

A majority of the theories of economic cause and effect explained thus far in this book were standard theories accepted by most economists before the Great Depression. However, there were some flaws and weaknesses in the theories, particularly with respect to work and wages, and the possibility of labor exploitation, which gave way to the acceptance of Marxism.[394] In the late 1930s, John Maynard Keynes published his famous book, *The General Theory of Employment, Interest and Money.* With its arrival, sound economics was thrown out the window and replaced with anti-capitalist theories which seem plausible on the surface, but could not withstand strong scrutiny. Yet few seemed to care.

Several years earlier, Keynes had presented a completely different theory of the workings of the economy, in his *A Treatise on Money;* but it, along with many other of Keynes' notions of how an economy really works, was shown to be incorrect by F.A. Hayek. When the *General Theory* came out, Hayek had grown tired of putting the time and energy into disproving Keynes, only to see him scrap his theories and start again with new ones. In the absence of a rebuttal, the *General Theory* caught on rapidly, and soon became the dominant economic theory in the world. Why did it catch on so fast? Because 1) it is in accordance with the common belief—and supposedly proves— that a free market cannot work without government control, and 2) it therefore gives government planners permission to intervene in the economy.

Today, Keynesian and other economic policies involving market manipulation are used by government central planners to try and control the economy. Were it not for this government control, the study of economics would be largely academic. For knowledge

---

[394] Marxism was discredited before the arrival of the twentieth century, and it is currently not even adhered to by left-wing economists. The only people who support Marxism are ignorant students and literature, arts, and history professors who have no idea what Marxism really is or how it has been thoroughly abandoned by all economists.

of economics is not needed for businessmen to carry on about their business of creating profits and wealth, or for workers and consumers to perform their jobs and live their lives. In a government-controlled world, economics—the study of human action—becomes a study of cause and effect of government intervention in the economy. It should be helpful to take a look at these tools of economic manipulation, focusing on Keynesianism, to understand its cause and effects in light of what we now know about how free markets operate.

The Meaninglessness of GDP as an Economic Indicator

A premier tool and indicator of government economists is that of Gross Domestic Product (GDP). While GDP is universally regarded as the prime measurement of economic growth and rising standards of living, in reality, this mathematical calculation is, first, mostly a measure of inflation and, second, a measure of spending on consumption of goods as opposed to spending on the production of goods.

GDP is held to reflect the value of national income and output simultaneously, or, more generally, the value of what a country produces. My intention is to show, in contrast, that it reflects primarily the amount of money, and therefore the amount of inflation, in the economy. As more money is created by the central bank and inserted into the economy, prices rise. Higher prices necessarily mean that the value of goods and services, corporate revenues, profits, wages, investments, and expenditures included in the calculation of GDP rise as well (as demonstrated in Chapter 3). Thus, GDP largely reflects inflation.

By way of illustration, if the quantity of money in the economy did not increase, neither could nominal nor real GDP. We have seen that there are only two ways that prices can rise: the supply of goods and services must fall or the supply of money must increase. Clearly, our volume of goods is not declining—at least not rapidly enough to cause price increases of 3–6 percent per year—but the quantity of money is increasing.

Prices in the GDP calculation are "deflated" with a price index in order to adjust for inflation, but they are only partially deflated because price indices significantly understate the actual inflation rate, as we learned in Chapter 3.

As evidence that creating money lifts GDP, consider the following scenario. If the money supply of the economy were static, i.e., if the central bank neither added to nor subtracted from the amount of paper bills and bank credit in the economy, GDP would be the same each and every year, because the fixed quantity of money would have to be distributed across an increasing amount of goods (and velocity, or the number of times we spent those same dollars, would also necessarily remain essentially unchanged each year[395]). In other words, no matter how many goods exist in the economy, the value of the amount of total spending and incomes in the economy would be the same every year because the quantity of money would be the same—an increased number of goods, each selling at lower prices, would leave the total sales value (price × quantity) constant. With a fixed money supply, our real economic prosperity would be measured by the extent to which prices of goods and services fell relative to our static incomes, since with the same amount of dollars chasing more goods, the price of each good would necessarily fall. This analysis demonstrates that prices and wages cannot rise without an increasing supply of money (likewise, having more money does not help to produce more goods), and that an increased production of goods would actually *reduce* prices. Thus, GDP measures inflation, not production.[396]

What GDP is ideally trying to measure is the physical volume of goods and services at our disposal. But since we can't add up oranges, trucks, movies and airplane tickets, and since there is not a stable and reliable monetary benchmark with which to measure all such items, we must accept that we can't fully count our domestic product in monetary terms (but we can calculate the rate of increase of units produced of individual products and services).

---

[395] Most of the changes in velocity are affected by changes in the money supply. Velocity does not, as most people believe, have a life of its own unrelated to other factors.

[396] While economists believe that deflators wipe out all excess increases in prices except those which account for new goods and services, the fact is that they do not.

The second major problem with using GDP as an economic indicator is that it counts mostly consumer spending and consumption, not the production of goods and services. Indeed, consumer spending is generally held to account for approximately 70 percent of GDP. However, since the production of goods, and not the consumption of goods, is what constitutes real wealth, an increase in GDP signifies mostly an increase in spending and consumption, not an increase in real economic prosperity.

As Reisman has shown, an increase in GDP in fact correlates with a decrease in economic progress because most business spending—productive spending—is subtracted from the calculation of GDP in order to avoid so-called double-counting (which will be explained below).[397] The greater the amount of productive spending in the economy, the greater is the corresponding number that is subtracted from the GDP calculation. As a result, the stated GDP is lower than would otherwise be the case. This is significant because productive spending, as I have shown, is virtually the sole means of wealth production.

Most business costs are subtracted from GDP in order to prevent "double counting," because it is thought that the value of most goods associated with business spending is reflected in the value of the final product, and should be counted as such. Therefore, GDP counts the final product as representing both the final product and all the products that went into it. It says that if we produced bolts, screws, and automobiles, in sum, we produced only automobiles. This is wrong because the screws and bolts were in fact produced, in addition to automobiles, and they have their own separate values, even if they are eventually used to create the composite automobile.

Since, then, most business spending is excluded from GDP, the resulting calculation over-represents the contribution of consumer

---

[397] GDP ≈ National Income; National Income ≈ profits + wages + interest; profits + wages + interest ≈ total business sales revenues − (total business costs − wages). Total business sales revenues minus only capital goods costs leaves profits, wages, and interest. Thus, GDP approximately equals total sales revenues minus only capital goods costs. This means GDP has capital goods costs subtracted out, leaving only (mostly) expenditures for consumer goods (mostly consisting of wages). Therefore, the greater the amount of capital goods expenditures, the more that is subtracted from GDP and the lower is GDP.

spending to total expenditures, and under-represents total productive spending, which far exceeds consumer spending and pays most wages—*business spending* is what is likely 70 percent or so of the economy. GDP, therefore, leads people to believe that prosperity comes about by means of spending and consuming our wealth. Wall Street and government officials, in turn, tell us to go and spend in order to "help" the economy. But it is savings, i.e., abstaining from consumption, which pays for the production of goods—real wealth—and increases our *ultimate* amount of consumption. Contrary to popular belief, savings do not usually sit under a mattress being hoarded, but are actively invested and financing production. All the assets companies possess are owned by capitalists (individuals), via their invested savings.

After all, if we spent all our savings on consumer goods, what money would finance factories, tools, and machines (and home mortgages and credit cards)? What money would pay the wages of workers producing products that have yet to be sold? As a reminder, machines and workers are paid for the products they make before consumers buy them. When we purchase a house, the hammer and the construction worker have already been paid for and have moved on to building the next house. Food, groceries, and CDs, as well as the tools and people that make them, have all been paid for before the consumer compensates (by purchasing these goods) the companies/employers who have paid to have the products created. Similarly, an automobile factory is paid for many decades prior to the complete reimbursement of the investors' capital (when the last cars are produced). Almost all workers and machines are paid in advance with savings, not with sales revenues from consumers.

In sum, economic progress consists of increased productive capabilities, not production-sacrificing consumption. Therefore, GDP does not measure our wealth-producing capabilities. It can give us an idea of the relative wealth between countries (assuming exchange rates can freely adjust to the relative quantity of money, production, and capital flows across countries). And it shows us an approximate rate of inflation and how much we are consuming. But it should not be understood as an indicator of economic progress or standard of living.

Additionally, GDP merely counts the *monetary* value of things produced; but what's produced may not be what really adds value to a society. For example, leftwing government economists such as John Kenneth Galbraith used to cite the Soviet Union's strong GDP growth as an example of successful socialist policies (similarly, Latin America had GDP growth rates as high as developed countries for many decades in the twentieth century, but its real standard of living did not grow comparably). The truth is that the Soviets created little of value. They had tons of screws, but not enough screwdrivers; they had scores of bricks, but not enough mortar with which to assemble the bricks into a building. According to the mathematics of calculating GDP, the Soviets could have produced nothing but screws, and seen their GDP rise. If they produced more screws each year, or even the same amount of screws while the quantity of money increased, they could have shown a rising GDP. To Galbraith this would represent wealth; but to the Soviet citizens, having tons of screws, but no new clothes, food, or houses, would mean death and poverty. Given the assumptions and methodology of GDP calculations, a nation could really increase its GDP by having each citizen simply pay their friends and neighbors to scratch their backs while the government simultaneously printed a lot of money. The more backs that were scratched, and the faster the government printed money, the faster GDP would rise. It should be clear from this that simply having an increase (or decrease) in GDP, like simply having jobs, does not necessarily mean anything. For real wealth to be created, both jobs and GDP must entail the creation of goods and services society needs.

The Keynesian Multiplier[398]

One of the tools Keynesians are most proud of is their so-called "multiplier," which they seem to think is equivalent to magic. The idea is that new additional spending of money creates new incomes. Keynesians believe that the formation of any additional spending in the economy, that is in turn spent by its receivers and re-spent in successive

---

[398] This, and the next six sections are largely paraphrased directly from George Reisman, *Capitalism: A Treatise on Economics* (1996).

rounds, will create additional incomes at a multiple of the original amount of spending. They consequently propose that government should engage in deficit spending during recessionary periods when businesses will supposedly not spend, so as to pump up the economy. They are so convinced of this magic multiplier that they even claim that if government invests in building such things as Egyptian pyramids, the spending on the pyramids would create subsequent additional incomes and create prosperity. Paul Samuelson, a leading Keynesian theorist, wrote in his textbooks that if the government printed money to pay for a million dollars worth of goods to be thrown in the ocean, the spending and re-spending of the million dollars which created those goods would create additional employment and production. Under that logic, if we threw *every new thing* we created in the ocean, we would somehow become *really* wealthy.

Indeed, the mathematics of the multiplier theory is sound, but the assumptions are not.[399] Since it is only productive expenditure, not consumption expenditure, which pays wages, the multiplier could only result in additional profit income, not wage income (the Keynesians specifically state that the multiplier works if incomes are spent, not saved and invested). To understand this concept better, suppose you spent $100 at the bookstore. Then the bookstore owner, instead of re-investing in his business, spent the money at the grocery store. The grocery store owner then takes the $100 out of the cash register and spends it on a new appliance. The appliance store owner spends it on movies, carnival rides, or whatever. The spending goes on and on in this fashion. In this case, the money was never *not* spent. If it were *not* spent, it would instead be *saved*.

If people spent all their incomes, there would be no funds available with which to invest and *to pay wages*. It is saving, i.e., not spending, that pays for additional capital goods and labor. Had any of the above businesses saved the $100 and invested it in their business, they could buy new machines or hire more workers. Had they saved the $100 in a bank, other businessmen, in borrowing these funds, could have expanded their operations or started new ones.

---

[399] This statement is true with regards to most economists' mathematical models.

	Change, Income	Change, Consumption	Change, Saving	Initial Change, Investment
Initial Increase	$5.00	$3.75	$1.25	$5.00
First Round	3.75	2.81	0.94	
Second Round	2.81	2.11	0.70	
Third Round	2.11	1.58	0.53	
Fourth Round	1.58	1.19	0.40	
Fifth Round	1.19	0.89	0.30	
All Other Rounds	4.75	3.56	1.19	
	$20.00	$15.00	$5.00	$5.00

Source: E. Ray Canterbery, A Brief History of Economics

Figure 10.1: The multiplier process.

If all monies were spent and not saved, we would soon consume all existing goods. Since we would not have produced any new goods to replace those consumed, we would soon have literally no goods of any kind, including food or housing (after our food was eaten and our houses deteriorated).

In sum, the only effect from any additional spending is to raise the rate of profit: business costs remain the same, but the additional spending increases sales revenues. But nothing new is created, no investments are made, and no wages are paid.

Keynes stated that if people were careful not to save too much, there could be full employment with interest rates of zero. But this is illogical thinking. For if people saved nothing, there would be no productive expenditure, thus there would be no employment (only self-producing for profit). In this scenario of not saving at all, profits would be equal to the entire amount of sales revenues, and the rate of profit would thus be infinite.

But the Keynesian multiplier has even deeper problems than assumed thus far. Any additional spending cannot create real additional wage income even if the spending was in fact saved. This is because increased real incomes can only come about from new and additional production; workers can't consume more goods if there have not been any additional goods created for them to consume.

The Case for Legalizing Capitalism | Kelly

The multiplier's math (**Figure 10.1**[400]) shows us that a single $5 million of "investment" expenditures by the government can create $20 million of new national income, if people spent 75 percent of their incomes and saved 25 percent. With a portion saved each round, the amount of money being spent eventually completely diminishes to zero. But, according to the Keynesian's own model, if people spent everything they earned, saving nothing, the amount spent each round would never diminish. In this case, each time the $5 million is spent it would create another $5 million in national income. This means that as long as the same money is spent and re-spent it will perpetually create an infinite amount of national income, forever. Obviously, this does not happen.

Now, a less important fact is that companies and businesses only receive so much income each year, and can only spend it once. And we know from studying how many times the same dollar is spent in the economy each year (velocity) that the same dollar is spent only several times in an economy on average—people don't just take the same dollar and pass it around faster and faster.

The more important insight to consider is that it is not just passing around dollar bills that creates new wealth. If it did, why would we need to pass around bills in order to encourage us to begin making things? It is not for lack of thought or incentive that we don't make more things; it's for lack of savings and real capital goods. If you think back to the desert island example in Chapter 1 where a barter economy existed, you will recall that money is a "receipt" or "claim" that represents ownership of real goods already produced. It's the real goods that are being exchanged, and once they are consumed they're gone. And adding more paper bills to the economy for people to pass around simply changes the money price of the goods, but does not create new goods. Can we imagine five people on a desert island creating goods faster by passing around paper bills than they would by not doing so? With or without the bills they need to find resources, to build things, and to have real, unconsumed and stored previously-created food and materials (i.e., savings) to sustain themselves while they produce more wealth. If we look at the Keynesian multiplier in the

---

[400] E.Ray Canterbery, *A Brief History of Economics* (2001), p. 220.

context of a barter economy the assumptions behind its mathematics break down and its façade disappears.

Lastly, if new spending comes from newly printed money, it does in fact result in increased incomes, but as incomes are spent, consumer prices rise in proportion (or even in disproportion, as consumer goods are used up), and no new wealth is created. Printing money is therefore not a realistic way to increase real incomes. Also, spending taken on by government necessarily reduces the ability to spend by others, because it either depletes savings via taxes or reduces purchasing power via inflation.

Still, since most of the government's economic advisors believe in the multiplier effect, the government continues to spend and spend, on any and everything, believing it will somehow bring prosperity. This is the basis behind our "stimulus" programs. Japan, too, has tried unsuccessfully to spend its way out of economic recession for the last 19 years; the Keynesian economist's only explanation is that Japan did not spend *enough*. The only thing the spending in Japan has created is the greatest amount of debt a country has ever had in history. But politicians don't have to worry about profits and losses, as it's not their money.

The Supposed Failure of Lower Wage Rates to Create Full Employment

A cornerstone of Keynesian theory is that it denies that allowing prices and wages to fall in the depths of a recession when unemployment is high—high because of the very fact that businesses are suffering profit and revenue reductions and need lower costs in order to invest and hire more workers—will result in the purchase of more workers or goods. Indeed, say Keynesians, if wage rates were lower, employers would not be able to take on any more workers (think back to our discussion in Chapter 1 where we showed that an employer would hire 10 people at $10 each instead of only nine people at $11.11, since his total monetary outlay is the same either way). They believe there is only a finite amount of work to be done. This argument is the same as saying that there are no more goods and services people want in their lives (i.e. as consumers we would have no more demand for the additional things we would make as workers). Keynesians believe that, given a static quantity of money, we only have so much we want to buy *in physical terms* and no more. No matter how cheap things are, we will not purchase any additional amounts of the things we buy because we always have enough of them. Keynesians therefore believe that we are capable of producing more than we can consume (the overproduction doctrine). But if one imagines a world in which everything is free it becomes clear that in fact we would all consume more of the things we want, given the ability to.

But for most of us living in the real world, if the price of most food, jewelry, or clothes, or anything that we need or want, was simply *less* expensive, most of us would consume more of these things. The same applies to employers "consuming" workers: if employers have a set amount of money they can spend on labor—which they do—with lower wages, more workers would be employed with that same amount of money (each earning less money). This is elementary to even most non-economists. All goods eventually get sold at some price. A purse that originally cost $300 at Macy's might end up being sold at outlet malls for $30, but it gets sold at the price people are willing to pay for it. The same applies to workers; if the government would cease its support of labor unions and minimum wage laws—laws that keep wages above the "market-clearing" price—employers would hire more workers since they could pay lower wages. In this case—a free market in labor—all those who wanted a job would have one, no matter what their skill level. And workers would be paid the value of the revenues they bring in (though salaries would be discounted enough to provide for the going rate of profit). The truth is that the Keynesian position is simply one refusing to recognize that their own socialist policies keep people out of work.[401] Wages are "sticky" in falling, as Keynesians claim, mainly because government policies prevent them from falling.

---

[401] Though government intervention in the labor market is really Marxist-based, these are socialist policies nonetheless, and Keynes himself clearly promoted socialism.

The Keynesian Explanation for Why There Cannot Be Full Employment

Most arguments by mainstream economists for why the free market will not work and how it needs to be manipulated are based on ill-conceived theories that are woven into mathematical and geometrical equations and graphs. The Keynesian argument that there cannot be full employment is enshrouded in the so-called IS curve (don't let these technical terms scare you away; they mean nothing), which is largely derived from a thing called the Marginal Efficiency of Capital (MEC). The MEC, which is essentially the rate of aggregate profits in the economy, is believed by Keynesians to be downward sloping, which simply means that the relationship between the rate of profit and the level of business investment is negative. Put another way, the more companies invest, the lower will be the going rate of profit. Thus, Keynesians therefore contend that if businesses invest too much money—which would come from too much savings arising from too much employment—the economy-wide rate of profit will be too low and companies will thus stop investing. This lack of investment due to a too-low rate of profit, in turn, causes "disinvestment" or, the hoarding of savings, and, therefore, unemployment.

The Keynesian assertion that increased investment leads to unprofitability (i.e., the downward-sloping IS curve and MEC) has three main components, all of which are wrong. The first is the claim that as more investment takes place as a result of falling prices and wages, the price of capital assets—the plant, machinery, and equipment needed for production—would rise from the increased demand arising from the additional investment. The theory is that a higher price of capital assets would lower the rate of return because it increases the initial investment, lowering profits. The reality is that, since falling prices and wages lead to lower unit costs, as well as increased production and supply, the price of capital assets would fall, not rise. Here the Keynesians are forgetting what they preach, which is not to confuse an increase in the supply demanded based on lower prices with an overall increase in demand for a product when the prices are unchanged. Additional investment that would take place due to falling prices and wages would be wholly *based on lower prices* of labor and capital assets, and would exist only in that case.

The Keynesian's second argument for why too much investment will cause the rate of profit to be too low and thus unemployment too high is that with more investment and therefore more capacity, the selling prices of products will fall relative to costs, thus squeezing profit margins. But this claim makes no sense: business costs would fall along with selling prices, thus keeping profitability intact. In fact, declining prices, under normal economic conditions, is *caused* by a fall in the cost of production (business costs). Keynesians assume that with additional investment, selling prices would fall but that the cost of producing them would not. Since costs in fact fall as fast or faster than revenues, profits would remain at least the same under this scenario where prices are falling due to an increase in production. For reasons explained below, increased investment and lower business costs and selling prices actually cause profits to *rise*.

The third main argument for why too much investment leads to lower profits and unemployment is the claim that with additional investment, businesses would experience diminishing returns on the same amount of capital that exists. The reality is that, in the context of the Keynesian argument—in the depths of a recession where there is mass unemployment—there is already unused capacity, and the rate of increased employment of the many unemployed would outpace the rate of increase in the supply of new capital goods. This increase of the ratio of labor to capital means increasing, not diminishing, rates of returns on capital. Even in the context of ongoing, non-recessionary periods, there are not diminishing returns because technology tends to increase along with production and supply so that fewer workers per unit of production are needed.

While the Keynesian's overall argument is that lower prices cannot lead to profitable investments and full employment, the Keynesians switch the context in the middle of their convoluted argument and do not specifically address the idea of lower prices resulting in increased demand for labor and production. Instead of discussing falling prices and lower costs of capital and production, they explain what would happen if there were instead, theoretically, *rising* prices and *constant or higher* costs of production. They basically state that if things were not as they are, they would be different. In fact, Keynes himself acknowledged that he knows of no actual case where his "unemployment doctrine" has existed.[402]

By arguing that mass unemployment during recessions cannot be alleviated with lower wages and prices and increased investment, the Keynesians are in essence claiming that recessionary periods are as good as things can get, that recoveries cannot exist in free markets without government assistance (which begs the question as to how things used to be better before the onset of recession). The reality is the opposite: profits are lower in recession than in recovery, and investment is weakest precisely during a recession, not during a recovery.

Liquidity Preference

Keynesians cite something called "liquidity preference" as the particular thing that explains why investors will not invest below a particular rate of interest (usually 2 percent). They argue that if the rate of return is lower than this rather arbitrary too-low level, lenders would choose instead to "hoard" cash. Keynesians also claim that, when interest rates are high, if these investors hoard too much cash, the rate of interest could not fall low enough to stimulate investment sufficiently to raise the economy out of the depression.[403] A primary assumption, therefore, is that liquidity preference (demand for money)—along with the quantity of money in the economy—determines the rate of interest. Thus, they propose that when investors won't invest due to expected low returns, the government should increase the quantity of money to lower interest rates enough to make investment spending profitable (which will actually set up a new boom and bust sequence, causing future losses and lack of investment).

But it is not true that the rate of interest will be too low or that holding cash determines the rate of interest. The actual fact is that the "hoarding" of cash, which would reduce the available supply of loanable funds, would act to *raise* the rate of return in a free market where the government did not keep interest rates artificially suppressed.

---

[402] John Maynard Keynes, *The General Theory of Employment, Interest, and Money* (1936), p. 378.

[403] As stated by Murray Rothbard, *America's Great Depression* (2000).

With higher rates of return, people would thus be induced to invest more.

Second, the relationship between the demand for holding money and the rate of interest Keynesians propose is backward, which reveals that the rate of interest is thus not determined by liquidity preference. Proof of this can be had by observing the levels of liquidity preference, or the demand to hold money, in actual cases of hyperinflation: when inflation and thus interest rates are high, people don't want to hold money; they want to trade it for real assets that don't lose their purchasing power. And when inflation and interest rates are lower, people do tend to hold money.

The lesson from these facts is that it is not true that investors might want to hold so much cash that it prevents business investment from taking place during recessions. The real story, once again, is that investors don't invest during recessions due to 1) the anticipation that prices will fall further due to a money supply collapse, 2) losses they already have from the central bank's boom and bust prevents them from investing more for the time being, and *mostly 3) that the government will not allow wages and prices to fall so that investment will be profitable and equilibrium restored.*

Lastly, not only does liquidity preference not determine the rate of interest, but neither does the quantity of money. The rate of interest is predominately determined by the (nominal) rate of profit (not vice versa): there would be no interest paid if companies did not already achieve a particular rate of profit with which to pay the interest.

Profits Rise, Not Fall, With More Investment

Contrary to the Keynesian claims of an inverse relationship between the "marginal efficiency of capital" (i.e., the rate of profit) and business investment, more aggregate, economy-wide investment means higher, not lower, profits. Net investment and profits move together almost in lock step, as was explained in Chapter 1. As new investment is undertaken the increased business spending results in increased revenues. The aggregate value of the corresponding costs associated with the revenues lags behind the aggregate value of the investment spending because much of the productive expenditures consists of purchases of capital equipment and inventory, whose appearance on financial statements are delayed due to common depreciation and cost of goods sold accounting principles, and thus do not show up immediately on profit and loss statements. The results of these facts are that when investment takes place, sales revenues outpace their corresponding costs; the revenue/cost gap widens, increasing the rate of profit.[404]

The opposite scenario takes place during recessions. As revenues fall, depreciation and inventory costs remain higher, and fall more slowly and in a delayed fashion. This is a primary reason profits sink so quickly and harshly during recessions (and again, falling spending and falling profits result from the fact that new money from the central bank stopped flowing into the marketplace).

Any net investment on the part of businesses by definition means an increase in profits. The fact that profits rise with increased net investment and fall with disinvestment completely obliterates the notion of the Keynesian's so-called MEC and IS curves. They are simply figments of the imagination, literally just made up. The overall point to understand is that the Keynesian argument that there must be government intervention because businesses will not invest and "jump-start" the economy because it will be unprofitable for them to do so is a complete fallacy. They will do so as soon as they can overcome the results of the previously-enacted government policies—to do so any sooner would be injurious to all.

Keynesian Self-Contradiction on Profits

With their Marginal Efficiency of Capital concept, Keynesians claim that more net investment reduces the rate of profit. But with their multiplier concept, they (implicitly) claim that more net investment raises the rate of profit. It is implicit because with an increase in aggregate demand that their multiplier would bring about, it would be expected that profits would necessarily rise. This is the case even if

---

[404] Reisman has shown that profits are the difference between sales revenues and costs; net investment is the difference between productive expenditure (which is almost equivalent to sales revenue) and costs.

the increase in profits and demand were in proportion, which, in reality, they could not be (profits increase faster than demand due to aforementioned lag in costs based on depreciation and costs of goods sold).

The Accusation that Savings is Destructive

Keynesians assert that since it is saving which funds investment (at least they admit this fact, sometimes), *too much* savings can cause too much investment, thus causing low profits and unemployment, as discussed above, and proven to be incorrect. The arguments behind this "Paradox of Thrift" theory have already been shown to be fallacious. But additionally, it should be remembered that there could never be such a thing as having too much saving because there is always more need for investment than there could ever be enough savings for (we can always use more and lower-priced things in our lives). But the Keynesian's false belief that too much savings causes unemployment is the basis for calling for the government to be the entity that acquires and uses these supposed "excess" savings—the additional amount of savings constituting "too much," and the amount which supposedly causes investment losses—since the government alone will invest in unprofitable ventures. The government, in their view, is supposed to run deficits (i.e., employ a "fiscal policy") as a means to sop up the excess savings. This is the crazy logic that is supposed to justify our current government policies of increased deficit spending during our current recession. The Keynesians believe this spending will somehow help the economy, but the truth is that it will serve only to take the equivalent amount of capital away from businesses producing wealth and squander it on unproductive activities.

In my Keynesian-dominated program in economics, I was taught that the need for savings is imaginary, and that instead paper bills can finance real production (and, as the **Figure 10.1** shows, that having the government spend savings actually somehow creates savings). But even Keynes himself said that savings were indeed needed. The problem was that he proposed both saving and the spending of savings simultaneously, stating, "There is room, therefore, for both policies to operate together: to promote investment and, at the same time, to promote consumption."[405] Since Keynes understood his own contradiction, he alternated terms so that when he referred to supposed harmful savings, he called it "hoarding," and when he referred to helpful savings, he called it as such. Nonetheless, Keynes' own formal definitions state that saving equals investment.[406]

Government Spending of our Savings

The Obama administration, with support from both aisles of Congress, is spending trillions in order to "get the economy going" by "investing" in it. But as we have learned, the government is not making real (profitable) investments, it is just spending money that produces very few real goods and services, if any. True, we need improved infrastructure, but that had already been budgeted for previously; and the infrastructure should already have been improved with those previous monies, but were instead used for redistribution. Now, the government is taking money from the productive private sector where it would otherwise be used to produce real wealth, and wasting it on government works projects. It is destroying capital, reducing our productive abilities, and making the economy worse.

Why Recessions Remain Recessions

As we saw in Chapter 3, a recessionary economy suffers from malinvestment caused by previously enacted government "policies," namely those creating fake money and tampering with market interest rates. Due to malinvestment, labor and capital have been allocated to places which the workings of the free market would have disallowed, but where they were placed by artificially low government-manipulated interest rates and fake money masquerading as real money. As a consequence, there has been too much production in some areas of the economy (i.e., dot-coms, financial services, housing, etc.) and too little in other areas (i.e., consumer goods industries). Once the money spigot stopped and these malinvestments were recognized as such, the market

---

[405] John Maynard Keynes, *General Theory of Employment, Interest, and Money (1936)*.

[406] Keynes formulas, as pointed out by Hans-Herman Hoppe, *The Misesian Case Against Keynes* (1992): "Income = consumption + investment; saving = income – consumption; therefore, saving = investment.

naturally acted to move capital and labor to where free market prices would dictate they be. But "stimulus" packages and the pumping of new money keeps these malinvestments in place, preventing the economy from righting itself by restoring its natural equilibrium.

Most economists erroneously think that the economy stays in recession because individuals and businesses will not spend; they say that there is a lack of demand. But these economists confuse artificial *monetary* demand arising from printing paper bills with *real* demand arising from having created something of value in the marketplace (which can then be exchanged for money and then other goods).[407] They don't understand that lack of demand means that there is a lack of spending *in money terms* due to the fact that the money that was created out of thin air by the banks has diminished or evaporated into thin air—in reverse fashion to how it was created—due to the ceasing of the previous credit creation and the ensuing business and bank losses which resulted (the reverse of the money creation process we saw in Chapter 3), in addition to the fact that people are hesitant to spend until the economy seems once again stable, since they are experiencing financial losses as a result of the crisis. Spenders, just like the banks, first want to get their financial situation improved, and they want to wait until the economy has settled down—has found its new "equilibrium."

Keynesians—who engage in statistical studies as a substitute for understanding real cause and effect—measure demand in terms of the calculated GDP number, not in terms of real goods and services created, as they should. They think that if monetary demand is restored, and that enough money is pumped into the economy to raise GDP, a mere number, to a higher level, that everything is fixed and that the economy is once again in good shape. They have no concept of the fact that what's wrong with the *real* economy is a misallocation of capital and an artificial, tenuous production structure. Artificially increasing a superficial indicator called GDP so as to read a higher number does not fix everything. This is analogous to having

---

[407] In the second case, one has to produce real wealth in order to obtain money. In the first case, one is simply handed money without first producing something to exchange for the money.

a plastic surgeon create an artificial smile on a depressed person and then calling that happiness.

The process of truly fixing the economy—allowing it to find its new equilibrium—involves allowing prices (and balance sheet values) to fall, businesses and individuals (such as homeowners) to incur losses, and allowing the movement of capital and labor to the places market prices would dictate. But just when the economy begins to do this, our Keynesian central bank, supported by the president and congress, disallows this adjustment and keeps printing more money in order to increase monetary demand; they thus keep in place the malinvestments and the artificial production structure. These pro-government economists don't even take into consideration the ramifications that creating fake money has on the production structure; they believe there is no real cause and effect. They think that if we simply print more money people will magically have more "demand" and spend, and the economy will once again take off. But we know now that real "demand" consists only of real goods, not paper bills, and that spending makes an economy worse, not better. Indeed, the economy might take off in monetary terms, but that does not mean that things are really fixed and that we are increasing our real wealth.

Printing Our Way Out of Recessions

Printing money is a core Keynesian tool also because this additional money is used to finance government expenditures that are supposed to create their multiplier effect and cause additional "demand." Starting the printing presses again can in fact work to raise GDP and get spending going as the economy receives more printed money at exponentially increasing proportions. However, this ultimately leads to either hyperinflation and a destruction of the monetary system, or a larger economic recession or depression (when the money stops flowing), causing even more unemployment and a larger-scale destruction of capital and wealth than existed before. Our most recent recession is so intense precisely because of the very fact that the economy was not allowed to adjust in 2001-2002, and trillions of dollars of new money were thrown at the problem.

Though these cycles of massive inflation and economic collapses have appeared over and over in various countries, socialists still stick to printing money as a means of trying to achieve economic improvement, since government economists believe printing paper bills or creating checking deposits on a computer screen can result in the creation of new physical goods. But surely, if printing money really created wealth, we would no longer have unemployment and scarcity—all a country would need in order to go from dirt poor to wealthy would be a central bank and a printing press. Unfortunately, the truth is that only physical production and the adequate devotion of savings to creating capital goods brings about economic improvements.[408]

Even if you do not understand an inkling of economics, doesn't it seem intuitively obvious that constantly manipulating an entire economy, pumping it up and then cooling it down, instead of letting it function normally on its own accord would result in a negative outcome? It's analogous to how Elvis and Michael Jackson both used artificial drugs to pump them up in the morning and keep them going through the day, and to calm them down so that they could sleep at night, instead of allowing their bodies to get the natural sleep, nutrients, and exercise they needed. The result in both cases was death.

Government spending, along with creating fake money, not only does not work, it makes the economy worse off in multiple ways, and *prolongs* the recession. These policies, along with all the other government economic manipulations not only cause the very depressions Keynesians think they can prevent, they result in less economic growth even in good times, prior to their causing the ensuing recessions. Keynesianism, its numerous variants, and all other socialist economics effectively consist of theories which state that prosperity can be created through the systematic destruction of wealth.

---

[408] In a free market there would also not be a push to save at the expense of consuming. How much was saved and invested would be determined by individuals and their personal desires.

Why are Keynesianism and other Socialist Policies So Popular?

Why do government economists promote such anti-capitalistic policies? Because it gives a salvific role to the government. Keynesianism is an ideal economic philosophy—as opposed to economic science—for government officials since it suggests that government should intervene in and manage the economy. Compare this to the boring free-market proposal of doing absolutely nothing. Which do you think politicians will choose?

But why do most economists in general support government intervention economics? There are three likely reasons. One is that no matter what logic or reason would tell them, they want to support socialist ideologies (e.g., Krugman), particularly because the ideologies *seem* moral and enlightened. So they stick their heads in the sand and pray only to socialist gods. The second reason is that they simply don't understand how the marketplace works if left on its own. If they understood free markets and were honest with themselves, they would naturally support capitalism because it's the path to greater prosperity for *all*. The third reason is that they have incentives to support government economics because they can often benefit from being hired to propose more optimal means of government intervention, as mentioned before.

But having the government sanction Keynesian and other pro-government economics means that most economists are *likely* to be pro-government economists. Since government controls our school systems and influences our universities (even private colleges usually receive some government funding), the government, or political groups, make sure that public schools and universities teach government (Keynesian) economics.[409] Also, the government funds most economic research; and when the government funds research it usually insists on the research revealing the story it wants told. I've heard way too many accounts supporting this assertion, from both academia and from business consulting firms.

---

[409] It should be noted that almost none of the free-market economics relayed in this book was taught to me in the seven years I spent in universities learning economics. Instead I was taught pro-government economics.

Therefore, most government funded or partially funded institutions are overwhelmingly comprised of government economists who prosper by producing pro-government research. This also, of course, includes actual government economists such as those at the Bureau of Labor Statistics, Treasury Department, Congressional Budget Office, FDIC, etc. It similarly includes economists at the World Bank, the IMF, USAID, WTO, OECD, etc.

Even most "private" financial institutions can be expected to largely have pro-government economists. Why? Because aside from the fact that they are taught Keynesian economics from government-issued textbooks in either left-wing universities, such as Ivy League schools (most universities are actually left-wing), or in government-funded schools, financial institutions make their living almost entirely off of government economics, primarily that of the Federal Reserve's printing press. If the government's central bank did not create money from nothing and provide the inflation for asset markets to rise and rise, financial institutions would simply make money by safekeeping funds or borrowing *real* savings from one group and lending them out to another, making money on the spread only (in addition to the other basic services such firms offer). Financial institutions in general, therefore, have every incentive to support socialist economics. They don't care about the real economy—they care about what will send the stock market higher again.[410] A majority of professional economists fall under one of these above categories; it should be clear now why most economists support left wing policies.

Another reason that most economists fail to understand that the marketplace works better without government intervention is that the very crucial details of the workings of capitalism are obscure and very difficult to understand. The intricacies can take many years to fully comprehend. Anti-capitalist economics, on the other hand, usually simply give a one-dimensional view of how virtually everything will go wrong if the marketplace is left to its own devices, and the logic makes sense on the surface. But any scrutiny of Marxism and Keynesianism will quickly reveal its fatal flaws. There are tens, if not

---

[410] As an investor in our current government-manipulated economy, I, too, benefit from central bank policies of inflating and have incentives to cheer on these policies. But as one seeking increased standards of living for everyone, I abhor them.

hundreds of free market books explaining, in gory detail, the flaws of Marxism and Keynesianism. Yet to my knowledge, no books have ever been written explaining, in detail, topic-by-topic, the systematic flaws of free-market economics. There are no developed and precise rebuttals to Mises, Hayek, Rothbard, Hazlitt, or Reisman. There are, however, many books which simply *state* that free markets don't work and others that attempt hit and run attacks on certain sub-topics. Most tellingly, none of the big works by Keynes, Marx, and other anti-capitalists explain how wealth and standards of living would improve under their regulated, socialist economies. They don't explain how labor laws can create higher wages or how stifling production creates increased production. They simply explain with half-cocked theories how capitalism must fail. This point is so important it's worth stating positively: Socialists have not and cannot explain how taxing, inflating, and regulating an economy can produce increased wealth for all of society. They have no viable, feasible, operable system of economic progress![411] Nor can they point to any society wherein socialism or communism has brought about more wealth for more people.

When they will actually listen to and consider free-market explanations, socialists will say that capitalism sounds plausible in theory, but there is no proof that it would work in reality. First, evidence such as what I've presented here in this book should suffice as showing that it works where and to the extent it's allowed. But the fact is, it is socialism that cannot be proved. All evidence empirical and circumstantial points to its failure. Even socialists propose marching full speed in the direction of communism, which they admit doesn't work, but pretend that no matter how hard or fast they approach it, they'll never get past that imaginary wall that is supposed to somehow separate socialism from communism.

No matter that capitalism seems to work and socialism doesn't, socialists want the government to enact their policies without any proof whatever that they work, steering us away from capitalism. They want us to take actions that will cause unemployment and a reduction in standards of living when they can't explain economically how these policies will truly help laborers and help create more goods

---

[411] In fact, many of them abhor economic progress.

and services. Thus, the onus should be on socialists to prove that what they propose will help us all before they are allowed to take away our freedoms and our prosperity.

Free Market Fantasy

Meanwhile, as the economic problems drag on, left-wing media such as the *New York Times* constantly question, ironically, why anyone still believes in a free market, as though we have one. They fully believe all of our problems were caused by utter freedom. As Jeffrey Tucker states:[412]

> So you can take a market and beat it, tax it, regulate it, sub-
> sidize it, flood it with fake money, punish its performers and
> reward its losers, hobble its capital sector, strangle consumers,
> nationalize stuff at will, and erect every barrier to trade and
> cooperation, and STILL call it a market. When the scheme
> fails, it's the free market that failed, so clearly we need the
> totalitarian state to sweep into action.

Similarly, in March of 2009, Harvard University sponsored an audacious conference called "The Free Market Mindset: History, Psychology, and Consequences,"[413] where "professional" economists and academics pondered why anyone would believe in the free market since we all know that it causes all our problems. To my knowledge, this group did not bother to invite an actual free-market economist or advocate to the conference to explain how the conference holders arrived at their confused state.

It would be a dream to have a type of courtroom battle where each side presents its economic arguments and counter arguments in full detail, where a societal jury would judge which system is likely to work and which isn't. If society had the time and patience to learn and understand in detail how markets work, there is no way that they would not choose capitalism if they were honest with themselves.

We have seen the results of Keynesian policies for the last 80 years. We have seen the results of similar types of policies of

---

[412] Jeffrey Tucker, "Crazy Economists Still Believe in the Free Market," http://blog.mises.org/9559/crazy-economists-still-believe-in-the-free-market/..

[413] Thomas E. Woods, "Supporters of Capitalism Are Crazy, Says Harvard," http://mises.org/story/3379.

government intervention before Keynesianism came along (i.e., the economic crises of 1873, 1896, 1907, 1921, 1929, etc.). These policies have harmed our economy. Yes, we are still alive and relatively prosperous, but at great costs. We would have much higher standards of living without inflation, unemployment, and recessions if we had had a true free-market economy all these decades.

It is often argued that free markets are fantasies, that they are a theoretical, idealistic world. This argument could not be further from the truth. *Were it not for laws specifically preventing free markets from functioning, free markets would exist today.* Saying free markets are theoretical is like saying that grass can't grow in a plot of land where a parking lot exists. Were it not for the asphalt, grass would be there instead. And grass does spring up through the cracks in parking lots unless it is prevented from doing so by cars driving on the asphalt, by chemicals, or by more asphalt being poured on top of it. Like the grass, the free market finds a way to try and operate daily, but they are constantly being suppressed. Fantasy? Abolish the central bank tomorrow, leaving only the dollars which currently exist. Watch and see if inflation and recessions continue to occur.[414] Idealistic only? Try allowing private companies to provide water and electricity and see whether we continue to have water shortages and power outages. Utopia? Just take away labor laws and see if unemployment persists. Just permit these things long enough to try them, I dare you.

Only YOU Can Prevent Socialism and Economic Regression

YOU, as a voter, are preventing free markets and prosperity from happening by continuing to vote for anti-capitalistic policies just because you are scared to see what would happen. I implore you: let's

---

[414] As a side note, it should be pointed out that this is exactly what happened in Iraq after the 2003 invasion. Iraqi banknotes were no longer produced, and the currency quickly began to outperform all other currencies. But then the Americans forced the U.S. dollar to be legal tender instead, so that Iraqi citizens would have no choice but to accept a depreciating currency that the U.S. government could print more of at their expense (the wealth redistribution effect).

just try it for 10 or 20 years in one area of the country. Not a government-sponsored and regulated "free market" with a thousand pages of rules—but a *true* free market. Let's have a real free market in say, eastern Oregon, or northern Nevada, places where there aren't many people living who might object to a lack of government domination. Instead of continuing to say it won't work, let's just give it a chance and see what happens. No true free market has ever existed in the history of the world. Our political leaders will never go for it on their own because if it is successful, people will no longer want the politicians to rule them. So this must be championed by the voters. Demand from your government a free-market experiment! As Mises stated, "What determines the course of a nation's economic policies is always the economic ideas held by public opinion. No government, whether democratic or dictatorial, can free itself from the sway of the generally accepted ideology."[415]

Otherwise, demand more free market legislation—which means demand to un-do previous legislation—on more and more issues. Instead of letting your politicians know that you want energy independence, let them know that you simply want free trade and a repeal of environmental legislation preventing the production of oil. Instead of demanding "change" in the way of more minimum wage laws or more union support, let your politicians know that you want the marketplace to determine wages. Instead of blaming free markets for financial crises and recessions and asking for yet more regulation, demand from your politicians that they quit printing money and quit attempting to manage and regulate the economy.

We can have increased safety and security. We can have more and higher-paying jobs. We can have prices falling daily. We can have a cleaner environment. We can have an absence of wars. We can have a higher quality of life every single month, no matter our age, skin color, or religious belief. We can have prosperity and freedom—but only if you will understand how it works and then vote for it. Let's give peace, freedom, and prosperity a chance.

---

[415] Ludwig von Mises, *Human Action: A Treatise on Economics* (1963), p. 850.

Chapter 11:

Political Quotes and News Blurbs

Armed with the knowledge we've learned, it should now be easier for the reader to interpret the real meaning behind government policies taking shape in the world today. Let's take a look at some recent news headlines and make sure that we understand the real story behind the news. It should soon become apparent that almost everything happening in society is dictated by government control, but that government leaders are not fit to "lead" anyone.

"Amazon pays $1,500 in daily fines in defiance of French law"
— January 14, 2008[416]

The French government is attempting to make Amazon.com's free shipping illegal. Why would a government intervene in the voluntary trade between two private parties and prevent its citizens from receiving free services from a bookseller that they obviously value? To protect local, independently-owned French booksellers, of course. Had French citizens cared as much about the book sellers as does the government, they would have chosen to purchase from independent

---

[416] Victoria Shannon, "Amazon.com is challenging French competition law," *The New York Times* (January 14, 2008).

stores instead of from Amazon. Who wins? The inefficient booksellers, the government, and those who support the independent stores. Who loses? All other French citizens.

"Bush: US is Not Headed into Recession"
— February 28, 2008 [417]

This one speaks for itself. Not only do politicians (nor their economic advisors) not understand that they cause recessions, but they have no clue when and whether recessions (or recoveries) might come about. Bush also said the strength of the dollar was fine during the time it was plummeting between 2002 and 2008. Though the dollar has fallen against most major currencies for the last 50 years or more, Treasury officials always state that the current administration supports "a strong dollar policy," at the same time they are actually printing money and devaluing the currency.

"Bill Gates Issues Call For Kinder Capitalism"
— January 24, 2008 [418]

Ok, this is not about government or politicians, but such comments as Gates' will necessarily call for government intervention. Gates does not understand that the very wealth his company created has helped the poor in numerous ways, the very least of which—by a mile—is in giving jobs directly to receptionists, janitors, parking attendants, and the like. To the extent that any poor person who wants to advance is not doing so is because they are being prevented by government. What Gates is really calling for in wanting to help the poor, but does not realize it, is for the legalization of capitalism.

"Some Chavez Allies Slow to Shed Luxuries"
— December 14, 2007 [419]

As would be expected, Venezuela's socialist leaders don't practice what they preach. The Associated Press reported that some of

---

[417] David Jackson, "Bush: U.S. is not headed into a recession," *USA Today* (February 28, 2008).

[418] Robert A. Guth, "Bill Gates Issues Call For Kinder Capitalism," *The Wall Street Journal* (January 24, 2008).

[419] Christopher Toothaker, "Some Chavez Allies Slow to Shed Luxuries," *Fox News* (December 14, 2007).

Chavez's cabinet ministers were caught living it up in the same way that Paris or Lindsay would (from their supposedly meager socialist government salaries). Chavez's buddies wear $180 Louis Vuitton ties, $500 Gucci shoes, drive luxury cars, and wear red Tommy Hilfiger jackets (financed by the poor, of course), all while denouncing capitalism.

Justice Minister Pedro Carreno, upon being put on the spot with accusations of hypocrisy, after stumbling, argued, "It's not contradictory because I would like Venezuela to produce all this, that way I could purchase things produced here instead of 95 percent of what we consume being imported."And Luis Acosta, the pro-Chavez governor of Carabobo state, stated last year that authorities can purchase expensive cars without sacrificing their revolutionary ideals. He said, "Is it that we revolutionaries don't have the right to have a Hummer...? If we make money, we can do it."

Obama: "China is rising and it's not going away. They're neither our enemy nor our friend. They're competitors."
— August 14, 2007 [420]

As we have learned, China is not a threat or a competitor.[421] It is an economic partner no less than a co-worker is. This assertion applies to the people and the economy, not to China's politicians, who will naturally want to be at odds with our own politicians. And as we also learned, Obama will likely turn China into an enemy who must be dealt with in the name of security and patriotism.

"Peru's Fujimori gets 25 years prison for massacres"
— April 8, 2009 [422]

Alberto Fujimori was a ruthless dictator who was found guilty by his own people of carrying out military death-squad massacres, and was previously condemned by Amnesty International, Human

---

[420] Foster Klug, "China becomes popular issue in 2008 race," USA Today (August 14, 2007).

[421] Individual Chinese companies might compete with American companies in the same industry, but this misses the larger point.

[422] Teresa Cespedes and Terry Wade, "Peru's Fujimori gets 25 years prison for massacres," Reuters (April 8, 2009).

Rights Watch, Americas and State Department Human Rights reports. No matter that he was heavily funded by the United States by way of numerous military advisers and trainers, Navy Seals and Green Berets, along with a slew of arms and equipment, surveillance flights, radar stations and more.[423] The official explanation for supporting him and his civil war, where nearly 70,000 people died, was that America was fighting the war on drugs. This was the alleged explanation even though many people in Fujimori's administration were directly engaged in the drug trade. Even Fujimori's closest advisor, Vladimir Montesino, was a drug kingpin, and was on the CIA payroll for many years.[424]

"German City Wonders How Green Is Too Green"
— August 6, 2008 [425]

Consumers and home-owners of the world have demonstrated that they don't want to pay the real cost of going green, by way of not voluntarily switching to higher-cost materials and energy sources. But the town of Marburg, Germany is forcing its citizens to use alternative energy against their will in dictating that residents must install solar panels on their homes or pay at least $1,500 in fines. This government force (along with property tax) completely violates private property rights. One can bet that if the law passes and a homeowner fails to install the panels, the government will do more than fine them $1,500; it will probably send them to prison or take away their home until they comply.

As should be expected, the citizens of Marburg have stated that they are much less concerned about the law being applied to office buildings. People of the town don't mind things being forced unfairly on others, only themselves. Additionally, people don't understand that if office buildings (or factories) are forced to go greener, it is they, as consumers, workers, and taxpayers who will pay the price.

---

[423] William Blum, *Rogue State: A Guide to the World's Only Superpower* (2006), p. 160
[424] Ibid, p. 160.
[425] Nicholas Kulish, "German City Wonders How Green Is Too Green," *The New York Times* (August 6, 2008).

(As an opposite scenario, consider the following. On an online community message board for my condo building, one resident proposed having solar panels installed on our roof. He stated in his online proposal: "I wonder if we could get [the city]/ the government to pitch in if we ever did any green improvements around here. I know they are too expensive to do with our budget, but we have a big roof that could be great for solar, wind, etc. technology." Examples abound of individuals wanting others to subsidize their lives.)

"Many doctors plan to quit or cut back: survey"
— November 17, 2008 [426]

A survey of 12,000 general practice physicians revealed that 60 percent of respondents would not recommend medicine as a career due to the long hours, stress, and paperwork. 78 percent of doctors surveyed believe there is a shortage of primary care physicians. Yet none apparently pointed to the AMA as the reason. This is likely because they don't understand that it is the AMA's policies of limiting the supply of doctors in the name of "safety" that causes the shortage and their stressful lives. Nearly half of all doctors plan to cut back on how many patients they see or quit medicine entirely (which will drive medical costs higher). A common reason cited is the amount of paperwork they must comply with. In other words, regulation is harming them and will harm their patients even more than it currently does when they reduce the number of patients they will see.

"Putting money in the hands of unemployed families... will create economic growth in America"
— Sen. Dick Durbin, D-Ill., November 20, 2008 [427]

With this quote Durbin claims that confiscating the incomes and savings of those who are producing wealth for society and giving the money to others to consume will somehow create additional real goods and services. With this logic, politicians could say—and they do—that virtually anything creates wealth. In fact, politicians,

---

[426] "Many doctors plan to quit or cut back: survey," *Reuters* (November 17, 2008).

[427] Jim Abrams, "Congress extends jobless benefits, stocks sink," *Fox News* (November 20, 2008).

and economists, often argue that having a hurricane destroy a city creates wealth (due to the spending involved in replacing all the wealth destroyed), that spending on unprofitable investments creates wealth (green energy, etc.), and that forcing citizens to purchase goods they don't want to purchase—like the solar panels above—creates wealth.

Also in this article was the quote that "economists put the positive impact at $1.64 for every dollar spent on jobless benefits because the money helps sustain other jobs and restores consumer confidence." These mathematical "economists" obviously believe the fallacious Keynesian notion that merely spending money to consume current goods without producing more goods to replace them somehow creates more goods (more wealth). They have astutely calculated that spending $1.00, while producing nothing, can create 64 cents of additional wealth. The truth is that it simply wastes a dollar and reduces our ability to produce increased economic growth.

"FDIC warns US bank deposit insurance fund may tank"
— March 5, 2009 [428]

We have seen that government is fully in bed with the banks (and having tons of nasty sex). We have also seen that allowing the government to permit and even encourage the banks to print trillions of fake dollars is what causes banks themselves to go bankrupt and collapse (after they cease or slow their previous rate of printing). We have seen that the government responds by bailing them out and insuring bank deposits with FDIC insurance, thus encouraging people to continue to trust these inherently bankrupt institutions. But there is enough FDIC insurance to protect only a handful of banks at a time, not the entire banking system. Since so many banks have gone under in the last year, it should be no surprise that the FDIC itself is on the verge of being bankrupt. If citizens finally lose all their money from collapsing banks, maybe they will finally see that government not only causes these problems but is also incapable of protecting us. Who am I kidding? People will continue to believe that our problems are caused by free markets and that government can fix the problems.

---

[428] "FDIC warns US bank deposit insurance fund may tank," *Agence France-Presse*, (March 5, 2009).

"Fed plans new rules to protect future homebuyers"
— December 18th, 2007 [429]

The media and the man on the street constantly blame evil greedy lenders for causing the subprime crisis and thus poor homeowners to lose their homes. In the small minority of instances where lenders were clearly guilty of wrongdoing, homeowners could rightfully sue the lender in court for damages. But most cannot because their predicament is their own fault. Yet few people want to admit this reality. We hear and read stories about people, and most of us personally know people, who were convinced that housing prices would always only go higher, [430] and bought houses they couldn't afford because they thought they could make up the difference when the house appreciated, which, they thought, must surely happen.

The subtitle of this article reads "Fed plans new rules to protect future homebuyers from dubious lending," and the writer states that "The rules will crack down on a range of shady lending practices that has burned many of the nation's riskiest 'subprime' borrowers." Yet the primary rules proposed by the Federal Reserve in the article were largely aimed not at any wrongdoings by the lender, but by the borrower, because it knows the borrowers were the guiltiest party. They are as follows:

- Restrict lenders from penalizing risky borrowers who pay loans off early

- Require lenders to make sure these borrowers set aside money to pay for taxes and insurance

- Bar lenders from making loans without proof of a borrower's income

- Prohibit lenders from engaging in a pattern or practice of lending without considering a borrower's ability to repay a home loan from sources other than the home's value.

The first proposed rule changes the structure of the loans that the borrower would have willingly agreed to. The lender's penalizing

---

[429] "Fed OKs Plan To Curb Shady Home Loan Practices," *CBS News* (December 18, 2007).
[430] Such as Anthony Snowball.

loans that are paid off early might enable them to charge lower interest for the loans. I don't know exactly what their business model is, but this practice does not involve misleading or cheating the borrower unless this term is not laid out in the contract, whereupon the borrower should not be responsible for honoring the term. The other rules simply involve putting the onus on the lender to act like a mother to the borrower, stopping the borrower from freely and willingly making possible irresponsible decisions. If people with bad credit—people who don't honor their debts—who make stupid choices should not be allowed to make their own future decisions, how can they be trusted to make the right decisions in voting for a politician to run our entire economy? They can't; but we can bet they will vote to take money from the rich so that they can buy more stuff they can't afford.

"The Real Scandal: How Feds Invited the Mortgage Mess"
— February 5th, 2008 [431]

In light of the previous headline, and considering how much blame supposed evil lenders and free markets receive for the current crisis, it is well worth presenting this *legitimate* article. As it would be difficult to summarize the details or to re-write the article in a better way, the entire article is presented here in its original form as it appeared in the *New York Post*:[432]

> PERHAPS the greatest scandal of the mortgage crisis is that it is a direct result of an intentional loosening of underwriting standards—done in the name of ending discrimination, despite warnings that it could lead to wide-scale defaults.
>
> At the crisis' core are loans that were made with virtually nonexistent underwriting standards—no verification of income or assets; little consideration of the applicant's ability to make payments; no down payment.

---

[431] Stan Liebowitz, "The Real Scandal: How The Feds Invited the Mortgage Mess," The *New York Post* (February 5, 2008).

[432] Written by Stan Liebowitz, the Ashbel Smith professor of Economics in the Business School at the University of Texas at Dallas.

Most people instinctively understand that such loans are likely to be unsound. But how did the heavily-regulated banking industry end up able to engage in such foolishness?

From the current hand-wringing, you'd think that the banks came up with the idea of looser underwriting standards on their own, with regulators just asleep on the job. In fact, it was the regulators who relaxed these standards—at the behest of community groups and "progressive" political forces.

In the 1980s, groups such as the activists at ACORN began pushing charges of "redlining"—claims that banks discriminated against minorities in mortgage lending. In 1989, sympathetic members of Congress got the Home Mortgage Disclosure Act amended to force banks to collect racial data on mortgage applicants; this allowed various studies to be ginned up that seemed to validate the original accusation.

In fact, minority mortgage applications were rejected more frequently than other applications—but the overwhelming reason wasn't racial discrimination, but simply that minorities tend to have weaker finances.

Yet a "landmark" 1992 study from the Boston Fed concluded that mortgage-lending discrimination was systemic.

That study was tremendously flawed—a colleague and I later showed that the data it had used contained thousands of egregious typos, such as loans with negative interest rates. Our study found no evidence of discrimination.

Yet the political agenda triumphed—with the president of the Boston Fed saying no new studies were needed, and the US comptroller of the currency seconding the motion.

No sooner had the ink dried on its discrimination study than the Boston Fed, clearly speaking for the entire Fed, produced a manual for mortgage lenders stating that: "discrimination may be observed when a lender's underwriting policies contain arbitrary or outdated criteria that effectively disqualify many urban or lower-income minority applicants."

Some of these "outdated" criteria included the size of the mortgage payment relative to income, credit history, savings history and income verification. Instead, the Boston Fed ruled that participation in a credit-counseling program should be taken as evidence of an applicant's ability to manage debt.

Sound crazy? You bet. Those "outdated" standards existed to limit defaults. But bank regulators required the loosened underwriting standards, with approval by politicians and the chattering class. A 1995 strengthening of the Community Reinvestment Act required banks to find ways to provide mortgages to their poorer communities. It also let community activists intervene at yearly bank reviews, shaking the banks down for large pots of money.

Banks that got poor reviews were punished; some saw their merger plans frustrated; others faced direct legal challenges by the Justice Department.

Flexible lending programs expanded even though they had higher default rates than loans with traditional standards. On the Web, you can still find CRA loans available via ACORN with "100 percent financing . . . no credit scores . . . undocumented income . . . even if you don't report it on your tax returns." Credit counseling is required, of course.

Ironically, an enthusiastic Fannie Mae Foundation report singled out one paragon of nondiscriminatory lending, which worked with community activists and followed "the most flexible underwriting criteria permitted." That lender's $1 billion commitment to low-income loans in 1992 had grown to $80 billion by 1999 and $600 billion by early 2003.

Who was that virtuous lender? Why—Countrywide, the nation's largest mortgage lender, recently in the headlines as it hurtled toward bankruptcy.

In an earlier newspaper story extolling the virtues of relaxed underwriting standards, Countrywide's chief executive bragged that, to approve minority applications that would otherwise be rejected "lenders have had to stretch the rules a bit." He's not bragging now.

For years, rising house prices hid the default problems since quick refinances were possible. But now that house prices have stopped rising, we can clearly see the damage caused by relaxed lending standards.

This damage was quite predictable: "After the warm and fuzzy glow of 'flexible underwriting standards' has worn off, we may discover that they are nothing more than standards that lead to bad loans . . . these policies will have done a disservice to their putative beneficiaries if . . . they are dispossessed from their homes." I wrote that, with Ted Day, in a 1998 academic article.

Sadly, we were spitting into the wind.

These days, everyone claims to favor strong lending standards. What about all those self-righteous newspapers, politicians and regulators who were intent on loosening lending standards?

As you might expect, they are now self-righteously blaming those, such as Countrywide, who did what they were told.

"Giuliani offers health care plan"
— July 31, 2007 [433]

During presidential campaigns politicians always come out with their healthcare "plans." They each have their own ideas of central planning for the healthcare industry. And most Americans embrace one plan or the other—as though one is much different the next—while simultaneously believing both that free markets exist in healthcare and that government officials should manage markets by way of their "plans" so that markets won't be too free and dangerous.

It was explained in Chapter 4 that healthcare costs rise so dramatically today because of a continually increasing healthcare demand arising from the printing of money and from corporate and government-subsidized insurance chasing a limited supply of healthcare services. So what was Rudolph Giuliani's plan in 2008? To have government give people yet more money to spend on healthcare. Giuliani claimed that as people buy more healthcare plans insurers will drop their prices. This is the opposite of the truth: healthcare prices will *rise*, not *fall* with more money thrown at the system.

The irony of Giuliani's proposed government handouts is his statement that "Government cannot take care of you. You've got to take care of yourself." Yet what he was proposing was for government to take care of people's healthcare costs while continuing its strict regulation of the healthcare industry. Letting people take care of themselves would involve the government going away all together and letting the marketplace work on its own.

---

[433] Holly Ramer, "Giuliani offers Health Plan," *USA Today* (July 31, 2007).

"Edwards promised to crack down on wealthy Americans who skirt paying their share of taxes"
— July 26, 2007 [434]

The quote above is from an article noting how presidential hopeful, John Edwards, pledged to crack down on offshore tax havens and on the rich engaging in tax evasion. It has been demonstrated that it is the rich who the rest of society milks for their wealth redistribution, and that they pay a majority of all taxes paid. Many rich people are so fed up with the rest of us stealing from them that they rightfully attempt to protect their assets. When they do, politicians and society call it not paying their "fair share." They also make it a crime for one to keep property that is rightly theirs to begin with.

But if *all* rich people would hide their assets offshore, there would be much more capital available to provide us with increased productivity, jobs, and incomes. We should cheer tax havens and tax evasion—these things are highly patriotic, as they are the means by which society is best served by the rich.

The U.S. government has become militant about such things as hiding assets (i.e., trying to protect one's property from being stolen). The U.S. has strong-armed so many nations into squealing on those hiding assets (and those not hiding assets) that it now has extradition treaties with over 135 countries. It is also legal for the U.S. to kidnap accused American tax evaders from other countries. And, the I.R.S. imposes so many regulations on international financial institutions that most of these companies will no longer deal with American citizens. Most Americans keeping money overseas do so legally, and they do so mainly because they want to 1) keep their money in a currency whose government does not devalue it and 2) keep their money in a banking system which is less liable to collapse and 3) have an increased amount of investment alternatives. These three things mostly cannot be done in America because the government 1) prints too much money and does not allow competing currencies, 2) has a *more* unsound banking system due to its printing of money and government-run financial system, and 3) imposes so much regulation and tax-oriented restrictions that it is

---

[434] "Edwards' plan would raise taxes," *The Associated Press, MSNBC* (July 26, 2007).

either illegal or unprofitable for American firms to provide the investment choices other countries do (such as annuity insurance wrappers, hedge fund mutual funds, multi-currency money markets, etc.).

The U.S. continually and increasingly makes its citizens financial prisoners. For citizens of most countries there is always the option of moving abroad and taking up tax residency elsewhere. That is not possible for American citizens, who are subject to U.S. taxation no matter what country they move to. Due to this country's extremely high personal and business tax rates, many citizens decide to leave the country all together. That option has now been made almost impossible or at least too expensive to be feasible. President Bush signed into law an exit tax on wealthy U.S. citizens and long-term green card holders who expatriate from the U.S., making it too costly to escape punitive taxation. John Edwards supports this Gestapo-like regulation, whose purpose is theft, simply because he had votes he needed to buy and the rich have the money that he could use to pay for the votes (via wealth redistribution programs).

"N. Korea's Kim Jong Il Makes Rare Election Pitch"
— February 18, 2009 [435]

Even dictators have to try and appease their citizens periodically for fear of possible revolution and rebellion. Communist North Korea's strongman had to tell the types of lies to his impoverished people that are customary to regular western politicians. He stated: "I will live up to the expectations of the entire electorate by devoting my all to the prosperity of the country and happiness of the people." Instead, of course, he has devoted his all to his own prosperity while his people live miserable, suffering lives, and periodically starve to death.

Similarly, Zimbabwean president, Robert Mugabe, who has almost completely destroyed a once prosperous country by redistributing farmland from the rich to the poor and causing hyperinflation, among other things, is now at risk of being overthrown by his impoverished people. Thus, he is making campaign promises in order to stay in

---

[435] Kelly Olsen, "North Korea's Kim Jong Il Makes Rare Election Pitch," *ABC News* (February 18, 2009).

power—in addition to killing opposition supporters. He has handed out over 450 cars and promised to buy houses for doctors, all with the monies he stole from his citizens and from foreign aid organizations. Politicians of any country will exchange other people's property for votes as much as needed to keep themselves in office; to hell with the economic consequences.

> **"I stand with the writers. The Guild's demand is a test of whether corporate media corporations are going to give writers a fair share of the wealth their work creates or continue concentrating profits in the hands of their executives. I urge the producers to work with the writers so that everyone can get back to work."**
> **— November 5, 2007** [436]

Little needs to be said of Obama's support of striking writers in 2007 considering all that I have explained about the evils of coercive unions. Obama here displays the typical Marxist argument that workers are not getting their "fair share." But as we now know, market forces dictate that workers are paid in accordance with the market value of the work they produce. But not only will Obama talk Marxist, he, like most politicians, will create more pro-Marxist, anti-capitalist laws that reduce productivity, employment, and salaries, all in the name of doing the opposite.

> **"Oui-Ha! France brings line dancing craze under state control"**
> **— May 31, 2008** [437]

Leftists want to regulate anything and everything, and to control the lives of as many as possible. In regulating line dancing, the French government believes its people need to be "protected" from foreign cultures and…and something else—I don't know what. But surely, they believe, people can't be trusted to act in their own best interest and enjoy their lives as they please. Government officials who are somehow superior must "lead" them.

---

[436] "Paul's November 5 fundraising push," *CNN* (November 5, 2007).

[437] Adam Sage, "Oui-Ha! France brings line dancing craze under state control," *The Times Online* (May 31, 2008).

Under new regulations, line dancing instructors must be taught by the government how to teach dancing (and one can bet that other regulations, such as limiting the number of dance studios, are included in the law). This will cost instructors about $2,500 for 600 hours of lessons for professionals and about $700 for 200 hours of training for amateurs. Such forced instructions include subjects like "the mechanics of the human body" and teaching dancing to the elderly (who as we know, are already taking over the club scene). Most of the costs, however, will be paid by taxpayers, not instructors. Thus, French citizens will be deprived of yet more of their incomes and will suffer a lower quality of life. Surely, if given the freedom to do so, French people would have chosen to spend their earnings in a different fashion than paying for line dancing regulations which aren't needed to begin with.

"South Korea's 'prophet of doom' indicted"
— January 22, 2009 [438]

South Korea's economic bust has paralleled the bust of every other developed world economy, since all developed economies are intimately connected via the various world central banks' coordinated monetary policies, and since their bubbles largely stem from our trade deficit. Yet South Korean officials have blamed and arrested an unemployed blogger for causing the decline in its economy, currency, and stock market because the blogger correctly forecasted most of these events (as did most free-market economists). The South Korean government charged the blogger with "false information" (even though it was far from false) and prosecutors said he hurt the local economy by posting incorrect information online.

So much for freedom. So much for stating opinions. It is now illegal in South Korea to forecast the negative results of the government's policies. Korean officials could have at least blamed the free market and a lack of regulation as other countries have—blaming a single blogger for disrupting the economy will not as easily fool even the ignorant public. Still, people are convinced that we need more of this regulation and government control.

---

[438] Jack Kim, "South Korea's 'Prophet of Doom' Indicted," *Reuters* (January 22, 2009).

Bibliography

Allen, W.B. (ed.) (1988). *George Washington, George Washington: A Collection.* University of Michigan Press.

Armentano, Dominick T. (1990). *Antitrust and Monopoly: The Anatomy of a Policy Failure.* Holmes and Meier Publishers Incorporated.

Bartlett, Bruce (1994). "How Excessive Government Killed Ancient Rome." *The Cato Journal, 14* (2).

Bator, F.M., D.L.M. Blackmer, R.S. Eckaus, E.E. Hagen, D. Lerner, M.F. Millikan, I. de Sola Pool, L.W. Pye, P.N. Rosenstein-Roday, and W.W. Rostow (1961). *The Emerging Nations: Their Growth and United States Policy.* Little, Brown, & Company.

Becker, Gary S. (1998). *The Economics Of Life: From Baseball to Affirmative Action to Immigration. How Real-World Issues Affect Our Everyday Life.* McGraw-Hill.

Block, Walter (1977). "Coase and Demesetz on Private Property Rights." *The Journal of Libertarian Studies,* 1 (2), 111–115.

Blum, William (2006). *Rogue State: A Guide to the World's Only Superpower.* Zed Books.

Boritt, G.S. (1994). *Lincoln the War President: The Gettysburg Lectures.* Oxford University Press U.S.

Bronzen, Yale. "The Antitrust Task Force Deconcentration Recommendation." *The Journal of Law and Ecomomics,* 13, 279–92.

Bronzen, Yale. (The Persistence of 'High Rates of Return' in High-Stable Concentration Industries). *The Journal of Law and Ecomomics,* 14, 501–12.

Brown, D., J. Haltiwanger and J. Lane (2006). *Economic turbulence: Is a volatile economy good for America?* University of Chicago Press.

Callahan, Gene. *Economics for real people: An introduction to the Austrian School.* Ludwig von Mises Institute.

Canterbery, E. Ray (2001). *A Brief History of Economics: Artful Approaches to the Dismal Science.* Penguin UK.

Case, Karl E. and Ray C. Fair (2002). *Principles of Macroeconomics.* 6th ed. Prentice-Hall.

Cooke, J., A. Kramer, and T. Rowland-Entwistle (1989). *History's Timeline: A 40,000 Year Chronology of Civilization.* Crescent Books.

Couch, J.F. and W.F. Shughart (1998). *The Political Economy of the New Deal.* E. Elgar Press.

Courtois, S., N. Werth, J. Panne, A. Paczkowski, K. Bartosek, J. Margolin, M. Kramer, and J. Murphy (1999). *The Black Book of Communism: Crimes, Terror, Repression.* Harvard University Press.

Denson, J.V. (2006). *A Century of War: Lincoln, Wilson and Roosevelt.* Ludwig von Mises Institute.

De Soto, J.S. (2006). *Money, Bank Credit, and Economic Cycles.* Unión Editorial, Madrid.

DiLorenzo, Thomas J. (1984). "The Origins of Antitrust: An Interest-Group Perspective." *International Review of Law and Economics, 5* (1), 73–90.

DiLorenzo, Thomas J. (2004). *How Capitalism Saved America: The Untold History of Our Country, From the Pilgrims to the Present.* Random House.

Duncan, Richard (2003). *The Dollar Crisis: Causes, Consequences, Cures.* John Wiley & Sons.

Engdahl, F.W. (1993). *A Century of War: Anglo-American Oil Politics and the New World Order.* Pluto Press.

Ferguson, Niall (1999). *The Pity of War: Explaining World War I.* Basic Books.

Freud, S., and W.C. Bullitt. *Woodrow Wilson: A Psychological Study.* Transaction Publishers.

Garrison, Roger W. (2001). *Time and Money: The Macroeconomics of Capital Structure.* Routledge.

Gordon, David (2002). *Secession, State and Liberty.* Transaction Publishers.

Greenspan, Alan. "Gold and Economic Freedom." *The Objectivist Newsletter, 2* (8).

Greider, William (1989). *Secrets of the Temple: How the Federal Reserve Runs the Country.* Simon & Schuster.

Hardin, Garrett (1968). "The Tragedy of the Commons." *Science, 162,* 1243–1248.

Halbrook, Stephen P. (1981). "The Alienation of a Homeland: How Palestine Became Israel." *The Journal of Libertarian Studies, 5* (4).

Harman, Nicholas (1980). *Dunkirk: The Patriotic Myth*. Simon and Schuster.

Hartwick, John M., and Nancy D. Olewiler (1998). *The Economics of Natural Resource Use*. 2nd ed. Addison-Wesley.

Hazlitt, Henry (1986). *The Conquest of Poverty*. University Press America.

Helleiner, Gerald K. (1981). *International Economic Disorder: Essays in North-South Relations*. University of Toronto Press.

Hopkins, Keith (1980). "Taxes and trade in the Roman Empire (200 B.C.-A.D. 400)." *Journal of Roman Studies*, 70, 101–125.

Hoppe, Hans-Herman (1992). "The Misesian Case Against Keynes." In *Dissent on Keynes: A Critical Appraisal of Keynesian Economics*. Praeger.

Johnson, Paul (1997). *A History of the American People*. HarperCollins.

Keynes, John M. (1936). *The General Theory of Employment, Interest, and Money*. Atlantic Publishers and Distributors.

Kirzner, Israel (1988). "Welfare Economics: A Modern Austrian Perspective." In *The Meaning of Market Process: Essays in the Development of Modern Austrian Economics*. Routledge.

Lomborg, Bjorn (2007). *Cool It: The Skeptical Environmentalist's Guide to Global Warming*. Alfred A. Knopf.

Lomborg, Bjorn (2007). *The Skeptical Environmentalist: Measuring the Real State of the World*. Cambridge University Press.

Machlup, Fritz (1940). *The Stock Market, Credit, and Capital Formation*. William Hodge & Co.

Mackay, Charles (1841). *Extraordinary Popular Delusions and the Madness of Crowds*. Richard Bentley.

Marshall, John A. (1881). *American Bastille: A History of the Illegal Arrests and Imprisonment of American Citizens in the Northern Border States, on Account of Their Political Opinions*. Reprinted 2004, Kessinger Publishing.

Marx, Karl, and Friedrich Engels (1867). *Das Kapital: A Critique of Political Economy*. Reprinted 1992, Penguin Classics.

Masters, E.L. (1931). *Lincoln: The Man*. The Foundation for American Education.

Mises, Ludwig von (1944). *Bureaucracy*, Reprinted 1972. Liberty Fund Inc.

Mises, Ludwig von (1963). *Human Action: A Treatise on Economics*. Yale University Press.

Mises, Ludwig von (2006). *The Causes of Economic Crisis: And Other Essays Before and After the Great Depression*. Ludwig von Mises Institute.

Mises, Ludwig von (1912). *The Theory of Money and Credit*, Reprinted 1981. Liberty Fund.

Mishkin, Frederic S. (1998). *The Economics of Money, Banking, and Financial Markets.* 5th ed. Addison-Wesley.

Moran, Daniel (2001). *Wars of National Liberation.* Smithsonian Books.

Nealy, Mark E. (1992). *The Fate of Liberty: Abraham Lincoln and Civil Liberties.* Oxford University Press U.S.

Phillips, C.A., T.F. McManus, and R.W. Nelson (1937). *Banking and the Business Cycle: A Study of the Great Depression in the United States.* Macmillan.

Powell, Jim (2003). *FDR's Folly: How Roosevelt and his New Deal Prolonged the Great Depression.* Crown Forum.

Quigley, Caroll (1975). *Tragedy and Hope: A History of the World in Our Time.* G. S. G. & Associates, Incorporated.

Randall, James G. (1951). *Constitutional Problems Under Lincoln.* University of Illinois Press.

Reed, Lawrence W. (2005). *Great Myths of the Great Depression.* The Mackinac Center for Public Policy.

Reisman, George (1996). *Capitalism: A Treatise on Economics.* Jameson Books.

Rogers, Jim (1994). *Investment Biker: Around the World with Jim Rogers.* Adams Media Corporation.

Rostovzeff, Michel (1926). *The Social and Economic History of the Roman Empire.* Clarendon Press.

Rothbard, Murray (1963). *America's Great Depression.* The Ludwig von Mises Institute.

Rothbard, Murray (1982). "Law, Property Rights, and Air Pollution." *The Cato Journal, 2* (1), 55-100.

Rothbard, Murray (1994). *The Case Against the Fed.* Ludwig von Mises Institute.

Rothbard, Murray (2000). *The Irrepressible Rothbard: The Rothbard-Rockwell Report Essays of Murray N. Rothbard.* Center for Libertarian Studies.

Schaffer, R., B. Earle, and F. Agusti (1996). *International Business Law and its Environment.* 3rd ed. West Publishing Company.

Simpson, Colin (1974). *The Lusitania.* Ballantine Books.

Soon, Wei-Hock W, and S.H. Yaskell (2003). *The Maunder Minimum and the Variable Sun-Earth Connection.* World Scientific.

Sperandeo, Victor (1993). *Methods of a Wall Street Master.* John Wiley and Sons.

Stiglitz, Joseph E. (1993). *Economics.* W.W. Norton Company, Inc.

Stinnett, Robert B. (2000). *Day of Deceit: The Truth About FDR and Pearl Harbor.* Simon and Schuster.

Stone, Lawrence (1979). *The Family, Sex, and Marriage in England 1500–1800.* Harper and Row.

Talbert, B.R. *Maryland: The South's First Casualty.* Rockbridge Publications.

Taylor, A.J.P. (1961). *The Origins of the Second World War.* Simon and Schuster.

Terrell, Timothy D. (2001). "A Pox on Government Vaccines!" *The Free Market*, 19 (4). Gateway Press.

Tilley, J.S. (1991). *Lincoln Takes Command.* Bill Coats.

Toffler, Alvin, and Heidi Toffler (1993). *War and Anti-War: Survival at the Dawn of the 21st Century.* Little Brown and Company.

Tompkins, David C. (1970). *Senator Arthur H. Vandenberg: The Evolution of a Modern Republican, 1884–1945.* Michigan State University Press.

Vargas Llosa, Alvaro (2005). *Liberty for Latin America: How to Undo Five Hundred Years of State Oppression.* Farrar, Straus, and Giroux.

Walford, Cornelius (1878). "The famines of the world." *The Journal of the Royal Statistical Society*, 41, 433–451.

Warburton, Peter (2005). *Debt and Delusion: Central Bank Follies that Threaten Economic Disaster.* WorldMetaView Press.

Zakaria, Fareed (1998). *From Wealth to Power: The Unusual Origins of America's Role.* Princeton University Press.

Index

About the Author

Kel Kelly has spent over 13 years as a Wall Street trader, a corporate finance analyst, and a research director for a Fortune 500 management consulting firm. Results of his financial analyses have been presented on CNBC Europe, and the online editions of CNN, Forbes, BusinessWeek and the Wall Street Journal.

Kelly holds a degree in Economics from the University of Tennessee, an MBA from the University of Hartford, and an MS in Economics from Florida State University. He has devoted many years to the study of economic thought, focusing on business cycles, financial markets, and monetary policy.

He lives in Atlanta and is a doting, adoptive parent of two greyhounds, Octavia and Daphne.